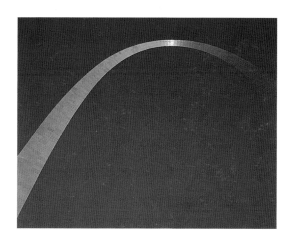

WONDERS OF WORLD ARCHITECTURE

EDITED BY NEIL PARKYN

WONDERS OF WORLD
ARCHITECTURE

WITH 352 ILLUSTRATIONS,
267 IN COLOR

Thames & Hudson

Contents

List of Contributors		8
Map		10
Introduction		12

© 2002 Thames & Hudson Ltd, London

All Rights Reserved. No part of this publication may be reproduced or transmitted in any form or by any means, electronic or mechanical, including photocopy, recording or any other information storage and retrieval system, without prior permission in writing from the publisher.

First published in 2002 in hardcover in the United States of America, under the title *The Seventy Wonders of the Modern World*, by Thames & Hudson Inc., 500 Fifth Avenue, New York, New York 10110

thamesandhudsonusa.com

First paperback edition 2009

Library of Congress Catalog Card Number 2008937296
ISBN 978-0-500-28400-1

Printed and bound in China by Toppan

ON THE COVER (front) The London Eye. Photo © Nick Wood; (back) The Taj Mahal. Photo Will Pryce © Thames & Hudson Ltd, London

Half-title The Gateway Arch, St Louis
Title-page The Golden Gate Bridge, San Francisco

Churches, Mosques, Temples & Shrines

	Introduction	18
1	Hagia Sophia	21
2	The Temple at Tanjavur	25
3	The Temple of Byodo-in	28
4	St Mark's Cathedral	30
5	The Leaning Tower of Pisa	34
6	Chartres Cathedral	39
7	King's College Chapel	44
8	St Peter's Basilica	48
9	The Mosque of Selim II	53
10	The Taj Mahal	57
11	St Paul's Cathedral	62
12	The Panthéon, Paris	66
13	The Sagrada Familia	68
14	The Chapel of Notre Dame du Haut	72

Palaces & Castles

	Introduction	76
15	The Alhambra	79
16	The Forbidden City	84
17	The Topkapi Palace	89
18	The Kremlin	93
19	The Escorial	98
20	Versailles	102
21	The Potala Palace	107
22	Schloss Schönbrunn	111
23	The Winter Palace	113
24	Neuschwanstein Castle	116
25	The Viceroy's House, New Delhi	119
26	La Cuesta Encantada: Hearst's Castle	123

The Pompidou Centre, Paris

The Forbidden City, Beijing

Public & State Buildings

	Introduction	126
27	The Houses of Parliament	129
28	The Crystal Palace	134
29	The Opéra, Paris	138
30	The Pentagon	141
31	The Guggenheim Museum, New York	143
32	Walt Disney World Resort	146
33	The Sydney Opera House	148
34	The Louisiana Superdome	153
35	The Pompidou Centre	156
36	Kansai International Airport	160
37	The Guggenheim Museum, Bilbao	164

Towers & Skyscrapers

	Introduction	168
38	The Washington Monument	171
39	The Eiffel Tower	174
40	The Empire State Building	179
41	The Gateway Arch	184
42	The World Trade Center	187
43	The Sears Tower	192
44	The CN Tower	195
45	The Hongkong and Shanghai Bank	197
46	Petronas Towers	201
47	New York-New York	205
48	The London Eye	207

The Forth Rail Bridge, Scotland

Bridges, Railways & Tunnels

	Introduction	210
49	The Iron Bridge, Coalbrookdale	213
50	The Thames Tunnel	216
51	Brooklyn Bridge	219
52	The Canadian Pacific Railway	223
53	The Forth Rail Bridge	225
54	The Jungfrau Rail System	229
55	The Moscow Metro	231
56	The Golden Gate Bridge	234
57	The Seikan Rail Tunnel	238
58	The Channel Tunnel	240
59	The Great Belt East Bridge	244
60	The Akashi Kaikyo Bridge	248

The Sears Tower, Chicago

Canals & Dams

	Introduction	252
61	The Erie Canal	255
62	The Suez Canal	257
63	The Panama Canal	260
64	Hoover Dam	264
65	Itaipú Dam	267
66	The Dutch Sea Barrier	271
67	The Three Gorges Dam	274

The Statue of Liberty, New York

Colossal Statues

	Introduction	278
68	The Statue of Liberty	281
69	The Statue of Christ the Redeemer	286
70	Mount Rushmore	288

Further Reading	292
Sources of Illustrations	297
Index	299

Itaipú Dam, Brazil

Contributors

Neil Parkyn is an architect and town planner, and Director of Huntingdon Associates. He has worked in over 20 countries, including China, Vietnam and France, as well as the United Kingdom, developing a particular expertise in large-scale master planning and urban design. He is a member of the Royal Institute of British Architects and the Royal Town Planning Institute, and a Fellow of the Royal Society of Arts and former Chairman of the Association of Consultant Planners. He is also a prize-winning journalist and illustrator. **25, 31, 44, 48, 49, 50**

Josep Bracons is an art historian and critic. He teaches and researches at the Escuela Superior de Restauracion de Bienes Culturales and the Open University (UOC) in Barcelona. He is president of the Catalan Association of Art Critics (ACCA) and has published articles and studies on medieval art and the art of the 19th and 20th centuries. **13, 15**

William Craft Brumfield is Professor of Slavic Studies at Tulane University. He has received a number of fellowships, including the Guggenheim Fellowship (2000–01). He is the author and photographer of several works on Russian architecture, most notably *A History of Russian Architecture* (1993). His photographs of Russian architecture have been exhibited at museums in the US and Europe, and are in the collection of the Photographic Archives at the National Gallery of Art, Washington, DC. **18, 23**

John B. Burland is a civil and structural engineer and is Professor of Soil Mechanics in the Department of Civil and Environmental Engineering at the Imperial College of Science, Technology and Medicine, London. A Fellow of both the Royal Society and of the Royal Academy of Engineering, he specializes in the effects on buildings of ground movement due to tunnelling and excavation. He was a member of the Italian Prime Minister's Commission for stabilizing the Leaning Tower of Pisa. **5**

John Bury is a student of the architecture and architectural treatises of early modern Europe, civil and military. His Escorial studies have been published in Britain (*Art History, Burlington Magazine*) and Canada (Calgary University) as well as in Spain (Patrimonio Nacional). **19**

Brian Carter is an architect who has worked in practice in Europe and is Professor of Architecture at the University of Michigan. He has written extensively on architecture and design. He is the author of several books on contemporary architecture, including one on Frank Lloyd Wright's buildings for Johnson Wax (1998), and co-author of *All American. Innovation in American Architecture* (2002). **41, 68, 70**

Robin Cormack is Deputy Director and Professor of the History of Art at the Courtauld Institute, London. He specializes in arts from antiquity to the end of the Middle Ages, notably Byzantine art, as well as theoretical issues, particularly the relationship between the written and the visual. His publications include *Painting the Soul. Icons, Death Masks, Shrouds* (1997) and *The Portrait of the Artist in Byzantium* (1997). **1**

Philip Denwood is Reader in Tibetan Studies at the School of Oriental & African Studies, University of London. He specializes in the Tibetan language and textile and architectural arts. His books include *Tibetan* (1999) and *The Tibetan Carpet* (1974/2001). **21**

Nils Francke is a freelance writer and journalist based in Copenhagen. He has written extensively about the construction and impact of the major public works which transformed the infrastructure of Scandinavia in the period 1988–2000. This includes the Great Belt link, the Øresund Link connecting Denmark and Sweden, and the Øresund Region. **59**

John Glover is a transport consultant, specializing in the railway industry, and is an Examiner for the Institute of Logistics and Transport (ILT). His publications include *National Railways, A Guide to the Privatised Railway* (1996), *London's Underground* (9th ed., 1999), *Railway Operations* (1999), *Principles of London Underground Operations* (2000) and *Southern Electric* (6th ed., 2001). **52, 54, 55, 57**

Godfrey Goodwin has retired from teaching architectural history at the University of the Bosphorus, Istanbul, where his courses included Ottoman and Byzantine art and architecture. He still gives summer courses. His publications include *A History of Ottoman Architecture* (1971), *Sinan, Ottoman Architecture and its Values Today* (1992) and *Topkapi Palace* (1999). **9, 17**

Jessica Harrison-Hall is Assistant Keeper in the Oriental Department, British Museum, London. She specializes in Chinese ceramics and Vietnamese art. She is the author of *Ancient Chinese Trade Ceramics* (with Regina Krahl, 1994), *Ming Ceramics – A Catalogue of Late Yuan and Ming Pottery and Porcelain in the British Museum* (2001) and *Vietnam: Behind the Lines* (2002). **16**

Alan Hess is an architect, historian and architecture critic for the *San Jose Mercury News* in California. His books include *Googie: Fifties Coffee Shop Architecture* (1985), *Viva Las Vegas* (1993), *Hyperwest* (1996), *The Architecture of John Lautner* (1999) and *Palm Springs Weekend* (2001). **26, 32, 47**

Ebba Koch is a professor of Asian Art in the Department of Art History at the University of Vienna. She has conducted major surveys of the architecture of the Mughals in the Indian subcontinent, focusing lately on the Taj Mahal. Her publications include the standard textbook *Mughal Architecture* (2nd ed., 2001) and *Mughal Art and Imperial Ideology* (2001). She has also co-authored the exhibition catalogue *King of the World. The Padshahnama: An Imperial Mughal Manuscript* from the Royal Library, Windsor Castle (1997). **10**

Annette LeCuyer is an architect who worked in practice in London for a number of years before joining the faculty at the University of Michigan as an Associate Professor of Architecture. She has written widely on contemporary architecture for professional journals in Europe and North America, and is author of *Radical Tectonics* (2001) and co-author of *All American. Innovation in American Architecture* (2002). **28, 37, 43**

Bert McClure is an architect, planner and former Loeb Fellow at Harvard University. He is currently head of the Masters Programme in Planning and Urban Development (AMUR) at the French École Nationale des Ponts et Chaussées and a planner in private practice. His publications include: *Promenades d'Architecture à Paris* (1999), a walking guide to Paris architecture; a guide to Le Corbusier's French buildings open to the public; *Promenades d'Architecture à Lille*, a walking guide to metropolitan Lille architecture; and *Plans et Dessins* (1991) – the communication of urban planning projects, for the French Ministry of Public Works. **12, 14, 20, 29, 35, 39**

George Michell studied in Melbourne and then took his Ph.D. in Indian Archaeology at the School of Oriental & African Studies, University of London. He has travelled extensively in India and worked on a number of sites there, notably at Vijayanagara. Among his numerous publications are *The Hindu Temple: An Introduction to its Meaning and Forms* (1997), *The Royal Palaces of India* (1994) and *Hindu Art and Architecture* (2000). **2**

David Morris is a geotechnical specialist who has worked in water resources engineering for almost 40 years. He has designed more than 20 dams and reservoirs worldwide and is closely involved with dam safety, having inspected more than 44 dams. He is the author of numerous papers on dam design, rehabilitation and performance, as well as on seismicity and landslides. He is presently an Associate with FaberMaunsell Ltd, consulting engineers, and is a member of the UK 'All Reservoirs Panel'. **62, 65, 67**

M. D. Morris has written and edited numerous articles and books on construction and related matters. He is recipient of the American Society of Civil Engineers Peurifoy Construction Research Award and the Construction Writers Association Silver Hard Hat Award. He is a Fellow of both the American Society of Civil Engineers and the Society for Technical Communication. He teaches non-fiction writing for industry and government. **34, 61, 63, 64**

Lawrence Nield is an Australian architect who has been responsible for a number of significant buildings, including the National Science and Technology Centre in Canberra, the University of the Sunshine Coast Library in Queensland, and Cook and Philip Park in Sydney. He had a major involvement in the planning and design of the Sydney Olympic Games in 2000 and is directing a number of projects for the Athens Olympic Games in 2004. He was visiting Professor of Architecture at the University of NSW from 1990 to 1992 and Professor of Architecture at the University of Sydney from 1992 to 1996. **33**

Linda S. Phipps is a visiting Assistant Professor of Architectural History at the University of California – Berkeley. She received her Ph.D. in the History of Art and Architecture from Harvard University, with a specialization in mid-20th-century modern architecture. She is currently preparing a book on the United Nations Headquarters. **42, 69**

Nicholas Ray is a Senior Lecturer at the University of Cambridge Department of Architecture, a Fellow of Jesus College and Director of the Cambridge Historic Buildings Group. He is the author of *Cambridge Architecture, A Concise Guide* (1994), and of numerous articles in professional journals. **7**

Peter Ross is a structural engineer and an Associate Director of Ove Arup & Partners, where he specializes in the assessment of historic building fabric and timber as a construction material. He held a term appointment as consulting engineer to the Historic Royal Palaces (Kensington Palace and Banqueting House). **3, 24, 36, 45, 58**

Ellen R. Shapiro is Professor of the History of Architecture and Director of the Program in Art History at the Massachusetts College of Art in Boston, and a Fellow of the American Academy in Rome. She has published extensively on the architecture and design of the Fascist period in Italy, and is a contributor to *Giuseppe Terragni: Opera Completa* (1996). Most recently, she co-edited *Mimmo Jodice: Inlands, Visions of Boston* (2001). **30, 38, 40, 46, 60**

Roger A. F. Smook is Professor of Design and Construction Management in the Faculty of Civil Engineering and Geosciences at Delft University of Technology, the Netherlands. After qualifying as an architect and planner, he moved to civil engineering and construction. He is author of *Inner Towns Change: The Atlas of the Process of Spatial Change of Dutch Inner Towns* (1984) and publications on construction management and real estate development. **66**

Ian Sutton studied the history of architecture under Nikolaus Pevsner, John Summerson and Peter Murray, before taking up a career in art publishing. He is the author of *Western Architecture, A Survey from Ancient Greece to the Present* (1999) and he co-edited *The Faber Guide to Victorian Churches* (1989). **4, 6, 8, 11, 22**

Alexandra Wedgwood was for many years the Architectural Archivist in the House of Lords' Record Office. She is a specialist in Victorian architecture, on which she has written widely. **27**

Mark Whitby was President of the Institution of Civil Engineers in 2001/2002 and is a founding director of Whitby Bird & Partners, one of the leading engineering practices in the UK. **51, 53, 56.**
51 with James Aitken, who is currently reading Engineering at Cambridge University and is being sponsored by Whitby Bird & Partners during his studies. **53** with **Scott Lomax**, Whitby Bird & Partners, who has worked on the design of pedestrian bridges, including the York Millennium Bridge and the River Lune Millennium Bridge. **56** with **Ai-Hua Tao**, formerly with Whitby Bird & Partners, who has worked in Singapore and London, and is currently with Alan Conisbee & Associates.

31 The Guggenheim Museum, New York

40 The Empire State Building

42 The World Trade Center

51 Brooklyn Bridge

68 The Statue of Liberty

52 The Canadian Pacific Railway

44 The CN Tower

61 The Erie Canal

70 Mount Rushmore

43 The Sears Tower

56 The Golden Gate Bridge

41 The Gateway Arch

26 La Cuesta Encantada: Hearst's Castle

30 The Pentagon

47 New York-New York

38 The Washington Monument

64 Hoover Dam

34 The Louisiana Superdome

32 Walt Disney World Resort

63 The Panama Canal

53 The Forth Rail Bridge

7 King's College Chapel

49 The Iron Bridge, Coalbrookdale

11 St Paul's Cathedral

27 The Houses of Parliament

28 The Crystal Palace

48 The London Eye

50 The Thames Tunnel

58 The Channel Tunnel

37 The Guggenheim Museum, Bilbao

19 The Escorial

15 The Alhambra

6 Chartres Cathedral

12 The Panthéon, Paris

20 Versailles

29 The Opéra, Paris

35 The Pompidou Centre

39 The Eiffel Tower

13 The Sagrada Familia

69 The Statue of Christ the Redeemer

65 Itaipú Dam

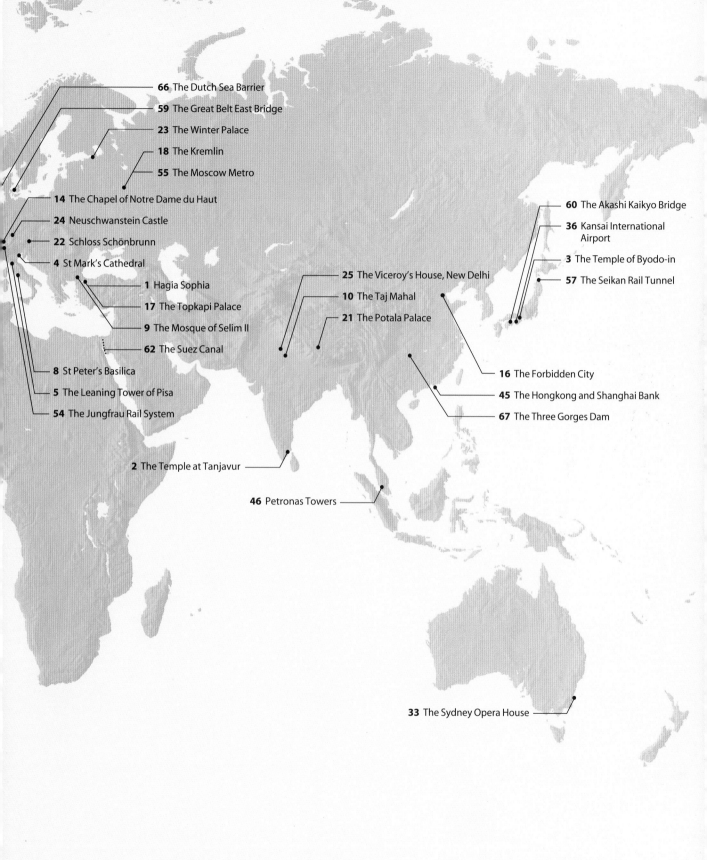

66 The Dutch Sea Barrier

59 The Great Belt East Bridge

23 The Winter Palace

18 The Kremlin

55 The Moscow Metro

14 The Chapel of Notre Dame du Haut

24 Neuschwanstein Castle

22 Schloss Schönbrunn

4 St Mark's Cathedral

1 Hagia Sophia

17 The Topkapi Palace

9 The Mosque of Selim II

62 The Suez Canal

8 St Peter's Basilica

5 The Leaning Tower of Pisa

54 The Jungfrau Rail System

25 The Viceroy's House, New Delhi

10 The Taj Mahal

21 The Potala Palace

60 The Akashi Kaikyo Bridge

36 Kansai International Airport

3 The Temple of Byodo-in

57 The Seikan Rail Tunnel

16 The Forbidden City

45 The Hongkong and Shanghai Bank

67 The Three Gorges Dam

2 The Temple at Tanjavur

46 Petronas Towers

33 The Sydney Opera House

Introduction

The Court of the Myrtles, with its rectangular pool, typifies the harmonious balance between architecture and water in the Alhambra palace in Granada, Spain. Courts are an important ordering element in this complex.

Even in our age of micro-miracles and astonishing miniaturization, the great works of mankind still retain their capacity to amaze. In making the selection for this volume, many criteria could have been applied with equal credibility. For our present purpose, the definition of what constitutes a 'Wonder' embraces those artifacts which are larger than the human scale, which are the products of the brain and hands of men and women, and which also somehow exemplify a notable landmark in the evolution of a particular genre – be it in the design of great bridges or the history of dams, canals or cathedrals.

By any measure of worth, the structures in this volume will continue to uplift and inspire, whether on a visit to them or simply by reading about them. Our search for candidates has been worldwide, since notable achievements have never been confined to western civilizations alone. The Wonders here are also worthy successors to earlier famous structures, stretching far back into human history, such as the pyramids of Egypt, the impressive temples of Greece or the Colosseum of Rome. There are many parallels and echoes across the ages, between great arenas or places of worship today, for example, and those completed several millennia past.

All these structures, built for a prime functional purpose, manage to transcend mere utility. While displaying the Vitruvian virtues of *firmitas* (strength) and *utilitas* (usefulness or functionality), they also impress as elegant, fully resolved solutions which can lay claim to the third ideal of Vitruvius – *venustas* (beauty). This achievement is seldom the product of self-conscious 'design' in the sense that modern artifacts are subjected to a process of styling and fine tuning to suit their intended markets.

As others see them

Sheer size, width and weight, volume enclosed or distance spanned do not, automatically, a Wonder make. There are many structures in the histories of engineering and architecture which, at their time of completion, were hailed as the last word in modernity, magnitude, technical daring or social improvement but which, with the benefit of hindsight, now rank as stepping stones to the next great leap in progress.

Fame is certainly fragile. Who better to know than those who promoted the Chrysler Building in New York, which briefly took the title of the world's tallest building, only to have the Empire State rise higher shortly afterwards? Or the builders of the medieval cathedrals of the Middle Ages in the Ile de France, from St Denis and Sens, through Chartres to Amiens and Beauvais, a sequence ending in the collapse of Beauvais?

If dimensional supremacy is not in itself a reliable measure of eminence and uniqueness, then the opinions of contemporary commentators often are. That most notable 'temporary' structure of them all, Joseph Paxton's Crystal Palace in London's Hyde Park, was correctly seen at the time as being of greater import than the contents of the Great Exhibition of 1851 which it housed.

Bastions of belief

For all their reminders of our earthly mortality, the major world religions have built themselves reassuringly permanent structures of power and majesty as settings for worship. Many of these owe their origins to an entirely secular concern for self-memorialization by rulers and priests intent on visible supremacy, leaving us with not only such familiar Wonders as St Peter's in Rome and St Paul's in the City of London, but also with lesser known yet no less remarkable structures such as Soufflot's Panthéon in Paris or the Hindu temple of Tanjavur in India. Such buildings have sometimes advanced construction technology through the efforts to erect larger and larger

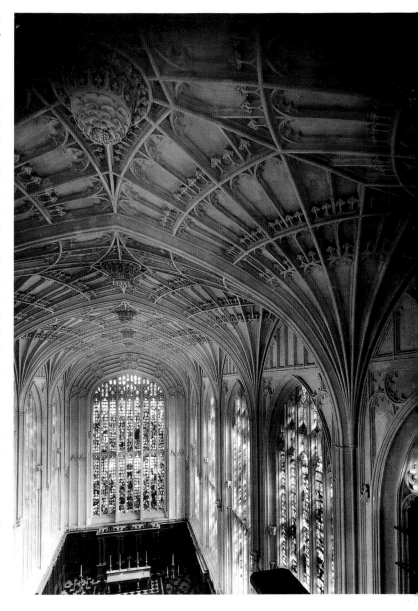

domes, or to make church naves higher and lighter. Sheer spectacle and magnificence are all. On occasions, innovation and aesthetic considerations are both satisfied, as by the spectacular fan vaulting of King's College Chapel, Cambridge, or by the sweeping concrete roof which Le Corbusier floated above his chapel at Ronchamp, France.

Palaces of power and pleasure

When secular rulers and regimes have wished to give expression to their ascendancy and temporal – often, as it emerged, *temporary* – status they

The spectacular fan vaulting of King's College Chapel, Cambridge – a complex form of masonry that is both structurally efficient and of great beauty.

Opposite *In his Petronas Towers in Kuala Lumpur, currently the world's tallest building, architect Cesar Pelli combined the use of innovative new materials and technology with Islamic symbolism.*

Below *The Potala Palace in Lhasa, Tibet, was built using traditional materials and methods, by a workforce made up of local farmers.*

have chosen to do so by the building of palaces where they could hold court and receive foreign emissaries in fitting style. These ambitious projects and megalomaniac desires could require a huge workforce – as the reportedly million labourers building the Forbidden City's 9000 rooms in Beijing, China – or a concerted attack on the national coffers, as in the case of Empress Elizabeth of Russia's recasting of the Winter Palace in St Petersburg.

Architects through the ages have risen to the challenge of delivering suitable splendour while satisfying the minutiae of court hierarchies, whether Johann Fischer von Erlach for the Holy Roman Emperor Leopold I at his Schloss Schönbrunn, outside Vienna, or Sir Edwin Lutyens in designing the Viceroy's House as the physical focus for the British Raj in New Delhi.

Where pure pleasure and personal comfort rather than prestige were paramount, palaces could flourish as oases of delight. One such is the Alhambra in the hills above the Andalucian city of Granada. Another is William Randolph Hearst's unfinished mansion on the rocky coast of southern California , immortalized by the young Orson Welles in his wonder of a film, *Citizen Kane* (1941), where architect Julia Morgan spent three decades working with the media mogul.

Challenges of nature

Much human endeavour has centred on solving the problems dealt us by the caprices of geography. An inconvenient isthmus here, an annoying mountain range there, or water barriers which hinder the passage of men and goods – all have eventually proved surmountable, often by some

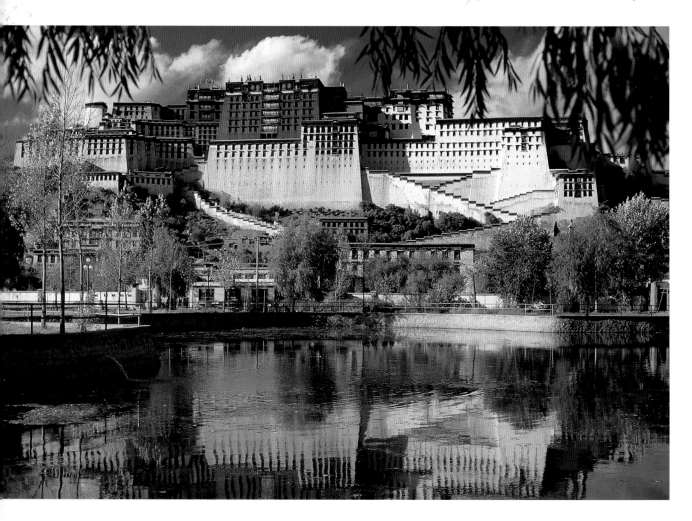

of the largest – and most daring – engineering solutions. The Canadian Pacific Railway opened up an entire continent; the Panama Canal linked the Atlantic and Pacific oceans; and the Suez Canal provided a shorter route to the east for ships which had hitherto sailed around the entire continent of Africa.

The technology of these great projects was sometimes simple enough – the deployment of huge workforces in often inhospitable climes:

The London Eye, or Millennium Wheel, is already an important and established addition to the London skyline – despite the fact that it is intended to be temporary.

over 125,000 Egyptian labourers perished while cutting the link through Suez.

Great bridges were made possible by dramatic advances in the use of materials such as iron and reinforced concrete, rather than by brute will. Engineers learned to use these materials in new ways, initially by trial and error, but later through experimentation and the gradual evolution of the theory of structures. This has led to bridges which can span greater distances for the same quantity of material, and which perform safely as dynamic structures under the pressures of their self-weight, the traffic they are designed to carry and the effects of external forces upon them – even earthquakes and typhoons in the case of San Francisco's Golden Gate Bridge or Japan's Akashi Kaikyo Bridge.

Tunnels represent a less visible but no less essential leap in technology. Their evolution stems from a key innovation of the 19th century: the tunnelling 'shield' patented by the pioneering engineer Marc Brunel. It was used, notably, in his 18-year endeavour to build the first tunnel under the River Thames. Later versions of Brunel's device have cut passages under the English Channel and through the Swiss Alps.

Yet nature can sometimes be turned to advantage. Lakes can be dammed and rivers diverted to generate hydroelectricity, improve navigation, promote irrigation or protect whole river basins from uncontrolled flooding. The impact of these massive structures – such as the Hoover (Boulder) Dam on the Colorado River or China's Three Gorges' Dam along the River Yangtse – on the prosperity and ecology of their entire regions can be dramatic indeed.

Rise of the urban icon

Paris would hardly be Paris without its Eiffel Tower, nor would Barcelona be the same without its extraordinary cathedral of the Sagrada Familia, still under construction. Even relative newcomers, such the Sydney Opera House in Australia, the Guggenheim Museum in Bilbao, northern Spain, or the Petronas Towers in Kuala Lumpur, Malaysia, have already established themselves as urban icons which now serve as international ambassadors for their host cities.

The benefits flowing from a single 'landmark' building designed by an architect of world standing can be considerable in terms of external perceptions, in addition to the economic and cultural advantages. What seems to matter most in the case of wonders as potential urban icons is that they present a memorable, ideally unique, skyline profile, and enjoy highly visible, prominent sites in the city centre as the focus for wider regeneration. Yet, as the tragic destruction of the World Trade Center's twin towers on the morning of 11 September 2001 demonstrates, icons can all too easily be reduced to a pyre of twisted metal and pulverized concrete.

Computers and the age of wonders

New materials, in themselves, will not lead to new wonders. They never have. In the past, the pioneers of engineering and architecture combined often entirely traditional and well proven materials, such as stone or iron, and subsequently steel and reinforced concrete, but in spectacular ways. We now live in an age where *anything* is technically feasible – at a price. Towers can rise higher; the central spans of bridges can be lengthened a little further and tunnels run a few more kilometres, but there are ultimately very tangible constraints of cost, construction programme or – more probably – ultimate utility.

What is arguably more interesting a development is the way in which construction technology has helped to liberate form. Frank Gehry at Bilbao – or indeed anywhere – can realize whatever forms his imagination can devise, aided by computers which can translate them into buildable components. Computers will even bar-code the structural components to speed assembly on site, as they did at Bilbao.

Will this all lead to an age of Wonders of whimsy and waywardness, driven on by the ambitions of city authorities and newly confident regions? Certainly the technology is readily available, as are accomplished designers who are willing and well used to taking their talents anywhere in the world. What should never be forgotten, however, is the thoroughly old-fashioned distinction often made between the labourer with a wheelbarrow who complains of the unremitting toil and his companion who explains, 'Yes, but *I* am building Chartres Cathedral!'

The unmistakable curves and reflective surfaces of the Guggenheim Museum, Bilbao, designed by Frank Gehry.

Churches, Mosques, Temples & Shrines

Of all the buildings in this volume, few have greater power to uplift and inspire than those created for that very purpose. Pay a pilgrimage visit to the chapel designed by the great Swiss-French architect Le Corbusier high in the foothills of the Vosges mountains at Ronchamp in eastern France, or view from a distance the Selimiye mosque in the Turkish city of Edirne, the masterpiece of 80-year-old Ottoman architect Sinan – and in both cases you are in the presence of sublime architecture. The chapel at Ronchamp is small, but its curving roof appears to float above massive-seeming walls pierced by openings filled with coloured glass which recall in their luminosity the great windows of Chartres Cathedral, dating from many centuries earlier. Also small, the exquisite temple of Byodo-in, near Kyoto, Japan, with a wooden roof structure of great elegance and complete structural stability, embodies centuries of temple building in the region.

The motives behind building such monuments of faith or remembrance can certainly be mixed. While the English king Henry VI made specific instructions in his will for the building of a simple and unadorned place of worship, his later successor Henry VIII saw the completion of King's College Chapel as an opportunity for artistic

Notre Dame du Haut, Ronchamp: the curved walls both create spaces of great sculptural expression and give the entire chapel its structural stability.

Looking up into Soufflot's dome for the Panthéon in Paris: he devised a complicated system of arches and pendentives to transfer the considerable weight of the dome to the supports. These were found to be inadequate, however, and later had to be strengthened.

pieces such as the Taj Mahal at Agra, the mausoleum Shah Jahan built for his favourite wife Mumtaz Mahal, could be built in a lifetime, larger undertakings might involve a succession of patrons and architects. St Peter's employed in turn the talents of Bramante, Raphael, Michelangelo, Maderno and Bernini, while the cathedral of Chartres, although a mere 30 years in the building, shows evidence of the handiwork of at least nine master-masons, each with their own 'lodge' of craftsmen. In more recent times, the Cathedral of the Sagrada Familia in Barcelona, to which the Catalan architect Antoni Gaudí devoted so much of his life, can be said to have been driven by a single, dedicated vision. This remarkable designer strove to realize his own, totally original form of organic architecture through models, drawings and full-size experiments on the building itself, which is still not complete.

Viewed strictly as functional structures, great churches and mosques share the same brief – that of spanning over a single large space for worship. Much ingenuity and considerable effort have been expended in creating larger and higher spaces with the minimum of obstructive supports. Istanbul's Hagia Sophia manages to achieve a breathtaking lightness in its dome through the use of transitional geometry between the circular dome and its supporting, square structure. Wren's St Paul's Cathedral in London and Soufflot's Panthéon in Paris combine the traditional Greek Cross domed central space with a linear nave. Unfortunately Soufflot underestimated the amount of masonry needed to support his dome, and it subsequently required reinforcement.

Seldom, it seems, is it a matter of the piety of the architect. Much as self-declared non-believers can compose great devotional music – such as the Requiems of Brahms or Verdi – many of the most memorable and inspiring places of worship have been created by architects with no declared faith or belief beyond that in their own ability to achieve spaces which could lift the hearts of others. The power of these buildings derives from their quality as architecture and their ability to embody effortlessly, through the ages, the 'image of the infinite', as Madame de Staël once wrote.

splendour and dynastic propaganda. And the marble and mosaic displayed on every surface of the church of St Mark's, Venice, as well as the treasures looted from Constantinople, convey a strong sense of the pride of a wealthy and powerful city-state. In the equally successful and confident city-state of Pisa, the authorities commissioned a cathedral with a bell tower – which shortly afterwards became the Leaning Tower – a structure which is a jewel of medieval architecture even without its lean, now happily stabilized as the result of recent international teamwork.

Strong personalities, papal or princely, provided the power, inspiration and often the funds for many of these structures. It was Pope Leo X's practice of promoting the sale of indulgences to raise money to continue work on the church of St Peter's in Rome that provoked Martin Luther's protest at Wittenberg and the Reformation which followed. Other patrons displayed their commitment to projects by personal gestures such as King Rajaraja I's ascent to the summit of his temple at Tanjavur to set its pinnacle, a copper water pot, in place.

Such patrons did not always live to see their church, mosque or temple completed. While set-

Hagia Sophia

Time: AD 532–37   Location: Istanbul, Turkey

Glory to God who has deemed me worthy of achieving such a work:
I have vanquished thee, Solomon.

<small>STATEMENT ATTRIBUTED TO JUSTINIAN ON INAUGURATING HAGIA SOPHIA IN AD 537</small>

Hagia Sophia is one of the great domed buildings of the world. Its exterior silhouette hints at the shock of the interior space, but the visual power and success of this dome, 31 m (100 ft) in diameter, can only be appreciated from inside. The church of Hagia Sophia – 'Holy Wisdom' – was built and decorated in just six years between 532 and 537. Its magnificence and great structural ingenuity belie any suggestion that Early Christian architecture on the threshold of the Middle Ages was in decline.

Origins

Hagia Sophia was in fact the third church on this site. It was preceded by the first Great Church of Constantinople, built in the middle of the 4th century in the ceremonial centre of the new capital city dedicated by the Roman emperor Constantine

Hagia Sophia from the south. The buttresses on either side of the dome were enlarged after it was built to strengthen the dome's support. The minarets date from after 1453.

the Great in 330. The prime location was next to both the Great Palace of the Byzantine emperors and the Hippodrome, the arena for chariot racing and other popular entertainments. By the early 5th century the first church of Hagia Sophia was a target in times of civil and ecclesiastic unrest; it was burnt down in 404, but rebuilt and reopened in 415. Its status as the public symbol of imperial power led to more trouble in the 6th century, and the (second) church was again burnt down in major riots in January 532. The huge new domed (third) church was built for the Byzantine emperor Justinian (527–65) by the architects Anthemius of Tralles and Isidore of Miletus (with the help, so legend has it, of 10,000 artisans), and was inaugurated on 27 December 537.

An earlier and smaller 6th-century church in Constantinople – SS Sergius and Bacchus – probably reveals the same architects already engaged in experimentation with domed architecture under the patronage of Justinian. This octagonal church has in common with Hagia Sophia an infinite variety in the interior forms and decorations, tantalizingly concealed within a scarcely articulated and heavy exterior frame.

The structural system of Hagia Sophia is based on opposing forces held in equilibrium, the thrust of the dome being countered by semidomes in the west and east and heavy buttresses north and south.

Conception and design

When Justinian commissioned his architects to build the new Hagia Sophia they clearly realized that this was a new style of church in the Early Christian world. Legend claims that the design was given to Justinian by an angel. Its complexity certainly reveals an extraordinary architectural confidence at a massive scale, requiring precise measuring and engineering boldness. The brief given to Anthemius and Isidore demanded the construction of a sacred space unprecedented in any other church, which had to be appropriate for the regular celebration of the Byzantine liturgy as well as for state ceremonial and pomp.

The rituals of the liturgy included processions in which the bread and wine were carried through the congregation to the eastern sanctuary for their consecration in the eucharist, Bible readings and a sermon. The culmination of the liturgy was celebrated by the Ecumenical Patriarch at the silver altar; the fittings of the sanctuary were replete with silver, gold and precious stones, and only the clergy and the emperor, who was seen as the representative of Christ on earth, were ever allowed to enter this Holy of Holies.

The architects worked at such a level of detail that the marble floor was divided by strips ('rivers') to assist the clergy of the church in the performance of the ceremonial. Although functional, this architecture at the same time offered the faithful an enveloping experience of light and space, especially beneath the centralized dome, soon to be understood in Byzantine theological exegesis as the symbol of heaven.

All the vaults of the ceilings and walls above the worshipper were covered with mosaics. In the 6th century subjects were confined to a myriad golden crosses and other non-figurative ornaments; it was only from the 9th century onwards that figurative subjects, such as the Virgin and Child between archangels in the apse, a Christ in the dome, and portraits of emperors and the main saints connected with Hagia Sophia, were added piecemeal, with imperial sponsorship. The church also progressively gained and displayed all manner of

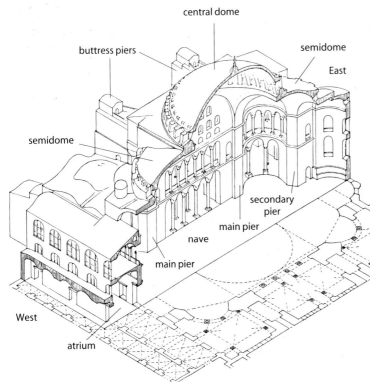

central dome

buttress piers

semidome

East

semidome

secondary pier

main pier

nave

main pier

West

atrium

The interior looking east, towards the chancel of the Christian church. Almost every surface is, or was, covered in marble veneer or glass mosaic, while the ring of windows at the base of the dome gives it an impression of weightlessness.

Christian relics, including a piece of the True Cross. This led to its use not only for vast congregational services, but also for private devotions and prayers.

The church was entered on the west from an atrium. A second monumental entrance lay on the southwest side of the church, next to the Patriarch's Palace, which was added to the church in the late 6th century, close to the separate Baptistery. The inner narthex had nine doors leading into the nave, and there were four ramps in the corners of the church giving access to the high galleries situated on the north, west and south sides.

Construction

Hagia Sophia was the largest church that had ever been built in the early Christian world; its scale is best appreciated in the dim light of dawn, the hour of the celebration of the liturgy, and flickering candles. Procopius, writing the official tribute to Justinian soon after its dedication in 537, expresses the perplexity of visitors ever since: how is the dome supported in mid-air?

The answer is that the structural engineering is concealed. Visitors see the central dome with buttressing semidomes on the east and west, and watch the shafts of sunlight from their windows illuminating the church. They see the marble

Hagia Sophia makes rich use of coloured marble for the columns and white marble for the capitals, which are exquisitely carved.

which were an integral part of the means of stabilizing the pressures within the structure. The combination of marble colonnades and brick vaults derives from imperial Roman concrete architecture in Italy, but the choice of materials depends on the local traditions of building in Roman Asia Minor.

Later history

Hagia Sophia remained the largest church of the Byzantine empire and the central monument of Orthodox Christianity. It was the cathedral, seat of the Patriarch of Constantinople and the main ceremonial church of the Byzantine empire up to 1453, except for a period as the Latin cathedral from 1204 to 1261.

The main later changes to Justinian's church consisted of the rebuilding of the dome higher by around 7 m (23 ft) after a collapse in 558 (the work was by Isidore the Younger), giving it its definitive modern silhouette as well as remedying the dangerous horizontal thrust of the first, lower dome; the probable rebuilding of the north and south tympana of the nave after an earthquake in 869; the rebuilding of the main west arch, semidome and parts of the dome after an earthquake in 989 by an Armenian architect, Trdat; the addition in 1317 of buttresses on the north and east sides; and the rebuilding of the east arch, semidome and parts of the dome after an earthquake in 1346.

In 1453 the city of Constantinople fell to the Ottoman Turks, whose troops broke into the church in the midst of the last mass ever to be held there. Hagia Sophia was converted into a mosque and soon gained four minarets and other Muslim additions – the apse at ground level was converted to include a *mihrab* orientated towards Mecca, a *mimbar* was added on the right and the sultan's box on the left; huge discs with Arabic inscriptions were suspended on the piers. Its architecture was impressively copied and developed in the mosque of Suleyman the Magnificent by the architect Sinan. The last major repairs to the structure were carried out by the Swiss architects Gaspare and Giuseppe Fossati in 1847–49 – a remarkable enterprise of consolidation and redecoration. The building became a museum in 1931.

colonnades (with coloured marble from various Mediterranean quarries) and the veined marble revetments (often set 'back to back' with their symmetrical veining suggesting mysterious forms within the stone) and deeply undercarved marble capitals, spandrels and cornices (the white marble from the Proconnesian quarries in the Sea of Marmara). But they will scarcely notice the limestone or green local granite, bricks, mortar, lead and iron cramps which are the supporting structural elements beneath all these facings; nor will they perhaps notice the wooden tie-beams between the columns and vaults

FACTFILE

Nave	78 x 72 m
Dome	
diameter	31 m
height	62 m
Materials	stone, bricks, mortar, plus iron and timber for ties and cramps

The Temple at Tanjavur

Time: *c*. 995–1010   Location: Tanjavur, South India

On the 275th day of the 25th year [of his reign = AD 1010], the king Shri Rajarajadeva gave one copper water pot to be placed on the copper pinnacle of the sacred shrine of the god Shri Rajarajeshvara.

INSCRIPTION, BRIHADISHVARA TEMPLE

The temple dedicated to Shiva erected by Rajaraja I at Tanjavur must be ranked as one of the greatest of all Hindu monuments in Asia, not only for its colossal scale but also for the perfection of its constructional technique and the clarity of its architectural conception. Much is known about the temple's patron and the circumstances of its construction thanks to the extensive inscriptions running along the basement of the building. Abandoned and remodelled on several occasions, the temple is now once again an active place of worship.

Rajaraja I (reigned 985–1014) was the first king of the Chola dynasty to select Tanjavur (the Tanjore of the British) as the capital of his rapidly expanding domains. From this city, which was

A view of the temple, with its steeply pyramidal tower rising over the linga sanctuary to the rear of the open pavilion for the Nandi bull.

strategically situated at the head of the fertile delta of the Kaveri River that runs through the middle of the Tamil country, Rajaraja set out on military campaigns all over South India, as well as to Orissa and Sri Lanka; his emissaries are even reputed to have reached Sumatra.

According to the inscriptions on the temple, Rajaraja took a personal interest in the construction of the monument, and was responsible for installing the pinnacle that marked its completion. Together with his queens, Rajaraja donated several gold and silver images for worship. The inscriptions also mention the 600 or so people employed by the temple and the wages that they received. The list includes dancing masters and

Side view of the columned halls in front of the linga sanctuary, with inscriptions covering the basement mouldings topped by a frieze of fantastic beasts, and sculpted figures in the wall niches above.

dancing girls, singers and musicians, conch-blowers, parasol-bearers, lamp-lighters, potters, washermen, astrologers, tailors, carpenters and florists. Though erected to glorify its royal patron, the temple was formally consecrated to Shiva under the name of Rajarajeshvara, later altered to Brihadishvara. As is usual in Shiva sanctuaries, the god was worshipped in symbolic form as a phallus, or linga; the emblem was fashioned out of polished basalt and was some 4 m (13 ft) high.

Construction

The Brihadishvara represents the climax of South Indian temple architecture. The temple stands in the middle of a vast rectangular walled courtyard lined by colonnades accommodating small sub-shrines. The courtyard is entered in the middle of the east side through a rectangular gateway structure topped with a barrel-vaulted roof; a short distance outside is a larger and higher free-standing gateway of the same type.

The temple itself comprises a square sanctuary housing the linga. This is surrounded by a passageway on two levels and is approached through a narrow vestibule with transverse doorways reached by flights of steps on the north and south. Two spacious columned halls extend to the east. The outer walls are supported on a double series of basement mouldings, the upper one incorporating a frieze of animal torsos. Above this are two superimposed wall series with pilastered projections overhung by curved eaves. Carvings of Hindu deities are placed in the deep niches on the projections, while flat pilasters standing in pots, all carved in relief, occupy the intervening recesses.

The pyramidal tower that rises above has 13 storeys that steadily diminish in height. Each storey is topped with a parapet of ornamental vaulted and dome-like roof forms, a characteristic feature of South Indian temples. The sanctuary-tower is capped by a large hemispherical roof on top of which is placed the copper pot-like finial installed by Rajaraja himself.

The temple is built entirely of granite blocks, laid one upon the other without any mortar. The sanctuary-tower is built with tiers of corbelled

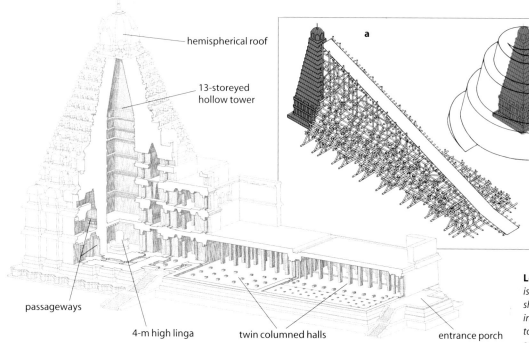

hemispherical roof

13-storeyed hollow tower

a

b

passageways

4-m high linga   twin columned halls   entrance porch

Left *Cut-away isometric drawing showing the interior of the tower, the linga sanctuary with a passageway on two levels, and the halls in front.*

Above *Two possible methods of lifting blocks to the summit of the tower:* **a** *ramp on bamboo scaffolding;* **b** *spiral earthen ramp.*

blocks that gradually cantilever inwards until they are closed off by the hemispherical roof. Though the tower is hollow, an enormous quantity of stone was utilized in its construction – estimated at almost 17,000 cu. m (600,350 cu. ft). Since granite was unavailable in the vicinity, roughly cut materials had to be transported by river from a quarry some 45 km (28 miles) upstream from Tanjavur.

Scholars have speculated about how the blocks were lifted to the upper storeys of the sanctuary-tower. Some 6 km (9 miles) northwest of Tanjavur is a village called Sarapallam, the Dell of the Scaffold. Here, so it is believed, began a ramp supported on bamboo scaffolding that led to the summit of the sanctuary-tower. Another theory postulates a spiral earthen ramp winding upwards around the tower, along which blocks were hauled. Whatever method was actually used, the tower survives complete as a testimony to the virtuoso building techniques of the Cholas.

Later additions

The plasterwork that ornaments the granite tower elements was added in the 18th–19th centuries when the temple was renovated under the Marathas of Tanjavur. However, it was the

Nayakas of the 17th century who completed the outer hall of the temple and built the pavilion for the colossal sculpture of Nandi, the bull mount of Shiva, that stands freely in front. The Nayakas were also responsible for the finely worked Subrahmanya temple and the goddess shrine which form part of the temple complex. The presence of these post-Chola period structures testifies to the significance of the Brihadishvara as a royal commemorative monument in post-Chola times. But the greatest achievement rests with Rajaraja and his master architect.

FACTFILE

Sanctuary tower	25 m sq. 60 m high
Hemispherical roof	7 m diameter 7 m high
Walled courtyard	241 × 121 m
Materials	drystone masonry of granite blocks
Decoration	carved granite covered with polychrome plasterwork
Renovations	17th and 19th centuries

3 The Temple of Byodo-in

Time: 1053 Location: Kyoto, Japan

If you doubt that there is a paradise, stand in worship before the bright temple at Uji.
CHILDREN'S VERSE, 12TH CENTURY

The temple of Byodo-in stands amid trees beside a small lake, as it has done for nearly one thousand years. Despite its early date, it is nevertheless a perfect example of a developed architectural style. This would be significant in itself, but in addition the building is made not of stone but of timber, a material susceptible to decay and fire, and stands in a land subject to earthquakes and past civil strife. Its survival over time, in more or less the form in which it was originally built, is indeed a minor miracle.

The temple's form originated in China, and came to Japan, with Buddhism, in the 6th century AD. The Japanese, as is their habit, adopted the basic model but took it to unparalleled heights of expression in a sequence of building that continues still.

The Byodo-in temple is located on an ancient highway leading out of Kyoto towards Nara, near the turbulent Uji River, at a place known for its scenic beauty. Aristocratic families from Kyoto built villas here, and in 1053 the regent Fujiwara-no-Yorimichi converted his father's villa into a monastery, erecting a group of buildings dedicated to the worship of Buddha Amida, of which the Byodo-in is today the sole survivor.

The building's style differs markedly from the European timber-framing tradition, most obviously in the attention given to the roofs, with their curved lines and ambitious projecting eaves. Apart from their beauty, these overhangs serve the practical function of keeping the frame dry in a country with notably high rainfall. Closer inspection reveals a more significant structural difference – the frame does not rely on triangulation, the fundamental basis of stability of its European counterpart. Instead, the roof members clasp the heads of the posts with complex joints capable of resisting large tensile loads. Thus the building stands like a table with many legs, and the slight flexibility in the frame has allowed the building to ride out periodic earthquake tremors.

In plan, the building consists of a central hall – the Hoo-do or Phoenix hall – with raised galleries projecting on either side which are terminated by short returns towards the lake. It is easy to imagine a bird with outstretched wings, and the general lightness of form and the lake setting all

Right *The Japanese timber-framing tradition differs from the European. It relies on a complex system of posts and joints, giving the building some flexibility. Useful in an earthquake zone, it is also of great beauty.*

FACTFILE

Total width	48 m
Width of façade of Phoenix Hall	14.24 m
Height of Buddha statue	3 m

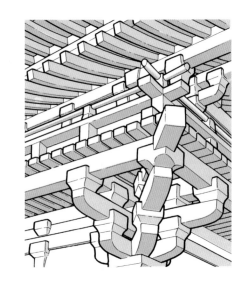

enhance this allusion. The two bronze phoenixes on the central ridge (copies of the originals) also emphasize the idea of death and reincarnation central to Buddhist teaching.

The purpose of all this lavish expenditure was to provide a sumptuous worship hall in which could be housed a large image of the Buddha, carved in wood and commissioned by Yorimichi from the famous sculptor Joche. Generally regarded to be the artist's masterpiece, it is nearly 3 m (10 ft) high.

There is a particular quality which ancient timbers give to an interior, stemming from the basic texture of an organic material. In view of the age of the building, it is of course too much to expect that all the fabric is original. However, it has been most sensitively conserved, for it has the

patina of age and yet is in good repair. It is also now a World Heritage site, one of the very few created for an all-timber building.

Above *The temple, with two phoenixes on its roof, is reflected in the pool in front. The garden is an important element of the complex.*

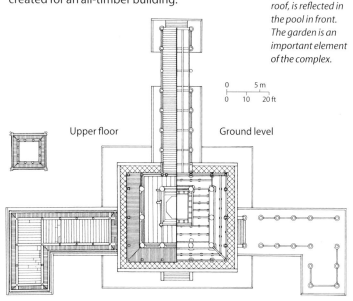

Upper floor   Ground level

0   5 m
0   10   20 ft

Right *Plan of the Byodo-in: two symmetrical corridors extend from the Phoenix Hall which houses the statue of Buddha.*

St Mark's Cathedral

Time: 1063–71 Location: Venice, Italy

… a multitude of pillars and white domes, clustered into a long, low pyramid of coloured light; a treasure-heap it seems, partly of gold, and partly of opal and mother-of-pearl, hollowed beneath into five great vaulted porches.

JOHN RUSKIN, 1851–53

The west front of St Mark's, facing the Piazza. The basic structure is that of the 11th-century church, but much of the decorative detail was added later, including the lace-like stone frill.

Venice was founded as a place of safety in the midst of its lagoons in 813. The body of the Evangelist St Mark, piously stolen from Alexandria in Egypt, was brought to the city in 828. An earlier church built to honour him was destroyed by fire in 976. The present church, adjoining the old Doge's Palace, was begun in 1063 and consecrated in 1094.

It is, and always was, a building unique in western Europe, partly because of its architectural form and partly because of the extraordinary richness of its mosaic decoration. Both are due to the fact that Venice, a commercial empire founded on sea-power, looked east, towards Constantinople, rather than west. The design, and perhaps also the architect, came from that

city. The model on which it was based was Justinian's much older church of the Holy Apostles in Constantinople, which was destroyed after the Turkish conquest.

Like that imperial church, St Mark's has a Greek-cross plan: four equal arms form nave, transepts and chancel, with domes over the arms and the crossing. The chancel ends in an apse and around the nave and transepts, outside the domes, run aisles. In elevation, St Mark's is two-storeyed; originally there were galleries over the aisles but these were later removed, making the aisles also two-storeyed, although there are narrow balustraded walkways at the upper level above the arcades. The result is a complex interlocking of spaces with mysterious vistas glimpsed between marble columns.

Around the nave, on the north, west and east, but not integrated into it, runs a single-storey atrium covered by a series of smaller domes. The mosaics in these domes are arranged in concentric circles to tell continuous narratives. Small in scale and close enough to be seen clearly, they are among the most exciting works in the whole church. The Creation of the Birds and Fishes, for instance, reveals an extraordinarily free fertility of invention. Visitors pass through this porch, or narthex, before entering the main interior space.

Above *The semidome over the northernmost door of the façade (far left in the photo opposite) contains the only medieval mosaic remaining on the exterior. It shows the front of the church as it originally appeared.*

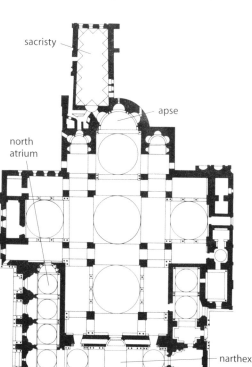

sacristy

apse

north atrium

narthex

Left *Plan of St Mark's, a Greek cross with domes over the four arms and the crossing, and with a narthex (also domed) surrounding the north, west and south sides.*

Construction

St Mark's is actually built of brick (the underlying structure can be seen clearly in the crypt, where the brick is not covered), but every surface is faced with precious marble or mosaic, so that the total effect is one of great richness. From the point of view of structural engineering, the church is not innovatory, and makes no attempt to match the scale or daring of Hagia Sophia in Constantinople (p. 21). Nor could it. The unstable subsoil of Venetian mud, even reinforced by a raft of timber piles, threatened disaster – a danger evident today in the uneven floor.

The church that was finished in 1071 is essentially the one we still see today. The west front keeps its five deep porches, lined with marble and surmounted by semicircular mosaic panels. They are matched on the upper level by larger mosaic lunettes, the central one now containing only glass. These are covered by a frill of late Gothic ornament, likened by John Ruskin to the spume of the sea.

The decoration

Wonderful as it is, St Mark's is much more than a splendid piece of architecture. For a thousand years it accumulated works of art; some, like the marble and mosaic decoration, are integral to the building, others, like the Pala d'Oro (Golden Altar) and the Bronze Horses, were assembled from

The glowing interior of St Mark's. Some early mosaics are visible on the pendentives and the right-hand arch. Those on the left-hand wall are Renaissance replacements.

elsewhere, sometimes under morally questionable circumstances.

The mosaics, in a style that is also ultimately Byzantine but the work of Italian craftsmen in a tradition going back to 6th-century Ravenna, constitute a complete scheme of Christian doctrine, from the Creation to the end of the world. They were begun soon after the building was finished and work continued on them through the 12th and 13th centuries. At ground level the facing of the walls is of marble, much of it using ancient Roman materials plundered from sites on the mainland. In the floor, red or green discs betray the fact that classical columns have been sliced to make patterned panels.

From the main west door, the visitor enters the atrium or narthex, where the dome mosaics are drawn from the Old Testament: the Creation, Adam and Eve, the Fall, Cain and Abel, Noah and the Flood, the Tower of Babel, the stories of Abraham and of Joseph and finally the story of Moses and the Exodus.

Inside the church it is the New Testament – the life of Christ, the Crucifixion and Ascension, the Acts of the Apostles, ending with the Last Judgment – that unfolds. The lives of the Apostles, especially of course St Mark, are related in considerable detail. Not all of them are medieval. In the Renaissance several areas of vault and wall were restored using designs by leading Venetian artists, including Tintoretto.

Of the treasures acquired during the Middle Ages, two of the most notable are the Pala d'Oro and the Bronze Horses. The first, the 'Golden Altar', was made by artists from Constantinople in 975, but much altered and added to. A large golden altar-screen, it contains pictures in coloured enamel and is studded with precious stones. Six large scenes along the top show the Passion story and the death of the Virgin, with the Archangel Michael in the centre. Other panels show the Life of Christ and rows of saints.

The Bronze Horses were part of the spoils from the sack of Constantinople in 1204 by the Crusaders – a shameful episode of the Fourth Crusade. They stand proudly over the western porch (or stood; they have now been taken down

and replaced by copies). Controversy still rages over their original date and provenance.

To see all the wonders of St Mark's takes many days. Some are now housed in a museum opening off the south transept. Indeed, the whole church is a museum, but one which retains its original function and meaning, uniquely redolent of the past, a monument as much to civic pride as to religious devotion.

The four great Bronze Horses above the central door were brought back from Constantinople after the Fourth Crusade, but their ultimate provenance is still a mystery. They are certainly Classical in origin, but whether Greek or Roman cannot be determined.

FACTFILE

Total length	76 m
Width of transepts	61 m
Width of atrium	47 m
Central dome	
diameter	13 m
interior height	29 m
exterior height	40 m

The Leaning Tower of Pisa

Time: 1173–c. 1370   Location: Pisa, Italy

*The stabilization of the Tower is as delicate an operation as the treatment of
an elderly invalid by a doctor who is forbidden to sound his chest but
who knows for sure that his patient reacts alarmingly to every medicine.*

Jean Kerisel, 1987

The Leaning Tower rises behind the Fountain of the Putti, with its group of three putti holding the coat-of-arms of Pisa, the work of Giuseppe Vaccà, 1764.

Imagine a tower, founded on material as soft as foam rubber, whose inclination is slowly and inexorably increasing to the point at which it is about to fall over. Moreover, the masonry composing the tower is so fragile that the stress generated by the increasing inclination is approaching the strength of the material – it could explode at any moment. The disturbance resulting from grouting or underpinning the foundations on the overhanging side would cause the tower to topple, while propping or pulling with cables could trigger the collapse of the masonry. This is an accurate picture of the marginal state of the Leaning Tower of Pisa, whose stabilization represents the ultimate civil engineering challenge.

The Leaning Tower of Pisa is not just some cranky tourist attraction, however. It is an architectural gem and would still be one of the most important monuments of medieval Europe even if it were not leaning. Standing in the Piazza del Duomo, it is part of the complex of four major gleaming white buildings, comprising the cathedral (Duomo), its bell-tower (campanile – the Leaning Tower), its baptistery and the cemetery (Camposanto). As with the other buildings in the Piazza, the bell-tower was intended to represent the civic pride and glory of the wealthy city state of Pisa, and as such it is beautiful, unique and enigmatic.

Details of construction

The eight-storey tower is 58.4 m (192 ft) high, it weighs 14,500 metric tonnes and its masonry foundations are 19.6 m (64 ft) in diameter, with a maximum depth of 5.5 m (18 ft) below ground level. The foundations slope towards the south at 5.5 degrees to the horizontal and as a consequence the seventh floor overhangs the first by 4.5 m (14.76 ft). Construction is in the form of a hollow cylinder surrounded by colonnades. The inner and outer surfaces of the cylinder are faced with tightly jointed marble, but the material

between these facings consists merely of mortar and stones in which extensive voids have been found. A spiral stairway winds up the tower within its walls.

The underlying ground consists of three distinct layers. Layer A is about 10 m (33 ft) thick and is made up of variable soft silty deposits laid down in shallow water less than 10,000 years ago. Layer B consists of very soft and sensitive marine clays laid down up to 30,000 years ago, and extends to a depth of 40 m (130 ft). Layer C is a dense sand extending to considerable depth. The water table in Layer A is between 1 m (3.28 ft) and 2 m (6.5 ft) deep. The many soil borings around, and even beneath, the tower show that the surface of Layer B is dish-shaped due to the weight of the tower above it. It can be deduced from this that the average settlement of the tower is 2.5 to 3 m (8 to 10 ft), showing how very compressible the underlying soil is.

History of construction

Construction of the tower began in August 1173 under the direction of Bonanno Pisano. By about 1178 it had risen to one quarter of the way up the fourth storey, when work stopped. The reason for this halt is not known, but had work continued much further the soil in Layer B would have had insufficient strength to carry the load and the tower would have fallen over. After a pause of nearly 100 years, Giovanni di Simone recommenced construction in about 1272, by which time the strength of the clay had increased due to consolidation under the weight of the tower (although this would not have been known). By about 1278 construction had reached the seventh level when work again stopped – possibly due to a local war. There can be no doubt that had the tower been completed at this stage it would have fallen over. In about 1360, when further consolidation of the clay had taken place, Tommaso Pisano commenced work on the bell chamber which was completed in about 1370 – nearly 200 years after construction began.

The tower must already have been tilting when work on the bell chamber began, as it is noticeably more vertical than the rest of the tower. Indeed on the south side there are six steps from the seventh cornice up to the floor of the bell chamber, while on the north there are only four.

A view of the cathedral of Pisa, with its leaning bell-tower beyond. Note that the bell chamber at the top is slightly more upright than the supporting tower.

The Leaning Tower from the north, with the temporary cable stays that were attached during soil extraction. These were a safeguard to hold the tower should anything have gone wrong.

History of tilting

In fact, there is evidence that tilting began early in the tower's history – its axis is not straight, but bends to the north. In an attempt to correct the lean, tapered blocks of masonry have been used at the level of each floor in order to bend the axis of the tower away from the lean. By careful analysis of the relative inclinations of the masonry layers, the history of the tilting of the tower has

The connection of the temporary safeguard cables to the third storey.

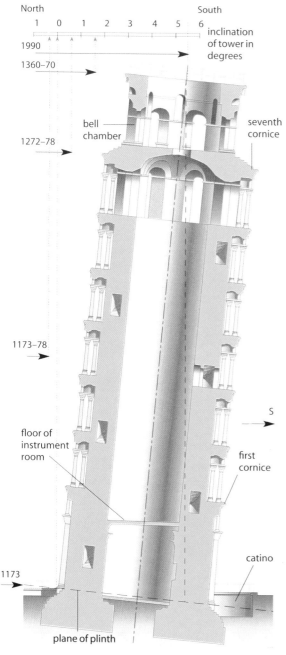

Left Diagram of the Leaning Tower, showing the increase in tilt as the different stages were built.

been revealed. At the end of the first phase it was actually leaning northwards by about one quarter of a degree. Then as construction advanced above the fourth storey it began to move towards the south so that by 1278, when the seventh level had been reached, it was inclining southwards by about 0.6 of a degree. This increased to about 1.6 degrees by 1360.

Advanced computer analysis has revealed that the rapid increase in inclination as the seventh level was reached and the bell chamber was added is directly analogous to constructing a tower from model bricks on a soft carpet. It is possible to build to a certain critical height, but no higher, however careful one is. The tower is just at its critical height and is very close to falling over.

In 1817 two British architects used a plumb line to measure the inclination and discovered that at that time it was 5 degrees. Then in 1838 the architect Alessandro della Gherardesca excavated a walk-way (catino) around the base of the tower to reveal the column plinths and foundation steps as was originally intended before the tower had sunk. The result was an inrush of water on the south side, since here the excavation was below the water table. There is evidence to suggest that at this point the inclination of the tower dramatically increased by nearly half a degree, to about 5.4 degrees.

Precise measurements, begun in 1911, show that the inclination of the tower has been increasing inexorably each year, and the rate of tilt has doubled since the mid-1930s. In 1990 the rate of tilt was equivalent to a horizontal movement at the top of about 1.5 mm (0.06 in) per year. Moreover, all interference with the tower has resulted

Stabilization of the tower

In 1990, following the collapse of a bell-tower in Pavia, which had not been leaning, a commission under the chairmanship of Professor Michele Jamiolkowski was set up by the Italian Prime Minister to advise on and implement stabilization measures for the Pisa tower. The internationally accepted conventions for the conservation of valuable historic monuments requires that their essential character should be preserved, together with their history and craftsmanship. Thus any intrusive interventions on the tower had to be kept to an absolute minimum and permanent stabilization schemes involving propping or visible support were unacceptable, and in any case could have triggered the collapse of the fragile masonry.

A solution was sought that would result in a small reduction in inclination which is not enough to be visible but which would reduce the stresses in the masonry and stabilize the foundations. After years of study, analysis and large-scale trials a method known as soil extraction was adopted. This involves installing a number of soil extraction tubes adjacent to and just beneath the north side of the foundations. Starting in February 1999, in an atmosphere of great tension, very gradually and in a carefully monitored step-by-step manner, small amounts of soil were removed from Layer A by means of a special drill. Due to the softness of the soil, the cavity formed by each extraction gently closed, resulting in a small surface subsidence and a minute rotation northwards of the tower.

The soil extraction operation took two-and-a-half years, and the inclination of the tower was reduced by half a degree. If southward tilt were to recommence it would be possible to repeat the soil extraction process at some future time. In addition to the soil extraction, a limited amount of strengthening of the masonry was undertaken at the most vulnerable locations on the south side.

This beautiful and enigmatic tower has been stabilized using a method which respects and preserves both its character and its fascinating interaction with the subsoil.

Above *Some of the drilling tubes in position for the process of soil extraction.*

Right *The arrangement of the drilling rigs for soil extraction beneath the north edge of the foundations of the tower.*

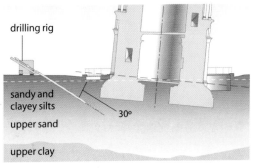

drilling rig

sandy and clayey silts

upper sand

30°

upper clay

in significant increases in tilt. For example, in 1934 consolidation of the foundation masonry by means of grout injection resulted in a sudden movement south of about 10 mm (0.4 in) and ground water abstraction from the lower sands in the 1970s resulted in an increase in movement of about 12 mm (0.5 in). These responses confirm how sensitively poised the tower is – and how delicate any method of stabilization would have to be.

FACTFILE

Height from foundations to belfry	58.4 m
Diameter of foundations	19.6 m
Weight of tower	14,500 tonnes
Work on the foundations commenced	9 August 1173
Work suspended at fourth storey	c. 1178
Construction to seventh cornice	c. 1272–1278
Construction of belfry completed	c. 1370
Excavation of catino around base	1838
Inclination of tower to the south	5.5 degrees
Settlement of the foundations	c. 3 m

Chartres Cathedral

Time: 1194–mid-13th century   Location: Chartres, France

*From the cross on the flèche and the keystone of the vault, down through the ribbed
nervures, the columns, the windows, to the foundation of the flying buttresses
far beyond the walls, one idea controlled every line.*
HENRY ADAMS, 1913

Chartres is the most complete survivor of a series of major cathedrals in the Ile de France, the region round Paris, which together established the Gothic style in Europe. St Denis and Sens, in the 1140s, were followed by Laon and Paris (1160s), Bourges and Chartres (1190s), Reims and Le Mans (1210s), and Amiens and Beauvais (1220s and 1240s). Each of these churches is original and individual, but together they set a pattern which would persist for a century and would spread to all parts of Christendom. Essentially this consisted of a system based not on the strength of solid masonry but on a balance of forces held in equilibrium. The pointed arch, which replaced the Romanesque round arch, meant that arches of varying width could all rise to the same height; the weight of the stone vault could now be concentrated upon certain points instead of being distributed along the whole wall, allowing the spaces in between to be opened up as increasingly large windows; and at those points the thrust could be carried down to the ground outside through flying buttresses, giving the whole structure a feeling of lightness and dynamic line that had never been achieved before.

Chartres followed the traditional plan of the Latin cross, with nave, transepts and choir meeting at a crossing. The choir ends in an apse with radiating chapels. The interior elevation is three-

The west front of Chartres Cathedral is an accidental mixture of styles. The towers were begun in the 1130s and 1140s, but the spire on the left was added nearly 400 years later. The rose window is Gothic, of about 1210.

The north side of the nave: the round flying buttresses with radiating colonettes were not functionally effective. The segmental ones above were added in the 14th century.

storeyed: an arcade of cylindrical piers carrying wide arches, with shafts in the four main directions, the inner one rising the whole height into the vault; a narrow triforium of five small arches per bay; and a very deep clearstorey with plate-tracery. Unusually, the clearstorey is extended downwards to a point below the springing of the vault. Of the nine towers originally planned for Chartres, only two were built.

While in many ways Chartres is typical of the early phase of Gothic, what makes it unique is that it still retains its full complement of sculpture and – even more exceptional – all its stained glass. As a total experience, therefore, Chartres has to count as one of the high points of world architecture.

Building Chartres

An earlier cathedral, a large Romanesque building with a spectacular three-bay porch – the 'Portail Royal' – had been built on the site in the 1140s. Fifty years later, on 10 June 1194, this cathedral was destroyed by fire, leaving only the porch. The rest had to be totally rebuilt.

It was decided to keep the old Portail Royal. Although this compromises the stylistic consistency of the building, it was a fortunate decision, since it meant the survival of some of the finest sculpture of the early Middle Ages. Nevertheless, the overall impression at Chartres is still one of a unified design, in which clear choices were made and aesthetic judgments followed. This suggests that it is the product of a single mind, a particular architect, whom historians customarily refer to as 'the Chartres master'. It has convincingly been shown, however, that over the 30 years it took to

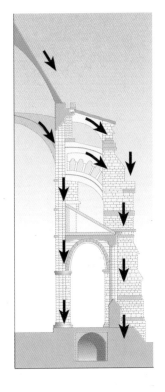

The constructional system used at Chartres and all the Gothic cathedrals: the weight of the vault being carried to the ground by flying buttresses.

FACTFILE

Total length	155 m
Width of west front	47.5 m
Width of nave	14 m
Length of nave	73 m
Height of the vaulting in the nave	37 m
Height of north tower	115 m
Height of south tower	107 m
Diameter of the large rose-windows	13.4 m

build, at least nine different masters were in charge, whose hands can be distinguished by a host of small details and some major decisions. Were they all following a master-plan, or did each one graft his own ideas on to what his predecessors had built? An intriguing question, but one that is impossible to answer.

Construction techniques

Gothic cathedrals were built by teams of construction workers under a master-builder, whom they would follow from site to site and sometimes from country to country. The team was known as the 'lodge', and consisted of specialized craftsmen, each with a separate skill. The stone was cut as precisely as possible at the quarry, in order to minimize the labour of transport, and the more elaborate elements, such as moulded arches or window tracery, would be laid out on the ground to match full-scale drawings. (A number of floors still preserve such drawings.) Ideally, the whole plan would be marked out and the foundations dug in one campaign.

The building would then rise layer by layer, and we can often follow the building history through the coursing of the masonry. In very large buildings such as Chartres, there are vertical breaks and changes in the coursing which indicate the building sequence.

It was normal to begin church-building at the east end, but this might not have happened at Chartres. The form of the nave flying buttresses – a quarter-circle wheel with spokes – is more prim-

itive than those of the choir further east, and the aisle windows, simple lancets in the nave, are more complex in the choir.

Scaffolding was expensive, and so the usual method was to construct wooden platforms supported on the walls that had already been built rather than resting on the ground. When the full height of the walls had been reached the internal space would be roofed over with timber before the vault was constructed, since this protected the builders from the weather. A skeleton of ribs would be made and then the spaces between (the cells) were filled out with a minimum of wooden centering.

Stones were carried up the scaffolding on ramps or lifted by cranes worked by treadwheels within the building. Decorative carving like capitals was carried out *in situ*. Figure sculpture was carved in the workshop and installed when finished – some medieval sculptures have numbers indicating where they were to be placed. Last of all came the glaziers, filling the windows with stained glass meticulously cut to fill the spaces in the stone tracery.

All these activities were governed by the master-mason, who was on the spot at all times. One medieval churchman complained that the master, 'holding a rod and gloves in his hand, says to the others "Cut it for me this way" and does no labour and yet receives a higher fee.'

Sculpture and glass

The architecture of Chartres seems deliberately to have been kept simple in order that the eyes should not be distracted on the exterior from the sculpture and in the interior from its glass.

The sculptural story must begin with the Portail Royal of the 1140s. Together with St Denis, it marks the beginning of free-standing figure-sculpture in the West, which took the form of *figures-colonnes*. These stood against, or replaced, the columns grouped round the door-ways of churches, with more sculpture in relief on the lintels and tympana above.

The north and south transepts were given even more elaborate porches. Created 80 or so years after the Portail Royal, they belong to a different world, that of 13th-century humanism, with life-like idealized figures combining spiritual intensity with heroic physical strength.

But the feature for which Chartres is most celebrated is its glass. A common reaction on entering the cathedral is one of dismay – it seems almost pitch dark. Early medieval glass was not radiantly transparent. The colours are deep and jewel-like and it takes some time to get used to the light level (and, it has to be said, it takes binoculars to appreciate the glass in any detail). These difficulties accepted, Chartres is an experience like no other.

The cathedral was glazed during the first half of the 13th century. The glass was paid for by the offerings of pilgrims, by noble patrons and by the merchants and tradesmen of the town, whose occupations are commemorated under their patron saints, linked with episodes from the Bible (for instance, the carpenters' window features the building of Noah's Ark). It is impossible to summarize the entire scheme; it includes the great cycle of the Old and New Testaments, the lives and miracles of the saints, and legendary history

A clearstorey window in the east side of the south transept. St Denis ('Dionisus'), the patron saint of France, hands the sacred banner, the 'oriflamme', to a knight who bears the Crusader's cross on his breast.

such as the story of Charlemagne and Roland. Most of these windows must always have required expert guidance to understand their meaning. The long lancets at aisle level often comprise 20 or 30 small scenes. Higher up, the scale becomes larger, and giant figures like that of Aaron, with his jewelled breastplate and wide staring eyes, gaze down.

Quite apart from the subjects of the windows, medieval theologians attributed a mystical quality to colour and light itself, expounded by Abbot Suger in his account of the building of St Denis. 'Material light, both that created by nature in the heavens and that produced on earth by human artifice, is an image of intelligible light and above all of the True Light Itself.'

7 King's College Chapel

Time: 1446–1515 Location: Cambridge, England

*I wol that the edificacion of my College procede in large fourme, clene and substantial,
settyng a parte superfluite of too gret curious werkes of enteille and besy moldyng.*
WILL OF HENRY VI, 1448

Part of the international fame of the chapel at King's College, Cambridge, derives from its choir, and the annual Christmas Carol service broadcast throughout the world, but the principal reason many thousands of people visit it each year is to experience a sublime work of architecture. It is the pre-eminent example of English Perpendicular, a late Gothic style distinguished, in its most magnificent manifestations, by its fan vaulting, a constructional form unique to English architecture of this period. The architecture provides large areas of glazing, filled in the case of King's with some of the finest stained glass in Europe. Finally, it contains an enormous piece of furniture, the screen and stalls, which Nikolaus Pevsner described as 'the purest work of the Early Renaissance style in England'.

History

Henry VI (1421–71) founded the college of St Nicholas (his patron saint) in 1441, changing its name in 1443 to 'the King's College of the Blessed Mary and St Nicholas'. Its buildings (now the University's 'Old Schools') formed a courtyard to the north of the present chapel. Henry's memorandum, or Will, of 1448 envisaged a much grander plan, with a great court to the south of the chapel, the dimensions of which he precisely determined. He also suggested that the character of the buildings should be restrained rather than ostentatious. It was not until the 19th century that the College completed the other three sides – on the east formed by the famous transparent screen by William Wilkins, which succeeds in imitating the style of the chapel to picturesque effect.

The chapel thus forms part of a court, like other Oxbridge chapels. As a chapel, not a church, and in recognition of its function as a royal chapel, like the Early Perpendicular St Stephen's Chapel at Westminster, the plan at King's is a high rectangular box, though it is grander and spatially simpler than any chapel in England before or since. Side chapels are suppressed, being contained between the buttresses either side and thus not affecting the main space at all.

Three phases of construction can be deduced. The first, from 1446 to about 1461, under master mason Reginald Ely, ended when Henry VI was deposed. There was little work for some 15 years before work resumed from 1476 to 1485, the end of Richard III's reign. The final phase was from 1508, the last year of Henry VII, to 1515. The vault (begun in 1512) and most of the elaborate carvings, by Thomas Stockton, date from this third period, during the reign of Henry VIII – the crowned roses, portcullises and fleurs-de-lis symbolizing the royal patronage. As Francis Woodman puts it, what began as 'an act of piety and of deep religious conviction' was seen at its completion as 'an object of artistic splendour and dynastic propaganda', contradicting the founder's call for restraint.

The great vault

The timber roof of the chapel – which is of course invisible from below – is one of the finest and largest late medieval roofs in England. It is concealed by the magnificent fan vault, erected in the final phase of construction. Mouldings of the piers, completed in the first campaign, imply a different

Opposite *The view eastwards, from the chapel nave towards the choir, showing the fan vaults and the central timber screen.*

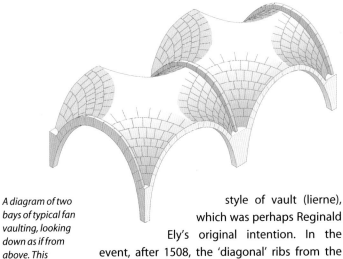

A diagram of two bays of typical fan vaulting, looking down as if from above. This particular form of vaulting is complex, and unique to English architecture of this period.

There are numerous examples of fan vaults in England, usually spanning relatively small chapels attached to earlier churches. But at Sherborne Abbey, which was re-fashioned from about 1475, the nave and transept are 7.9 m (26 ft) wide, and in four other buildings the span is 8 m (26.25 ft) or over: the Henry VII chapel at Westminster; Bath abbey; the so-called New Buildings at Peterborough Cathedral; and King's College, where the span is 12.7 m (42 ft). As in other late Gothic buildings, decorative ribs are applied to the surface of the vault, but the shell in a fan vault is fundamentally different in principle from other surfaces. A pointed quadripartite vault, for example, is curved in only one direction, and its structural performance can be calculated by considering a typical section. A fan vault is curved in two directions, and this means that its structural analysis, as with a dome, is much more complex. Professor Jacques Heyman has employed membrane shell theory to demonstrate the structural action of the form. At a first estimate, the horizontal forces in each bay at King's approximate to 16 tonnes. But the conoid hollow of each vault is partially filled with rubble, and this assists in the stability of the vault, reducing the horizontal thrusts to each buttress to about 10 tonnes.

style of vault (lierne), which was perhaps Reginald Ely's original intention. In the event, after 1508, the 'diagonal' ribs from the piers branch out into the five ribs of each quarter fan. Who actually designed the fan vault is still debated, though John Wastell, master mason from 1508, is usually credited. John a Lee, Henry Smith, William Vertue and Henry Redman, all royal masons, visited the college at various stages during its construction.

John Wastell had also designed the crossing vault at Canterbury Cathedral. His style is distinguished by a certain clarity: the fan vaults at Westminster, of almost exactly the same period, are lush but visually confusing. Wastell's vaults at King's are structurally efficient, and their form is also clarified by the subdividing ribs on each bay. The quality of construction was also exceptionally high – it is 'undoubtedly the best-planned, best-cut and best-executed stone vault in England' – and this standard of execution continues in Stockton's carved decorations on the walls: the roses, portcullises and crowns are almost entirely undercut.

The stained glass

The stained glass at King's is the most complete set of church windows preserved from the time of Henry VIII, and even the contracts for their design and execution survive. Barnard Flower seems to

A detail of the east window, showing Pontius Pilate washing his hands. The stained glass at King's College Chapel is among the finest in Europe.

have subcontracted some of the work to six other glass-painters, but there is some argument about responsibility for the overall design of the windows. Whoever it was – if not the Dutchmen Adrian van den Houte or Dierick Vellert (who seem most likely) – they were certainly familiar with continental woodcuts and engravings, from which the designs are in large part derived. The compositions are sophisticatedly pictorial, crossing from one panel to the next, with subtle line-work and intense portrayal of emotion. The main theme is the life of Christ, supplemented by scenes from that of the Virgin Mary; much of the iconography is typological so that correspondences are drawn between, for example, Jonah who spent three days in the belly of the whale, and the crucifixion and resurrection of Christ. The architectural detail portrayed refers to Renaissance rather than Gothic elements, and there are frequent references to Tudor patronage, especially in the glorious east window. At a more abstract level, the colour combinations are remarkable, and the windows can be appreciated purely as a pattern.

The screen

The screen, or 'pulpitum', was probably installed between 1530 and 1535. It carries the organ above and continues eastwards to form the back of the choir stalls. Its execution was clearly the work of many hands, and the King's College Accounts do not reveal the name of the designer. In style it is more closely related to French or Dutch classicism than Italian, but despite its elaborate decoration it does not seem to be as 'mannerist' as the work at Fontainebleau, for example. Its repetitive round arches, subdivisions of base, shaft and entablature, and the careful hierarchy of its composition ensure a classic sense of order, but within this are cherubs, animals, birds and stylized plant forms woven into the panels of the pilasters, friezes and covings.

The monograms HR and AR, and quartered arms of Henry VIII and Anne Boleyn, who reigned as Queen from 14 November 1532 to 9 May 1536, provide the best evidence for its date. The elaborate coats-of-arms on the backs of the side stalls

and St George and the Dragon with figures above and below are especially rich. In its own manner, the screen attains an authority to match that of the late Gothic masterpiece in which it is situated.

In the 1960s, after some debate, Rubens' *Adoration of the Magi* was installed under the east window and the end of the chapel re-ordered. So now the chapel contains a 17th-century Dutch masterpiece of painting in dialogue with its late Gothic stonework, exceptional glass and Renaissance timber screen.

View of the exterior of the chapel from the southwest, showing it in its architectural setting.

FACTFILE

Length	88 m
Width	12.7 m
Height	24.4 m
Windows	25 completed

St Peter's Basilica

Time: 1506–1666   Location: Rome, Italy

*This temple is an image of the infinite, there is no limit to the feelings it inspires,
to the ideas it recalls, to the enormous number of years it brings to mind,
whether of the past or the future.*

MADAME DE STAËL, 1807

In the summer of 1505 Pope Julius II decided to demolish the most venerable monument in Christendom – the church that Constantine had built more than a thousand years earlier over the tomb of St Peter – and rebuild it. His new basilica was to be one of the wonders of the world, on a scale never attempted before. Over the next two hundred years a succession of great architects worked on it, and the result did indeed eventually very largely fulfil Julius's ambition. St Peter's is an astonishing statement of sustained confidence, grandeur and authority.

The architect Julius chose was Donato Bramante, a man of genius who was responsible for introducing the style of the High Renaissance to Rome. Characteristic of both him and of Julius was his bold plan for the new St Peter's: a centralized church (symmetrical in all four directions) – a Greek cross with four arms ending in apses, to be surmounted by a hemispherical dome. This dome was to rest on four substantial piers, flanked by square chapels covered by smaller domes. There were to be two towers on the façade. Almost our only information about this church comes from a fragmentary plan and a foundation medal issued in 1506.

At first work proceeded rapidly, concentrating on the four great arches that were to support the dome, but after the death of Julius in 1513, followed by Bramante's a year later, the pace slack-

The medal struck in 1506, when the new St Peter's was begun, is almost our only record of Bramante's original intention.

ened. One problem was cash. Julius's successor, Leo X, raised money by selling indulgences – documents that guaranteed the forgiveness of sins – which provoked Luther's protest at Wittenberg. St Peter's was thus one of the causes of the Reformation.

As Bramante's successor, Leo X appointed Raphael, a curious choice, since he was not primarily an architect and he relied for technical advice on Antonio da Sangallo. The altar-end of the old basilica had been demolished and a little temple-like structure built over the shrine of St Peter to protect it. Work now virtually ceased while a debate took place on how to proceed – whether to continue with Bramante's scheme of a centralized church, or to follow a more traditional plan with a longer nave.

There are a number of drawings from the 1520s and 1530s showing the huge arches of the crossing looming over the temporary shrine, while the bare walls of Constantine's nave still stand bleakly in front of it. Nearly all the accumulated treasures of centuries, including the tombs of popes, were ruthlessly smashed.

Between the death of Raphael in 1520 and the appointment of Michelangelo in 1546 a number of schemes were drawn up, some centralized, some longitudinal, but very little progress was made on the ground. Antonio da Sangallo made a

Opposite *A view of St Peter's from the roof of Bernini's colonnade shows the dome very much as Michelangelo meant it to be seen, dominating the façade in a way that is now obscured by Maderno's long nave.*

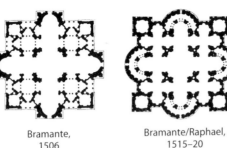

Right *Four stages in the evolution of St Peter's, showing the various solutions proposed by four of its architects. In the event, liturgical considerations led to the building of a long nave, compromising the ideas of Bramante and Michelangelo.*

Bramante, 1506

Bramante/Raphael, 1515–20

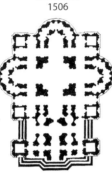

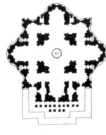

Antonio da Sangallo, 1539

Michelangelo, 1546–64

detailed model, which survives, but this scheme was never begun. These were difficult times for the papacy, including the Sack of Rome and the rise of Protestantism.

A new beginning

Michelangelo was the choice of Pope Paul III. He undertook the task reluctantly, without a fee, 'for the love of God'; he also immediately returned to Bramante's initial scheme. 'Whoever departs from Bramante', he said, 'departs from the truth.' His concept of architecture, nevertheless, was almost the antithesis of Bramante's. Instead of geometrical forms logically related, he saw volume and space as the embodiment of irresistible forces. This is an essentially sculptural concept and makes him as much a forerunner of the Baroque as a child of the Renaissance. He vastly increased the thickness of the central piers and of the exterior walls, convinced (rightly) that they were too weak to support the enormous dome. By the time he died, in 1564, St Peter's had risen as far as the top of the drum, and a detailed model of the dome had been prepared which made his intentions clear.

The succeeding architect, Giacomo della Porta, did not follow his design exactly, but the main outline and structure are still Michelangelo's. The dome consists of a double shell: an inner hemispherical one seen from inside, and another, slightly more pointed, which is seen from outside. Divided into segments by the dynamic lines of ribs converging at the top, it has exercised a continuing influence on dome design ever since.

The real force of Michelangelo's imagination can now be appreciated only from the Vatican garden. From here the complex hierarchy of forms – the giant order of pilasters, with openings squeezed into spaces apparently too small for them, the attic storey with its elaborate window-frames, the powerful ring of paired columns round the drum, and the soaring shape of the dome itself – creates an unforgettable impression of energy.

Michelangelo assumed that this would be the effect from the front as well, but his planned

façade was never built, and the old idea of a long nave (the Latin-cross plan) once again came to the fore. In 1607 a committee of ten architects made the final decision, and Carlo Maderno, one of the first generation of Baroque architects, was put in charge. Within ten years the nave was finished.

Completing St Peter's

Over the long period that St Peter's took to complete, the actual techniques employed in building inevitably changed. In some years, when work was proceeding fast, the labour force could number up to 2000. This was the case at the beginning, when Bramante drew up contracts with five sub-architects, who in turn employed teams of craftsmen paid piecemeal, down to the

level of detail of so much per square foot of pavement, wall and roof.

As mentioned, Bramante's crossing would never have supported the dome he had in mind and it was left to Michelangelo to devise a remedy. Under his leadership the army of labourers grew again. As the structure rose he provided spiral ramps for loaded donkeys to carry up the stones. Always, much depended on the energy of the current pope. When della Porta was building the dome, every available resource was pressed into service and we know that 800 labourers worked in shifts day and night to finish it.

A similar climax of activity marked the building of Maderno's nave. In 1600 a team of specialists had been formed, consisting of masons, painters, stuccoists, glaziers and gilders, reflecting the fact

From the air Bernini's piazza, embraced by oval colonnades, comes into its own. He intended a central section that would have made the piazza more enclosed. Instead of that, it was opened out even more by Mussolini.

Opposite below
The full grandeur of Michelangelo's conception is now visible only from the Vatican garden and is rarely seen by the public.

Inside the central crossing of St Peter's: the space is Michelangelo's, but the decoration – including the baldacchino, the altar, the giant statues and the mosaics – belongs to Bernini. This watercolour by Louis Haghe depicts a papal procession (1864).

Most of the stone used in St Peter's was quarried in the surrounding region – tufa from Porta Portense and travertine from Tivoli. The wooden centering required for Maderno's barrel vault was a feat of engineering in itself, and whole tree-trunks were brought to Rome. Over 1000 men were employed in the building work and in the demolition and carting away of the last vestiges of the old basilica.

Maderno's was an unenviable task. For the elevations of his building, exterior and interior, he had to follow Michelangelo. To design a new façade turned out to be even less rewarding, and the result does not reflect Maderno's talents fairly. Instead of a truly Baroque front, he adapted Michelangelo's earlier scheme, but interpreted it in flat, heavy, unexciting terms, which no one has ever greatly admired. Particularly unfortunate was the abandonment (for structural reasons) of the towers which were to flank the central bays. It is now disproportionately wide, while the length of the nave behind it means that the dome, which should be the climax of the whole building, is invisible except from a distance.

Bernini's contribution

The last great architect to be involved with St Peter's was Gianlorenzo Bernini, master of the Baroque. It is not unfair to say that for most visitors, the dominant impression of both interior and exterior is due to him: in the interior, his vast baldacchino (finished in 1633) over the shrine of St Peter, a towering bronze canopy supported on barleysugar columns; and on the exterior the great oval colonnade of Tuscan columns four deep (finished in 1666), which encloses the Piazza S. Pietro and supplies just that element of sublimity that Maderno's façade lacks.

The immensely lavish decoration and furnishing of St Peter's – the mosaics, the statues (many over-life-size), the wood-carving, stucco and numerous papal tombs – are also Bernini's, in inspiration if not actually by his hand. St Peter's is inexhaustible, and if it cannot claim the unity of a single controlling vision, it is uniquely an expression of two centuries of a nation's creative genius.

that from now on the work would be decorative as much as structural. These specialized functions would be handed down from father to son, the whole team being known as the 'Sampietrini'.

FACTFILE

Length of interior	183 m
Total length, including portico	213 m
Width of transepts	137 m
Height of dome with lantern	138 m
Diameter of dome	42 m
Width of nave	25 m
Width of portico	71 m
Width of Piazza San Pietro	198 m
Number of columns in colonnade	284

The Mosque of Selim II

9

Time: 1569–75 Location: Edirne, Turkey

The body of the mosque is one prodigious dome. I understand so little of architecture
I dare not pretend to speak of the proportions; it seemed to me very regular.
This I am sure of it is vastly high; and I thought it the noblest building I ever saw.
LADY MARY WORTLEY-MONTAGU, 17 MAY 1717

The mosque of Selim II at Edirne is the masterpiece of one of the greatest architects of world history, Sinan. The climax of all his experiments, it expresses monumental form, intellectual structure and sublime space to a degree that would never be surpassed. Sinan strove to achieve unity, balancing strength with lightness, visual excitement with spiritual peace. Edirne is the crown of his long career.

The architect and his masterpiece

Sinan was born in the humble Central Anatolian village that now bears his name. Trained as a carpenter, he was conscripted into the Janissary companies, the infantry élite, and soon impressed his officers with his skills in building roads, bridges and causeways at great speed. He was also a commander in the field and the inscription on his tomb refers foremost to his military honours and his great Büyükçekmiçe bridge across marshes on the Istanbul to Edirne road.

On reaching retiring age as a general, Sinan immediately became Royal Architect and effectively minister of works. He held the office until he died, aged 96–100 in Islamic years, and trained generations of architects. Sinan was 80 when he began work on the Selim II mosque.

Selim II (1566–74) was a poet and receptive patron who left the government of his vast empire to his Grand Vizir Sokollu Mehmet Pasha,

Sinan's masterpiece: the mosque for Sultan Selim II, with its four minarets, the tallest in Islam, and its semidomes which support the thrust from the massive main dome.

Above *A view looking up into the great dome of Edirne, which matches in size that of Hagia Sophia, supported on large piers. The painted decoration is not original.*

Opposite above
At Edirne light and airy colonnades surround the courtyard, which is the same shape and size as the mosque itself.

Opposite below
Plan of the mosque, courtyard and other related structures.

himself an aesthete. There was no hilltop left for an imperial mosque in Istanbul and so the only high ground available in the summer capital of Edirne was chosen – with its rivers, meadows and woods this city is still beautiful.

To approach Edirne from Greece is to see a unique skyline of domes and minarets dominated by the mosque of Selim II and its four minarets. To arrive from Istanbul is to see the mosque from 10 km (6 miles) away, as one does with many cathedrals of Europe; and with a diameter of 31 m (103

ft), its dome matches that of Hagia Sophia in Istanbul (p. 21), which for a thousand years was the largest in the world. Downthrust is the overriding problem with domes, as they have a tendency to expand. At Edirne, two semidomes support the thrust, which is mainly carried directly down the piers. The solution to this structural problem was refined by Sinan at his earlier mosque of Suleyman the Magnificent in Istanbul.

The basic structure of Roman-proportioned blocks of limestone separated only by a dusting of sand was repeated at Edirne. But Sinan's great coup was the revolutionary removal of the massive central piers. He replaced these with eight piers in effect set into the walls, with corresponding towers above. Sinan was also proud of the four minarets – each reaching 71 m (233 ft), they are the tallest in Islam.

In preparing for the construction Sinan's military training was invaluable. Every conceivable material had to be ordered and then assembled and stored in the order in which it would be used.

FACTFILE

Area of courtyard	60 × 44 m
Dome	
diameter	31 m
height	43.5 m
Minarets	4
height	71 m
Number of workers	20,000

The stone was largely local, but marble columns came from all over the Ottoman empire. Also needed were carved shutters, window frames and much else, down to the iron grids and tie-beams that helped support the arches.

Wages were accounted for each man. Apart from military recruits on army pay there were teams of craftsmen from villages which specialized in carpentry, carving and laying drains. In the three winter months when their ships were laid up, galley slaves were also used. A total of 20,000 men might be employed, plus grooms and muleteers. This is why it was possible to build the mosque in just six years.

Exterior and interior

Outside the mosque, the spacious courtyard occupies the same area as the interior. The traditionally large arcade before the great door has a rhythm arising from the insertion of a pair of smaller arches carrying inscribed discs that may be read as the sun and the moon. Lateral colonnades of impressive size and the ablution fountain in the middle, which has escaped the addition of a dome, complete the courtyard.

With grilles gilded and marble polished – best appreciated after rain – the open space is only rivalled by the vistas from the lateral doors. The flanks of the mosque are deeply recessed to create shadows at the entries and in the arcaded recesses between – this is important to an appreciation of the interior, which is a revolution in Ottoman architecture.

The entire space is opened up by the removal of the central piers. To this is added the effects of shadow at ground level caused by the externally recessed windows which reduce the light reaching the lower areas of the interior. Temporal and celestial are in this way divided – galleries extending above the height of the recesses have large windows which let unimpeded light stream in, as do tiers of windows above.

For the first time the large platform from which the muezzins make the final call to prayer is set exactly under the centre of the dome and over a symbolic fountain of life, also unique. The rich paintwork on the sides of this platform is in good

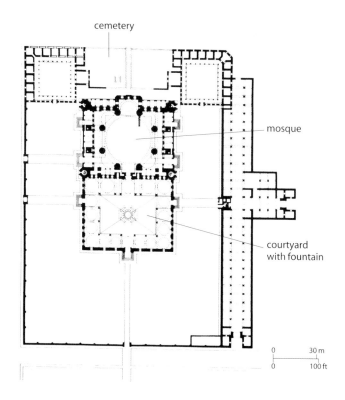

cemetery

mosque

courtyard with fountain

0   30 m
0   100 ft

The muezzin's gallery and the mimbar. One of Sinan's many innovations in the Edirne mosque is the positioning of the muezzin's gallery directly beneath the centre of the dome.

condition. The tall white marble *mimbar*, from which the Friday sermon and announcement of new laws were delivered, is deliberately carved with flowers symbolic of Eden. The *mihrab* apse is the centre of all prayer because it indicates the direction of Mecca. Here there are large windows to create the light of sanctuary, and the decorative restraints of the prayer hall give way to walls covered with the flowers of paradise, using the full colourscape of the Iznik kilns at their greatest. Elsewhere, except for the sultan's loggia, the use of ceramics is restrained. At the corners of the lateral arches that support the projecting galleries, carefully curved tiles fit irregular spaces like bouquets and must have given their designers in the royal studio deep satisfaction.

At night, the great candles beside the *mimbar* were lit, their smoke trapped in bronze hoods producing the finest of black ink. They face the hall and a low ceiling of flickering oil lamps that cut off the area from an invisible divine. The foundation document of the mosque shows that there were two officers to prevent people coming to dip their crusts in the olive oil in the days before electricity. It also records that the chief muezzin was to marry a young and beautiful girl so that he would never be tempted to take another.

To reach the ultimate splendour of the sultan's loggia, a broad staircase in the thickness of the wall leads to a landing and a tiled doorway giving access to a chamber resplendent with the finest tiles of all – missing one carried off by the Russians when they invaded in 1878 and now in the Hermitage Museum in St Petersburg. The tiles reach a climax at the small entry alcove where the *mihrab* is set. It was a retreat for prayer and abstinence which should last forty days. No ruler could be absent for so long. Forty is a magic number, however, so perhaps days became hours. The *mimbar* is striking, made of inlaid wood of extraordinary delicacy. And here is another of Sinan's coups – the wall is in fact shutters, and so a sultan on his knees could pray directly to paradise. This was as emotional a moment as ever architect could achieve.

The sultanate ended in 1924, but the mosque flourishes as the most important, outside Istanbul, in modern Turkey. The building was recently surveyed and found in excellent condition in spite of the depredations of the Russian army. No other architect, even his senior pupil Mehmet Agha, could approach Sinan in skill or imagination. By crowning the Ottoman achievement, Sinan made it impossible to have a creative successor within the same tradition. History has never been otherwise.

The Taj Mahal

Time: 1632–47   Location: Agra, Uttar Pradesh, India

*A magnificent edifice was founded – the like and peer of which the eye of the Age
has not seen beneath these nine vaults of heaven, and the resemblance and equal
of which the ear of Time has not heard of in any of the past ages.*
MUHAMMAD AMIN QAZWINI, HISTORIAN OF SHAH JAHAN, EARLY 1630s

When the Mughal emperor Shah Jahan (reigned 1628–58) built a mausoleum at Agra in northern India for his favourite wife, Mumtaz Mahal, he envisaged that it would become a universally admired work of architecture – the Masterpiece of Days to Come. It has certainly fulfilled his expectations: the Taj Mahal is the best-known monument of India and a principal attraction for all the many thousands of visitors to the subcontinent. Begun in 1632, the Taj Mahal expresses the characteristic Mughal concept of a tomb set in an architecturally planned garden in its most monumental and ideal form.

The design

The success of the Taj Mahal lies in its aesthetic, romantic and symbolic appeal, and in something more specific: it expresses in canonical form the architectural principles of the period, which the Mughals did not set down in writing. First comes a rational and strict geometry, ensured by the use of grid systems based on the Shahjahani *gaz* (*c.* 80–82 cm/32 in); second, consistent symmetrical planning, with an emphasis on bilateral symmetry along a central axis, into which further centralized schemes are integrated; third, a hierarchical grading of materials, forms and colours down to the most minute ornamental detail; and

The Taj Mahal seen from the Yamuna River; the mausoleum is flanked by two identical buildings: on the left side the Assembly Hall (Mehman Khana, literally 'Guest House') and on the right side the Mosque.

Plan of the entire Taj Mahal complex as built. The southernmost section (D) no longer survives.

A Terrace
B Tomb Garden
C Complex of Forecourt (Jilau Khana)
D Cross-axial Bazaar and Caravanserai Complex
E Waterworks

1 Mausoleum
2 Mosque of Mausoleum
3 Assembly Hall (Mehman Khana)
4 Garden Pavilion
5 Garden Gate
6 Tower Pavilion
7 Quarters for the Tomb Attendants (Khawasspura)
8 Bazaar Street
9 Subsidiary Tomb (a and b Saheli Burj, c Saheli Burj and Sandli Masjid)
10 Caravanserai
11 Outer Tomb
12 Outer Mosque (Fatehpuri Masjid)

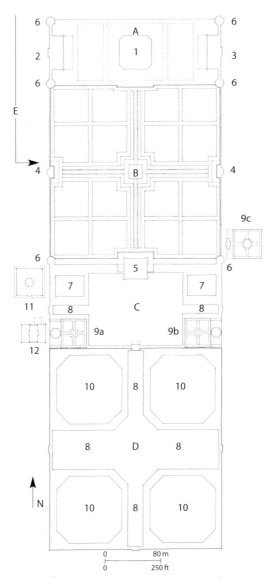

as a monumentalized version of the waterfront garden, a specific Mughal variant of the Persianate fourfold garden or *chaharbagh*: this consists of a raised rectangular riverfront terrace (A) on which are placed the main buildings, and, on the landward side, a square, centrally planned four-part garden (B).

The two courtyard complexes with subsidiary structures echoed the configuration of the tomb garden; but here the buildings consisted of narrow wings and arcades around open courtyards, typical of the residential and utilitarian architecture of the period. The rectangular unit (C)

finally, a sophisticated symbolism in the programme, expressing the building as the earthly realization of the mansion of Mumtaz in the garden of Paradise.

The mausoleum stands in a vast walled enclosure which originally measured 1113 × 373 *gaz* (c. 897.3 × 300 m/2944 × 984 ft); the southernmost third has since been built over by the city quarter called Taj Ganj. The tomb and its garden, with elaborate waterworks, lie at the northern end (A, B, E on the plan); to the south were two courtyard complexes with subsidiary structures (C and D, the latter not surviving). The tomb garden is laid out comprises the forecourt of the tomb garden, framed by two residential courtyards for the tomb attendants (7) and two subsidiary tombs for lesser wives of Shah Jahan (9a, b); they are separated by open bazaar streets (8) which provide access to the forecourt. The squarish unit to the south (D) consisted originally of two cross-axially arranged open bazaar streets and four open caravanserai courts, reflecting the *chaharbagh* design of the main tomb garden. The connection was functional as well as formal: the income of the bazaars and caravanserais went to the upkeep of the mausoleum.

The builders

The identity of the architect of the Taj Mahal is not definitely known because the official histories of Shah Jahan's reign place the emphasis on the emperor's involvement. We do know that it was planned by a team of architects working under his close supervision: named among them are Ustad Ahmad Lahauri, who was credited by his son with building the Taj; and Mir 'Abdul Karim, who had been the favourite architect of Shah Jahan's father Jahangir (1605–27). The craftsmen left numerous masons' marks, scratched into the stones of the garden walkways and the slabs

The mausoleum stands at the end of the water channel, which is sunk in the central walkway of the garden.

facing the buildings – stars, swastikas, fishes, flowers, intersecting figures and also names, both Muslim and Hindu, written respectively in Persian and Devanagari letters.

Constructing the tomb

The site chosen for the Taj Mahal lies on the southern bank of the Yamuna River: it was originally one of the gardens that lined the river on both sides in a band constituting Mughal Agra. Mumtaz Mahal died in June 1631 at Burhanpur. Work had started by January 1632, when her body arrived at Agra and was temporarily buried under a cupola in the area of the tomb garden. Jean-Baptiste Tavernier, a French jeweller, saw the Taj in 1640 and claims that 20,000 men were employed over the years in its building.

The greatest technical challenge was to secure the foundations of the terrace in the unstable sands of the riverbank so that it could support the domed mausoleum, some 68 m (223 ft) high, including plinth and pinnacle. Shah Jahan's court poet Abu Talib Kalim, an unlikely but here unique source for technical data, reports that this was done by means of wells cased in wood and filled with rubble and iron, and his information was supported by 20th-century investigations.

The tall double dome – one dome is visible from the outside, the other from the inside – is not built of solid marble as is generally assumed, but of brick faced with white marble. The bricks are a standard

size, at that time usually *c.* 19 × 12.5 × 3 cm (*c.* 7.5 × 5 × 1.25 in), or slightly smaller. In a typical Shahjahani structure they are set in courses composed largely of stretchers, but alternating at times with headers, in a thick bed of lime mortar; the vaults are built up in concentric rings of courses, set in an even thicker mortar bed. This construction technique gave the masonry the strength needed to support the curvature of the partly spherical shell of the inner dome and the high bulbous dome above it, without any inner stiffening walls.

All the subsidiary structures of the complex are also built in brick, but faced with red sandstone; special features such as domes may be clad in white marble. This hierarchical colour dualism of white marble and red sandstone is generally characteristic of imperial Mughal architecture, but it is here explored with unparalleled sophistication. It connects with the ancient Indian architectural theory that assigned white stones to Brahmins and red ones to the princely warrior caste of the Kshatriyas. The Mughals thus associated themselves with the two highest levels of the Indian caste system.

The marble for the Taj was brought by bullock cart over more than 400 km (250 miles) from Makrana in Rajasthan. The sandstone came from the quarries of the Vindhyan system in the region of Fatehpur Sikri and Rupbas, which have furnished building materials throughout the centuries to the cities of the adjoining plains.

Above *Selection of characteristic masons' marks of the Mughal workmen collected from the paved walkways of the garden.*

Right *Cross-section through the mausoleum, showing the double dome.*

The *pietra dura* decoration

The screen around the cenotaphs of Mumtaz Mahal and Shah Jahan in the central hall, which attracts all visitors today with its naturalistic flowers and plants, was put up in 1643 to replace an earlier one of enamelled gold, deemed too precious. The same technique of inlay with semiprecious stones appears on the cenotaphs themselves.

It has now been established that while Mughal stone intarsia or *parchin kari* is based on an indigenous tradition, the inlaying of hardstones into a marble surface is of Florentine origin – hence its name, *commesso di pietre dure* or *pietra dura*. The elaborate Quranic inscriptions which frame the arches were designed by Amanat Khan al-Shirazi and executed in simple stone inlay; they focus on the Day of Resurrection, the Last Judgment and the Reward of the Faithful.

Completion, costs and future

According to two inscriptions, one inside and one in the portal of the west façade, the tomb structure of the Taj Mahal was completed in 1638/39. The histories report that the entire complex was completed in 1643, but an inscription on the garden façade of the main gateway indicates that work on the decoration went on at least until

FACTFILE	
Entire complex	897.3 x 300 m
Preserved complex	561.2 x 300 m
Height of mausoleum	68 m
Height of inner dome	24.74 m
Diameter of inner dome	17.72 m
Height of inside of upper dome	29.61 m
Height of garden gate	23.07 m
Workforce	20,000 men?

1647. Suggestions of the overall costs of the monument range from 40 to 50 *lakhs* of rupees (4–5 million rupees). Masons at the top of the hierarchy of Mughal builders earned between 9 and 20 rupees a month.

The structure of the Taj Mahal has endured for three and a half centuries, but its unique facing, with inlaid and carved marble and sandstone, is suffering increasingly from the effects of environmental pollution, from chemical cleaning, and from natural factors like pigeons who nest around the inner dome. Another problem is its appeal to visitors, who want to associate themselves with Shah Jahan's Masterpiece of the Days to Come by inscribing their names on its walls.

A flower in pietra dura *from the top of the cenotaph of Shah Jahan.*

Left *The cenotaph of Mumtaz Mahal inscribed with the date of her death, 1631, next to that of Shah Jahan, added in 1666, and surrounding screen, covered with flowers and plant motifs in* pietra dura *inlay.*

11 St Paul's Cathedral

Time: 1675–1711   Location: London, England

Christopher Wren's St Paul's cathedral, England's greatest Baroque building, would never have existed had it not been for the catastrophe of the Great Fire of London in 1666, which destroyed its medieval predecessor and reduced most of the city to ashes. The story of Wren's involvement, however, and in particular the feature that dominated his thinking from the very beginning – the dome – goes back to before the Fire. In 1663 the old cathedral, which had long given cause for anxiety, showed alarming signs of instability underneath the crossing tower. Wren's proposal was to demolish the tower, rebuild the crossing on a larger plan, and cover it with a dome culminating in a giant pineapple; the proposal was accepted.

A dome was something that every architect wanted to build. But opportunities, understandably, were limited. Brunelleschi had built that of Florence Cathedral in 1420. Michelangelo's dome of St Peter's (p. 48) had followed in the late 16th century. In Paris, François Mansart's Val-de-Grâce and Jacques Lemercier's church of the Sorbonne were beginning to rise in 1665, when Wren probably saw them under construction on his only trip abroad.

The final plan of St Paul's, with conventional nave and chancel, evolved through many trials and variations. Wren originally wanted a centralized Greek-cross plan, with the dome more dominant.

Evolution of the design

After the Fire, all the previous schemes became irrelevant and Wren started afresh. Between then and the building's completion in 1711, a profusion of plans and drawings survive from Wren's office,

which ought to make the process of design clear but in fact sometimes does the opposite.

The main stages of the evolution are these. In 1670 Wren produced a curiously modest design consisting of a domed vestibule and a fairly small rectangular church. When this was judged to be insufficiently impressive he made further designs, some based on a Latin cross with a domed crossing and some on a Greek cross (with arms of equal length), also with a dome, like Bramante's original scheme for St Peter's.

This Greek-cross plan was Wren's favourite and in 1673 he made a model, the so-called 'Great Model', to win approval for it. In the end, just as at St Peter's, the church authorities insisted on the more traditional plan with a long nave (it was, they said, 'not enough of a cathedral fashion'). But the Great Model remains a vivid testimony to Wren's imagination. As architecture it would have been more exciting than the church as built: four equal arms plus a spacious vestibule at the west end and a huge central dome. The arms are con-

FACTFILE

Total length	156 m
Length of transepts	76 m
Width of nave	37 m
Width of west front with chapels	55 m
Height to balustrade	33 m
Height to Golden Gallery	86 m
Height to cross on top of dome	110 m
Height of western towers	68 m
Area	5480 sq. m

The west front of St Paul's was the last part to be designed. The scene in the pediment representing the conversion of St Paul on the way to Damascus is by Francis Bird (1706), a rare and under-appreciated work of monumental Baroque sculpture in England.

nected not by straight sides but by curves, a superbly original idea, unique in England and in the world. The play of curves – the concave walls of the lower storey meeting the convex curves of the dome – would have been the epitome of Baroque bravura.

The next stage is the most puzzling, a design in which the confident expertise of the Great Model is replaced by what seems grotesque amateurishness. Here Wren returns to the longitudinal plan, but crowns the crossing with a four-storey combi-nation of dome and tower: a bulbous base sup-porting a circular drum with coupled columns, then a small dome and finally a pagoda-like tower similar to the one he eventually provided for St Bride's, Fleet Street. It was this design that received the Royal Warrant in May 1675, but Wren always reserved the right to change his mind as building progressed.

This he did almost at once, and from here the evolution of the finished work is fairly straightfor-ward. The Warrant Design's extraordinary

In order to maintain the impression of eight equal arches under the dome, Wren disguised the four diagonals (one is in the centre of the photograph) to look the same width as those in the main directions.

dome rests not upon the four main piers where nave, transepts and chancel meet but – by abolishing the end-bay of the aisles in all four corners – upon eight. As originally conceived, and demonstrated in the Great Model, the arches between the eight piers would be equal, but in the event Wren was obliged to strengthen them to such a degree that the diagonal arches became much narrower than those in the main directions. To overcome this discrepancy optically, he introduced large lunettes or balconies in the diagonals which match the main openings, continuing their lines over the surfaces of the adjoining piers. To the eye the effect is of a ring of eight equal arches. The fact that they are not concentric with the segmental arches below them has been seen, surely rightly, as a defect.

Predictably, these structural supports of the dome gave Wren more trouble than anything else in the cathedral. He had built the eight piers of rubble (material salvaged from Old St Paul's) with Portland stone facing. But he soon realized that this was not strong enough and had to embark on the delicate process of replacing the cores with layers of solid masonry. For increased safety a 'Great Iron Chain or Girdle' made by the ironmaster Jean Tijou, best known for his splendid wrought-iron screens to the chancel aisles, was placed around the base of the dome in 1706 to stop it spreading, and further metal chains were added the year after.

Another ingenious deception concerns the dome itself. Previous domes, such as Florence Cathedral's and St Peter's, had been double – an inner dome seen from the inside and an outer dome seen from without. Wren, who wished to crown his dome with an unusually heavy cupola, added a brick cone, invisible from both within and without, which rises from the level of the gallery and supports the cupola. The inner dome is of masonry, the outer of timber and lead.

Finally, Wren built a screen wall all round the cathedral on top of the aisle walls, creating a two-storey elevation rather than the single storey which would have represented the true height of the aisles. This completely conceals the fact that the main vessels (nave, transepts, chancel)

concoction was replaced by the dome we know, and the carefully detailed elevation was finalized. The only elements left unresolved were the towers and the west façade, which did not take shape until after 1700.

Building St Paul's

In realizing his vision Wren encountered a number of problems, which he solved brilliantly but which left him open, from 19th-century writers wedded to the principles of A. W. N. Pugin and John Ruskin, to charges of 'dishonesty'. The plan consists of the conventional elements: an aisled nave, aisled transepts and aisled chancel. The

receive their light from high clearstorey windows just as in a medieval cathedral, and (in the same tradition) that the vault is supported by flying buttresses. From inside this is not noticed, and very few visitors are aware of it from the outside either; it can only be seen from above. The effect, as Wren intended, is visually to provide a solid base for the soaring dome, and structurally to give additional buttressing to the dome's thrust.

All three of these ingenious devices work, and St Paul's would be the poorer without them. But they gave Pugin an excuse for his gibe that 'one half of the edifice is built to conceal the other.'

The last part to be finished was the west front. There is some evidence that Wren would have preferred a giant Ionic order for the portico but could find no stone long enough to span the intercolumniations. The two towers reflect influence from Italian Baroque (Francesco Borromini's S. Agnese in Rome), which parallels the other late features of St Paul's, such as the transept ends which show knowledge of Pietro da Cortona's S. Maria della Pace, also in Rome. This may be a development of Wren's own taste (derived from engravings) or possibly the contribution of younger men in his office. The part played by his many draughtsmen, some of whom were architects in their own right, such as Nicholas Hawksmoor, has still not been finally settled.

Wren was a designer, not a mason, and he assembled a large and highly specialized team to carry out the work. During the nearly 40 years that it took to build St Paul's, 14 contractors were employed. They supervised every step of the operation, from the quarry at Portland to the final detailing on site. In a busy year (1694) 64 masons are recorded at work, besides carpenters, plumbers, stone-carvers and plasterers. Of the sculptors the most notable was Grinling Gibbons, who was responsible with Edward Pearce for the stone carving on the exterior, where delicious cherubs peer out of the friezes and window-frames, as well as the wood-carving of the stalls.

Right *Seen from above (a view Wren never imagined possible), the screen walls concealing the buttresses become disconcertingly visible.*

Wren was badly treated in his old age and dismissed from his post of Surveyor General. One of the cathedral commissioners' last decisions, against his wishes, was to place a balustrade all round the top of the walls. 'Ladies', said Wren acidly, 'think nothing well without an edging'.

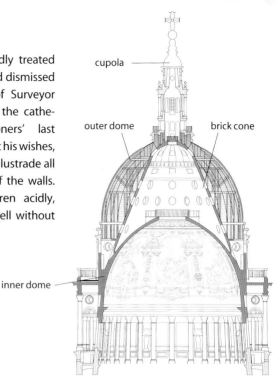

cupola

outer dome

brick cone

inner dome

Wren's three domes: the outer one is not load-bearing; the invisible cone supports the cupola; the inner one is visible from the interior.

12 The Panthéon, Paris

Time: 1757–90   Location: Paris, France

*Sainte Geneviève will combine the lightness of Gothic structures
and the purity of Greek architecture.*
ATTRIBUTED TO SOUFFLOT BY HIS ASSISTANT AND SUCCESSOR RONDELET

The Panthéon, originally the church of Sainte Geneviève, makes an immediate impression on every visitor: light, elegant, sophisticated and spatially complex, it has none of the heaviness associated with Neoclassicism. This is not accidental. Its designer, Jacques-Germain Soufflot, was fascinated by Gothic architecture and at Sainte Geneviève he attempted to build a Classical church using the Gothic system of forces held in equilibrium rather than that of direct load-bearing supports. It has to be said that this is not at all obvious to the spectator, since every detail is meticulously Classical.

Soufflot knew Wren's St Paul's (p. 62) well, as his dome clearly demonstrates, and, like Wren, he made use of concealed flying buttresses. In fact, it is only through a knowledge of Soufflot's theories that one can truly appreciate this aspect of the building.

Evolution of the project

The project began in 1744, with Louis XV's illness and vow to construct a magnificent church to Paris's patron saint Sainte Geneviève. In 1757, the Director of Royal Buildings, Marigny, who had named Soufflot Director of Paris's Royal Buildings five years earlier, accepted his protégé's design for the church. This design was (like Bramante's, Michelangelo's and Wren's) for a centralized plan, but (like them) he was obliged to lengthen the nave and make it longitudinal.

The magnificent west façade and cupola of the Panthéon, originally the church of Sainte Geneviève, invite comparison with Rome's St Peter's and London's St Paul's cathedrals.

FACTFILE

Length	110 m
Width	83 m
Height	92 m
Materials	stone, iron ties

Soufflot opened up the interior space by reverting to Gothic building technique, carrying roof and cupola on a continuous course of free-standing columns. Careful examination of roof domes, vaults and buttresses overhead reveals a sophisticated transfer of weight directly over interior columns.

The magnificent cupola, however, required a more complicated system of arches and pendentives to transfer its considerable weight to the transept's corner pillars and columns; parapet walls hide a structure which can only be clearly understood through analysing the plan. Particularly at the transept, the delicate 'gothic-like' blending of vaults, pendentives and columns creates a visual openness in the upper structure and a physical continuity for the side aisles which are exceptional indeed for a Classically inspired building.

Evolution and revolution

Sainte Geneviève evolved slowly over many years. When Soufflot died in 1780, building had only reached the drum of the dome (it was finally completed in 1790). After Soufflot's death drastic changes had to be made. As at St Peter's and St Paul's, the piers supporting the dome were found to be inadequate and had to be strengthened. This was done by building solid walls across spaces that in Soufflot's plan were open arches, thus seriously compromising his ideal of lightness. Another change that had the same unfortunate effect was the walling-up of the 42 lower windows, when, following the French Revolution, the church was deconsecrated and turned into a public monument for French heroes, which it remains today.

Viollet-Le-Duc, the French architect, restorer and writer, would cite Soufflot's Sainte Geneviève (with the Gothic cathedral at Beauvais) to make the point that structural systems' proportions can be magnified only to a certain point before failing – noting that 'the surface area of the floor plan increases as a function of two dimensions, while the weight of the structure is a function of three'. Structural iron systems, followed by the development of steel-reinforced concrete at the beginning of the 20th century, would soon allow architects and builders to clear this hurdle.

Over the course of the 19th century, the building alternated between secular and public use to end as the Panthéon with the state burial of French writer Victor Hugo in 1855. The transept even served as the arena for a public demonstration of Foucault's Pendulum, illustrating the earth's rotation, a replica of which is now in place.

The crypt contains the remains, amongst others, of Pierre and Marie Curie, Voltaire, and Jean-Jacques Rousseau. The crypt's last resident, French Resistance hero, writer and culture minister André Malraux, was installed here by order of President Jacques Chirac in 1996.

The surprisingly light and airy classical interior uses vaults and pendentives to distribute the structural loads between visible columns and hidden buttresses. The piers were found to be inadequate to their task and were strengthened by building walls across spaces that were originally intended to be open.

13 The Sagrada Familia

Time: 1882– Location: Barcelona, Catalonia, Spain

This is not the last cathedral, but probably the first of a new line.

ANTONI GAUDÍ

Above *The Sagrada Familia under construction around 1912, when apse walls and eastern façade were already completed and its towers were beginning to rise.*

Right *Architect Antoni Gaudí in a religious celebration in Barcelona, 1924.*

It may seem paradoxical, but it is perhaps simply two sides of the same coin: in Barcelona, throughout the 19th century, churches were knocked down in the name of progress, and outbreaks of violence resulted in the burning, looting and destruction of religious buildings. Yet in the same city, towards the end of the 19th century, work began on a monumental church that was destined both to revive the old ideals of Gothic cathedrals and to become one of the greatest examples of contemporary religious architecture.

The initiative for this grand plan came from a modest religious organization dedicated to the cult of St Joseph. Its president, Josep María Bocabella, announced a scheme to build a church dedicated to the Holy Family, Jesus, Mary and Joseph, as a model for all Christian families. The church was to be expiatory in nature – it was to be financed only through alms and donations.

The first collections did not bring in enough to buy land near the old city centre, so a site was chosen in what at that time were the outskirts of Barcelona, the so-called Ensanche, where the city had begun rapidly to expand due to the 1859 town plans by engineer Ildefons Cerdà. The land was bought for 170,000 pesetas (around £700) and the first stone of the new church was symbolically laid on the feast day of St Joseph, 19 March, in 1882.

Work began under the direction of the architect Francisco Villar y Lozano, and the original neo-Gothic design was directly inspired by the Basilica of Loreto in Italy. However, the project was completely rethought when, at the end of 1883, Villar was replaced by Antoni Gaudí.

Gaudí, who had qualified as an architect in 1878, took over the Sagrada Familia just as his career was beginning to flourish, and he remained closely linked to the project until his death in 1926. From 1918 onwards he devoted himself exclusively to the Sagrada Familia, setting up his home and studio within the site itself. Because of this, the church can be considered the culmination of Gaudí's architecture, a work which brings together all the experiences and innovations of his entire career.

Style and spirituality

Gaudí's architecture was born within the context of Art Nouveau, although his strong personality distances his work from the typical features of that style. Within Gaudí's buildings are elements that prefigure other contemporary styles – Expressionism, for instance, in his use of materials. The plasticity of his work was later developed by organicist architects, and his singularity of vision fits well within a postmodern context. The architecture of Frank O. Gehry, to mention but one, is full of Gaudian resonances.

In spite of all these innovatory concepts and anticipations of postmodernism, the striking fact remains that the Sagrada Familia is essentially a Gothic building. Gaudí used the Gothic principle of forces held in equilibrium and took it further than any medieval architect had done. The piers of the nave lean inwards, becoming their own buttresses – a logical development of the system of thrust and counter-thrust. Gaudí made a schematic model of the interior out of cords, coated it with plaster and hung it upside down. When the plaster set he reversed it, producing the design that we now see. The technical name for this structural arch is 'catenary' (from *catena*, a chain).

One of the most striking features of Gaudí's architecture is his capacity for formal invention. Forms which appear whimsical and random are in fact based on deeply logical reasoning. The architecture of the Sagrada Familia grows up from a solid geometric base, and the whole building is modulated according to a fixed system of proportions. Dominant forms include paraboloids and hyperboloids, which Gaudí worked out empiri-

cally; today such calculations are done using computer-aided design (CAD) systems.

Another aspect of Gaudí's architecture made manifest in the Sagrada Familia is a deep sense of religious exaltation. Although his orthodoxy is disputed by some, in the year 2000 the Catholic church began the process which may lead to Gaudí's beatification. The Sagrada Familia was designed as an expression of the Church triumphing over the contradictions and upheavals of the modern world, and for this reason Gaudí

The Nativity façade of the Sagrada Familia, with its three porches and dense sculpture. The design of the church is full of religious symbolism: the four towers, of an eventual 12, represent apostles.

Above *The Sagrada Familia today, from the eastern side. The Nativity façade and the walls of the apse were finished in Gaudí's lifetime; the naves (left) are under construction.*

Opposite *The polychrome tops of the Sagrada Familia. The cypress, at the top of the central body of the Nativity façade, symbolizes the Catholic church.*

wanted to place it in a dominant position on the Barcelona skyline. It is this religious motivation, together with Gaudí's concept of architecture emulating nature, that provide the keys to understanding the building's dense symbolism.

FACTFILE

Maximum exterior height (projected)	170 m
Interior length	90 m
Maximum width (the crossing)	60 m
Width of main nave	45 m
Height of the naves	
central	45 m
lateral	30 m

Plan and symbolism

The church strives upwards, reminiscent of a mountain, and has sometimes been compared to the mountain of Montserrat, a rock formation near Barcelona which is the site of an important religious shrine. The highest peak of the Sagrada Familia will be a large cupola or dome, intended to reach 170 m (558 ft) high when completed. Around it, another four spires, none yet built, 130 m (426.5 ft) tall, will represent the four Evangelists, while a fifth spire, to be 140 m (460 ft) tall, over the apse of the church, will represent the Virgin Mary. The vertical theme is completed by the four towers that top each of the three façades. These 12 towers, representing the 12 Apostles, are, or will be, each around 100 m (328 ft) tall. At the time of writing, eight have been completed.

The eastern façade, facing the rising sun, represents the Nativity, while the western façade, facing the setting sun, is dedicated to the Passion of Christ. The south-facing main façade is dedicated to Glory. The church interior is intended to resemble a forest, whose tree-like columns branch out at a certain height to support a vault, formed by a rich geometric network of starlike shapes.

Gaudí laid down the master plans for the project in around 1890. In 1892, construction began on the Nativity façade, the only one that was actually finished under Gaudí's direct supervision. By the time of his death, he had completed detailed plans for the Passion façade and the naves, as well as the symbolic and iconographic programme for the whole church complex. The main reference sources for the project were 1:10 and 1:25 scale models, which were destroyed in 1936 when the Sagrada Familia was looted during the course of the Spanish Civil War, but later reconstructed. Between 1936 and 1952, building work was suspended; it was restarted with the intention of staying as true as possible to Gaudí's plans, although allowing for the incorporation of new technology and materials such as concrete.

At the same time, views were expressed that opposed the continuation of work on the Sagrada Familia, and the validity of the project is regularly called into question, both on religious grounds – what does a monumental church mean in the modern world? – and aesthetic – is it right to continue in Gaudí's own, extremely personal style, or should new artistic languages be incorporated?

Building work goes through phases of greater and lesser activity, since its sponsors wish it to be financed entirely through donations and personal bequests. In 1976, the Passion façade, with its four towers, was completed, and sculptor Josep M. Subirachs has been working on the sculpted decoration of this façade since 1986. In 2002, work was underway on the naves, which have now been partially covered over. No date for possible completion of the Sagrada Familia has been set.

The Chapel of Notre Dame du Haut

Time: 1950–54 Location: Ronchamp, Vosges, France

A vessel of intense contemplation and meditation ....
LE CORBUSIER

For those who have visited Le Corbusier's chapel of Notre Dame du Haut at Ronchamp, no combination of text and image can match the feeling of magic and spiritual intensity that the building evokes. This extraordinary though modest chapel synthesizes the many influences present in Le Corbusier's post-Second World War architecture, revealing a sensitivity for the project's site much less evident in many of his more easily accessible urban buildings. The chapel is equally important as a remarkable demonstration of Dominican Father Alain Couturier's efforts to convince his fellow clergymen to revitalize ecclesiastical art through commissioning the best modern artists and architects.

Father Couturier had already commissioned Henri Matisse to decorate a Dominican chapel in Saint Paul de Vence; well aware of Le Corbusier's work, he advised the Belfort Diocese to commission the architect to replace the Notre Dame du Haut chapel which had been destroyed during the Second World War. Though a professed atheist, Le Corbusier (Charles-Édouard Jeanneret) was strongly sensitive to the space created in many religious structures he had visited, and he accepted the commission. Father Couturier later commissioned Le Corbusier to design the much larger La Tourette monastery near Lyon.

The environment

Perched on a prominent hilltop, not far from Le Corbusier's native Jura, the site had been occupied first by sun worshippers, then Romans, and finally, since the Middle Ages, by a pilgrimage shrine to the Virgin Mary. Le Corbusier was immediately taken with the location and gradually determined the general form which assistant André Maisonnier would refine and detail.

A small team of workers under Maisonnier built the chapel largely by hand following Le Corbusier's frequent personal instructions. The spontaneous nature of its construction more closely resembles the production of sculpture than that of a highly predetermined work of architecture.

Right *The rough, grey concrete roof hovering over a variety of white wall surfaces celebrates Le Corbusier's masterful play of light and textures.*

Opposite above *Sunlight falling upon the chapel's rich forms records the daily passage of time.*

4/1/57

When viewed from afar, the building seems to rise up out of the hilltop. When approached from the village below, the gradual revelation of the chapel's sculptural forms is astonishing; at no time does the visitor lose the remarkable sensation of discovery and surprise. The reasons for the sense of both drama and harmony are certainly complex, but probably arise from the architect's dedication in designing every last detail.

Harmony is inherent in the fact that overall proportions, flooring patterns, window-sizes and spacing – all dimensions – derive from the Modulor system of proportional measurements based on multiples of human dimensions and applications of the Golden Section that Le Corbusier had developed. The sense of discovery is sustained through a subtle evolution of concave and convex forms, rough and smooth textures.

Above *Le Corbusier's early sketches clearly indicate the chapel's final form.*

Nave	
length	25 m
width	13 m
max. height	
at altar wall	10 m
Half-domes	
height	15 and 22 m
Materials	reinforced concrete, stone infill, sprayed concrete

Structure

The three curved walls serve a dual purpose: they create external and interior spaces of great sculptural expression, while giving the entire chapel its structural stability, allowing the roof and three chapel towers to stand largely by themselves. Each of the three structural walls is formed by concrete panels and masonry infill (with stones from the earlier chapel) which were then covered with metal mesh and sprayed with concrete. Each wall received a different texture, heightening the play of light on the chapel throughout the day.

The massive concrete roof, generally thought to have been inspired by the form of the horseshoe crab, which the architect admired, is in reality a lightweight concrete shell, reminiscent of an aeroplane wing in section. This last analogy seems appropriate as the roof indeed 'floats' over the east and south façades. Very small supports, hidden from exterior view by shadow, disappear from interior view due to the brilliant strip of light admitted at the junction of wall and roof, giving the impression that the massive roof is hovering over independent walls. Le Corbusier would use the same detail at La Tourette.

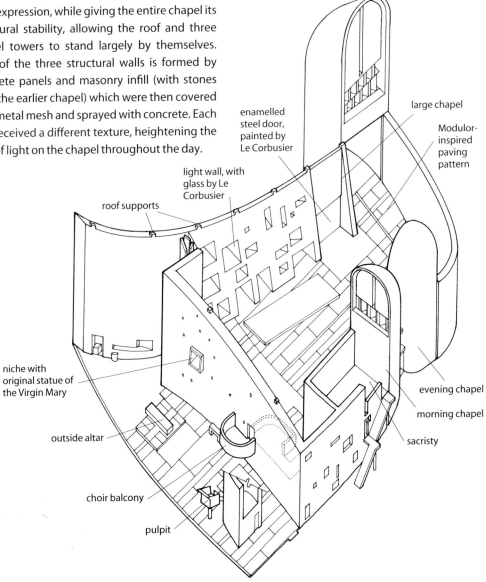

Cut-away diagram of the chapel. Rebuilt on the site of a previous chapel, an ancient statue of the Virgin Mary was incorporated into a niche visible from both outside and within.

enamelled steel door, painted by Le Corbusier

large chapel

Modulor-inspired paving pattern

light wall, with glass by Le Corbusier

roof supports

niche with original statue of the Virgin Mary

evening chapel

morning chapel

sacristy

outside altar

choir balcony

pulpit

The eastern façade contains an outdoor altar, pulpit and choir tucked under the overhanging roof to allow services for overflow pilgrimage crowds; grading has given the eastern lawn an amphitheatre configuration. The ancient statue of the Virgin occupies a niche visible from both interior and exterior.

Facing south is the extraordinary wall of light – a heavy masonry wall 1.5 to 4.5 m (5 to 14.75 ft) thick, curved in plan and tapering in section. Set into this plastered stone wall are Modulor-determined openings with stained glass inserts by Le Corbusier; the great fired-enamelled steel processional south door is also decorated by him.

A symphony in light

The visitor soon discovers that the building is also a giant sundial whose rich collection of textures, edges, forms and cavities accurately record the passage of time. The transition of the sun's rays past the hard edge of the southeastern 'prow' to the southern wall of light seems to last an eternity. From dawn to dusk, the building retains the visitor's attention, continuously changing form and character.

The fascinating play of light and shadow continues in the interior, where the changing atmosphere created by light-towers with differing orientations determines the appropriate time of day for use of each of the three chapels. The rough, shuttered concrete of the roof, the smooth stone of the floor, rough-hewn wood of the benches, stained glass windows and fired-enamel door all combine to create a rich palette of materials and textures.

The combined effect of the suspended roof, the light wall and the rich acoustics generated by the curved surfaces, gives the chapel a rich, intimate and very modern environment, confirming Le Corbusier's and Father Couturier's intuitions.

The openings in the light wall and all the interior furnishings respect the architect's Modulor system of dimensions. The coloured glass is also by Le Corbusier.

Palaces
& Castles

When rulers and regimes are about to fall, popular protest has frequently found a convenient focus in the gates and walls of a palace or fortress. Such an event was portrayed memorably, if not with complete historical accuracy, by Soviet director Sergei Eisenstein in his re-staging of the storming of St Petersburg's Winter Palace in 1917.

Not for nothing were the great palaces of the 17th century onwards consciously conceived as unified architectural compositions designed to impress by their scale and dignity. What better way of giving form to, and creating a physical reminder of, the continuing hegemony of the British Raj in India than commissioning Sir Edwin Lutyens to select a site for and then design a new capital for the subcontinent? Its centrepiece was the magnificent Viceroy's House, which was anything but domestic, rather a palace rivalling in its dimensions and architectural swagger Louis XIV's Versailles of three centuries earlier.

Through his architecture, Lutyens linked India's new masters with past dynasties who had once ruled these same plains. Empress Elizabeth of Russia had similar aspirations with her Fourth Winter Palace at St Petersburg, begun largely for reasons of prestige and with little concern for the national coffers, at the height of the Seven Years War. Beijing's Forbidden City combined palatial accommodation with the buildings required to administer the relocated capital of the Ming Dynasty – a total of 800 individual structures providing over 9000 rooms, and reputedly requiring a workforce of one million to complete it.

The Kremlin, the citadel at the heart of Moscow, contained the residence of the ruler, as well as major cathedrals, administrative buildings, monasteries and smaller churches.

Neuschwanstein Castle in Bavaria was entirely the vision of its creator, Ludwig II, and was built as a retreat from the world rather than a display of political power and wealth, as many other palaces were.

Princely residences such as the Ottoman Sultan Mehmet II's Topkapi Palace in Istanbul could be more correctly described as an accretive and organically growing complex of rooms for both state and private use, magnificent individually but hardly conforming to any master plan or consistent intention. The Kremlin in Moscow developed from its beginnings as a defensive citadel engineered by imported Italian specialists, through fine classical architecture to less elegant creations of the Stalinist era.

Palaces might also be more private affairs, retreats for a ruler and his or her entourage intent upon escaping the heat of summer or the attentions of foreign emissaries. King Ludwig of Bavaria sought to build a safe haven from reality itself in his fantastic Castle of Neuschwanstein.

Rulers often took a close personal interest in such projects. In 1238 Sultan Muhammad I sought a location for what was later to become the Alhambra Palace above Granada in Andalucia on horseback; King Philip II of Spain himself chose the site for the huge complex, almost a complete town in itself, of the Escorial, which sits high on the southern slope of the Sierra de Guadarrama, some 50 km (30 miles) northwest of Madrid. William Randolph Hearst, arguably the world's first media tycoon, chose to site his pleasure palace with great prescience on an isolated site near San Simeon along the coast of California, where he had camped with his parents as a boy long before. Julia Morgan, his architect, travelled every weekend for 28 years to the site of Hearst's never-to-be-completed mansion, to design and supervise the ever-evolving complex.

Almost by definition, a royal palace or castle has but a single client at any point in its evolution, who may place very forceful requirements on the architect, making the functional challenge of planning a large number of rooms of differing sizes and importance very demanding indeed. Johann Fischer von Erlach, 'imperial and royal architect' to the Austrian Emperor Leopold I, had to juggle with some 1400 individual rooms in his planning of Schloss Schönbrunn near Vienna, while still respecting his overarching conception of the palace as the ideal residence of the Holy Roman Emperor. Juan Bautista, Philip II's architect for the Escorial, managed to harmonize myriad requirements – not only the mausoleum that was its main function, but also a large monastery, apartments for the king, his extensive library, a processing plant for herbal medicines, galleries for indoor exercise, a hospital and convalescent facilities, a college for religious instruction and a seminary – into an austere but assured building respecting Vitruvian proportional systems.

Tibet's Potala Palace, running along a low crest overlooking Lhasa, grew by extension and remodelling over time, a process rendered simpler by the traditional materials and construction methods used. These buildings were hardly the place for technical innovation and, it could be argued, new ways of building things were irrelevant when the vernacular could offer such exquisite models.

The Alhambra

Time: 1238–1527   Location: Granada, Andalusia, Spain

Call it both a fortress and a mansion of pleasure. It is a palace replete with splendour. Between its roof, floor and four walls, in the stucco and the tiles, there are marvels, but its carved wood ceilings are even more extraordinary.
IBN AL-YAYYAB, 1333–49

The Nasrid kingdom of Granada was the last stronghold of Al-Andalus, the Islamic dominion in the Iberian peninsula which formed the western edge of the medieval Islamic world. Following the decisive battle of Las Navas de Tolosa (1212), the great cities of Al-Andalus were conquered by the Christians: Cordoba, the former capital of the caliphate, fell in 1236 and Seville in 1248. Only the tiny kingdom of Granada kept its autonomy, when the founder of the Nasrid dynasty, Muhammad I (1232–72), declared himself a vassal of the King of Castile. The kingdom of Granada survived until 1492, when it was conquered by the Catholic monarchs, Ferdinand of Aragon and Isabella of Castile. America was discovered that same year, marking for Spain the end of the *reconquista* and the beginning of the conquest of the New World.

An affirmation of Islamic culture

The greatest achievement of the Nasrid sultans was without doubt the Alhambra palace, designed as a declaration of the culture, taste and refinement of Islamic civilization. This affirmation of identity was closely connected with the kingdom of Granada's awareness of its own weakness, and perhaps for this reason, the Alhambra is dominated by a mood of nostalgia, fantasy and poetry. In fact, one of its most distinctive features is the use of poems to decorate rooms and spaces, some written by the great court poets such as Ibn al-Yayyab, Ibn al-Jatib and Ibn Zamrak.

The theme of a return to the past can also be seen in the architectural structure of the palace. Beyond its specifically Islamic references, it draws on many of the characteristic forms of palace

A view of the Alhambra from the north, with the massive Comares Tower standing out; behind it is the palace of Charles V.

architecture from Greek and Roman antiquity. The Alhambra thus contains not only poetry, but also a certain Classical erudition.

History of construction

The Alhambra is built on a hilltop overlooking the city of Granada. Its name is derived from *al-Qalat al Hamra*, meaning 'the red castle', because of the colour of the bricks and earth from which the first fortress was made. The complex is surrounded by a walled enclosure that protects and isolates it from the city. The oldest sections of the fortress date from the 11th and 12th centuries, but it was Muhammad I who began construction of a residential palace on the site. Historical sources explain how, in 1238, the sultan 'went up to the place called the Alhambra, inspected it, marked the foundations of the castle and left the building to be supervised. Construction of the walls was

Detail of a wall decoration carved in stucco. Poems and other texts on the Alhambra's walls are the voice of the building.

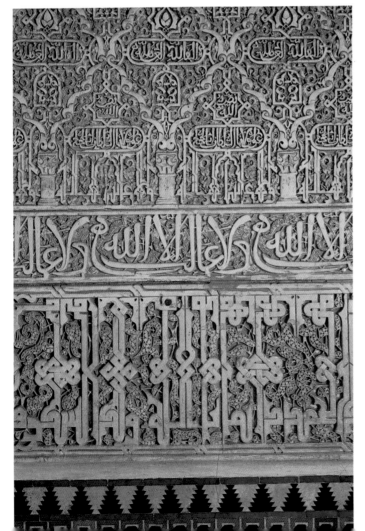

completed before the year was over. He also opened a channel to bring water from the river.'

This first, 13th-century, Alhambra was a sober affair, with a characteristically military feel. The earliest sultan to keep a residence there was Muhammad IV (1303–09), but it was under Yusuf I (1333–54) that the interiors of some of the Alhambra's towers were richly decorated according to courtly taste. To this period belong the decoration of the Torre de Comares (Comares Tower) and the Torre de la Cautiva (the Captive's Tower); inside the latter can be found epigraphic poems, composed by the poet Ibn al-Yayyab (1274–1349) in praise of the works of Yusuf I.

The Alhambra was to reach its most glorious heights under Muhammad V, who ruled from 1354 to 1359 and again from 1362 to 1391, his reign divided by the internal dissent that was so common in the history of Granada. It was he who created the Palacio de los Leones (Palace of the Lions), around the court of the same name, as well as the Patio de los Arrayanes (Court of the Myrtles) and other areas of the Palacio de Comares.

Design and organization

There is no surviving documentation referring directly to the construction process, so it is impossible to obtain any information about the architects who built the Nasrid palaces, the craftsmen who worked on them, or even the cost of the work. The Alhambra is anonymous. Nor is there any precise information concerning everyday life in the palaces, or even the original names of many of the rooms and halls. Because of this lack of detailed sources, the dating of different parts of the Alhambra can only be ascertained by using hypothesis and external references.

The buildings of the palace complex are made principally from brick, together with concrete and

The star-shaped lantern of the Sala de los Abencerrajes, with spectacular muqarnas – *stucco ceiling ornamentation. This room is part of the Palace of the Lions constructed under Sultan Muhammad V.*

cement. Carved stone is used relatively little, and marble is restricted almost entirely to paving and columns and capitals. The decoration that covers the walls, ceilings and floors is mainly of wood, ceramic and stucco. One magnificent example of wood carving is the ceiling of the Sala de Comares or Sala de Embajadores (Room of the Ambassadors). Polychrome ceramic tiles fill many of the interior and exterior spaces, their geometric compositions full of reflections and intense colour. But undoubtedly the Alhambra's most striking feature is its stucco work, decorated with vegetal motifs and inscriptions; it is also used for the spectacular ceiling *muqarnas* in the Sala de las Dos Hermanas (Room of the Two Sisters) and the Sala de los Abencerrajes.

Within the walled enclosure of the Alhambra are three distinct sections: the Alcazaba, on the highest point, used for strictly military purposes, the Medina and the palaces. There were once up to seven palaces, but the only two that survive are those that best represent the

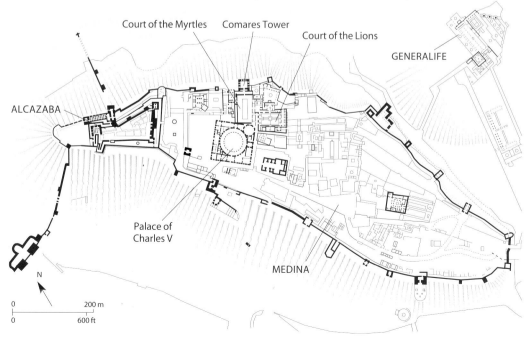

Court of the Myrtles Comares Tower
Court of the Lions
GENERALIFE
ALCAZABA
Palace of
Charles V
MEDINA
N
0   200 m
0   600 ft

Plan of the Alhambra palace. Within the enclosing walls are three main sections: the Alcazaba, for military purposes; the area of the palaces, of which there were originally seven; and the Medina. Outside the Alhambra proper lies the smaller Generalife palace, almost a summer villa.

Nasrid Alhambra: the Palacio de Comares and the Palacio de los Leones. Courts form an important ordering element, with water in the form of pools and fountains also playing a major role.

The court in the Palacio de Comares (Patio de los Arrayanes) has a rectangular shape and is crossed by a pool running in a north–south direction. Much more complex and elaborate is the Patio de los Leones, within the palace of the same name. This court is surrounded by a portico with a total of 124 marble columns, and is centred around the famous Lion Fountain. Its cruciform structure is emphasized by the water channels that run through it, as well as the arrangement of the four surrounding rooms along the transversal and longitudinal axes.

Close to the Alhambra, but outside its walls, lies the Generalife palace. Resembling a country villa, it was built by Sultan Muhammad II (1272–1302) and is noted for its gardens, which faithfully reflect the most typical features of Islamic garden design.

Later history

For most of the 15th century, from the reign of Muhammad V until the Christian conquest, the Alhambra largely retained its 14th-century configuration, with no substantial changes being made. Then from 1492 onwards, the rulers of Spain began a series of developments of great symbolic and political significance in Granada. Emperor Charles V even left his imprint within the walls of the Alhambra itself. His major creation was his palace, designed by the architect Pedro Machuca (1527): a classical-style construction, whose sober decoration and geometric composition (a circle within a square) present an intentional contrast between Islamic and Christian styles. Charles V never lived in the palace, however, and after his reign, no new buildings were added. Only restorations and maintenance work followed, as well as demolitions.

It was the Romantics, and British artists in particular, who rediscovered the Alhambra and brought it back to the attention of the western world in the 19th century, idealizing it and transforming it into a mythical place, imbued with exoticism and sensuality. This image is reflected in the art of David Roberts and John Frederick Lewis, as well as in the evocative writings of Chateaubriand, Théophile Gautier and above all Washington Irving, in his *Conquest of Granada* (1829) and *Tales of the Alhambra* (1832). Another notable contribution to the revival of Islamic art came from Owen Jones, with his *Plans, Elevations, Sections and Details of the Alhambra* (1842–45). Since the 19th century, the Alhambra has become a major tourist attraction. In 1984, both the Alhambra and the Generalife were made UNESCO World Heritage Sites.

The wonder of the Alhambra lies not in its monumentality, its grandeur or its richness; nor does it possess any stylistic unity, having been constructed, deconstructed and reconstructed in different eras. Instead, the Alhambra's charm rests mainly on its extraordinary decoration and above all, in the balance and wisdom with which nature and architecture have been brought together. Everywhere within it, water and plants play an active and harmonious role.

16 The Forbidden City

Time: 1406–21 Location: Beijing, China

*No one of our European capitals has been conceived and laid out with
such pageant always dominant, especially that of imparting an imposing
effect to the appearance of the emperor.*
PIERRE LOTI, 1902

The Forbidden City is the largest complex of intact historic buildings in the world, comprising some 800 buildings with 9000 rooms. It is a calm oasis situated in the heart of China's bustling capital city, Beijing. Now called the Palace Museum (*Gu gong*), it acquired its former name, Purple Forbidden City (*Zi jin cheng*), because entrance was forbidden to the common people unless they were granted special permission. Basic Chinese construction principles link this collection of buildings to China's ancient past. Indeed, its buildings exemplify traditional Chinese architecture, with a timber frame supporting the weight of the roof, which was constructed using a complicated bracketing system, upturned eaves, sloping roofs, decorative

roof tiles, and brick and masonry infill for the walls.

For over 500 years, from its completion in 1421 until 1925, when it became a museum, the Forbidden City was both the centre of government administration and also the private residence of 24 Ming and Qing dynasty emperors. The last emperor of China, Aisin Gioro Pu Yi (r. 1908–11) lived in it until he was five as emperor, and was allowed to live there once more under house arrest after the Republic was founded in 1911, but was finally forced by warlords to flee to Tianjin in 1924. The following year, the Forbidden City became a museum.

Today it is the largest museum in the world, belonging to the world's most populous nation. It houses some of China's most important art treasures, antiquities and paintings and is visited by tens of millions of people each year. In 1987, UNESCO declared the Forbidden City one of the world's cultural and national heritage sites.

History of construction

Construction began in 1406, on the orders of the Yongle emperor (r. 1403–24), Zhu Di, a powerful military general and a cunning political strategist who had seized the throne from his young nephew on spurious grounds during a bloody civil war. Initially, the Yongle emperor maintained the existing capital in Nanjing, but soon realized the potential for disloyalty in the south and set about moving the capital to the north, to Beijing, nearer his own power base. The new palace was built on the site of the earlier Yuan imperial palaces which had been destroyed by the first Ming emperor, Hongwu (r. 1368–98), during his conquest of the Mongols.

The structures we see today do not, in the main, date to the early 15th century. As the buildings were predominantly made of wood, several devastating fires led to major reconstructions throughout the 600 years of the Forbidden City's history. For example, the Qianlong emperor (r. 1736–95) extensively refurbished, rebuilt and extended the Forbidden City, creating further exquisite gardens and a Nine Dragon Screen, 27.5 m long by 5.5 m high (90 ft by 18 ft), decorated

with colourful ceramic tiles. His son and successor, the Jiaqing emperor between 1797 and 1799, also had to rebuild the three main private halls after fire damage.

Orientation and colour

According to traditional Chinese principles of architectural orientation, the Forbidden City is arranged, more or less symmetrically, on a north–south axis. Coal Hill (*Jing shan*), created from the earth excavated from the wide moat which surrounds the imperial complex, is to the north, while Tian'an men square lies to the south. The area covered by the city is equivalent to more than one hundred football pitches. Essentially it is

Above Detail of glazed yellow roof tiles in the Forbidden City; they probably include modern or Qing replacement tiles.

FACTFILE

Area	250,000 sq. m
Width of moat	54 m
Height of walls	10 m
Buildings	800
Rooms	9000
Workforce	1,000,000 (estimated)

Opposite General view of the Forbidden City, illustrating the vast area which it covers and the numerous individual buildings with their yellow glazed roofs and red walls.

Across a vast open space, the Hall of Supreme Harmony is situated at the top of two flights of marble steps and a central carved dragon way, over which the emperor's sedan chair passed.

formed from a series of buildings set in courtyards divided into two main sections: the front palace to the south (*Qian chao*); and the inner palace (*Nei ting*) to the north. The front palace consists of three great halls on three-tier marble platforms, used for civil and military ceremonies and audiences. The inner palace encompasses three major palaces on single-tier platforms for the royal household, and other less formal accommodation for the imperial family, as well as storehouses, libraries, gardens and temples for royal worshippers.

Water is supplied from a pool in the northwest and then directed to the south of the complex, where it is crossed by beautifully carved marble bridges. Protecting the buildings of the Forbidden City are the broad moat and thick walls of rammed earth and brick, with large, arched gateways at the cardinal points and tall watch towers at the four corners.

Open spaces punctuate the grand constructions, as the visitor moves from south to north, while low buildings at the sides emphasize the grandeur of the three imperial audience halls. The first of these is the Hall of Supreme Harmony

(*Taihe dian*), which is the largest and most impressive edifice within the complex. It covers a total area of 2730 sq. m (29,386 sq. ft), equivalent to nine tennis courts, and the building measures 64 m (210 ft) wide by 37 m (122 ft) deep. The scale, shape, decoration and furnishings of the hall all enforce a sense of the emperor's power and supremacy over those summoned for grand ceremonies, such as enthronements, weddings, coming-of-age ceremonies, announcement of the results of the final civil service examinations and the reception of newly appointed officials.

During the Qing dynasty (1368–1644) it was used for three major festivals: New Year's Day; the Imperial Birthday; and the Winter Solstice. For special ceremonial occasions, up to 100,000 people could pack into the Hall of Supreme Harmony's courtyard, including guards in full uniform and hosts of court musicians. At such times the air would be thick with the smell of aromatic incense, burning in large tripods. Behind this, the middle hall, called the Hall of Central Harmony (*Zhonghe dian*), was used for preparation before major ceremonies. The last main administrative building, the Hall of Preserving

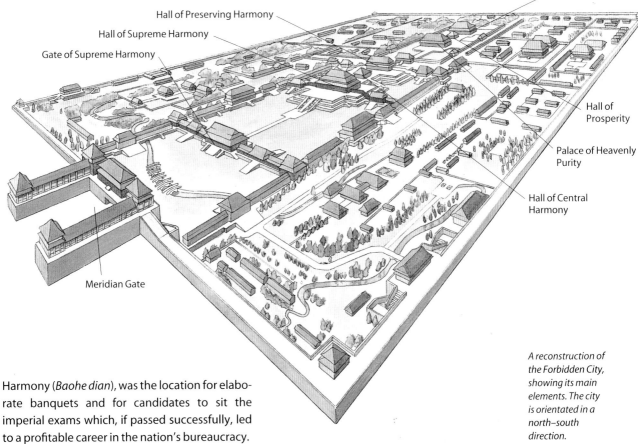

Palace of Earthly Tranquillity

Hall of Preserving Harmony

Hall of Supreme Harmony

Gate of Supreme Harmony

Hall of Prosperity

Palace of Heavenly Purity

Hall of Central Harmony

Meridian Gate

A reconstruction of the Forbidden City, showing its main elements. The city is orientated in a north–south direction.

Harmony (*Baohe dian*), was the location for elaborate banquets and for candidates to sit the imperial exams which, if passed successfully, led to a profitable career in the nation's bureaucracy.

illustrates the resources available to the emperor and his construction team. It took 20,000 men 28 days to drag this stone more than 48 km (30 miles) into position. Scholars suggest that this work was carried out in winter when ice paths could be created to slide the stone along.

Behind the official halls are the three inner palaces. The first, the Palace of Heavenly Purity (*Qian qing gong*), was the Ming emperors' official residence. Here, in 1542, the despotic and unpopular Jiajing emperor (r. 1522–66) survived an assassination attempt when a group of palace ladies tried to strangle him but failed because of their poor skill at tying knots. Once they were betrayed, they were all put to death. The second is the Hall of Prosperity (*Jiao tai dian*), which has been used for receiving birthday greetings from imperial concubines and princesses and for storing 25 imperial seals since 1746. The Palace of Earthly Tranquillity (*Kunning gong*) was the bedchamber of empresses in the Ming dynasty. The last Ming emperor's wife killed herself here as the Manchu troops approached. Later, in the Qing era, it was used as the bridal chamber for the first three days after a wedding. On either side of these are the six western and six eastern palaces, where concubines and other members of the royal household lived.

Above *A colourful tiled gateway, titled in Chinese characters and Manchu script.*

Below *Detail of the Nine Dragon Screen.*

Leading from this hall are two staircases with a central ramp, carved with nine dragons chasing pearls through auspicious clouds. The emperor would be carried above this emblem of power and good fortune by bearers of his chair. The ramp was crafted from Fangshan marble and weighs an estimated 200–250 tons. Its installation

By contrast with contemporary royal palaces built in the West, the Forbidden City is incredibly colourful from the outside, with red walls, scarlet pillars and upturned roofs decorated with glistening yellow tiles with ornamental figures. Curved semicircular clay roof tiles, derived from halved bamboo stems, were placed alternately in concave and convex positions on the roofs. Tiles fitted at the ends of the roof ridge pole were in forms associated with water, such as dragons or fishes, in the hope of preventing fire. Colour on the roofs, walls and pillars is further emphasized by the marble and pale grey bricks used in the courtyard spaces in between the buildings.

Lavish official banquets were held in the Forbidden City. In 1796 more than 5000 guests aged 60 and above dined at 800 tables to celebrate the handing over of power from the Qianlong to Jiaqing emperor.

The Topkapi Palace

Time: 1463–1853   Location: Istanbul, Turkey

He was concerned with the collection of the most expensive and most rare materials and took care to summon the best workmen from everywhere. For he was constructing great edifices which should vie in every respect with the greatest and best of the past.
KRITAVOULOS, SECRETARY TO MEHMET II, 1451–67

In 1453, when the Ottoman Sultan Mehmet II conquered Constantinople (later known as Istanbul), the city was dilapidated and depopulated, making a grand palace as a seat of government irrelevant until the city had been repopulated and rebuilt. It was only in 1472 that Istanbul became the capital of his empire, and the Topkapisaray (literally 'palace of the Gun Gate', a 19th-century name) began to play its role as a royal residence and administrative centre. The site was a promontory with spectacular views over the Bosporus, the Golden Horn and the Sea of Marmara.

To call the Topkapi a 'palace' may evoke the wrong image to a modern reader, suggesting an architecturally unified building like Versailles (p. 102), designed to impress by its size and dignity. In the 15th century there were no palaces in this sense. Royal residences and seats of government were collections of buildings created piecemeal as the need arose (the Kremlin in Moscow (p. 93) is a good surviving example).

The decoration of the Topkapi was of the highest order, and it is this consistent level of luxury and the fact that it has survived largely intact that make it unique – a living symbol of an absolutist court that was one of the most powerful in the world. The Topkapi still retains an atmosphere of wealth, sophistication and slightly sinister charm that can hardly be matched anywhere else.

The First Court

As it eventually evolved over the centuries, the palace now consists of a series of disparate buildings grouped round four courts. The First Court, entered from the west, nearest to the city, is the largest and most public. It was – and is – dominated by the 6th-century Byzantine church of Hagia Irene, used by the Ottomans as an armoury, and by a large hospital where pages could escape the rigours of college discipline. There was a mint, and large store-wagons brought in heavy goods, including 500 shiploads of timber a year.

The Revan Kiosk, built for Murat IV in 1635, was intended as a place of royal retreat. It is faced with reused elements from older Byzantine structures.

The Court was entered through the Gate of Majesty, displaying traitors' heads like London Bridge. It still stands, massive and medieval. The original gate became the Gate of Welcome with prison towers embellished by Murat III in the 1570s. Here, everyone except the sultan dismounted and entered on foot.

Silence was strictly enforced within the palace and besides officers with wands, the visitor was watched by dwarfs and mutes, who could read and write. Only the most important new ambassador made a visit with his train of presents, such as William Harborne, who was the first English envoy. In the 16th century, Francis I of France forgot to pay Pierre Gyllius whom he had sent to buy Greek manuscripts and he was allowed to join the élite Janissary Corps. Some details were recorded by him, such as the stripping of the tiles of the inner gate. The Venetian Alvise Gritti became a close friend of Suleyman the Magnificent, who visited him in his mansion in Pera, but it was not possible for such hospitality to be returned. And there was Hasan, a penniless prisoner from Lowestoft, England, who was happy to be gelded and grow rich as a teacher at the College where the staff were white eunuchs. He was allowed out and was an invaluable friend of English merchants, useful for gossip; he knew that the juicier the scandal, the larger the reward.

The Second Court

The Second or Divan Court still has grass and a few of the old trees, walled to protect them from the gazelles that wandered there. Behind a long terrace are the kitchens, now the porcelain museum, barracks for cooks and scullions, and extensive storerooms. Opposite is the Divan Hall, dating from early in the 16th century and redecorated both in the 18th century and under the Republic. On another side is the large Barrack of the Halberdiers rebuilt by Davut Agha at the end of the 16th century and the only such barrack still standing. Davut was the most gifted of all the students of the great architect Sinan and much work attributed to the master in his old age was carried out by the pupil. Sinan's vital work was the discovery of two Byzantine wells of great depth, and the building of four waterwheels. In the 1590s Davut built the grandest of the waterside pavilions, the Pearl Kiosk, of which only the foundations remain.

A bird's eye view of the palace, from the Second to the Fourth courts.

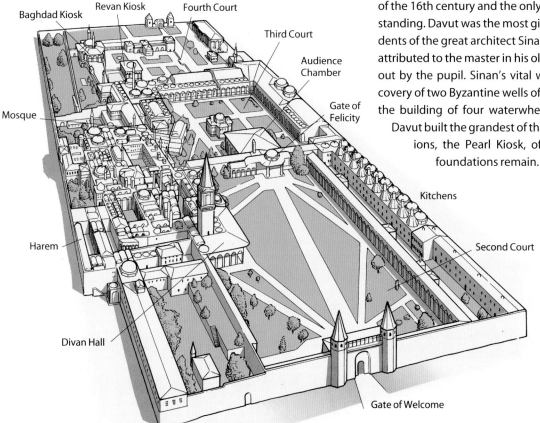

Baghdad Kiosk
Revan Kiosk
Fourth Court
Third Court
Audience Chamber
Gate of Felicity
Mosque
Kitchens
Harem
Second Court
Divan Hall
Gate of Welcome

Between the barracks and the Divan Hall was the tower from which the sultan could survey the palace. Its classical top was added in the mid-19th century, perhaps by the Swiss architects, the Fossatis, who had worked in St Petersburg. Beyond the Divan is another of Mehmet's original buildings – the massive stone hall of the Treasury Without. This is followed by the baroque Gate of Felicity.

In the Divan Court it is still possible to visualize the palace grandees, in their gorgeous embroidered kaftans, seated in the arcades of polished columns with gilded capitals. There might be as many as 600 witnesses and petitioners on the grass, who would be fed and who drew water from the fountains. This gives some idea of the splendour on Divan days.

The Third Court

Through the Gate of Felicity one comes face to face with the Audience Chamber. This was built by Ala'ettin Agha, royal architect from 1515 to 1529, who carried out a considerable programme of renovation for Suleyman, in part as a result of the severe earthquake of 1508. The Audience Chamber is surrounded by splendid verandahs, and next to the entry are exceptional panels of tiles from Iznik and a beautiful fountain named after Suleyman. Inside, the walls were covered with cloth of gold studded with pearls, as were the floors. But these were boiled down in a period of economic crisis in the 18th century. On the left of the pavilion is the large mosque of the college, now the palace library, angled to face Mecca.

Three sides of the court are enclosed by the dormitory halls of the college: the first two were burnt down in 1857; the others are ghosts but are bounded by the original walls and form museums of costume, fine arts and the palace directorate. The best students graduated to attending the sultan, if a post – such as Sword Bearer or Master of the Horse – was vacant. The halls were based on another original building, which now houses the

Right *The door to the Pavilion of the Holy Mantle. Once the Royal Pavilion, the suite of rooms now houses treasures of the Prophet Muhammad.*

treasures of the Prophet Muhammad brought back by Selim I after the conquest of Egypt. There is a grand entry hall with tiles and a large fountain of Murat III by Davut Agha. The former bedchamber can only be glimpsed because it stores the standard and robe of the Prophet. The walls bear the finest 16th-century Iznik tile panels. Opposite and overlooking the Marmara, are the daytime apartments of Mehmet II, a series of lofty chambers culminating in a belvedere and open fountain. These now form the Treasury Museum.

The Harem

The Harem is reached through the Court of the Eunuchs, past their lofty barracks. Guarded by black eunuchs, the Harem was the residence of the sultan's wives, mistresses and female relatives, many of whom wielded real power. It is not grandiose, even the hall of the Valide or the Queen Mother. The 17th-century tiles are not rich in colour but dramatic in design, and at the end of

Above *A detail from one of the glowing Iznik tile panels, dating from 1572.*

The Hall of the Throne, within the Harem, is a grand space and was used for formal meetings. It was built for Murat III in 1588.

the 18th century a whole suite of Rococo apartments was added, with mirrors and bright paintings of countryside, which have a life of their own. The finest room is that of Murat III, with a fountain, but the windows are blocked by an extension of Ahmet I. Beneath it is a vast basement swimming pool for the Harem. The Hall of the Throne is probably the work of Davut, but has suffered from changing fashions. The Pavilion of the Heir is very fine and possesses the only surviving original early 17th-century dome, intricately painted with flowers and gilded borders.

FACTFILE

Total area	700,000 sq. m
Second Court	160 x 130 m
Length of walls	5 km
Gates	6 major
Population in 1640	40,000 estimated

The Fourth Court

The terraces of the Fourth Court possess the two finest kiosks in the palace – probably the work of Hasan Agha – which celebrate victories of Murat IV. The Baghdad Kiosk is the largest and has the finest tiles and inlaid woodwork. On each side of the tall hooded fireplace are gazelle tilescapes which echo those at the far end of the terrace. There is a gazebo with a pool, beside which sultans relaxed. The poetry of private life is encapsulated here because of the fine domes and the classical proportions. Many of the pavilions in the park have gone, including the Pearl Kiosk. There Dallam came to set up his organ which was the gift of Elizabeth I of England.

In one sense, these gilded tents created in marble and stone epitomize Ottoman architecture, as does the inter-relationship of interior and exterior spaces. Topkapisaray, the palace of the Gun Gate, was simply called the New Saray when sultans lived there. And the loneliness of their august office leaves behind a sad shadow.

The Kremlin

Time: 1475 onwards   Location: Moscow, Russia

There is nothing above Moscow except the Kremlin,
and nothing above the Kremlin except Heaven.
RUSSIAN PROVERB

Few architectural forms have acquired greater resonance than the Moscow Kremlin. For decades the very term 'Kremlin' symbolized the mysterious, menacing forces of Soviet communism. In fact, many medieval Russian towns had a 'kremlin' – or fortified citadel – yet no other kremlin acquired the fame, or notoriety, of Moscow's. This can be explained on many levels, but the basic reason is simple: power.

Although Moscow, founded around 1147, was a relative newcomer among ancient Russian cities, it grew through ruthless manipulation of circumstances until all the Russian lands came under its sway. The Kremlin, the citadel at the heart of the city, occupied a roughly triangular plot next to the river. As the seat of power in the Muscovite principality – and later in Russia as a whole – the Kremlin contained the domain's major cathedrals as well as the residence of the ruler, until Peter the Great moved the capital to St Petersburg in 1711. The Kremlin also contained major administrative buildings, monasteries and smaller churches used by the court.

History of construction

The Kremlin walls, which have become so potent a symbol of Russian power, owe much of their famous appearance to the Russian imagination – especially the tower spires added in the 17th century by local architects. Yet the main towers

The east towers of the Kremlin – an architectural collection dating from between the 15th and 19th centuries – in the evening sun before a summer storm.

and walls are very much the product of Italian fortification engineering of the Quattrocento, already long outdated in Italy by the time they were built in Moscow.

In the 1460s, the condition of the Kremlin's existing limestone walls, dating from the late 14th century, had reached a dangerous state of disrepair. Local contractors were hired to patch them; but for a fundamental reconstruction, Ivan III turned to Italy for specialists in fortification. Between 1485 and 1516, the old fortress was replaced with brick walls and towers. The walls extended 2235 m (7332 ft) and ranged in thickness from 3.5 to 6.5 m (11.5 to 21 ft); their height varied from 8 to 19 m (26 to 62 ft), with the distinctive Italian 'swallowtail' crenellation.

Of the 20 towers that punctuate the Kremlin's walls, the most elaborate were placed on the corners or at the main entrances to the citadel. Among the most imposing is the Frolov (later Spassky, or Saviour, Tower), first built in 1464–66 by Vasily Ermolin but rebuilt in 1491 by Pietro Antonio Solari, who arrived in Moscow from Milan in 1490. The decorative crown was added in 1624–25 by Bazhen Ogurtsov and the Englishman Christopher Halloway. At the southeast corner of the walls, the Beklemishev Tower (1487–88, with an octagonal spire from 1680) was constructed by Marco Friazin, who often worked with Solari. This and similar Kremlin towers suggest comparisons with the fortress at Milan.

Solari played a major role in the renovation of the Kremlin, not only with four entrance towers, the Borovitsky, the Constantine and Helen, the Frolov, and the Nikolsky (all 1490–93), as well as the magnificent corner Arsenal Tower and the

The east wall of the Kremlin, with the Lenin Mausoleum in front and the reviewing stands.

Kremlin wall facing Red Square, but also in the completion of the 'Faceted Palace' (*Granovitaia palata*), so named for the diamond-shaped rustication of the limestone main façade. Used for banquets and state receptions within the Kremlin palace complex, the building was begun in 1487 by Marco Friazin.

FACTFILE

Area	24 ha
Walls	
length	2235 m
height	8–19 m
towers	20
Bell Tower of Ivan the Great	81 m high

The Kremlin cathedrals

The rebuilding of the primary cathedral of Moscow, the Dormition of the Mother of God, began in the early 1470s with the support of Grand Prince Ivan III and Metropolitan Philip, leader of the Russian Orthodox church. Local builders proved incapable of so large and complex a task, and when a portion of the walls collapsed, Ivan obtained the services of another Italian architect and engineer, Aristotle Fioravanti, who arrived in Moscow in 1475. He was instructed to model his structure on the Cathedral of the Dormition in Vladimir. While his design incorporates certain features of the Russo-Byzantine style (particularly the large central cupola, with lesser cupolas at the corners), the architect also introduced a number of structural innovations: stout oak piles for the foundation, iron tie-rods for the vaulting and strong bricks (instead of stone) for the vaults and cupola drums.

The limestone exterior reflects the perfect proportions of the equilateral bays of the plan, and the interior – with round columns instead of massive piers – is lighter and more spacious than any previous Muscovite church. The same period also saw the construction of smaller churches in traditional Russian styles, such as the Church of the Deposition of the Robe (1484–88) and the Annunciation Cathedral (1484–89).

Schematic drawing of the Kremlin, showing the different elements, from east (bottom) to west (top).

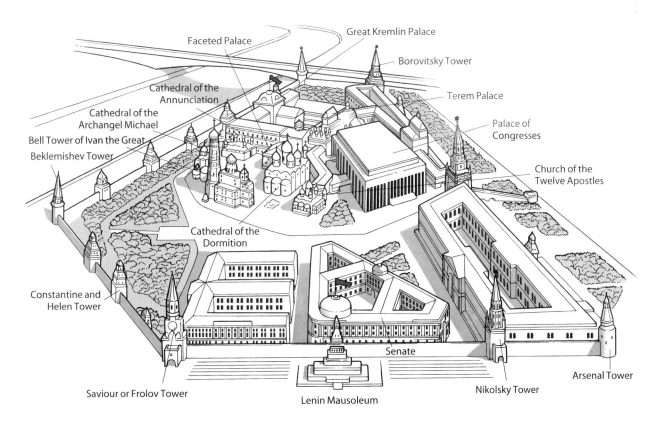

The ensemble of Kremlin cathedrals commissioned by Ivan III concludes with the Cathedral of the Archangel Michael, built in 1505–08 by Aleviz Novy. The building displays the most extravagantly Italianate features of the Kremlin's 'Italian Period', and yet it also represents a return to the more traditional forms of large Russian cross-inscribed churches. The 'scallop' motif – a Venetian feature soon to enter the repertoire of Moscovy's architects – provides an emphatic accent to the exterior walls, which are divided with an array of cornices, arches and pilasters. The wall paintings on the interior date from the mid-17th century and contain, in addition to religious subjects, the portraits of Russian rulers, including those buried in the cathedral from the 16th to the end of the 17th centuries.

The final, and culminating, monument in the rebuilding of the Kremlin is the Bell Tower of Ivan

the Great, begun, like the Archangel Cathedral, in 1505 and completed in 1508. Virtually nothing is known of its architect, Bon Friazin. Yet he was clearly a brilliant engineer, for not only did his bell tower – of 60 m (197 ft), in two tiers – withstand the fires and other disasters that periodically devastated much of the Kremlin, but it also survived intact a French explosive charge in 1812 strong enough to level two large adjacent structures. The tower, whose height was increased by an additional 21 m (68 ft) during the reign of Boris Godunov, rests on solid brick walls that are 5 m (16.5 ft) thick at the base and 2.5 m (8 ft) in the second tier. The walls of the first tier are reinforced by iron beams set within the masonry.

The most significant 17th-century addition to the Kremlin was the Church of the Twelve Apostles, commissioned by Patriarch Nikon as part of the Patriarchal Palace in the Kremlin. This large church was originally dedicated to the Apostle Phillip, in implicit homage to the Metropolitan Phillip, who had achieved martyrdom for his opposition to the terror of Ivan IV. The design and detailing of this large brick church, built in 1652–56, were derived from the 12th-century limestone churches of Vladimir. Nikon intended that his church serve as a model for the return to the symbolically correct forms of church design.

The Imperial Kremlin

During the first part of the 18th century, Russia's rulers were preoccupied with the building of St Petersburg, the new capital city. But in the reign of Catherine the Great, the Kremlin once again became the object of royal attention. Indeed, Catherine sponsored plans to rebuild the entire ensemble, walls included, in a Neoclassical style. Fortunately, little came of these plans. None the less, Catherine commissioned Moscow's gifted Neoclassical architect Matvei Kazakov to design one of the most important state buildings of her reign – the Senate in the Kremlin. After a reform in the legal system in 1763, Moscow, the second capital, was designated as the seat of two of the country's highest judicial bodies.

Kazakov's design masterfully exploited a large but awkward space wedged in the northeast

The south wall of the Kremlin, with the cathedrals and the Bell Tower of Ivan the Great rising behind.

corner of the Kremlin to create a triangular four-storeyed building. The plan is symmetrical, with two interior wings that allow more convenient passage between the sides of the triangle and create three courtyards. At the apex of one of these is the dominant feature of the entire structure – the great rotunda, which is visible over the centre of the east Kremlin wall. The rotunda was the main assembly space for the deliberations of the Senate, or high court. Encircled on the outside with a Doric colonnade, the interior was magnificently finished with Corinthian columns and bas reliefs by Gavrill Zamaraev on allegorical subjects. The upper part contained large plaster medallions with portraits of Russian princes and tsars in classicized form.

In the 19th century, Nicholas I initiated the rebuilding of the Great Kremlin Palace (1839–49), which had been severely damaged in the 1812 French occupation and subsequently repaired. In his design the architect Konstantin Ton created an imposing façade for the Kremlin above the Moscow River, and provided a stylistic link with the Terem Palace, the Faceted Palace and the Annunciation Cathedral within. For the design of the palace interior, Ton was joined by the court architect Friedrich Richter, who combined Neo-classical, Baroque, Gothic and medieval Russian motifs. Ton also designed the adjacent building of the Armoury (1844–51), whose historicist style reflected its function as a museum for some of Russia's most sacred historical relics.

The Soviet Kremlin

With the transfer of the Soviet capital to Moscow in 1918, the Kremlin once again became the seat of power in Russia. That, however, proved a mixed blessing as some of its most venerable monuments were destroyed in order to clear space for government buildings. Only after the death of Joseph Stalin was the Kremlin once again opened to tourists.

The most noticeable Soviet addition to the ensemble was the Palace of Congresses (1959–61) designed by Mikhail Posokhin and others. It has the appearance of a modern concert hall (one of its uses), whose marble-clad rectangular outline is marked by narrow pylons and multi-storeyed shafts of plate glass. The one virtue of its bland appearance is the lack of conflict with the historic buildings of the Kremlin, which remain the most important cultural shrine in Russia.

A view of the Kremlin across the river, from the southwest, with the Great Kremlin Palace, dating from the 19th century, dominating the scene.

The Escorial

Time: 1563–84   Location: northwest of Madrid, Spain

*This palatial cloyster it selfe, I confesse, excelleth in beauty that
Constantinopolitan Seraglia, the Pallace of the Great Turke, though not
in divisions, and ground distances, yet for a maine incorporate house.*
WILLIAM LITHGOW, 1623

A view of the Escorial from the southwest: beyond the square pool are the blind arches of the retaining wall of a terrace-garden designed to contrast with the plain wall above it, pierced by 259 windows.

The royal monastery of St Lawrence of the Escorial was already cited by the metaphysical poet John Donne in his *Funeral Elegie* of 1611 as an embodiment of vast size, and it still has the power to impress visitors by its magnitude. From the first, astonishment was expressed that this huge edifice should have been planned, executed and completed within the lifetime of its founder, King Philip II of Spain (r. 1556–98). We are fortunate in having an exhaustive contemporary description of the Escorial, published in 1605, by a scholarly monk, José Sigüenza, who later became prior of the monastery.

Conception

Philip II's primary intention was to establish an appropriately dignified mausoleum for his father, the emperor Charles V, and for himself and his descendants. The mausoleum needed to be located within a large monastery so that

continual prayers could be said for the souls of the royal departed. The dedication to St Lawrence, a Spanish martyr venerated by Philip since childhood, was intended as a thanksgiving for the Spanish victory over the French at St Quentin in 1557 on St Lawrence's Day, 10 August, but the often repeated story that the Escorial's groundplan was inspired by the gridiron on which St Lawrence was martyred is a myth.

First and foremost, the Escorial is a mausoleum and monastery, but within its rectangular plan it was designed to incorporate a series of other functions. About a quarter of the groundplan (east and northeast sides) is occupied by a royal palace. Normally resident in Madrid, the Court could retire to the cooler Escorial, at an altitude of 1125 m (3390 ft), during the summer, a practice probably anticipated when the site was chosen near the tiny village of El Escorial or Escurial at the foot of the Sierra de Guadarrama.

Other purposes for which space was made available were educational and medical. The Council of Trent (1545–63) recommended that every large religious institution should establish a college for religious and secular instruction and a seminary. These occupy most of the northwest section of the building, while the southwest corner contains rooms for visitors and hospital and convalescent accommodation, together with a pharmacy supported by a considerable medicinal manufacturing capacity.

Design and construction

The architect chosen by King Philip was Juan Bautista Alfonsis de Toledo (*c.* 1515–67), for 11 years royal architect and engineer in the service of the viceroy of Naples, and before that second architect, under Michelangelo, at St Peter's, Rome (p. 48). The plan finally agreed by the king in 1562 was determined by a Vitruvian geometrical construction of equilateral triangles inscribed within a circle. A close study of the groundplan seems to indicate that in establishing internal divisions,

Juan Bautista employed a module of one-sixth of 100, or approximately 5 m (17 ft).

The outline plan comprises a main rectangular block 204 m (670 ft) north–south by 160 m (530 ft) east–west, with projections to the east (private royal apartments) and southwest (convalescents' galleries). Surrounding the block, and integral to the design, are paved or garden terraces about 30 m (98 ft) wide (60 m or 196 ft on the western – entrance – side). Juan Bautista's original design envisaged 10 towers round the perimeter of the block, but this number was reduced to six, one at each corner and two in the middle, when alterations to the design were made in 1563 and 1564.

Juan Bautista's 1562 ground plan remained unaltered, but he twice had

Above *Marble royal sarcophagi in the circular vaulted mausoleum beneath the high altar of the Escorial church.*

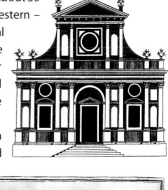

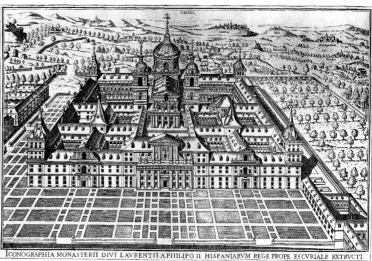

ICONOGRAPHIA MONASTERII DIVI LAVRENTII A PHILIPO II. HISPANIARVM REGE PROPE ESCVRIALE EXTRVCTI

Right *Engraved aerial view of the Escorial (1657, after an original of 1587), showing the multifunctional complex from the west. Above is an engraving from Serlio's* Architecture *(1537) which inspired the central feature of the façade.*

FACTFILE

Main block	204 x 160 m
Terraces	30 m wide (60 m on west)
Towers	6

to redesign elevations. First, in 1563, soon after building had begun, the design of the church had to be revised in response to radical suggestions made by an Italian consultant architect, Francesco Paciotto of Urbino. Secondly, in 1564, the height of the western half of the building had to be raised by an extra storey to provide the additional accommodation needed when Philip II agreed that the number of monks should be increased from 50 to 100.

The untimely death of Juan Bautista in 1567 caused consternation. But the foundations had been laid and many walls started. The architect had also left a wooden model and a comprehensive set of drawings which had been agreed with the king. Some continuity was provided by Juan de Herrera (1530–97), a regular soldier who had been seconded from military service in 1563 to assist Juan Bautista as a draughtsman. After the latter's death Herrera retained control of the drawing office, and was thereby able to exercise some influence over the construction. Recently, attempts have been made to credit him with the redesign of important parts of the Escorial, including the church and the great processional staircase in the monastery, but these conjectures are contradicted by specific statements made by José de Sigüenza who must certainly have known what occurred. He clearly states that the church as built followed the revisionist design given by Francesco Paciotto, and the staircase that of another Italian architect, G. B. Castello of Bergamo, who we know from other evidence was an experienced staircase designer. However, Herrera certainly did redesign the roofs, which was indeed the only design contribution that he himself claimed to have made.

At various times during the 21 years of construction, teams of artisans and labourers were directly employed by the monastery, on a piece-work basis, whereas at other times specific tasks were put out to tender and competed for by building contractors, each system having its advocates and critics.

Pen and ink drawing showing the Escorial under construction in 1576. On the back an inscription in the hand of Lord Burghley, Queen Elizabeth I's minister, reads 'the king of Spayne's howse'. Only the monastery (left) and private royal apartments (foreground) had then been completed, and building work is shown concentrated on the church (centre) where 16 cranes are operating. On the adjacent hillside (right) the hutted camp of the workforce can be seen. Agustín Bustamente has plausibly ascribed the drawing to a Netherlandish artist, Rodrigo de Holanda.

All exterior walls were built, or faced, with cut stone – the local grey Guadarrama granite, which harmonizes the building with its setting. Transport of stone from quarry to site was effected by carts, each drawn by a pair of oxen –two hundred were assembled for this service, and a senior monk made responsible for their care and well-being.

The style of the Escorial, decided by the king himself, was that of the Renaissance in its later phase, associated in Italy with such architects as Giorgio Vasari and Giacamo Barozzi da Vignola. We know that Philip particularly admired Vignola's Palazzo Farnese at Piacenza (begun 1558). Contemporaries such as Sigüenza saw the style as Vitruvian and there certainly are numerous references in the building to precepts in the ancient Roman architect's treatise. Emulation of the ancients was a principal ambition of Renaissance patrons and architects, and as early as 1578 the Escorial was being spoken of as the *octavo milagro* or Eighth Wonder of the World, surpassing the seven ancient ones.

The external façades of the main block have been criticized for their plainness (*estilo desornamentado*). But this fails to recognize the architect's intention to create contrasts between plain walls and adjacent spaces – hanging gardens, with orchards and park below, to the south and east; and to the west and north, wide stone terraces (*lonjas*) which extend the pilaster articulation of the façades in a third dimension by pavement patterning. And similarly, the plain elevations of the courtyards contrast with, and thus accentuate, the highly decorated interiors of the building.

Interior decoration

Philip II took as close an interest in the painted and sculptural decoration of the interior of the Escorial as he did in its architecture. Extensive fresco cycles were painted by Luca Cambiaso and Pellegrino Pellegrini (Tibaldi) in the church, principal cloister and library. Numerous altarpieces were commissioned from Italian and Spanish painters, including martyrdoms by Titian (St Lawrence) and El Greco (St Maurice), the latter famously rejected by the king because, unlike the work of the Spaniard Nararrete, El Greco's altar-

piece failed to inspire devotion. Philip II's successors continued his practice of presenting paintings to the monastery, which are displayed in the chapter rooms. They include works by Tintoretto, Rubens and Velázquez.

Every detail of the design and decoration of the Escorial was referred to and decided upon by Philip II. He even personally intervened to ensure that the hanging gardens should be planted well ahead of time so that the plants, which he chose, should be well established when building was completed. Building had been one of his principal interests at least since the age of 14 when he began to acquire architectural treatises. He could even be described as an architect manqué. Among his titles was that of King of Jerusalem, so he may well have seen himself as successor to the six Jewish builder-kings whose colossal statues look down on to the front entrance courtyard, known from them as the Patio de los Reyes.

Chancel and high altar of the Escorial church viewed from the crossing. In the south wall (right side) of the chancel, above a royal family oratory between tall Doric columns, are the over-life-size effigies, in gilded bronze, of Philip II and his family, kneeling in perpetual prayer, by Pompeo Leoni of Milan. The panel paintings and the frescoes on the vault are by the Italian artists Zuccaro, Pellegrini (Tibaldi) and Cambiaso.

Versailles

Time: 1623–1820   Location: outside Paris, France

And moreover, I can assure you, without exaggerating,
that you have never seen anything comparable.
MADEMOISELLE DE SENDÉRY, 1682

The Marble Courtyard is the last vestige of Le Roy's original château built for Louis XIII, which was remodelled by Le Vau.

At Louis XIII's death in 1643, Louis XIV was just five years old, and the French royal residence was installed in the Louvre and Saint-Germain-en-Laye palaces. On his marriage in 1660, however, Louis XIV moved the royal residence to Versailles. This had originally been built by his father in 1623 as a hunting lodge, but had been subsequently enlarged to become a château.

Through 50 years of Louis XIV's reign, Versailles would incorporate or receive much of the best work of French artists and architects. It became the largest and most beautiful palace in Europe; its subtle combination of Italian-Baroque-influenced Classical façades separating exuberant Baroque interiors from similarly lavish gardens came to define the style now known as

French Classicism. Palace and grounds would exert a strong influence on all 18th-century European royal residences.

Louis XV and XVI continued to add to the palace – redecorating and completing a stylistic cycle from Renaissance (Louis XIII) and French Classicism (Louis XIV), through Rococo (Louis XV) and then Neoclassical (Louis XVI). After the revolution, Napoleon I made minor additions before Louis-Philippe turned the palace into a Museum to the Glories of France. In its final form the building is simply colossal, with more than 700 rooms, 51,000 sq. m (549,000 sq. ft) of floor area and no fewer than 65 stairways.

The designers

Work on Louis XIV's Versailles began in 1661. The king's choice of Louis Le Vau, Charles Lebrun and André Le Nôtre – as, respectively, architect, decorator and landscape designer – owed little to chance. The previous year, a celebration for the king had been organized at Finance Minister Fouquet's new château at Vaux le Vicomte, near Melun. Louis XIV, as much impressed by the magnificent château and park as by the pretensions of its owner – whom he promptly imprisoned – engaged the château's designers for the extension of his comparatively modest Versailles residence.

Le Vau (1612–70) was from a family of architect-builder-developers and was named Royal Architect in 1654. He first remodelled Philibert Le Roy's 'Louis XIII' Versailles, before adding an Italian-Baroque-inspired extension encompassing the original building on three sides and a terrace. After Le Vau's death, his work – now State Apartments – was completed by his assistant, François d'Orbay.

Jules Hardouin (1646–1708), nephew and successor to architect François Mansart (whose name he adopted), succeeded Le Vau as Royal Architect and, following Louis XIV's decision in 1682 to install the court at Versailles, added several major elements to the palace – increasing the total floor area five-fold. Among Hardouin-Mansart's most notable Versailles accomplishments are the magnificent Hall of Mirrors (Galerie des Glaces, 1678), achieved by filling in a recessed façade designed by Le Vau, and the 13-m (43-ft) tall orangery, whose massive walls maintain an almost constant temperature throughout the year. At the end of his life, Hardouin-Mansart designed the highly decorated Royal Chapel, completed by his brother-in-law Robert de Cotte in 1710.

Louis XV's reign saw delicate Rococo decoration (the term originally refers to intricate Italian bead and sea-shell decoration) replace the existing Baroque, and the construction of another

Le Vau's garden façade consisted originally of two projecting pavilions with a recessed centre of 11 bays. Jules Hardouin-Mansart, carefully copying the earlier elevation, filled this recess with his Hall of Mirrors.

royal retreat within the vast park – the Trianon Palace. In 1770, under King Louis XVI, Jacques-Ange Gabriel added the palace's last major edifice, the splendid wood-construction Neoclassical opera which seated 700–1000; his best Neoclassical building, however, was the subtle Petit Trianon (1768).

Decoration

Charles Lebrun (1619–90) trained with the painters François Vouet and then Nicolas Poussin, resident in Rome. Louis XIV, appreciative of Lebrun's highly classical painting and frescoes, engaged the painter in 1661 to supervise every aspect of Versailles' decoration, naming him Royal Painter in 1662.

As Louis XIV's life – and the château – were largely public, palace rooms are large and Lebrun's interiors are extraordinarily exuberant; every effort was made to impress. The essence of Baroque art lies in using decoration and light to create the illusion of movement and infinite space; the architecture of enclosure disappears as the viewer feels drawn into the rooms and then up into ceiling frescoes. Astrological and mythical themes constantly remind the visitor of the king's association with the sun – Apollo, the giver of light and life.

The wealth of noble materials and superb craftsmanship from all over Europe is deliberately astonishing. One of the world's finest spaces, Hardouin-Mansart's immensely beautiful Hall of Mirrors, overlooking the park, combines the first use of mirrors on a massive scale (17 tall mirrored panels reflect similar, full-height windows opposite), while 30 Lebrun ceiling frescoes depict Louis XIV's accomplishments.

Versailles owes much of its rich collection to the lavishness of its original architecture, decor and furnishings, and to the art acquisitions of successive, discerning kings. King Louis-Philippe commissioned more than 3000 paintings to fill in missing segments in the history of France from the Middle Ages to the 1830s. (No paintings of defeat will be found here, however.)

Landscape

André Le Nôtre (1613–1700), son of Louis XIII's master-gardener Jean Le Nôtre, grew up a skilled botanist and gardener. Formal training with the painter François Vouet and the architect François Mansart taught Le Nôtre the principles of perspective and architecture that he would employ in all his designs.

A prolific landscape architect, Le Nôtre also designed the Trianon gardens, those for the châteaux of Saint-Cloud and Chantilly, as well as the parks of Saint-Germain-en-Laye and Fontainebleau. His talent was widely recognized

and he may even have been responsible for St James's Park, London (1662). His students and collaborators spread his style of landscape planning and garden design across Europe. The highly geometric plans for several North American cities (L'Enfant's plan for the US capital at Washington, DC and others) also reflect Le Nôtre's influence.

Le Nôtre's gardens look deceptively simple in plan, but a visit reveals his mastery of large-scale compositions and subtle details. A complex web of evolving perspectives, changes in level and scale, and lavish architectural compositions gradually unfold as the visitor progresses through the park. Versailles' apparently simple organization on a grand and lavish scale constantly produces surprising vistas and details. Louis XIV was so pleased with the result that he wrote his own guide, with itineraries to help visitors discover his favourite compositions.

The parterres – geometric compositions of low box hedges, flowers and lawn – are close to the château and were designed to be seen from high vantage points from within, without impeding the view. The Grand Canal, used for nautical

FACTFILE

Château	
length	680 m
area	51,210 sq. m
rooms	700
Park	
area	800 ha
walls	20 km long
grand canal	1650 m long, 65 m wide
petit canal	1070 m long, 80 m wide
Gardens	
area	100 ha
bosquets	14 (9 surviving)
fountains	50,3600 cu. m water per hour
plumbing	35 km

Le Nôtre's deceptively simple Baroque grand axis reveals a seemingly endless series of views, architectural compositions and interesting details.

events, is also a dramatic example of the Baroque technique of drawing the viewer's perception of the central axis right to the horizon.

Once in the park, however, the central axis becomes a delightful alignment of basins, statues to France's rivers and geometrically trimmed trees, punctuated by fountains and secondary axes. The latter, in turn, lead to more intimate fountains for each of the seasons, as well as to the unexpected groves, or bosquets (9 of the original 14), hidden in the surrounding forest.

The most impressive garden element is arguably the presence and treatment of water – provided by pumping a supply up from the River Seine at Marly. The grand canal (covering 23 ha or 57 acres) and other basins, like the mirrors in the grand hall in the château facing the park, transform the sky into a constantly changing decorative element, reinforcing the Baroque illusion of infinite space. The fountains once again emphasize the Sun King's association with the Classical sun god: the two major fountains recall the passage of the sun through the heavens – fea-

turing Apollo, to the west, and Leto, mother of Apollo, to the east.

At Versailles, the use of water in all its dynamic forms – vertical water canons, arcing geometric compositions, cascades – delight all the senses in a way that unaccompanied, interior sculpture could never attain. Visitors to the 'Grandes Eaux' – when the original 35 km (22 miles) of hydraulic networks bring the 50 fountains to life – experience a truly magical moment, unequalled in any other garden.

Versailles today

Today, Versailles continues to serve as both state museum and state palace, as well as an important venue for national events such as the signing of the treaty ending the First World War, conferences for European heads of state and the assembly of the French Parliament's two chambers when considering constitutional reforms. In spite of changes made by succeeding rulers, Versailles still remains essentially the work of Louis XIV's talented designers and decorators.

The Potala Palace

Time: 1645–94 (with later additions)   Location: Lhasa, Tibet

The roadway was but a gully, and we had to dismount and pass through in single file. But once through, what a sight lay before our eyes! … Immediately to our left we were face to face with the gigantic structure of the Potala Palace, which covered the whole of the hill.… I halted almost dumbfounded before its splendour.
W. MONTGOMERY MCGOVERN, 1924

The Potala was conceived as a symbol of the Tibetan polity at a time when the country was newly united under the rule of the Buddhist Dalai Lamas. It has admirably fulfilled that function – it provides the quintessential visual icon of Tibet for outsiders and its image has been displayed by diverse groups in their claims of control over or affiliation with Tibet. At the same time it evokes the Indian roots of Tibetan Buddhism, the practical Mongol backing which made its construction possible, and Chinese modes of architectural embellishment.

Named after the mythical south Indian palace of Tibet's patron Buddhist deity Avalokiteshvara, the Potala is built on the alleged site of a small palace of the 7th-century founder of Tibet, King

A photograph by Hugh Richardson, the British representative to Tibet, taken in the 1940s. A banner with images of the Buddha hangs from the building during a festival.

Songtsen Gampo, who, like the instigator of the Potala, the Fifth Dalai Lama (r. 1642–82), is reckoned as a reincarnation of Avalokiteshvara. Thus the continuity and renaissance of the Tibetan state after periods of disintegration are consciously reasserted.

The Potala runs along the crest of a low ridge overlooking the town of Lhasa to the south, and is part of a fortified complex which includes a rectangular walled precinct at the ridge's foot. Its core comprises two main elements, the White Palace to the east and the Red Palace to the west.

After being installed as ruler of Tibet by the Mongol Gushri Khan in 1642, the Fifth Dalai Lama constructed the White Palace between 1645 and 1648 and made it his official residence. His last Regent, Sangye Gyatsho, built the Red Palace between 1690 and 1694 to incorporate the Dalai Lama's mausoleum.

Both the White and the Red Palaces are ultimately a development of ancient Indian monastic design. A rectangular ground-floor assembly hall is surrounded by inward-looking cells over which are superimposed two or more storeys of further cells, leaving a galleried, open, inner terrace over the hall. The internal spaces are mostly chapels, monastic rooms, the living apartments of the Dalai Lamas or their funerary shrines.

The tomb of the Thirteenth Dalai Lama (r. 1895–1933) is housed in a western extension to the Red Palace built between 1934 and 1936. Peripheral buildings such as monastic living quarters at the western end, storerooms and outer fortifications seem mostly to go back to the late 17th century, though many minor modifications have been made over the years. Access is by narrow, defensible gateways reached by a number of stepped ramps whose gentle gradient is easily negotiable by a loaded horse.

Despite several brief sieges, the ever-present dangers of fire and earthquake, and the ravages of the Cultural Revolution, the Potala has never been seriously damaged and has generally been kept in reasonable repair.

Despite the spread of Lhasa in recent decades, with a proliferation of buildings in modern style, the Potala still dominates its townscape.

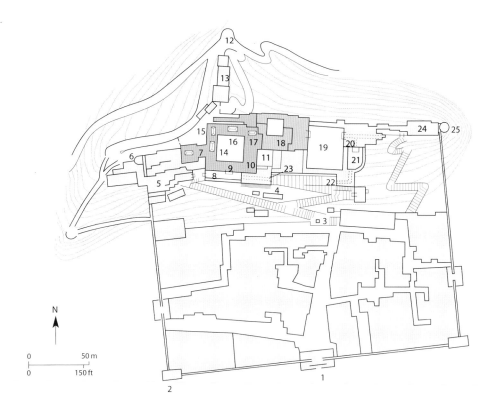

Plan of the Potala Palace

1 Central tower
2 Corner tower
3 Lower landing of southern ramps
4 Building for *thangkas*
5 Monks' residences
6 West round tower
7 Funerary shrine of Thirteenth Dalai Lama
8 Exterior court of Red Palace
9 Vestibule of Red Palace
10 Red Palace
11 Chapel
12 Bastion on northern road
13 Buildings on northern spur
14 Funerary shrine of Fifth Dalai Lama
15 Funerary shrine of Seventh Dalai Lama
16 Funerary shrine of Eighth Dalai Lama
17 Funerary shrine of Ninth Dalai Lama
18 White Palace
19 Exterior court of White Palace
20 School of religious officials
21 Southern bastion
22 Ramp leading to southern entrance
23 Ramp leading to western entrance
24 East fort
25 Round tower

Construction

The crest of the hill seems to have been levelled into a terrace by cut and fill, a standard Tibetan technique; the outer walls of the buildings descending below the terrace to various levels give the impression of growing out of the ridge. In technology and use of materials, the Potala differs hardly at all from the ordinary Tibetan farmhouse – not surprising since the bulk of the workforce can only have been recruited from the local peasantry.

The structural technique is one of massive outer loadbearing masonry walls – in this case of roughly dressed stone mortared with mud – into which are set heavy wooden ceiling beams, which in turn support wooden floor joists. Internally the beams are supported by wooden columns via long brackets. Thus masonry on the outside gives way largely to timber on the inside. One minor difference from farmhouse construction is seen in the small defensive towers at the eastern and western extremities, with their curving rather than straight walls. Much of the stone was transported from sites upstream to the northeast of Lhasa, on the backs of porters and by coracle, while the mud was largely dug from immediately behind the site, leaving pits which were later converted into an ornamental lake.

The inner and outer skins of the walls are made of horizontal courses of stones, typically about 25 cm (10 in) deep and 30–50 cm (12–20 in) long, separated by thin layers of much smaller, flattish stones packed with mud to form a level bed for the course above. In the lower parts of the walls and defensive outworks the main stones are often only very roughly shaped and the packing layers form a greater proportion of the total. In places the main stones are completely surrounded by the packing stones, a technique known as 'diaper' style.

FACTFILE

Storeys	13
Height	117 m
Materials	stone, wood, mud
Altitude	3700 m

The façade of the White Palace is typical of Tibetan religious architecture, with its inward-sloping walls, vivid colour contrasts and concentration of ornamentation towards the top.

Metal-covered roofs in Chinese style bear finials of Indian origin. Textile awnings shade doors and windows and decorate parapets.

Typical of Tibetan architecture is the inward slope or batter of the outer walls of 6–9 degrees from the vertical, often slightly greater in the coarser lower section. This necessitates careful grading of the packing layers towards the corners. Between the inner and outer skins, the walls – up to 5 m (16.5 ft) thick – are filled in with earth, rubble and interlacing willow branches. References to the use of molten bronze in the foundations may be just a literary convention.

The inward slope of the walls is visually counterbalanced by columns of timber-framed windows, slit-like in the lowest tier and widening out sometimes to balconies in the upper tiers. Their lintels are capped by projecting joist-ends and mud canopies. The flat roofs are bounded by parapets, vertical rather than battered, into whose outer face is set a stack of willow or tamarisk brushwood, ends outwards and painted red. This is a fossilized version of the stack of fuel or fodder still heaped round the roofs of Tibetan farmhouses. The walls are decorated by a wash of lime or red ochre, regularly renewed by pouring from above. The rough texture of the outer surfaces at close quarters reinforces the rustic feel of the building.

Internal woodwork and wall surfaces are heavy with painted and carved decoration. The most important points within the complex are marked at the highest level by small gilded roofs of Chinese type and gilded ornaments of Indian origin, almost certainly made by Chinese and Nepalese craftsmen respectively, and another departure from the farmhouse style.

Schloss Schönbrunn

Time: 1696–1700   Location: Vienna, Austria

The furniture, all rich brocades, is so well fancied and fitted up, nothing can look more gay and splendid, and throughout the whole house a profusion of gilding, carving, fine paintings and statues of alabaster and ivory.
LADY MARY WORTLEY MONTAGU, 1716

Schloss Schönbrunn, the summer palace of the Austro-Hungarian monarchy, is one of the grandest and most splendid Baroque palaces in Central Europe. Even so, it is only a fragment of what its architect, Johann Bernhard Fischer von Erlach, originally dreamed.

Fischer, 'imperial and royal architect' to the Emperor Leopold I, was a key figure in the development of Austrian Baroque. In 1671, aged 15, he went to Italy and stayed there for 16 years, studying both Classical remains and the works of Borromini, Bernini and Fontana. (He later wrote and illustrated the first history of architecture.) He was also in touch with French architects and knew their buildings through engravings. When he returned to Austria in 1687, he found Vienna recovering from the Turkish siege, newly confident and ready for ambitious building projects. Very soon he found important patrons and was moving in the imperial circle, becoming a tutor to the Emperor's son Joseph, the future Joseph I. In 1696 he was raised to the nobility and took the title 'von Erlach'. In 1704 he travelled to Germany, Holland and England and met Christopher Wren.

Plan and reality

It was probably for Joseph that Fischer von Erlach drew up the first scheme for Schönbrunn. The date is unknown, but the scale is so vast that he cannot seriously have imagined that it could ever

The vast palace of Schönbrunn, outside Vienna, was designed by Fischer von Erlach but drastically remodelled in the 18th century by Nikolaus Pacassi, who raised the top floor and inserted a mezzanine.

The so-called 'Millions Room' (Millionenzimmer), part of Pacassi's remodelling in the 18th century. Exuberantly Rococo, it incorporates over 200 Indian miniatures.

version, it is still vast by any normal standards. The large courtyard, with its two fountains, was realized, and the façade still reflected Versailles, with the main hall in the centre and wings for Emperor and Empress to left and right. Joseph I succeeded his father in 1705 and died in 1711, with the palace still unfinished.

Fischer's interiors were suitably impressive, with lavish stucco-work and ceiling-paintings by leading artists. Not much can be said about them, however, because the whole palace was radically remodelled in the 18th century by Nikolaus Pacassi, court architect to the Empress Maria Theresa. Pacassi changed the exterior too, raising the top floor, inserting a mezzanine and giving the north front a row of Ionic columns – thus seriously compromising Fischer's elevations.

Maria Theresa's palace

Pacassi's interiors, however, are major works of Rococo art, and so soften the blow of the loss of Fischer's. The Great Gallery takes up the centre of the façade, once occupied by Fischer's main hall. Fluted pilasters carry acanthus capitals against gilt mural decoration and mirrors. The Blue Staircase was once Fischer's Dining Room and retains the only ceiling painting of his time, Sebastiano Ricci's Apotheosis of Joseph I.

The 'Millions Room' is panelled in rosewood inlaid with 260 Indian miniatures on vellum depicting life at the court of the Mughal emperors. The room named after Napoleon, where he slept in 1805 and 1809, is hung with 18th-century Brussels tapestries of battle scenes. The 'Vieux-Lacque' Room was Maria Theresa's private sanctum, combining Viennese Rococo with black lacquer panels from East Asia. The circular Chinese Room, once Joseph I's study, has Chinese lacquer, again in a Rococo setting.

The park of Schönbrunn is as impressive as the palace, its meticulously trimmed hedges forming topiary walls as high as a three-storey house. Of its buildings, the most notable are the Gloriette, a monumental Neoclassical colonnade designed by Ferdinand von Hokenberg, and the almost equally monumental Palm House constructed for Franz Joseph I in 1882.

be built. Conceived as the ideal residence of the Holy Roman Emperor, it was on a grander scale even than Louis XIV's Versailles (p. 102). The huge palace was to stand on top of the hill of Schönbrunn outside Vienna. An entrance between two replicas of Trajan's Column in Rome would lead to a large open space for jousting, flanked by ponds with fountains. Behind it rose terraces ascended by ramps imitated from Versailles. At the top, the palace itself was divided into a central section and lateral courts connected by quadrant wings.

Construction began in 1696, and though Schönbrunn as built was inevitably a reduced

FACTFILE

Length	190 m
Area of park	1200 x 1300 m
Rooms	1400

The Winter Palace

Time: 1753-62   Location: St Petersburg, Russia

What unity! How all the parts do answer to the whole!
KONSTANTIN BATIUSHKOV, 1814

The Winter Palace in St Petersburg has been one of history's fateful buildings. The site of epochal events from the 18th century to the end of the 20th, its current status as the great Hermitage State Museum in no way diminishes its importance. The early Winter Palaces were created during the reign of Peter the Great: the first in 1711, and the second in 1716–19 by the architect Georg Mattarnovi. During the reign of Empress Anna Ioannovna, work began in 1732 on a much larger, third, Winter Palace, designed by Bartolomeo Francesco Rastrelli, but this, too, eventually proved inadequate for imperial purposes.

Discussions for the creation of a new, fourth, Winter Palace for Empress Elizabeth began in the early 1750s, and by 1753 Rastrelli had submitted the final variant of his plan. The project was complicated by the need to incorporate a substantial existing structure (his own third Winter Palace) into the design of a still larger work, staggering in both size and cost. As construction proceeded during 1754, Rastrelli concluded that the new palace would involve not simply an expansion of the old, but would have to be built over its foundations, thus necessitating the razing of the previous structure.

Rastrelli had no hope of meeting Elizabeth's expectations for constructing the Winter Palace within two years, yet he exerted his considerable experience in directing the vast project, organized to a degree unprecedented in St Petersburg.

The splendour of the Winter Palace is seen to full effect from the Neva River.

The rich Baroque decoration on the west façade, with an array of ornamental motifs.

the 859,555 roubles originally allotted for construction of the Winter Palace were to be drawn, in a scheme devised by her courtier Petr Shuvalov, from the revenues of state-licensed pothouses – frequented, no doubt, by Rastrelli's army of labourers, most of whom earned a monthly wage of one rouble.

Despite the huge sums designated for the Winter Palace, cost overruns were chronic, and work was occasionally halted for lack of materials and money at a time when Russia's resources were strained to the absolute limit by involvement in the Seven Years War. Ultimately, the project cost some 2,500,000 roubles, drawn from the alcohol and salt taxes placed on an already burdened population. Elizabeth did not live to see the completion of her greatest commission. She died on 25 December 1761. The main state rooms and imperial apartments were ready the following year for Tsar Peter III and his wife Catherine.

Plan and decoration

The basic plan of the Winter Palace is formed by a quadrilateral interior courtyard decorated in a manner similar to the outer walls. The exterior façades – three of which are turned towards great public spaces – are among the world's most imposing. On the river side the palace presents from a distance an uninterrupted horizontal sweep of over 200 m (656 ft), while the Palace Square façade is marked in the centre by the three arches of the main courtyard entrance, immortalized by Sergei Eisenstein and numerous lesser artists, who portrayed, in exaggerated form, the 'storming of the Winter Palace'. The façade overlooking the Admiralty is the one area that preserves substantial elements of previous palace walls; and the decorative detailing of its central part, flanked by two wings, reflects the earlier mannerisms of Rastrelli's style.

Although a strict symmetry reigns in the articulation of the façades, each has its own formulation in the design of pediments and the spacing of attached columns, whose distribution provides an insistent rhythm to the horizontal expanse. The 250 columns segment some 700

Construction continued year round, despite the severe winters, and the empress – who viewed the palace as a matter of state prestige during the Seven Years War (1756–63) – continued to issue orders for its completion and requests for supplemental appropriations. Indeed, it is a telling comment on the state of Elizabeth's finances that

FACTFILE

Main façade	approx. 225 m
Side façade	approx. 185 m
Rooms	over 700
Bricks	5,000,000
Materials	marble from Italy, red granite from Finland, other stone Ural Mountains
Workforce in 1757	2300 masons

windows (not including those of the interior court), whose surrounds are decorated in 20 different patterns reflecting the array of ornamental motifs – including lion masks and grotesque figures – accumulated by Rastrelli over a period of three decades.

The three main floors of the Winter Palace are situated over a basement level, whose semicircular window surrounds establish an arcade effect that is followed in the tiers of windows above. The horizontal dimensions of the palace are emphasized by a string course separating the two upper floors from the first, and by the complex profile of the cornice, above which is a balustrade supporting 176 large ornamental vases and allegorical statues.

Troubled history

Changes have inevitably occurred in the structure and decoration of the Winter Palace. In the 1890s the stone statuary above the balustrade, corroded by St Petersburg's harsh weather, was replaced by copper figures; and the sandy colour originally intended for the stucco façade has vanished over the years under a series of paints ranging from dull red (applied in the late 19th century) to the present green.

The interior of the Winter Palace, with its more than 700 rooms, has undergone far greater modifications. Rastrelli's original designs used decorative devices similar to those of his earlier palaces: gilded plaster and wooden ornamentation, elaborate pilasters to segment the walls of large spaces such as the Throne Room, and intricate parquetry for the floors. Yet little of Rastrelli's Rococo interior decoration has survived.

Work on so elaborate a space was to continue for several decades, as rooms were changed and refitted to suit the tastes of Catherine the Great and her successors. Still more damaging was the 1837 fire that burned unchecked for over two days. During the reconstruction most of the rooms were decorated in eclectic styles of the mid-19th century or restored to the Neoclassical style used by Rastrelli's successors, such as Giacomo Quarenghi. Only the main, Jordan Staircase, with the corridor leading to it (the Rastrelli

Gallery), were restored by Vasilii Stasov in a manner close to Rastrelli's original design

Yet the Winter Palace remains, rightly, associated with the name of Rastrelli. For all Elizabeth's apparent caprices and the problems inherent in a project on such a scale, Rastrelli's genius succeeded in creating not only one of the last major Baroque buildings in Europe, but also – in light of subsequent events – one of the central monuments in the history of the modern world.

The grand ceremonial entrance to the Palace is the Jordan, or Ambassador, Staircase. This is the only part of the Palace that was restored in a style close to Rastrelli's original design.

24 Neuschwanstein Castle

Time: 1869–86   Location: Bavarian Alps, Germany

Completed is the immortal work! On mountain peak the gods' abode …
RICHARD WAGNER

The castle of Neuschwanstein, set on a rocky crag towering over the wooded foothills of the Bavarian Alps, is one of the world's most familiar romantic images. What sets it apart from the majority of other castles and palaces described in this book, however, is that it was built not as a public display of wealth and power, but for the private use of its creator, Ludwig II, and a few retainers.

Ludwig's father, Maximilian II, had built the nearby castle of Hohenschwangau in 1837, as a summer residence. The style was Gothic, for by the beginning of the 19th century style was something to be chosen from the pattern book of history. Here Ludwig grew up, and here, in the music room, he was first introduced to the composer Richard Wagner, whose operas were to have such an impression on the young prince. Ludwig became king at the age of 18 without having received any formal education, and quickly found himself at odds with his ministers of government. As he realized that he had no inclination or talent for politics, he withdrew increasingly from day-to-day reality into the world of myths and legends.

At that time the site of Neuschwanstein was occupied by the ruins of a former castle, and in a letter to Wagner dated 1868 Ludwig wrote, 'I intend to have the old ruins rebuilt in the true style of the castles of the ancient German knights … here the Gods will come and dwell with us on the steep summit, cooled by celestial breezes.' The castle would become a private place, where the heroes of Wagner's musical dramas would not only come to life in performance, but would always be present as images.

Design and style

Appropriately enough, the original sketches for Neuschwanstein were made in 1868 by the set-designer of the Munich Court Theatre, Christian Jank. These were then turned into practical architectural drawings by Edouard Riedel and work began the following year. The site itself presented significant problems, since it was some 200 m (650 ft) above the existing road, on a waterless outcrop. Eventually a spring was found and piped to the castle, as it still is to this day. Riedel was in charge until 1872, after which two more architects took over, until the king's death in 1886 brought work to a halt. By that time most of the structure was built and the decoration of the royal apartments was complete, although other interiors remained unfinished.

The dominant style is German Romanesque of the 13th century, albeit freely interpreted. Certain features are taken from real buildings, but as a whole it is an original composition; its irregular massing and high towers with conical roofs make an unforgettable impression amid trees and distant mountains. Small wonder that at night the king would go up to the bridge on the north side to enjoy the fairytale sight of his castle illuminated by chandeliers and banks of candles.

The exterior of the castle impresses by the arrangement of the various elements and the massive stone walls are relieved by very little decorative detail. The visitor is therefore quite unprepared for the richness and complexity of the interior decorative schemes – it is difficult to find any surface without some form of pictorial or applied decoration. Ludwig's bedchamber is particularly sumptuous, an effect achieved by the use of the Gothic style, with engraved oak panels and paintings by A. Spiess illustrating the legend of Tristan and Isolde. The living-room is dedicated to the myth of Lohengrin, the Swan Knight (Neuschwanstein means 'the New Stone Swan'), depicted in tapestries by Hauschild.

The two grandest rooms in the castle are the Throne Room and the Singers' Hall. The first is surrounded by elaborate Byzantine arcades; sadly

Neuschwanstein rises from a precipitous rock, the perfect combination of genuine Romanesque elements and romantic stage-design.

FACTFILE

Area	5935 sq. m
Altitude	965 m
Rooms completed	15 (of 228 planned)
Cost (at Ludwig's death)	6,180,047 marks

Opposite *The Throne Room, based by Ludwig's decision on Hagia Sophia, was designed by Edouard Ille, and was originally conceived as the Hall of the Grail in Wagner's* Parsifal.

The Singers' Hall, inspired by the original in the Wartburg, which in its turn had inspired Wagner's Tannhäuser.

the throne, to be located at the focal point of the room, was never made. The Singers' Hall is based on an original in the Wartburg, and has a raised ceiling with panels infilled with decorative motifs based on the signs of the zodiac. These rooms allowed Ludwig to play out historical roles such as Lohengrin amid surroundings in which 'imagination is the model from which reality is created'

The end of the staircase in the north tower, with a crouching dragon greeting those who reach the top. Designed by Riedel's successor, Julius Hofmann, this was one of the last parts of the castle to be finished, in 1884.

– an observation made by Walt Disney; the image of the castle from the north resembles the emblem of Disneyland.

Unfortunately, Ludwig's own story does not have a happy ending. In 1880 it was estimated that an annual expenditure of around 900,000 marks would be required to complete the Castle by 1893. By this time Ludwig had started to build two more castles, and the combined demands outran his resources, since he paid for all the work from his treasury allowance as king, and did not draw on public funds. It may have been for this reason that his subjects generally regarded him as a lovable eccentric, but his government, increasingly hostile to his apparently hallucinatory behaviour, arranged for a commission of psychiatrists (who never actually examined Ludwig) to declare the king mentally ill, and appointed his 60-year-old uncle as Regent.

Ludwig, in great distress, finally agreed to abdicate, and was taken from Neuschwanstein. Three days later, on 13 June 1886, the king was found drowned, together with his doctor, in Lake Starnberg. Contrary to his wishes, the castle was opened to visitors some three weeks after his death, and brought Ludwig an ironic immortality – history's most private king had created Germany's most visited tourist attraction.

The Viceroy's House, New Delhi

Time: 1912–31   Location: New Delhi, India

The dome of the Viceroy's House … seems not to have been built, but to have been poured compact from a mould, impermeable to age, destined to stand for ever.…
(It) recalls the architectural intentions of Antiquity, of Egypt, Babylon and Persia.
ROBERT BYRON, 1931

In April 1912, from their precarious perch on top of an elephant, three middle-aged Englishmen, appointed in London earlier that year by the Permanent Secretary for India, were surveying the ridges, foothills and plains around Delhi. They were looking for a site on which to build the new capital of the British Empire's greatest possession. The decision had been taken to move India's capital from Calcutta to Delhi, and to build a city for 30,000 people, including Secretariat buildings from which the Dominion would be administered and, as its centrepiece, the Viceroy's House from which it would be ruled.

The Commissioners, including Edwin Lutyens, the architect, finally found their location, 5 km (3 miles) southwest of Delhi. It included Raisina

King's Way – the axial avenue leading west to the Viceroy's House, with the Jaipur Column rising in front of it.

Hill, on which, with the top levelled, the Viceroy's House, a free-standing structure of truly palatial proportions, was to crown the grand composition. From this building one axis would run to the Friday Mosque (Jumma Masjid) in Shahjahanabad, the historic Mughal city of Delhi, and another, the Rajpath or King's Way, would run due east, forming the grand processional route up to the Viceroy's House.

Lutyens was probably the inevitable choice as architect. He had already emerged as the leading British architect of his generation, designing a remarkable series of grand houses for the Edwardian mercantile élite, as well as staking his claim as the architect of Empire. New Delhi was to prove the commission of a lifetime. Sir Herbert Baker, another distinguished English architect, was his colleague in this great adventure.

East and West

In designing the Viceroy's House on steamship voyages to and from India and in his London studio, Lutyens was able to draw upon what he had seen and noted on his first visit to India. One morning he had visited the Red Fort in Delhi and managed to have its historic fountains set in motion, the better to understand the aural and visual effects of cascading water. This memory was later transmuted into his use of water throughout the city and, most splendidly, in the water-lily fountain within his Mughal garden and on the roof of the huge building where he inverted its dome motif to create bowl fountains.

Assailed by advice, often little short of instruction, as to the need to include what were claimed to be vernacular or traditional elements of Indian architecture, such as the Indo-Saracenic pointed arch, the architect responded by returning not to style books but to first principles. Lutyens understood that in the unforgiving glare of the Indian plains, colour and form count for little. Hence he followed the great Mughal architects by painting in shadow, borrowing their invention of the *chujja*, a thin, blade-like cornice of stone which casts a deep band of shadow and further underscores the horizontality of the façade. Additional

'Painting with shadow' – Lutyens used a thin, blade-like cornice, borrowed from the chujja *of Mughal architecture.*

Left *The grand staircase of the Viceroy's House, with the opening above letting in strong sunlight and views of the stars at night – a suitably dramatic setting for state arrivals.*

Below *The west side of the Viceroy's House, with its gardens modelled on Mughal principles.*

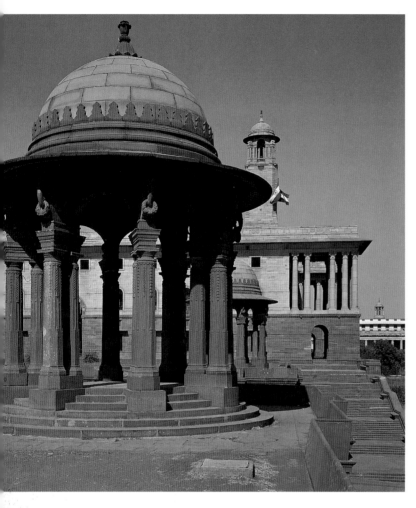

The resulting synthesis of these elements with Lutyens' own abstracted Classical vocabulary is unique. The telling play of solid and voids, more Italian in proportion than the larger openings needed to light the interiors of northern Europe; the small, deep-set window openings used to powerful effect; the magnificent Staircase Court set under its dome open to the stars; the inter-weaving of terraces and verandas, colonnades and courts, echoing the vernacular typologies of the subcontinent – all are convincingly resolved within a single building of enormous size. It contained 340 rooms, yet Lutyens still found the time to design delightful child-sized furniture for its nursery.

Beneath the huge dome, which is the building's most famous feature, is the circular Durbar Hall where the Viceroy's throne was positioned facing the main entrance. A set of state apartments, including drawing room, ballroom, library and dining room occupy the principal floor. Yet this building was also intended as a house – if on a vast scale – and there are 54 bedrooms.

Unfortunately antagonism arose between Lutyens and Baker; the most notable falling out revolved around the key issue of site levels. As designed by Baker, the axial road which led up to and between his two Secretariat buildings rose at a steep gradient and then levelled out. The result was that the view when approaching from the east up the King's Way to Government Court and the Viceroy's House was fatally compromised: only the upper part of the dome was visible for most of the route. When he realized this, Lutyens had proposed that the slope be cut back, but his plea was rejected.

Yet even this cannot detract from the architects' joint achievement. When New Delhi was inaugurated in 1931, it moved many a distinguished guest of His Excellency to tears by its greatness. Other planned capitals followed: Chandigarh in the Punjab by Le Corbusier, and Brasilia, designed by Lucio Costa and his architect Oscar Niemeyer, but New Delhi remains in a class of its own, timeless beyond the short span of 14 years when it served so splendidly as the pinnacle of the Raj.

Lutyens brilliantly utilized the Mughal architects' chattri, or roof-top pavilions, and the red Dohlpur stone.

emphasis is given by Lutyens' use of two-colour banding of the rhubarb-red Dohlpur stone from which the Viceroy's House and Baker's two Secretariats were built to a standard of craftsmanship which remains breathtaking to this day.

FACTFILE

Area	18,580 sq. m
Length	192 m
No. of rooms	340
Height of dome	50.5 m
Durbar Hall	22.8 m diameter
Number of workers at peak of construction	23,000 men and women, including 3000 stone cutters

La Cuesta Encantada: Hearst's Castle

Time: 1919–51   Location: San Simeon, California, United States

… this is the one unique romantic architectural event in America …
Bruce Porter, 1923

La Cuesta Encantada, William Randolph Hearst's opulent 'enchanted hill' retreat, is literally on the edge of the world. While his fellow turn-of-the-century plutocrats preferred to rest and rehabilitate in the eastern United States, Hearst revelled in his westernness. From a mountaintop site in the Santa Lucia range overlooking a sublimely rugged coastline of rocky coves and the blue Pacific 490 m (1600 ft) below, he was literally master of all he surveyed. Only a simple ranch road – a couple of wagon-wheel ruts – led to the site when he began the project in 1919, and there was no coastal road north to Monterey or San Francisco. A train arrived in San Luis Obispo 64 km (40 miles) away, connecting the region to Los Angeles and the rest of the nation.

Yet in this remote site he created an extraordinary home as both a pleasure ground for entertaining friends and celebrities – including the glittering likes of Charlie Chaplin and George Bernard Shaw – and a nerve centre from which he ruled his business empire. Hearst, the 20th century's first multi-media mogul, as proprietor of newspapers, magazines and a movie studio, would by day keep close control over his financial interests via telephone and by night host lavish dinners, balls and movies.

At first Hearst imagined a cottage retreat on his 109,270 ha (270,000 acres) of ranch and

Like many elements of Hearst's never-ending project, the Neptune pool was designed, built, ripped out, redesigned and rebuilt several times. It blends an authentic Roman temple fragment with new Neoclassical colonnades and sculpture.

With characteristic immodesty, Hearst fashioned the main residence, or Casa Grande, after a Spanish cathedral, dominating a small village of guest cottages. The towers contain bedrooms.

coupled with the emerging influence of Japanese architecture seen in the Craftsman style. Morgan could not have foreseen the 20-odd year project on which she was about to embark.

Building a palace in the wilderness

Despite the demands of business, Hearst found time to collaborate closely with Morgan on architecture, one of his loves. As the scope of the project grew, so did the challenge to Morgan to organize workers, materials and the shiploads of priceless antiques for the project. All supplies and furnishings were brought to the site by tramp steamer. A pier and warehouses were built in the small settlement of San Simeon at the base of the mountain. Housing for the workers, who had to be brought to the site – there were no large towns nearby – was provided. From the warehouses, supplies were sorted and sent up the hill by chain truck on a specially constructed road.

Working from a small shack on site, Morgan commanded a staff of draughtsmen and -women, and a platoon of workers. The structures, Hearst and Morgan agreed, should be built of reinforced concrete to survive on California's seismically active central coast, and yet they would be as gracefully proportioned and opulently ornamented as a Spanish Renaissance palace.

Planning began immediately for three cottages, finished in 1921 – actually large guesthouses ranging from 10 to 18 rooms and spilling several levels down the hillside. The entire hilltop was re-graded for 51 ha (127 acres) of gardens, terraces, tennis courts and a riding trail shaded by a high trellis so that Hearst could ride comfortably with his guests. The main house, or Casa Grande, was conceived, none too modestly, as a 5640-sq. m (60,645-sq. ft), 130-room twin-towered Spanish Renaissance cathedral, modelled after that at La Ronda in Spain. Facing the three cottages across a landscaped plaza, it created an idyllic hilltop village, lavishly landscaped as an Eden-like garden in the middle of the mountainous wilderness.

As work progressed, nothing ever seemed to be finished. If Hearst wanted to try a larger fireplace in a room, or a larger pool, or he found a new architectural fragment he prized, a wall, ceil-

mountain range. Julia Morgan had been one of his mother's favoured architects and when Hearst asked for a 'Jappo-Swisso' bungalow, he probably was thinking of the chalet-like homes of Berkeley,

FACTFILE

Area (house and gardens)	51 ha
Rooms (total)	165
Main house:	
area	5640 sq. m
height	42 m
rooms	130
Outdoor pool	155 sq. m

ing or concrete fireplace would be ripped out and redesigned. The 155-sq. m (1665-sq. ft) Neptune outdoor pool was enlarged when a Roman temple façade and a colonnade were added. Casa Grande was finally ready to be occupied in 1927.

There was also a sumptuous indoor bath house and blue-tiled pool of Byzantine opulence, a zoo with lions, zebras and other exotic species, 41 fireplaces, 61 bathrooms, 38 bedrooms in Casa Grande alone, and libraries, suites, kitchens, a movie theatre and refectory – all constructed under the eye of Julia Morgan. For 20 years she travelled every weekend to San Simeon by overnight train after a full week's work in her San Francisco office to oversee construction and design details and confer with her client.

An unfinished dream

La Cuesta Encantada was never finished. Construction continued unabated until 1937 when even Hearst's vast fortune came close to deple-

tion. Heavily in debt, he was forced to restructure and cut back on his extravagant lifestyle. A final, fourth floor was added in 1947, when an 84-year-old Hearst left San Simeon for the last time. After his death in 1951, a planned ballroom wing was left unfinished – the bare concrete walls where it would have connected to the house are still visible.

The daring building celebrated Hearst's wealth and his iconoclastic personality that helped shape the 20th century. Despite the antique coffered ceilings brought from Spanish monasteries, La Cuesta Encantada was not a museum or a re-creation of an historical building, but a living house that combined the modern and the past in a seamless tapestry. After his death, it no longer had a purpose for any single individual. His family deeded the home to the State of California in 1957 as a state park, where it continues its life as one of the most popular tourist attractions in the state.

The blue and gilt tiles of the indoor pool shimmer like a Byzantine throne room. Architect Julia Morgan, the first woman to graduate from the École des Beaux-Arts in Paris, commanded a small army of gifted craftsmen.

Public & State Buildings

Tremendous advances in our knowledge of the potential of construction materials and in engineering design have liberated space in great public buildings to a degree unthinkable in the ancient world. Structures built by the Greeks and Romans, or during the Middle Ages, relied on timber and stone, and were constrained by the enormous self-weight of these materials and their limited strength in tension. Typically, up to half the total floor area of such buildings was given over to structural supports coming to ground, obstructing the spectators' view of events. By contrast, it is now feasible to hang a roof of 210 m (680 ft) in diameter in the Louisiana Superdome without the need for internal supports.

Displays of structural virtuosity seem wholly appropriate for places of public assembly which are centred on a single, large space of simple plan, such as the world's longest building, Kansai Airport in Japan, which extends for 1800 m (5905 ft). Despite the potential banality of such length, Kansai convinces as architecture as well as great engineering because its basic cross-section, as designed by its architects, the Renzo Piano Building Workshop, and engineered by Ove Arup & Partners, is elegant and suggestive of the magic of flight itself, while efficiently handling the movements of thousands of passengers.

Harnessing current building technology, or turning it to new applications, has often proved a

Charles Barry's design for the Houses of Parliament was in a deliberately archaic, Gothic, style, but contained all the facilities required by a modern state legislature.

The lavish decoration of Charles Garnier's Opéra in Paris produces an effect of spectacle and luxury, but in a setting that functioned well for both audience and performers.

crafted product which rather self-consciously presents an industrial aesthetic to the viewer.

More recent public buildings of international stature, notably the Sydney Opera House and the Guggenheim Museum in Bilbao, explore the potential of expressive, iconic form to the full. Their distinctive profiles appear to owe nothing to a limited range of standard building products, yet they are both assembled from a small family of components. Computers, whether calculating the size of the lids which carry the million ceramic tiles covering the roof of the Opera House, or the computer-driven machine tools which cut and bar-coded the steelwork supporting the titanium skin of the Guggenheim, are now essential design tools for major pubic buildings. It is interesting to think what use Brigadier General Brehon B. Sommervell, builder of the Pentagon in Washington, might have made of computers in scheduling construction of what remains the world's largest office building. As it was, 1000 draughtsmen were needed on site to draw up the mammoth design.

There is little in the descending spiral form of Frank Lloyd Wright's Guggenheim Museum facing Central Park in New York which suggests a rationalized building process, but other noted designers have managed the feat of delivering a public building as memorable as Charles Garnier's Opéra in Paris while exploiting a rational design process. Garnier set the framework – the colours, shape and location – for his carefully selected group of artist-decorators rather than concern himself with each individual piece. Rationality also entered into the realization of Charles Barry and Augustus Pugin's Houses of Parliament in London, for which much of the wood carving was carried out by patented machines, while leaving free rein to the craftsman's personality in the most prominent installations.

Perhaps the most accomplished and knowing blend of fantasy and supportive technology is found in Florida's Walt Disney World Resort, where the Magic Kingdom and other visitor attractions are built on an artificial level some 4.8 m (16 ft) above ground level, allowing the entertainers to step up on to the stage in front of their audience, then disappear.

fruitful generative force in creating buildings in which large numbers of people can gather and be entertained or instructed. When Joseph Paxton, the former head-gardener at the English stately home of Chatsworth, submitted his radical solution to the Royal Commissioners' challenge of a structure to protect the public and the exhibits at the forthcoming Great Exhibition of 1851 in London's Hyde Park, he brought his unrivalled expertise in building huge glasshouses on the estate directly to bear. His idea was to throw a 'tablecloth' of strictly standardized glazing components over the whole area, including several existing large trees.

In certain respects, Paxton's Crystal Palace can be hailed as the forerunner of such later structures as the Pompidou Centre in Paris, since it provided a model of an all-embracing, weatherproof enclosure which could comfortably house a changing parade of diverse exhibits or activities. But there is an important distinction to be drawn. While the Crystal Palace was the outcome of Paxton's rigorous application of logic to the construction process and its potential for rationalization, the Pompidou Centre is, in reality, a huge hand-

The Houses of Parliament

Time: 1840–60s Location: London, England

[There is] no building in Europe, whether ancient or modern, which could compete with that which is deservedly termed the New Palace of Westminster.
WILLIAM CUBITT, 1850

The Houses of Parliament is a building that is known all over the world. It is made memorable particularly by its long frontage beside the River Thames, its rich Perpendicular Gothic detail and its three contrasting towers – the massive square Victoria Tower at its southern end, the octagonal spire of the Central Tower and, at the northern end, the slim Clock Tower with its steep and ornate roof above its bell-chamber, the sound of whose great bell, Big Ben, is closely connected with Parliament in the public imagination. Its 19th-century character

Aerial view of the Houses of Parliament from the northeast, showing the long river frontage.

the river bank. There he also rebuilt the great Abbey of St Peter, and the history of the Palace and the monastery are closely linked until the 16th century.

The Palace remained the principal residence of the Norman kings, and the spectacular surviving great Hall, added by William II between 1097 and 1099, was probably the largest of its date in Europe and certainly a wonder in itself. From 1292 a new royal chapel was built, dedicated to St Stephen, with the undercroft completed in 1297 and the upper chapel in 1348, when a college of canons was established. It was decorated with great splendour, but only the undercroft and fragments from the upper chapel remain.

Between 1397 and 1399 the final medieval wonder was added, the beautiful hammerbeam roof of Westminster Hall. This spans the great width of the Hall without any intervening supports and is substantially unaltered to this day. It is still not definitely proved how the estimated weight of the roof, 660 tonnes, is carried. The latest theory is that it is supported directly by the walls and not by the flying buttresses that were provided.

Soon after the suppression in 1547 of religious collegiate foundations, which included the college of St Stephen, Parliament began regularly to use the substantial empty buildings on the site – the House of Commons the upper chapel of St Stephen, and the House of Lords a large room further south in the former apartments of the medieval queens. It is presumed that the seating in the House of Commons, with members facing each other across a central aisle, subsequently copied in the House of Lords, derives from its collegiate origin. The arrangements were inadequate and inconvenient for their purpose, but various proposals for grand Neoclassical buildings came to nothing. From the beginning of the 19th century there were many alterations and additions, but at the centre the old buildings, unsuitable but hallowed by tradition, remained until they were completely gutted by fire in October 1834.

The New Palace of Westminster
Comprehensive rebuilding was decided upon, with the architect chosen in a competition that

Above *A view of Westminster Hall towards St Stephen's Porch, with its 11th-century walls and 14th-century roof.*

Opposite above *Working drawing showing the construction of the iron trusses for the roof of St Stephen's Hall.*

and its present use, however, mask its origin as a royal palace with nearly a thousand-year-old history and some magnificent medieval survivals. This explains the name, the New Palace of Westminster, which is often given to the Houses of Parliament.

The Old Palace of Westminster
The foundation of the Palace goes back to Edward the Confessor, who started to build in the late 1040s on what was then Thorney Island, low-lying and marshy ground dug out by ditches from

stipulated that the entries should be in either Gothic or Elizabethan Revival style. Although the stylistic details of the building looked back to earlier periods in order to harmonize with their surroundings, particularly Westminster Hall and Westminster Abbey, a modern legislature with up-to-date facilities was required. In January 1836 it was announced that Charles Barry had been chosen. His plan was well organized, with efficient circulation for the different categories of user: the monarch, members of each House, officials and the public. It provided a unified Principal Floor on which all the main rooms were located, with the two Chambers on the central spine, facing each other across corridors and the octagonal Central Lobby. His entry, sadly lost, had been drawn by A.W. Pugin, whose skilled draughtsmanship and knowledge of Gothic detail probably influenced the judges.

The site for the new building covered about 3.25 ha (8 acres), greatly increased by embanking the river. The first thing to be provided was a huge cofferdam behind which the embankment could be built. It took nearly 16 months to build by traditional methods, which were also used for the excavation of the river wall and Terrace. The river wall was built of granite and carried down 7.6 m (25 ft) below the Trinity High Water mark. The granite was laid on a bed of concrete, and behind it and the east wall of the main building the space was also filled with concrete. Then a mass-concrete raft of varying thickness formed the foundations for the entire superstructure. Using concrete on such a large scale was a comparatively new development and had been introduced for the foundations of the British Museum only a few years earlier.

The basement was built of brick with groined vaults and rubble infill. Above that the principal materials were the traditional ones of brick and stone, together with iron, both cast and wrought, wood being used only for fittings. With the recent fire in mind, great emphasis was placed on making the building as fire-proof as possible. Usually

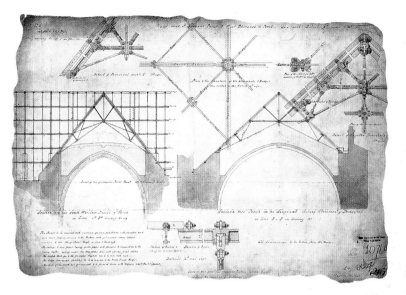

Right *View of the House of Lords looking towards the throne where the monarch sits for the State Opening of Parliament.*

View across Old Palace Yard towards St Stephen's Porch with the West Front in the foreground and the Central Tower in the background still under construction; a lithograph of c. 1852.

the floors had shallow brick jack-arches between inverted cast iron T-beams, but the floors of both Chambers were made entirely of cast iron. (Every beam had to be 'proved' on the site.)

More remarkable are the roofs throughout the building, with their cast iron trusses covered with interlocking cast iron plates. The three great towers of the Palace are also major examples of structural engineering, with much ingenuity

being shown in their construction. The grand and ornate lowest stage of the Victoria Tower was designed as the monarch's entrance and the nine floors above were to be used as the repository for parliamentary records and so were also of fire-proof construction. Both this and the Clock Tower were constructed on the thickened concrete raft, with brick walls faced with stone, and were built without external scaffolding. The Central Tower

Plan of the Principal Floor of the Houses of Parliament.

St Stephen's Porch

Old Palace Yard

House of Lords

Victoria Tower

Westminster Hall

House of Commons

New Palace Yard

Central Hall

Clock Tower

Royal Court

Peers' Court

Commons Court

Speaker's Court

Lobby

Lobby

was added specifically for ventilation and has a huge inner cone of brick and masonry with a lantern and spire above. At the base of the cone there are wrought iron tie-rods tied to eight cast iron cotter-plates at the angles of the octagon and also held down on the masonry.

The scale of the work was unparalleled and had important implications for its organization. Charles Barry increased his office staff to deal with the great number of drawings and measurements needed and the supervision on the site. Most of the materials were brought by water, often by barge, including the stone from Anston in Yorkshire. In 1843 about 300 men were working in the quarry. The main contractors, Grissell & Peto, were employing more than 800 men at Westminster in 1845 to 1846; and in the Thames Bank workshops where the carvers and carpenters worked, a peak of 300 men was reached in 1847. For the joinery some mechanization was possible using a carving machine designed by Messrs. Taylor, Williams & Jordan, although much was done by hand and the quality and consistency of the finished results are outstanding.

Many of the men took great pride in their work, and some of the carvers and painters have left their signatures on the building. Nevertheless, in October 1841 there was a masons' strike which was aimed at George Allen, Grissell's overbearing foreman. The strike did not collapse, but was wound up at the end of May 1842.

Heating, ventilation and lighting were among the requirements for which new, modern solutions had to be found. For the lighting gas was widely used, at first either on Michael Faraday's principle or following Goldsworthy Gurney's scheme, although the House of Lords was first lit by candles. Heating and ventilation proved far more intractable problems: Barry suggested the appointment of a practical engineer, and from April 1840 the ventilation of the building was placed entirely in the hands of Dr David Boswell Reid, a chemistry teacher from Edinburgh. His upcast shaft system involved building a central tower to act as a great chimney for both 'vitiated air' and smoke, plus a number of smaller ventilation shafts and innumerable flues in the walls.

Barry accepted all these changes as improvements to his design, but by 1846 the relationship between him and Reid had deteriorated. It was finally settled that Barry would ventilate the House of Lords and Reid the House of Commons, for which he brought air from the Clock Tower. Barry replaced Reid's system with a downcast one with air coming from the Victoria Tower, but neither was satisfactory. Reid was dismissed in September 1852 and in 1854 Goldsworthy Gurney, a rival expert, was appointed. He changed things yet again but Members continued to complain. Finally, in the 1860s, Dr John Percy established a reasonable system with fresh air coming from the river terrace.

The Clock Tower is an unforgettable feature; the history of the clock and its bells is a complicated one. The lifting of the bells, particularly the great bell, nicknamed 'Big Ben' probably after Sir Benjamin Hall, the First Commissioner, and which had cracked once and been recast, was a major challenge. It was successfully raised in October 1858 and has rung ever since.

The Houses of Parliament is a building that has always been much loved, and one whose architecture was considerably influenced by the modern services which it contained.

View of the top of the Clock Tower, which contains the great bell known as 'Big Ben'. In the foreground is part of St Stephen's Porch.

FACTFILE

River front	286.5 m long
Clock Tower	94.5 m high
Victoria Tower	102.5 m high
Cost	£2,167,000
original estimate	£700,000
House of Lords opened	April 1847
House of Commons opened	February 1852
bombed May 1941, reopened October 1950	

28 The Crystal Palace

Time: 1850–51   Location: London, England

It is probable that no other people in the world could have achieved such a marvel of constructive skill within so brief a period. It is to our wonderful industrial discipline – our consummately arranged organization of toil, and our habit of division of labour – that we owe all the triumph.
THE MORNING CHRONICLE, LONDON, 1 MAY 1851

Built in Hyde Park in central London to celebrate the cultural and economic achievements of the British Empire, the Crystal Palace was conceived as an open-ended system made from a kit of industrially produced parts.

As a product of industrial processes of fabrication and assembly, Joseph Paxton's Crystal Palace was one of the most innovative buildings of the 19th century. It was instantly regarded as an icon of modernity, and many of its achievements remain unequalled to this day. Designed and constructed in less than eight months, it was at the time the largest enclosure ever built, creating an artificial environment of huge dimensions wrapped in an ineffably thin, transparent envelope. Conceived as a temporary building, it stood in Hyde Park for only a year and

was then dismantled as quickly as it had been built – a spectacular but fleeting achievement.

The idea for a Great Exhibition celebrating peace, individual prosperity and free trade – all viewed through the lens of the British Empire – grew out of the Royal Society of Arts, whose patron was Prince Albert, consort of Queen Victoria. In early 1850, the Royal Commission formed to oversee the project launched a design and build competition for a 74,350-sq. m (800,000-sq. ft) building with a budget of £100,000 to be completed in just 15 months. The competition

documents explicitly stated that 'any cheap mode of construction will be fully considered'. Although hundreds of schemes were submitted, the members of the Commission could not agree on a winner and decided to design the building themselves. The result bore all the hallmarks of a committee effort and, designed to be built of some 17 million bricks, it clearly would be unable to meet the prescribed budget and timetable.

Building in glass

The project was rescued by Joseph Paxton, a gardener with 20 years of experience building glasshouses. His most notable achievement up to that time was the Great Stove, completed in 1840, at Chatsworth in Derbyshire, where he was head gardener. Many of his innovations on that project would be applied directly to the building for the Great Exhibition, albeit on a much larger scale.

In collaboration with glassmaker Robert Lucas Chance, sheets of glass were made for the Great Stove which were 1.2 m (4 ft) long but a mere 2 mm ($1/13$ in) thick and extremely light. As the largest sheets ever produced, this glass conformed to Paxton's concept of the 1.2-m (4-ft) module, and its light weight enabled him greatly to reduce the size of the glazing sashes and supporting structure. Structure was further lightened by his ridge-and-furrow glazing system which reduced the span of the sash bars by running them crosswise from ridge to furrow instead of lengthwise.

To save time and money – and to increase precision – Paxton developed a steam-powered machine to standardize the fabrication of the wooden sash bars which were designed to incorporate grooves for gathering condensation internally and rainwater externally. Finally, he developed the 'Paxton gutter', a flat wooden gutter cambered by a tension truss on its underside to carry rainwater away.

Paxton's innovations for the Great Stove focused on wood and glass, and he used iron sparingly, only where essential for structural purposes. He conceptualized his glass and wood envelope as a systematic, repetitive constant – a 'tablecloth' over a variable iron frame which could adjust itself to the particular requirements

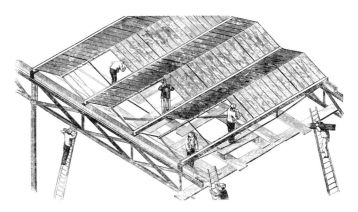

of site and building programme. The stiffness and lateral stability of the table enabled the 'tablecloth' to be thin and lightweight. In 1849 Paxton built another glasshouse at Chatsworth for the famous *Victoria regia* waterlily, and he claimed that the strong ribs on the underside of its leaf inspired his two-way-spanning structural table.

In June 1851 Paxton learned from friends on the Royal Commission of their difficulties in arriving at a satisfactory design and convinced them to let him submit an alternative. Collaborating with Chance Brothers and engineering contractors Fox Henderson & Co., and using the systems which he had developed on his previous glasshouses, Paxton's was the only bid to meet the

The glass and wood envelope of the Crystal Palace, developed as a ridge-and-furrow glazing system based on a 1.2-m module, employed a number of innovations that reduced the weight of the structure and standardized the fabrication of the building's components.

FACTFILE

Length	554.4 m
Width	122.4 m
Height of nave	19.2 m
Height of transept	32.4 m
Usable floor area on 3 levels	92,000 sq. m
Building footprint	7.7 ha
Cast iron	3800 tons
Wrought iron	700 tons
Timber	55,762 cu. m
Glass	293,655 panes, 250 mm x 1225 mm, 83,610 sq. m
Guttering	38.6 km
Tender	£79,800
As built (inc. fixtures & fittings)	£169,998

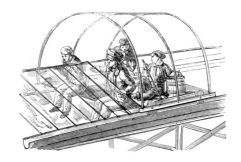

restrictions of budget and timetable, which by now had been reduced to eight months.

The process of construction

Two weeks after Paxton's tender for the building was accepted, Fox Henderson began work on site. The detailed design, fabrication and assembly of

the building proceeded at a breakneck pace. The project was hailed as the first architectural application of Adam Smith's principle of the division of labour. In startling contrast to the architectural ethos of the day, the building was not conceived as a form, but instead as a *process*. Like the railways, which were the focus of so much engineering innovation in the 19th century, it was a formally indeterminate, dynamic, open-ended system made from a standardized kit of parts.

Every component was designed to conform to Paxton's 1.2-m (4-ft) planning module. To reduce the number of components and lighten the construction, each element was designed to do more than one job: glazing sash bars doubled as gutters; hollow cast iron columns as rainwater pipes; and the site hoarding was subsequently laid as floorboards. Components were fabricated in workshops throughout Britain on assembly lines, with each labourer described by the architectural critic Matthew Digby Wyatt as 'acting precisely as the various portions of a well-devised machine, skilled in his own department, profoundly ignorant in others'. Building elements were transported to London by rail and delivered to site where they were erected almost instantly so that stockpiling was minimized.

The scale of components was broken down so that nothing weighed over a ton and the building could be assembled largely by manpower, with the occasional aid of horses. The 22.8-m (74-ft) span of the central vaulted aisle was achieved by iron and timber semicircular ribs, which were fully assembled on the ground and hoisted ingeniously at an angle in order to clear the slightly narrower internal width of the vault. Special equipment was designed by Fox Henderson to speed site assembly. Ingenious wheeled trolleys which ran on the Paxton gutters as rails eliminated the need for scaffolding for the glaziers. Using the trolleys, a team of 80 men was able to fix 18,000 panes of glass in one week. By December

To speed the construction process, the prefabricated structural components of the central vault were assembled on the ground. To clear the narrower width of the central aisle, the completed vault was hoisted at an angle.

1850, there were 2260 labourers on site working in tightly co-ordinated sequences of operations.

This new dry construction – in which components fabricated remotely were simply assembled on site – was fast and safe compared with conventional construction practices, and was exhilarating for both the labourers and the public alike. The construction of the building became a public spectacle, attracting large numbers of onlookers and daily coverage in the press, which dubbed it the 'Crystal Palace'.

The construction process, which organized men, machines and material on a vast scale, became a vivid public demonstration of the logical efficiencies of time, rate and motion that would subsequently inspire the assembly lines of Henry Ford. Because of its transparency and the clarity of its systems, the construction of the Crystal Palace became a celebration of the power of industry far more sophisticated than the Great Exhibition itself.

Just six months after work had commenced on site and four months after the first cast iron column was erected, the Crystal Palace was completed and handed over to the Royal Commission for the installation of the exhibition displays. On 1 May 1851, the Great Exhibition was opened by Queen Victoria and was an enormous success, attracting over 6 million visitors in just five months. In addition to making a substantial profit, the exhibition gave birth to the idea of large-scale public entertainment, ushered in the era of the consumer and spawned a new building type in which goods of all kinds were displayed and sold – the modern department store.

Incorporating existing mature trees in Hyde Park within its vaulted transept, the delicate glazed enclosure created a new experience, dissolving the distinction between interior and exterior space, and between art and nature. The Crystal Palace also fuelled a debate about the distinction between architecture and engineering. Considered a fine example of engineering practicalities and processes but not beautiful, the building was disowned by the architectural profession.

The Great Exhibition closed, as planned, in October 1851. The dismantling of the Crystal Palace in 1852 was as rapid and remarkable as its erection, bringing to a close its brief but glorious life which had so captured the public imagination. The components were purchased by a new company headed by Joseph Paxton who, after making substantial design modifications, reassembled the building on a site in South London, in an area now known as Crystal Palace. It took two years to complete and was used for concerts and miscellaneous exhibitions, though it was never a popular or economic success. The building finally burned to the ground in 1936.

The largest enclosure ever built at that time, the Crystal Palace enveloped existing mature trees in Hyde Park, and its thin transparent skin created a new ambiguity between interior and exterior space.

The Opéra, Paris

Time: 1861–75 Location: Paris, France

In sum, the Opéra was like a temple, with art as its divinity.
CHARLES GARNIER

The Opéra – now re-named the Palais Garnier in honour of its architect – is one of the most prominent buildings in Paris, as it was intended to be. When Napoleon III and Baron Haussmann re-planned the city in 1852, with wide boulevards and long straight vistas, they placed certain key buildings at points that would unify the whole design. The Opéra, on an island site at the confluence of major radiating streets, was one such.

The choice of architect was determined by an open competition, held in 1860, the entries for which were anonymous. When the judges had made their decision, the winner, rather to their surprise, turned out to be young (33) and virtually unknown – Charles Garnier, a graduate of the École des Beaux-Arts and the French Academy in Rome. Inexperienced as he was, he instinctively understood what was required: a building that functioned smoothly from the point of view of both audience and performers and was at the same time an expression of the richness and pleasure associated with a night at the opera.

Conception

As his starting-point, Garnier took the most admired theatre in Europe, the Grand Théâtre of Bordeaux by Victor Louis. This noble Neoclassical building, begun in 1773, was among the first to make a theatre a major civic monument. The visitor comes first into a spacious entrance hall focused upon a grand staircase leading to the upper tiers of seats and providing ample circulation space during the intervals. The auditorium is covered by a domed ceiling resting on a ring of columns. Garnier followed this scheme quite closely but expressed it in Neo-baroque, not Neoclassical language.

A cut-away model of the Opéra, in the Orsay Museum: the pivotal auditorium brings public and performers together in a common celebration; note the dramatic proportions and central placement of Garnier's grand staircase.

His staircase is even grander and full of opulent curves, the decoration much richer, making the spectators' ascent to their seats a dramatic experience in itself. A polychrome marble cascade of balustrades, caryatids, columns and stairs creates a daunting spectacle, especially when each of four levels is crowded with the evening's audience. In the auditorium itself, Garnier improved the sight-lines by concentrating the supporting columns in pairs in the corners rather than in a continuous ring.

Back-stage facilities were equally well organized, with a large rehearsal stage at the rear, making the whole building symmetrical. The Emperor was given a separate entrance at one side (partly for security – he had been nearly assassinated going into the previous opera house), matched by a small museum at the other. The exterior massing of the whole building is indeed both logically and aesthetically satisfying.

Interior decoration

In the interior, organization and materials serve functional purposes, while the overall effect of an intense decorative effort creates a strong sense of theatre throughout the building. Before Garnier, marble and mosaics were not familiar Parisian building materials. Garnier combed Europe and even had ancient quarries reopened to extract the precise materials he wanted. Once the marble had been acquired, he then convinced his sculptors to reinterpret their classical canons and

Recent cleaning has restored Garnier's original polychrome façades, greatly improving the Opéra's appearance.

FACTFILE

Area	11,237 sq. m
Length	97 m
Width (max.)	125 m
Height (from foundations to Apollo's lyre)	73.6 m
Grand Staircase	30 m high
Auditorium	20 m high 32 m deep 31 m wide (max.) seats 2200
Chandelier	8 tonnes

grout, allowing them to be placed in panels. Garnier's research revealed that only certain decorative surfaces that catch the light needed gold highlights; other surfaces were simply painted the tone of gold in shadow. Instead of casting decorative statues in expensive bronze, Garnier used an electro-plating process requiring far less material.

No surface, however small, escaped Garnier's full attention, though he did not in fact design every detail. A large part of his talent lay in determining the scale, profile, palette of colours and theme he wanted for a surface or sculpture, and then letting the artist he chose develop his own ideas. The two would then decide the final composition. While Garnier was personable and persuasive, he took few chances and selected highly qualified artists and assistants who had the same Beaux-Arts training and Prix de Rome background as he had. His choice of Jean-Baptiste Carpeaux for a sculpture called *The Dance* clearly demonstrated his own self-confidence as a designer. The headstrong and talented Carpeaux's final proposal overrode Garnier's initial ideas and even caused a major scandal at its unveiling; Garnier strongly defended the famous sculptor and history has confirmed his conviction.

execute caryatids and busts, combining different coloured marbles in the same piece so that the polychrome effect would not be lost over time.

In spite of the apparently lavish decoration, Garnier fiercely negotiated contracts and devised new techniques to control costs. Mosaics were not directly laid by hand in the expensive traditional manner but organized 'face down' on paper backing and then cast in a thin coat of

J-B Carpeaux's marvellous The Dance *offended many at the time, but Garnier quite rightly stood by his sculptor. (The original statue is now in the Orsay Museum.)*

Garnier's legacy

Garnier was aware of his originality and proud of it. When the Empress Eugénie complained that she could not tell what style the building was in – 'Was it Henri IV or Louis XIV or Louis XV?' – Garnier replied: 'It is in the Napoleon III style'. His remark must be considered as his recognition, first, of the importance of his client's unfaltering support and, second, of the reality of the collective efforts of a very large team of talented artists working under his direction.

This is not intellectual, contemplative architecture, but a building intended to be festive and amusing. Architecture as entertainment, the Opéra is one of the first expressions of an emerging nouveau-riche society – of unanchored taste perhaps – confident in itself, ready to take on any challenge. More than a century after its opening, the Palais Garnier's magic is still intact.

The Pentagon

Time: 1941–43   Location: Arlington, Virginia, United States

You know, gentlemen, I like that pentagon-shaped building. You know why?
I like it because nothing like it has ever been done before.
PRESIDENT FRANKLIN D. ROOSEVELT

Considered the largest office building in the world with a total floor area of 616,518 sq. m (6.6 million sq. ft) and 28.15 km (17.5 miles) of corridors, the Pentagon, located on the Virginia side of the Potomac River across from Washington, DC, is the home of the United States Department of Defense and of the Army, Navy and Air Force. It boasts three times the floor space of the Empire State Building (p. 179), and the United States' Capitol building could fit into each of the Pentagon's five wedges. Despite its massive area, the Pentagon is a study in efficiency: 10 spoke-like corridors connect the different sections of the building, making it possible to walk to any given point in only seven minutes.

Designed by George Edwin Bergstrom and built in 1941–43, the stripped Neoclassical, five-sided building recalls historical fort structures in plan. The Pentagon, however, goes one step further than its predecessors in its pentagonal imagery: its structure consists of five pentagons arranged concentrically; it contains five floors, excluding mezzanine and basement levels; and its central court covers an area of 5 acres (2 ha). Its distinctive five-sided profile was influenced not only by fort design, but also by the original intended site, which was five-sided. And while ultimately the building was constructed at a slightly different location, its pentagonal design remained its most prominent feature.

Created to consolidate the 17 buildings of the United States War Department under one roof, the Pentagon was an engineering marvel, with construction completed in only 16 months.

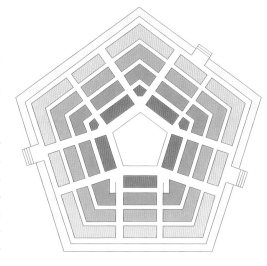

The Pentagon, as its name reflects, is based on the number five: it consists of five rings, it has five floors and its central courtyard has an area of 5 acres.

Brigadier General Brehon B. Sommervell, Chief of the Construction Division of the Office of the Quartermaster General, conceived the idea for

The Pentagon under construction – it was completed in just 16 months.

FACTFILE

Length of each façade	280.72 m
Height	23.56 m
Total length of corridors	28.15 km
Total floor area	616,518 sq. m
Workforce at peak	13,000
Cost of building	$49,600,000

the massive structure, and insisted that the basic plan of the building, intended as a temporary headquarters, be created in just four days. Construction began only after the completion of extensive land reclamation at the site – part of it known as 'Hell's Bottom' – which was occupied by swamps, dumps and ruined buildings.

Once the site had been prepared, engineers moved in 4.2 million cu. m (5.5 million cu. yd) of earth and 41,492 concrete piles for the foundations. The Potomac River itself was used as the source for building materials: 617,000 tonnes of sand and gravel were extracted, which were then processed into 332,000 cu. m (435,000 cu. yd) of concrete. With the approach of the Second World War, structural steel was in short supply in the United States, a fact that contributed to the decision to use reinforced concrete as the main building material, along with Indiana limestone for the outer façades. It was noted, incidentally, that by using concrete as the main building material, enough steel was saved to build a battleship.

Under a tightly organized construction schedule, beginning in August 1941, shifts of 13,000 workers laboured day and night, seven days a week, and over 1000 architects worked in a nearby hangar to produce construction drawings as work progressed. Employees were able to begin working as each part of the building was completed, with 300 workers moving into the first completed section in April 1942, and 22,000 by the following December. To facilitate transportation to and from the massive structure, 48 km (30 miles) of access roads were constructed. The Pentagon also has its own police and fire-fighting forces and water and sewage facilities. In 1956, a heliport was added, and today the complex has its own taxi and bus terminals, as well as a subway stop.

Since 1993, the Pentagon has been undergoing a massive, $1.2 billion overall renovation project due to be completed in 2006, the first since its construction. This will not only upgrade electrical, mechanical and communications facilities, it will also add 18,581 sq. m (200,000 sq. ft) of office space in a newly created mezzanine area in the basement. In addition, the building will have passenger elevators for the first time, 40 in all, and will see all 7748 of its windows replaced. Renovation teams are tackling the task in much the same way as the contractors who built the Pentagon in the 1940s: one wedge at a time, with the difference that the renovation should take 13 years to complete, as opposed to the original 16 months it took to build.

But on 11 September 2001, the Pentagon became the locus of unspeakable tragedy when part of its west façade was destroyed by terrorists who crashed a commercial airliner into the building, killing 189 people.

Aerial view of the Pentagon; despite its vast size, its efficient organization makes it possible to walk to any point in only seven minutes.

The Guggenheim Museum, New York

Time: 1956–59 Location: New York City, United States

Amazing, different, startling, forceful, bold, hypnotic, unique – all these adjectives and more can be used to describe [the Museum], but beautiful it isn't.
BERNARD LEVIN, 1989

Of those architects often dubbed the 'Big Four', the Founding Fathers of the Modern Movement in architecture – Le Corbusier (Charles-Éduoard Jeanneret), Alvar Aalto, Mies van der Rohe and Frank Lloyd Wright (FLW) – it is the last in the list who perhaps achieved the greatest dexterity in the form-generating use of geometry in his buildings. Whether in his virtuoso detailing of the Imperial Hotel in Tokyo (1916–22; demolished 1968), the 'Mayan' geometry of his earliest houses in California, such as the Hollyhock House (1919–21), or the hexagonal and 45-degree planning grids he used in some of his most notable houses, Wright proved himself a master at modulating patterns and volumes.

Circles as well as circular and frequently spiral or helical forms held a particular fascination for Wright, evident as early as an unbuilt proposal of 1925 for the Sugar Loaf Mountain Planetarium. His Annunciation Greek Orthodox Church in Milwaukee (1959–61, built after Wright's death) and the C. V. Morris Shop (1948–49) in San Francisco, amply demonstrate Wright's ability to transmute what might initially appear to be banal, mechanical geometry into dynamic, memorable spaces.

Quite late in a long and eventful career – he lived from 1867 to 1959 – Wright found a fully supportive patron. Solomon R. Guggenheim commissioned him to build a museum for his collection of (mostly) non-representational art assembled under the steely eye of Baroness Hilla

Frank Lloyd Wright with the model of his museum, showing the glass lid.

Rebay, who was to become the first director of the Museum. This was also Wright's first commission in New York City; the design was published in 1944, but delayed both by the Second World War and by the founder's death five years later.

Site and solution

Founder and director alike were certainly treated to a singular solution to the problem of displaying the collection. Whereas conventional curatorial

The museum in the course of construction – the structure is reinforced concrete, poured in place.

Below *The Museum is sited in a prime location in the city of New York, directly facing Central Park. The 1992 extension rises behind.*

wisdom, even in the 1950s, would most likely have favoured a sequential arrangement of well-defined gallery spaces, there were already notable exceptions, especially in the United States, such as Louis Kahn's Yale Art Gallery of 1954.

Nearly half a century earlier, Wright had already presaged the grand central volume of the Guggenheim, as well as the many hundreds of top-lit atria subsequently built across the world, in the design of an office building for the Larkin mail order company in Buffalo (1904, demolished 1950). On the site on Fifth Avenue, sandwiched between East 88th and East 89th Streets and looking due west on to Central Park, he was able to combine this concept with a powerful spiral geometry which recalled the historic ziggurats of the Near East, albeit inverted. This comparison is a just one, since Wright himself scrawled the term on one of his exquisite pencilled cross-sections of the museum.

The museum is built of reinforced concrete, with 12 structural fins linking the gallery levels. Wright deliberately and masterfully plays down the low-ceilinged entrances and foyer areas, the better to stun visitors as they step out into the radiant central volume, soaring upwards through four floors to the domed skylight. These are not four conventional floors, however, but rather a single spiral ramp, on the sloping wall of which much of the art collection is displayed.

FLW's intention was that gallery-goers would take the lifts to the top level and then descend the spiral ramp, stopping off and viewing exhibits displayed in the less dramatic, rectangular galleries opening off each floor. There was also the option of ascending the ramp from the entrance level. In either case visitors encounter a basic and – to Wright scholars – entirely typical paradox of the architect, that the Guggenheim may not be the most propitious setting for art. Should the paintings displayed be hung precisely horizontally, or follow the 10 degree slope of the ramp? In addition, the sloping walls tend to showcase the pictures as individual vertical planes, free of the usual visual backing of a wall. The emphasis on each picture is further compounded by the vertical fins which form an integral part of the

The spectacular view straight upwards to the skylight, and the spiral descending ramp.

building's structure and tend thereby to fragment the continuity of the display.

These and other debates will continue – as they have done from the moment the Guggenheim opened in October 1959. In 1992, the extension by the New York architects Gwathmey Siegel & Associates, broadly following Wright's own volumetric concept, provided much-needed additional gallery space and curatorial facilities. A more recent facelift has brought the Guggenheim's facilities up to international standards and it remains a 'must-see' destination for both domestic and overseas visitors. Certain critics, including the British columnist Bernard Levin, have described it, affectionately, as FLW's last practical joke on mankind, but the Guggenheim will continue to delight as a magnificent architectural space which happens to house a world-class collection of art.

FACTFILE

Ramp	3 m wide
Typical gallery height	2.9 m
External finish	concrete with cement & crushed marble render

32 Walt Disney World Resort

Time: 1959–71 Location: Orlando, Florida, United States

I'm tired of museums and fairs where you have to walk your legs off.
WALT DISNEY

W alt Disney was a man easily bored. After he helped invent the sound cartoon, he turned his restless imagination to making the first full-length colour animated film. After losing interest in films, he reinvented the amusement park at Disneyland in Anaheim, California, in 1955, but he was not totally satisfied with the results and sought a broader canvas. Disneyland thus turned out to be the first draft for an even larger, more expansive recreational landscape – Walt Disney World.

It would include not only a larger version of the Magic Kingdom in Anaheim, with its fairytale castle, 1890s Main Street, Adventureland, Tomorrowland and Frontierland, but resort hotels, a mass-transport system and, Walt envisioned, an experimental prototype community of tomorrow, 'EPCOT', where slums would not develop, blight was banished and the fruits of modern technology were brought to daily life. And still there would be room for more experiments.

Having scouted for sites near east coast centres since 1959, he chose the central Florida site and began buying property. He eventually spent $5 million on 10,927 ha (27,000 acres) of flat pastureland and swamp, an hour's drive from the Florida beaches. He did not, however, live to see his new venture completed. He died in 1966, still plotting and refining the plan of his dream. It fell to his partner and older brother Roy O. Disney to fulfil his vision. By 1969 bulldozers had started reshaping the area into reliably dry land. An elaborately engineered 64-km (40-mile) canal system was created to drain the land – the water table was only 1.2 m (4 ft) below the surface. Recreational lakes were dug into the white sand.

Roy Disney postponed the experimental city as impractical. Yet some of its large-scale planning concepts and technical innovations survive. For example, service and functional activities are kept strictly separate from the entertainment and pleasure areas. The ground level of the Magic Kingdom was built 5 m (16 ft) above actual ground level, creating a hidden city of tunnels, storerooms, offices and service areas, allowing the public realm of rides, restaurants and lawns above to be unobtrusively and efficiently supplied and maintained. Waste is removed by a large vacuum system to a central recycling plant. Employees can get into costume or take breaks below, and then return to their jobs, appearing anywhere in the park via special entry points.

Two hotels were built on the lake across from the Magic Kingdom Park. The 500-room Polynesian Hotel is low-rise and South Seas in style,

A geodesic dome at Epcot's entrance features an exhibit on the history of communication, sponsored by AT&T. The monorail linking Epcot with the Magic Kingdom Park glides silently by on the right.

while the 1000-room Disney's Contemporary Resort is a 15-storey, A-frame structure with a lofty central atrium. It suggests a sleek high-tech future, accentuated by the monorail passing through the atrium as it circles the lake. It connects the hotels and parking to the Magic Kingdom, as do water taxis and bus shuttles.

Although dramatically different in appearance, the two hotels are much more alike than might be supposed. Both use an experimental mass-production method of hotel construction developed by US Steel and designed by architect Donald Wexler. Hotel rooms were prefabricated off site as units, including walls and bathrooms, trucked to the hotel sites and then stacked in place by crane in the hotel framework.

Roy Disney was 78 when Walt Disney World Resort finally opened on 1 October 1971, at a cost of $400 million. He had spent his final years fulfilling his brother's dream; taxed by the tremendous undertaking, he died two months later. But it was never finished as Walt Disney had envisaged it. The Disney team reworked Epcot as a theme park in the image of a permanent World's Fair rather than a living city. Ultra-modern pavilions feature exhibits on transport (sponsored by General Motors), imagination (sponsored by Kodak) and communication (sponsored by AT&T); the latter's geodesic globe serves as the park's unmistakable theme building. Around a nearby artificial lagoon, companies and organization in Mexico, Great Britain, Italy, Canada and in other countries sponsored pavilions based on their native architecture. This version of Epcot, costing $1.2 billion, opened in 1982. Two more theme parks were added (Disney-MGM Studios in 1989; Disney's Animal Kingdom in 1998) as well as new hotels, motels, water parks, nightclubs and other attractions.

In an economy and culture shaped by tourism and entertainment, Walt Disney World Resort set the standards. It was repeated by Disney in Tokyo and Paris, and by other entertainment corporations in amusement parks, water parks and wild animal parks around the world. As the factory became the emblematic architecture of the Industrial Revolution, the amusement park typified our era.

FACTFILE

Area	10,927 ha
Cost	$400,000,000
Hotel architect	Welton Becket Associates

The Magic Kingdom, a more spacious version of the Disneyland park in Anaheim, California, rises out of an artificially engineered landscape of lakes and plantings.

The Sydney Opera House

Time: 1959–73   Location: Sydney, Australia

The rim of the cape, the original view and my building had to be a unity.
JORN UTZON, 1965

The Sydney Opera House is one of the most celebrated architectural icons of the 20th century. Its name alone evokes a special form and place. The Opera House became part of a reconsideration of architecture in the 1950s, developing from the Modernism of the 1930s and 1940s. Here, in a new country, a young architect provided new visions and new celebrations.

Located on Bennelong Point, a low promontory which defines Sydney Cove, the 'hub' of Sydney Harbour and place of initial white settlement in Australia, the Opera House transforms the site into a series of plateaux, with white shells sailing above them. It was the result of an international architectural competition organized by the New South Wales Government in 1956. On 29 January 1957, the 38-year-old Danish architect Jorn Utzon was announced as a winner from 233 submissions.

Concept and construction

In concept, the building is simple: a platform with two amphitheatres incised from it. Lightly arching over these two auditoria and their associated foyers and bars are great white-tiled shells. These hover like sails or clouds and, in fact, Utzon drew sketches of plateaux and clouds to explain the design. Freely designed in the original competition drawings, these shell roofs were difficult both to design in engineering terms, and to construct.

From 1957 to 1961, three or four different approaches were explored by Utzon and the engineers, Ove Arup. The problem centered on the lack of geometric form and repetition in the shape of the shells. In 1961, however, while still in Denmark prior to emigrating to Australia in 1963, Utzon resolved the structural problems of the shells in a flash of inspiration. His solution was that each segment of the shell of the Opera House should be cut, as it were, from the same sphere. It is variously recounted that Utzon confirmed his idea with a beach ball in a bath, or an orange. In this account, Utzon's four-year-old son, Kim, was

A building study model, showing the shells. Jorn Utzon is on the left, explaining the structure.

peeling an orange and showed it to his father. The peel revealed how each part's curved surface could be obtained from the sphere. According to Philip Drew, Jorn Utzon is reported to have said 'it is a big sphere with parts cut out of it, just like an orange'. He then went to a shop and returned with an orange to demonstrate his geometry.

Once the basic geometry had been solved it followed that the shells could be made out of prefabricated ribs. All parts of the shells were precast on site; precast ribs were 'threaded' with cables and were stressed together to make an arch. The completed arches fan out to make each side of the shell.

Prefabricated trays, or 'lids', with ceramic tiles spanning the space between the ribs, form the surface of the shells. A total of over 1,000,000 tiles cover the 4240 lids. The tiles are patterned, with shiny ones in the centre and matt ones at the edges, creating an extraordinary radiating pattern of textures which, according to Utzon, 'interact like fingernails and flesh'. As he also rightly said, 'The sun, the light and the clouds will make it a living thing', so that viewers will 'never be finished with it'.

This brilliant resolution of the complex shell shows Utzon's interest in an architecture of additive forms – a 'kit of parts' which he plays with in different ways. Additive form becomes a theme of his design approach, from the building to the furniture – it appears in his own house in Sydney and his completed project for the Kuwait Parliament House. Le Corbusier, who interested Utzon, designed a hospital in Venice with repetitive roof elements used poetically. Utzon had a vision of the mass production of elements, such as roofs, walls or structure, which could lead to a new architecture of freedom.

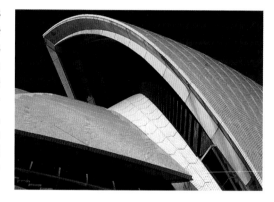

The completed shells, showing the intricate tiling pattern.

Below *The Opera House under construction in 1960, with the rib arches and tiled lids being installed.*

The Opera House under construction in 1967, with Circular Quay and central Sydney in the background.

Phases of completion

The Sydney Opera House was designed and constructed in three main phases: first, the platform, secondly the shells, and thirdly the exterior 'cladding' and glass walls. The auditoria's plywood walls, ribs and interiors formed part of the third stage. The architectural ideas of each of the three parts were put forward simply and directly by Utzon in two books: the *Red Book* of 1958 and the *Yellow Book* of 1962. These described to his client his thinking, design intentions and design drawings – the *Yellow Book* particularly relied on drawings. Under his design direction the platform

and the shells were implemented. He was not to complete the third stage.

The tragic story of Utzon's resignation is as dramatic as his architectural design. In 1964 the government of New South Wales changed and the new government began to attack Utzon publicly and in private, and did not pay his fees and claims. Utzon wrote to the new Minister that 'you have forced me to leave the job!' Utzon and his family left Australia secretly on 28 April 1966. He was replaced for the third stage of the project by Hall, Todd & Littlemore. From 1966 Peter Hall, of this specially formed team, was the design architect, completing the Concert Hall and Opera Theatre, as well as detailing the windows and stairs.

Utzon's design had the two largest halls side by side upon the great platform, with their stages to the south and their foyers opening out over the Harbour. With this plan it was not possible to have conventional side and back stage spaces. Utzon proposed a series of lifts to service the stages. In 1967 this was reviewed by Peter Hall, who proposed that the major hall should no longer have a stage but be merely a concert hall, and that opera be confined to the smaller of the major halls. This is how the building was completed.

Audience and visitors arrive on the city-side of the building by foot in the austere space beneath the grand stairs roofed by sculptured concrete beams. They then ascend stairs to the main platform level as though 'passing from a low narthex or crypt to a grand Gothic cathedral'. The foyer is light and the rib vaults soar to the top of the shells. From the southern foyer, the audience is led by rising side corridors to northern foyers and bars – heroic multi-level spaces with panoramic views of the Harbour. Both major auditoria are entered from the northern foyers and side corridors. The Concert Hall is a series of faceted and inflected white birch veneer forms, with the seating for 2679 people in a radius around a rostrum for the orchestra. Behind the orchestra and choir galleries is an organ designed and built by Ronald Sharp of Sydney. This was finished in 1979, after the completion of the Opera House, and is the largest mechanical-action organ in the world.

The Opera Theatre has a more traditional form with open boxes and galleries steeply raked, with 1547 seats surrounding the proscenium stage. Lined with timber painted matt black, a vibrant stage curtain 'The Curtain of the Sun', by John Coburn, relieves the sombre tone. Both the Concert Hall and Opera Theatre have an external acoustic carcass in brush box timber. This external wall combines with the shell ribs and steel mullions

FACTFILE

Ground area	1.8 ha
External dimensions	186 x 116 m
Height of tallest shell	67 m
Weight of roof	26,700 tonnes
Precast segments in roof	2914
Surface area of roof	18,500 sq. m

to provide a natural palette of colours to the corridors and foyers outside the major halls.

The Opera House was opened by Her Majesty Queen Elizabeth II on 20 October 1973. The Queen said 'Controversy of the most extreme kind attended the building of the pyramids, yet they stand today – 4000 years later – acknowledged as one of the wonders of the world. I believe this will be so for the Sydney Opera House.'

Why is the Sydney Opera House a modern wonder of the world? It certainly provided effective new facilities for Sydney, it responded to its site and there was also great human drama in its

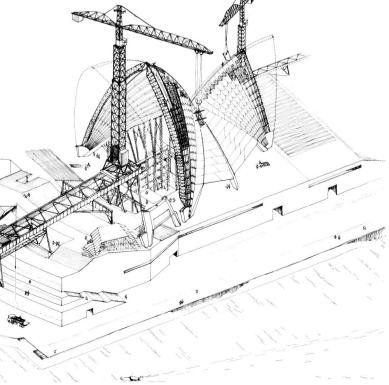

The construction method showing a tower crane on tracks and the mobile rib-arch support.

'Looking at a Gothic church, you will never be finished with it – when you pass around it or see it against the sky. It is as if something new goes on all the time and it is so important – this interplay is so important that together with the sun, the light and the clouds, it makes it a living thing' –Jorn Utzon. The Sydney Opera House in the flickering morning light, surrounded by Sydney Harbour.

implementation. But the Opera House is more than this, it has become a symbol of Sydney – it has, with its three-dimensional form, its floating shells, become identified with the city. It is the first of a series of great modern landmark buildings that not only contribute to their respective cities but show the power of architecture in transforming and enhancing a city. There have been many such buildings since the Sydney Opera House – for example the Pompidou Centre, Paris (p. 156), the Hongkong and Shanghai Bank, Hong Kong (p. 197) and the Guggenheim Museum, Bilbao (p. 164). Utzon's Opera House was the first.

And in a coda to this remarkable story in 2001, after a gap of 35 years, Jorn Utzon agreed to act as a consultant to the Sydney architects Johnson Pilton Walker on a £9-million refurbishment of his great building.

The Louisiana Superdome

Time: 1971–75   Location: New Orleans, Louisiana, United States

In Xanadu did Kubla Khan A stately pleasure-dome decree …
It was a miracle of rare device; A sunny pleasure-dome with caves of ice!
SAMUEL TAYLOR COLERIDGE, 1798

The world's pre-eminent domed facility is also the world's largest steel-constructed room, with interior views unobstructed by any support. Furthermore, it is the first privately managed, publicly owned, multi-purpose facility. The Louisiana Superdome, the dominant structure in New Orleans, has sufficient area in its main arena for two football fields. Covered by a 4-ha (9.7-acre) roof-dome, in September 1987 it accommodated an audience of 80,000, who had come to hear Pope John Paul II.

Some ancient Greek and Egyptian temples may have had equal or larger footprints, but 60 per cent of their interior floor-space was occupied by roof support columns, leaving scant usable space in proportion to the structure's size. What

The Superdome, resplendently the dominant structure in New Orleans, can hold 87,000 people safely, for events from Papal visits to football games or pet shows.

153

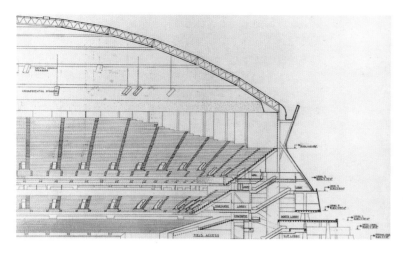

Above A cross-section, showing structural design details.

Birth of the project

Originally the dream of New Orleans' business-man Dave Dixon, this Wonder was conceived as a means of luring a major league football franchise. In 1966 the Louisiana Legislature agreed with the lobbyists, politicians and financiers, and passed a Constitutional Amendment to allow the state to sell bonds to finance the project.

Built in a depressed area of the town, the Superdome sparked a $2-billion local construction boom; good hotel room availability was increased 150 per cent in the neighbourhood. Economic academics have called it: '… the most usable public building ever designed …' and '… one of the wisest investments that the state has ever made.' The project soon became a financial success. Constructed for $163 million between August 1971 and August 1975, the Superdome created an economic impact of $4.6 billion in its first 20 operational years. Of that, $16.8 million came back to the state in taxes, and $83.6 million went into local government tax coffers.

makes the difference is that today's more effective design techniques, construction materials and methods create more efficient structures.

Football, basketball, baseball, tennis and track events share bookings in the Superdome's 3.5-million cu. m (125-million cu. ft) interior, along with the Mardi Gras party, music festivals and concerts, as well as home, garden and motor shows. In addition, the circus and ice events consistently bedazzle sellout crowds.

This edifice is also an engineering construction Wonder, as designed by architect Arthur Q. Davis.

Football games are one of the Superdome's prime attractions: they draw capacity crowds who enjoy a view completely free of support columns.

All its technical innovations worked, and natural obstacles were successfully overcome without mishap.

New Orleans is a city built below sea-level on reclaimed swampland, and the playing-field had to be built at a level above the high water table. Runoff of the abundant annual rainwater from the 4-ha (9.7-acre) dome area required a 1,305,000-litre (345,000-gallon) capacity gutter-tub system ringing the dome circumference. The accumulated water can then be fed gradually into the drainage system.

Innovations

Simply stated, 96 structural steel columns, arranged in four lines, support a tension ring that rests on 10-cm (4-in) rocker bearings. Those allow the ring (and thus the roof) a flexibility of movement of about 8 cm (3 in) in any direction, to compensate for expansion or contraction due to temperature changes, preserving the structural integrity of the building. For wind bracing, a frame of 'K' supports extends outwards from beneath the ring's nearly 0.8-km (0.5-mile) perimeter.

The Superdome holds the Guinness World Record as the largest clear-span structure, literally held together by and hanging from the 210-m (680-ft) diameter roof. The dome has a lamella

Opposite Erection of the vast main framework nearly complete. The skin is made of steel, polyurethane and plastic.

configuration – a series of overlapping triangles extend outwards at the apex from a central ring. The vast interior required specially designed facilities: electrical and TV systems, advertising space, a non-feedback balanced sound system, lighting, telephones, ventilation and climate control, fire precautions and people-moving systems. In addition to all this are a convertible artificial playing surface, known locally as 'Mardi Grass', movable stands to switch between football and baseball, luxury boxes for spectators, and de-luxe facilities for the gladiators.

In New Orleans, the Louisiana Superdome survives and prospers, while some later stadia have succumbed to name changes for commercial gain (the former Indiana Hoosierdome), and others have disappeared completely (Seattle's Kingdome). The Louisiana Superdome is a monumentally beautiful, stable structure which consistently performs multiple public services, is maintainable and financially viable. It is indeed a modern Wonder.

FACTFILE

Main arena	50,685 sq. m
Height	82.3 m
Concert capacity (max.)	87,500
Cost	$163 million

The Pompidou Centre

Time: 1972–77 Location: Paris, France

… then we took a decision: are we going to show all of this, or cover it with a false façade?
That was it! Our design. It was absolutely super simple.
RENZO PIANO, QUOTED IN N. SILVER, 1994

The west façade: the totally column-free interior required moving all structure, public circulation and access to the exterior.

In December 1969, French president Georges Pompidou launched an international design competition for a new public library and art museum. It was a widely applauded move. The future site would be the barren Beaubourg neighbourhood where four decades of demolition had created a vast city-centre parking-lot sandwiched between the City Hall and the recently evacuated Les Halles central food market.

But this ambitious project involved much more than enlightened urban renewal, for the French cultural élite had already sensed that Paris was gradually conceding its place as the world's pre-eminent art capital to New York and to London. Precursor to the Orsay Museum, the Bastille Opéra, the Louvre renovation, the Bibliothèque Nationale and a series of smaller cultural projects throughout the country, Beaubourg would be the first – and arguably the most extraordinary – of the many prestigious projects launched by French presidents over a 30-year period.

Beaubourg became an instant icon, successfully embodying the spirit of its country and its times. In the process, it also set a very high standard which would weigh heavily on future projects. But the realization of the Beaubourg project is remarkable also for the unwavering commitment of President Pompidou. He was personally responsible for launching an open international competition (drawing 700 submissions), and for giving free rein to a jury under French industrial designer Jean Prouvé to award an important public building to an astonishing design by a previously untested team of Italian and British architects, Renzo Piano and Richard Rogers. Pompidou's only reaction on seeing the result was reputedly a bemused 'We haven't heard the end of this!' ('Ça va crier!').

Beaubourg's immediate success with tourists and visitors had the desired effect on the French capital's cultural reputation, dramatically raising the stakes in 'city-marketing' in the process.

Architecture as art

The opening of the Beaubourg in 1977 marked a significant evolution in the social and cultural life of Paris. For the Georges Pompidou Centre for Modern Art – so named after Pompidou's death in 1974 – does not simply house a modern art collection and a library, but combines in one structure many aspects of modern culture, including architecture, industrial design and contemporary music. The symbiotic assemblage almost unique to Beaubourg plays a major role in the building's continuing cultural successes and popular support.

As for the building itself, Beaubourg appears to be 'high-tech' industrial architecture rooted in 19th-century civil engineering, inter-war Bauhaus design theories and the contemporary urban creations of the British Archigram group. Still criticized for its awkward assemblage of 'off-the-shelf' oil-platform components, Beaubourg is in reality an extraordinarily intricate and complex building, from its overall composition right down to the chairs and door-handles. Every last item was chosen, designed and custom manufactured at considerable cost.

With over 25,000 visitors a day, Beaubourg has become a major modern art 'destination' in its own right. And, while many visitors enjoy its facilities, others enjoy exploring a building apparently turned inside out, taking escalators to the top floor to enjoy magnificent Paris roof-scapes.

The winning design

In 1970, Ove Arup were internationally renowned civil engineers who had been responsible for Jorn Utzon's Sydney Opera House (p. 148); relatively unknown architects Renzo Piano and Richard Rogers had been drawn into the competition by

The Pompidou Centre in context: many visitors take the red escalators to the popular top-floor view of Paris rooftops, with Montmartre in the distance.

FACTFILE

Dimensions	60 x 166.4 m
Height	42 m
Total built floor area	135,000 sq. m
superstructure	70,000 sq. m
substructure	65,000 sq. m
Cost	476,000,000 FF

Above *The competition model, with the west façade visible, facing on to the piazza. Some details, such as the escalators, changed in the final building.*

Arup. Both Piano and Rogers quickly confirmed the promise revealed by Beaubourg and have gone on, each in very different ways, to realize many significant buildings. Further, the exceptional architectural and engineering talents assembled for Beaubourg's team, including engineers Edmund Happold and the late Peter Rice, and many others, also confirmed their place in the history of late 20th-century design.

While most competitors focused their attention on spreading low-rise projects over the large Beaubourg site, dutifully respecting Paris's medieval core, the competition's highly detailed design brief also called upon architects to provide maximum 'internal flexibility' in the use of exhibition spaces. The Piano and Rogers design team – early proponents of flexibility in building design – seized upon this requirement as their central organizing principle. The result was a 42-m (138-ft) tall stack of six column-free floors, each 45 × 160 m (148 × 425 ft), facing a large open piazza. With the help of their Arup's colleagues, the team managed totally to banish all the building's structure, circulation, air-conditioning and services beyond the free floorspace.

Building organization can be very simply described: 'visitors on the west façade, services on the east, free exhibition space in between'. Visitors access the various floors by the west side's suspended caterpillar of escalators and walkways, which create Beaubourg's distinctive façade and provide an animated spectacle for the crowds in the piazza below. Distribution of services to each floor is on the other (eastern) side.

The designers' aim of maximum flexibility soon created problems of co-ordinating structural and functional systems. The building could not employ conventional steel-frame columns with cross-bracing and a central core, but had to be designed and built with external columns and bracing alone. Borrowing from bridge construction practice, Arup engineers proposed 13 full-height transverse frames, 12.8 m (42 ft) apart, composed of floor frames and vertical columns. The floors' concrete panels sit on twin full-width floor frames resting on *gerberettes* (steel rocker arms cast in one piece). Horizontal elements every two floors and a diagonal grid of thinner tie-rods provide additional wind bracing to the façade without obstructing the building's interior. The entire structural system, completed by truss-like composite cross-bracing on north and south façades, is clearly evident at each corner.

Fire- and weather-protection posed additional problems for which elegant solutions slowly emerged. Non-combustible materials were used

for all interior furnishings and vulnerable steel elements were covered with metal-clad insulation or special protective finishes

Functional elements, such as wiring, air conditioning, plumbing and vertical circulation, usually 'designed' by contractors and buried inside the building behind ducts and shafts, had to come outside. This meant that they had to be architect-designed, appear elegant and resist the elements. A colour code indicated each service, consisting of industry-standard colour codes, plus white for the structure, red for lifts and circulation, blue for water, yellow for electrical, and blue or white for air-conditioning.

On closer inspection, the east façade's initially confusing final composition appears less like an oil platform (a constant complaint by Beaubourg's detractors) than a Fernand Léger painting.

Bespoke architecture – on time

Despite an approach requiring the full design – or selection – of every last component, the building was delivered within budget (476,000,000 FF) and on time (five years) – a spectacular performance requiring a special set of circumstances.

Once a courageous President Pompidou had decided to proceed with an ambitious project from untested architects, and in the face of the predictable criticism, there could be no risk of failure. A strong public authority, under high-ranking civil servant Robert Bordaz, received the instruction to keep the project on the rails, respect the budget and solve administrative problems. This arrangement, known as 'client authority', is now standard practice for large public architectural projects in France and has influenced practice in many other countries.

Contrary to customary French practice, however, it was not possible to delegate design responsibilities to contractors; the Piano and Rogers–Ove Arup team quite rightly insisted on controlling all aspects of design and specification. Their success over five years of constant negotiations – including Pompidou's death in 1974 and the arrival of the new president Giscard d'Estaing in mid-project – benefited largely from Bordaz's talent, authority and support as mediator.

In practice, solving the Beaubourg puzzle quickly proved too complex for a centralized architectural team and considerable delegation had to be distributed within the team itself. Arup's talented civil engineering team handled conceptual structural design and calculations, while architectural design and services were delegated to internal team leaders according to their design specialism: building systems, interior design or circulation. A strong central philosophy shared by the entire team allowed each specialism considerable latitude to work directly with equipment suppliers to get exactly the performance, appearance and finishes desired. This freed lead architects Piano and Rogers, with Ove Arup engineers Happold and Rice, to concentrate their efforts on negotiating and overseeing essential issues.

That the final building is so surprisingly close to the competition entry, and that so few important initial concepts were lost in the process must be considered a tribute to a widely shared design philosophy, the design team's talents and the unceasing efforts of all those involved.

Opposite below *Movable partitions and stairs adapt vast interior spaces to a variety of exhibitions.*

Below *The east façade: the vertical circulation, services and air conditioning also serve to isolate exhibition spaces from local traffic noise.*

36 Kansai International Airport

Time: 1990–94   Location: Osaka, Japan

Kansai is a precision instrument, a child of mathematics and technology.
RENZO PIANO

You may, if you so wish, walk the entire length of the departure lounge in Osaka's Kansai International Airport, but be aware that you will walk a distance of 1800 m (1.2 miles), because this is the world's longest building, situated off-shore on a manmade island. These facts might seem to be record-seeking gimmicks, but they are in reality rational responses to the city's need for new airport facilities.

The Kansai region is the second largest in Japan, with a population of some 20 million. The existing airport, hemmed in by urbanization, was incapable of further expansion but there was no obvious alternative, as building development had reached the encircling mountains. Studies showed that the optimum solution was to create an island in Osaka Bay, away from conurbations. Runways could be arranged so that take-off and landing took place over water, reducing noise pollution and permitting 24-hour operation. Expansion could readily be achieved simply by enlarging the island. These factors could be set against the considerable capital cost of such a scheme.

Below and opposite below
Kansai airport is essentially a single building, 1.8 km long, with aircraft docking along the wings that stretch from each side of the main, central hall. Passengers can easily orientate themselves at all times.

The island

The manmade island measures approximately 4.5 × 2.5 km (3 × 1.5 miles). The sea at this location is around 20 m (66 ft) deep, but the bed consists of the same depth again of very soft clay, which, it was estimated, would settle by 11 m (30 ft) as fill was deposited to form the island. It took five years to place the enormous quantity of fill needed, obtained by levelling two nearby mountains. The material was transported to site in barges, which were positioned by computers linked to satellites before dropping their load. In the event, settlement was more than predicted, leading to a necessity for yet more fill – and a year's delay.

The terminal building

The building was the subject of an international design competition in 1988, based on a brief proposed by Aéroports de Paris. It was won by the Renzo Piano Building Workshop, with Ove Arup & Partners as engineers. Their proposal was in line with the brief – essentially a new airport form, handling domestic and international flights in a single building, with aircraft docked along

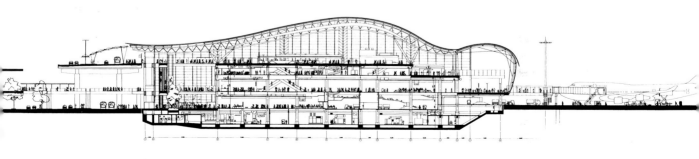

extended wings. Such a long, narrow structure is efficient in terms of the island plan form, which has essentially been determined by the runway.

While the majority of ground settlement had taken place before building commenced, some residual settlements would be inevitable. If they were not uniform, the structure would be subject to distortion and possible damage. In order to counter any such distortion, the entire building is mounted on jacking points, which, if necessary, can each be operated independently to re-align the structural frame.

Clarity and movement

From the beginning, clarity of orientation was a paramount design objective. It should be obvious at all times to incoming passengers (unlike at many other airports) which is the land-side and which is the air-side. To achieve this, two major decisions were made – all the concessions (cafés and duty-free shops) were put on a mezzanine level, and a narrow hall (the 'canyon') was introduced on the land-side. The purpose of the canyon is to allow passengers to move to the appropriate building level by means of lifts and escalators set against the outside wall. The colours in which the canyon is decorated (blues and ochres) may initially be a surprise, but they can be found in traditional Japanese architecture.

The space is lit from above, and planted with trees to enhance the 'street' concept. Departing passengers, crossing the canyon at high level, get their first sight of the departure hall and its roof – a curving, almost skeletal structure, which has already become the airport's signature.

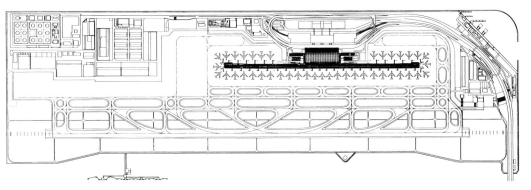

Above *The 'canyon', a tall, light-filled atrium where the routes to the embarkation gates converge. The trusses supporting the roof are over 80 m long.*

The lines of the roof of the departure hall indicate the flow of movement of passengers through the airport.

– earthquake resistance. Depending on the degree of risk, buildings in seismic zones are required to be designed for some fraction of their weight as a horizontal load. In Japan, a generally high-risk area, the building laws required that the Kansai structure should not collapse under a lateral load actually in excess of its own weight. As the engineers are fond of pointing out, the structure could be built on a wall and remain perfectly stable. They could not have known how soon their design would be tested: in January 1994, before the building had even been handed over, a major earthquake measuring 7.2 on the Richter scale occurred near the city of Kobe, with its epicentre only 30 km (19 miles) from the airport. Although the island suffered some local settlement at its perimeter, the terminal building itself, both in terms of the structure and its cladding, came through completely unscathed.

The ceiling of the hall is remarkable for the absence of clutter usually associated with spaces which are air-conditioned and artificially lit. The design solution to both these problems lies in the fabric shells fitted between the trusses which both catch and guide the jet of air emitted from sculptural nozzles, and act as reflectors for the uplighters mounted below. This is a brilliant technical response to performance criteria, but the greatness of Kansai lies in the way that this solution is integrated into the design as a whole.

The international departure hall

The roof of the departure hall is made up of a series of steel lattice beams with strong directional lines. They indicate to passengers their onward and downward movement through the building, first to customs clearance, and then to the departure lounge at low level. The visual clarity, however, is not achieved at the expense of structural logic: since the roof follows the general mass of the structure below, the volume of air to be controlled is minimized.

The prominent splayed legs of the trusses, which give them lateral support, remind the visitor of an important design parameter in Japan

The departure lounge

The departure lounge has no restriction to movement along its entire length of 1800 m (1.2 miles), and can thus be regarded as the world's longest room. While this is efficient in terms of passenger movement, it is unexpected, as the conventional response to the containment of fire in large buildings in Japan (as in other countries) is to introduce compartment walls at regular intervals. The omission of such walls has been achieved by a combination of innovative engineering and the co-operation of enlightened Japanese authorities. The proposed strategy was described as the 'cabin and island' concept. The main fire hazards (such as the concessions) are grouped under the sprinklers and rapid-venting smoke hoods (the

Computer diagram of the structure of Kansai. The form is functional in channelling air from the passenger side (left) to the runway side (right).

'cabins'). The lesser hazards (such as the seat groups) are set sufficiently far apart, as 'islands', to avoid fire transmission from one to another.

Construction achievements

A brief description of the airport construction abounds in superlatives. Although Osaka Bay hosts other manmade islands, Kansai is much further from the shore (5 km/3 miles) and in deeper water than its predecessors. After the placing of 178 million cu. m (6286 cu. ft) of fill, the mile-long terminal building, with a total floor area of 300,000 sq. m (3,230,000 sq. ft) was completed in only three years. In order to achieve this, separate contracts were let to two consortia, led by Takinaka and Obayashi, who each built one half of the building – a convenient joint on the exact centreline of the building dividing the contracts.

But the building does not overwhelm the traveller with its achievement. The spaces are of human scale, and the rigour of the design, together with the attention to detail, have an elegance and clarity unequalled in the field of airport construction.

The spectacular departure lounge stretches the entire length of the structure.

FACTFILE

Length	1800 m
Area	300,000 sq. m
Workforce (max.)	10,000
Cost of building island	$17 billion
Flights per year	160,000
Runway	3500 m

The Guggenheim Museum, Bilbao

Time: 1991–97   Location: Bilbao, Spain

What cannot be easily explained, much less argued into existence, is the sheer exhilaration that this building gives off, the jubilant excess of its presence.
KURT W. FORSTER, 1998

In contrast with the rational form-giving which has dominated western architecture for centuries, the Guggenheim Museum in Bilbao is the product of intuitive form-finding. The marriage of intuition with computer-controlled processes of design, fabrication and assembly has produced a building that is a dazzling technical achievement and an exuberant demonstration of the potential of the computer to transform design and construction.

The 1991 competition to design the Bilbao Guggenheim was won by the Los Angeles architect, Frank O. Gehry. Gehry had risen to prominence in the 1980s, initially with a series of provocative houses in California that challenged the conventions of light, wood-frame construction, and subsequently with larger public commissions including the Toledo Art School (1989) and the scheme for the Disney Concert Hall in Los Angeles (1989–). Gehry was awarded the prestigious international Pritzker Prize in 1989. The commission to design a satellite

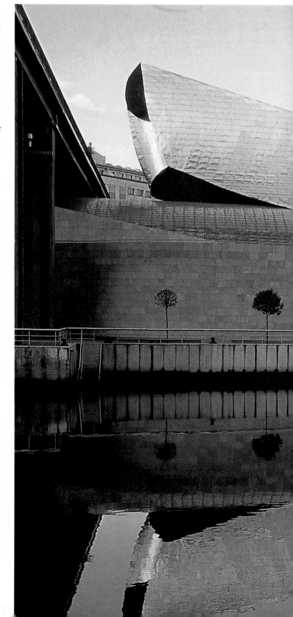

The Bilbao Guggenheim is both contextual and alien. The building is finely tuned to the difficult geometry of the site, yet its billowing titanium-clad volumes are unfamiliar.

FACTFILE

Structure	braced steel frame
Cladding	titanium, stone and glass
Area	24,628 sq. m
Budget	10,859 million pesetas ($59,205,000)

museum for the Guggenheim – based in Manhattan in a well-known building designed by Frank Lloyd Wright (p. 143) and one of the premier institutions for contemporary art – was ideal for this architect who collaborates closely with artists and whose own formal language is highly sculptural.

The Guggenheim, together with other new cultural amenities and an improved public transport system, is a key component of the strategic plan to regenerate the city of Bilbao. The prominent but difficult site of the museum on the banks of the Nervion River is surrounded by shipping container yards, railway lines and the access ramps of an elevated bridge.

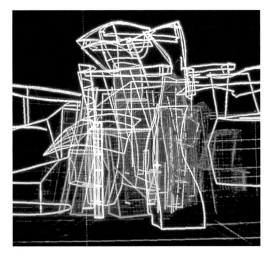

Computers were essential to transform physical models into a digital model with continuously curved surfaces, and then to translate this digital database into fabrication drawings and computer numerically controlled milling data.

Above *Two layers of substructure were built off the primary steel frame.*

Computer modelling

While the formal configuration of the building was initially developed intuitively through a series of rough, handmade cardboard models,

it is the computer which made the scheme technically and economically feasible. Gehry is the first architect to exploit the potential of CATIA – software developed by the French aerospace industry. Unlike most architectural software, CATIA is based on surfaces rather than polygons. For Bilbao, Gehry's cardboard models were digitized to generate a continuously curved surface model in CATIA. From this computer model, interior and exterior control surfaces were identified which would be used as setting out points for the building.

Offsetting from these control surfaces, a structural zone was established. The braced steel frame, comprising wide flange sections on a 3-m (10-ft) grid, is remarkably straightforward. Most members are straight sections, and the plasticity of the overall form is achieved purely in the connections. Between the faceted frame of the primary steel and the control surfaces are two layers of secondary structure, inside and out. Horizontal ladders of steel tubes, 60 mm (2.4 in) in diameter, establish horizontal curvature. The ladders are split frames straddling the primary structure at 3-m (10-ft) intervals and are connected to it with a universal joint, allowing fine adjustment in all directions. Vertical curvature is defined by the innermost and outermost layers of secondary structure, with vertical light-gauge steel studs at 600 mm (2.4 in) centres. All tubes and studs are curved in one or more directions.

While CATIA could precisely locate and size every structural member, the computer model remained a wire-frame line drawing. BOCAD, new proprietary software developed for bridge and road construction, was used to translate the CATIA wire frame into a comprehensive three-dimensional computer model of the structural steel. From this model, BOCAD could automatically produce either two-dimensional fabrication drawings or computer numerically controlled (CNC) milling data.

Left *In contrast with the flexible metal cladding and the curved surfaces of stone achieved by CNC milling, the glass in the Guggenheim is flat and the desired complex curvatures are approximated by faceted assemblies.*

Because of unique end cuts, no two pieces of steel in the building are alike. However, using BOCAD, the primary structure was fabricated so accurately that the need for field measuring, cutting and welding was virtually eliminated. Borrowing construction practices once again from the aerospace industry, each structural component was bar coded during fabrication. On site, bar codes were swiped and laser surveying equipment linked to CATIA enabled each piece to be precisely placed in position, defined by co-ordinates in the computer model. This method avoided the accumulation of tolerances, or margins of error, and ensured that the precision needed to realize such complex geometries could be achieved.

Cladding

The computer model did not, however, completely eliminate the need for empirical data. During design development, full-scale mock-ups were used to ascertain the extent to which sheet metal could be subjected to complex curvature without buckling, and the precise amount of tolerance required in the seams. CATIA was subsequently used to rationalize the metal surfaces of the building to conform with the parameters established by the mock-ups.

The cladding for Bilbao was supplied flat and only four standard panel sizes were needed for 80 per cent of the surface area of the metal skin. While the galvanized underlayer is absolutely taut, the slight pillow on the outer surface of the titanium cladding has been intentionally deployed to soften the appearance of the building. In contrast, all the glass in the building is flat and, because glass has no capacity to warp, complex surfaces are achieved through triangulation of the panels rather than bending. Consequently, and in contrast with the metal cladding, nearly 70 per cent of the glazed panels are unique sizes.

Although the structure and cladding of Bilbao could have been fabricated using CNC machines linked to the CATIA database, most subcontractors opted instead to fabricate manually because of their highly skilled labour forces. The stone clad-

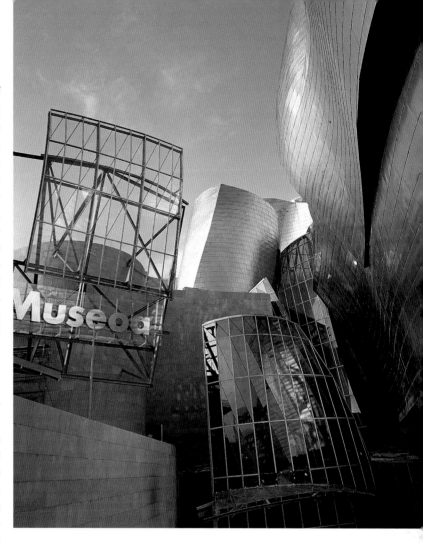

ding is the only component of the building that was robotically milled and this, the most technically sophisticated fabrication process, took place *in situ* rather than on the shop floor. While the architects had envisioned the stone being milled in a workshop and delivered to site in finished form, the subcontractor installed a milling machine on site.

When the new Guggenheim opened in 1997, it became the centre of worldwide media attention. By bringing the technology of other industries to bear upon building construction, Bilbao has gone far beyond the limits of what was formerly understood to be possible both aesthetically and technically. And by making complexity and uniqueness as economic as mass production, the computer has overturned the conventions of industrial production, offering the potential once again for a craft-centred architecture in the post-industrial world.

Software has been used to rationalize the surfaces of the building to conform with the maximum curvature of the titanium-sheet cladding, which was established by full-scale mock-ups.

Towers & Skyscrapers

The nearest peace-time equivalent of war', was how Col. W. A. Starrett described the process of building skyscrapers. Starrett could certainly speak with authority. When he made the remark in 1928, his company, Starrett Brothers and Eken, was poised to embark upon their greatest challenge yet – the construction of the Empire State Building, the world's tallest building for 40 years after its completion in 1931.

National monuments and commemorative structures have always proved more telling if they are visually pre-eminent above the surrounding urban fabric. The Washington Monument, completed in 1884, is not only still the highest free-standing stone structure in the world, it is also confirmed by Act of Congress as the highest building which can be erected in the Capitol. Further west, on the banks of the River Mississippi at St Louis, the great Finnish-American architect Eero Saarinen's soaring arch, which forms the Jefferson Westward Expansion Memorial, marks the point of departure for the countless pioneers who opened up America's West. The Gateway Arch's power resides not only in its sweeping simplicity of form, but also in its location, unchallenged by the high-rises of downtown St Louis.

Building ever higher points of vantage for pure pleasure continues to make good business and civic sense. The Eiffel Tower has become an icon so intertwined with its host city that the two are forever inseparable. More recent examples of such towers forming what could be dubbed 'city signatures' include Toronto's CN Tower, still the

New York's Empire State Building still towers above Lower Manhattan; it was built in record time and under budget, despite the difficult construction and economic conditions.

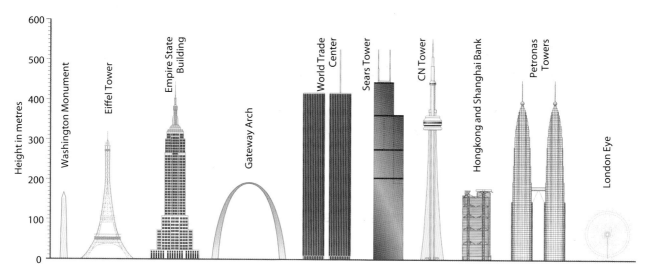

The Petronas Towers currently holds the title of the world's tallest building. This title is adjudicated by the Council on Tall Buildings and Urban Habitat, which defines a building as 'a structure that is designed for residential, business or manufacturing purposes', and an essential characteristic is that it has floors. Buildings are measured from the pavement level of the main entrance to the structural top of the building. Spires are included, but not television and radio antennae or flag poles.

world's tallest free-standing structure. The newest example, the British Airways London Eye, on the South Bank of the River Thames, has already firmly caught the public imagination.

High-rise buildings are often required to house a host of functions, from office space of various configurations, residential units, conference centres, restaurants, observation decks and even transport interchanges at their bases. In effect, they are complete vertical cities, in which several thousand people live and work, constructed on restricted urban sites while life goes on all around them. A creative partnership between designer and contractor is a pre-requisite of success. Site work began on the Empire State Building before structural design of all floors was completed, yet it was built within a scant 20 months.

In part, this success was due to innovations in component design and site logistics, which still remain models for the construction industry. Steelwork for the building frame was scheduled as self-contained packages; beams and columns trucked in on a split-second timetable from the rolling mills of Pittsburgh were almost still warm to the touch; temporary canteens set up on inter-mediate floors fed the workforce without the time-consuming use of busy lifts; and component design allowed all external cladding units to be fixed and self-sealed from the inside.

In the course of what now seems the first Golden Age of skyscraper design, exemplified by the Empire State and its contemporaries, the genre reached new heights, not merely dimen-sional, but also as mature works of architecture. Subsequent evolution sought to exploit the emerging possibilities for building ever higher, facilitated by leading structural engineers such as Fazlur Khan, who developed the 'bundled tubes' concept which made possible Chicago's Sears Tower, or the potential of loading-bearing exter-nal walls, a system pioneered by architect Minoru Yamasaki in the twin towers of the New York World Trade Center and traumatically put to the test on 11 September 2001.

Now that sheer height has become a secure technical possibility, the focus has turned to teasing out a form of expression for the sky-scraper which can embody regional, cultural or ecological themes. Cesar Pelli's Petronas Towers in Kuala Lumpur, currently the world's tallest building, are based on an eight-pointed star plan modelled on Islamic symbolism. The Hongkong and Shanghai Bank, designed by Norman Foster, includes devices to funnel sunlight into its spec-tacular first-floor banking hall, and to the new urban plaza which is part of the site development, thus giving something back to the public realm of the city of Hong Kong.

The last word on the potency of the skyscraper as icon must go to the hotel 'New York-New York' in Las Vegas, remarkable even in the company of all the other memorable and gigantic hotels on offer. The hotel's theme is a huge re-creation, or re-enactment, of the skyline of the Big Apple, peopled not by the wage slaves of Wall Street but by 100,000 daily visitors and guests.

The Washington Monument

Time: 1848–84 Location: Washington, DC, United States

*… the Washington Monument stands … as one of the most beautiful of human creations.
Indeed, it is at once so great and so simple that it seems to be almost a work of nature.*
FREDERICK LAW OLMSTED JR & CHARLES MOORE, 1902

Still the tallest free-standing stone tower in the world at 169.3 m (555.5 ft), the Washington Monument, designed by Robert Mills and completed in 1884, remains, by congressional mandate, the tallest structure in Washington, DC. Until the completion of the Eiffel Tower in 1889 (p. 174), it was also the loftiest structure in the world.

Its protracted building campaign – almost four decades – was fraught with political intrigue and the tribulations of war, as well as problems relating to funding, delivery of materials and the construction of the foundation. Intended to honour George Washington, the nation's first president and 'father of his country', Congress decided upon a number of different forms for the monument over the years, including an equestrian statue and a mausoleum. The monument as finally built was made possible by the privately funded Washington National Monument Society,

A view of the Washington Monument from the Mall. By congressional mandate it is, and has to remain, the tallest structure in Washington, DC.

The original competition design by Robert Mills, 1833. The colonnade at the base intended for statues of American heroes was never built.

created in 1833, which launched a competition won by Robert Mills. His original design was for a marble obelisk with a pantheon at its base ringed by a colonnade with statues of heroes of the American Revolution. Only the obelisk would be built, and construction did not begin until 12 years after the approval of Mills's design.

Initial construction

In 1848 a stone-handling wharf was set up on the banks of the Potomac River to supply the construction site. With Mills as site architect and engineer, the foundation was excavated and huge blocks of bluestone were sunk into it and bound together by lime and hydraulic cement. Construction proceeded until 1854, a year before Mills's death, when the monument had reached a truncated 46.32 m (152 ft). Then, with the country in turmoil because of the events leading up to the Civil War (1861–65), and with erosion of funding and public support, construction was effectively halted for two decades.

New building campaign and completion

Only in 1878 did a building campaign begin that would lead to successful completion, after years of funding fiascos and doubts over the integrity of the foundation. That year, Lieutenant Colonel Thomas Lincoln Casey of the Army Corps of Engineers was given the task of redesigning the foundation and completing the monument. His ingenious strengthening of the foundation entailed removing about 70 per cent of the earth under it, and filling that space with a concrete footing, as well as covering the stones of the original foundation in a pyramid of concrete. The whole was more than twice the area of the old foundation, and 4.11 m (13.5 ft) deeper.

Having abandoned the idea of Mills's pantheon and colonnade, Casey concentrated on the form and construction of the obelisk itself. After consulting George Perkins Marsh, United States ambassador to Italy and an authority on Egyptian obelisks, Casey abandoned the planned height of almost 183 m (600 ft) for the shaft, and instead adopted the true Egyptian proportional system of 10 times base to height, resulting in the final

The Monument in 1879, soon after building work had recommenced after a gap of around two decades. The foundations were widened and deepened.

FACTFILE

Height	169.3 m
Weight	81,630 tonnes
Materials	marble, granite, bluestone, iron, aluminium, glass
Stone blocks	36,000
Steps	897
Cost	$1.8 million

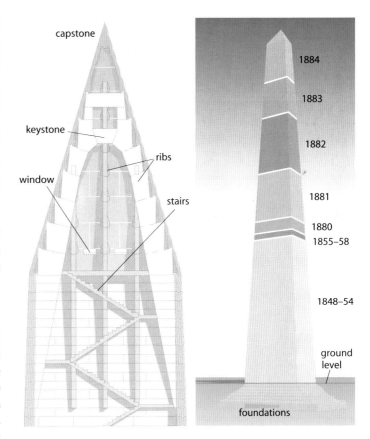

Cross-section of the pyramidion supported by tapering ribs; and the stages in the construction.

height of the Washington Monument at 169.3 m (555.5 ft). The design of the pointed apex of the obelisk, the 16.76-m (55-ft) high pyramidion, was likewise dictated by ancient proportions.

Construction

Casey devised an interior iron framework held together by I-beams and channel bars, anchored to the granite stones of the interior. This structure went up at a faster rate than the setting of the stones of the obelisk itself, and cranes attached to its columns could hoist up the blocks. A steam-operated hoist was employed that was later used to carry visitors. The gradual thinning of the walls, from 4.6 m (15 ft) at the base to 17.8 cm (7 in) at the summit of the pyramidion, lightened the pressure on the base. The marble capstone was secured to the structure on 6 December 1884, and was topped by a tip made of aluminium – then an expensive, new material and used here for the first time in American architecture. The dedication ceremony was held one day before George Washington's 153rd birthday, on 21 February 1885. Construction had taken 37 long years.

Recent history

In the last century, the great stone obelisk was the setting for some of the most symbolically charged events in American history, from protests by Suffragettes to massive rallies by Civil Rights advocates and Vietnam War protesters. Most recently, a comprehensive two-year, $9.4-million restoration, completed in 2000, included the repair and cleaning of the 193 memorial stones on the inner walls. The Washington Monument has thus been returned to its former majesty and remains a celebrated and dramatic tribute to its namesake.

Left *A crane was used to hoist the blocks of stone into position on to the rising shaft of the Monument.*

The Eiffel Tower

Time: 1887–89 Location: Paris, France

For my part, I believe the tower will have its own beauty. Is one to believe that beauty does not figure in our designs simply because we are engineers? That while we are engaged in building solid and lasting structures, we are not also attempting to achieve elegant solutions?

GUSTAVE EIFFEL, 1887

For many people, the mention of Paris immediately evokes an image of the Eiffel Tower; the two are inseparable – just as New York and the Statue of Liberty are (p. 281). Interestingly, both structures are by the same talented engineer, investor, scientist and showman – Gustave Eiffel. In a prolific career spanning nearly half a century of invention and construction, the tower remains his best-known work. Its story is inextricably bound up with that of its designer, and illustrates what sort of person Eiffel was and why the tower should bear his name.

Born in 1823, Eiffel trained first as a chemist at the École Centrale in Paris before joining a metalworking shop which was soon absorbed by a larger railway company. His first mature project, aged 35, was for the construction of a railway bridge, 500 m (1640 ft) long, in difficult conditions and within the space of just two years. This project demonstrated his prodigious energy and imagination when confronted by construction problems. Other early projects for train stations for Toulouse and Agen in 1865 confirmed his talent for efficient, elegant structures. After several projects abroad, and work as a structural engineer on the Halle des Machines at the 1867

August 1888 – just 18 months after groundbreaking; a high degree of detailed design planning and off-site prefabrication allowed safe, rapid construction of the Eiffel Tower.

World's Fair in Paris, Eiffel acquired the workshop of a structural iron construction company near Paris. Eiffel was now engineer *and* builder. By 1885 he had designed and constructed a wide variety of civil engineering projects, including the structure for Bartholdi's Statue of Liberty and the record-breaking 165-m (540-ft) long Garabit Viaduct in the Auvergne.

The concept and competition

When, in 1884, the French president decided to launch the 1889 World's Fair to celebrate the Republic's 100th anniversary, the call went out for appropriately spectacular projects. In spite of a flurry of suggestions, nothing convincing emerged, and the imaginative Eiffel was asked to propose something. The idea of building a tower 300 m (around 1000 ft) high – a magical figure – was a popular challenge of the period and several plans had already emerged in Europe and the United States, though none had been successful.

Fortunately, two talented engineers in Eiffel's office – Maurice Koechlin (who had calculated the Statue of Liberty structure) and Émile Nougier – had already patented the design for a 300-m high tower, which Eiffel had considered but abandoned. Seizing the opportunity, Eiffel now bought the patent from his engineers and the team refined the project with the help of architect Stephane Sauvestre. Commerce Minister Lockroy had the project he needed. In mid-1886, a hastily prepared competition lasting two weeks (and drawing 107 entries) selected Eiffel's project – negotiations could begin.

In January 1887, the contract to build the tower was awarded to Eiffel, who then had two and a half years to complete the world's tallest structure. Foundation works began three weeks later and building proceeded at a breakneck pace. Financial conditions for the project awarded Eiffel a subsidy of 1,500,000 Francs (about 20 per cent of total construction costs), plus the right to exploit the tower commercially

Over a century after its inauguration for the 1889 World's Fair, the tower's delicate structure still remains a remarkable construction feat.

Gustave Eiffel and his assistant Adolphe Salles pose proudly near the tower's summit.

for the duration of the World's Fair. At the end of the Fair, the tower would become the property of the City of Paris, but Eiffel would retain the right to exploit it for a 20-year period. The genial engineer sensed he was on to a good investment – and he was proved correct.

Construction innovations

As might be expected from Eiffel's background, the tower was an astounding accomplishment in civil engineering design. First, Eiffel did not proceed by trial and error, as many of his contemporaries did, but was one of the first to calculate the stresses his structure would experience from applied forces such as the wind. His engineering prowess allowed him to produce a filigree iron structure which presented a minimum surface to the wind. Modern calculations have confirmed the validity of his methods.

The result is an extraordinarily light construction for its height; at 7300 tonnes, the tower's structure represents less than 9 cu. m (318 cu. ft) of iron, and weighs less than a cylinder of air equivalent to the circumference of its base, 300 m (1000 ft) tall. The wind force calculations which determined a large part of the tower's final form show the top moving just 12 cm (5 in) when subjected to winds of 180 km (112 miles) per hour – a deflection the tower has never experienced.

Academic architects of the period – including Opéra architect Charles Garnier (p. 138) – criticized the aesthetic form of the tower. But Eiffel staunchly defended it, claiming that as an engineer he, too, was concerned by the beauty and elegance of his structures; wind resistance calculations, he claimed, generated forms revealing hidden rules of harmony. Even today the structure still appears extraordinarily fine and elegant.

A second innovation involved the high level of organization and prefabrication Eiffel employed in all his structures. More than 18,000 structural members were individually drawn, made to exacting specifications and partially prefabricated in Eiffel's workshops before they were numbered and sent to the site by barge. Workers at the tower then hoisted structural members into place and riveted them – no further drilling or adjustments were necessary. Safety was an important consideration as well as speed: building the tower only claimed a single life – a major accomplishment for the time. (Construction of New York's Brooklyn Bridge (p. 219) had claimed 20 lives, and Scotland's Forth Rail Bridge (p. 225) – built at the same time as the tower – 57.)

Finally, to meet the contracted delivery date, Eiffel had to employ his considerable communication talents in motivating his workers. Work began promptly at 6.30 a.m. and continued to

FACTFILE

Height	300.51 m
with antenna	320.75 m
Platforms	57 m; 115 m; 276 m
Steps	c. 1700
Base	1 ha
Weight	7300 tonnes
Workforce (max.)	250
Cost	$1.5 million

dusk throughout the year, and in all weather. To keep workers on the job and construction progressing smoothly, Eiffel departed from usual practice by employing only a limited number of skilled iron workers (80 to 250 maximum), paying them reasonably well for the period and providing canteens serving meals on the tower itself. Eiffel was also a strict disciplinarian and solved disputes and drinking on site by firing offenders. The result was a proud, tightly knit construction team bent on a single purpose – delivering the structure on time for the World's Fair.

The tallest structure

Three hundred metres tall, the Eiffel Tower was complete for the opening on 31 March 1889, and would become the fair's major attraction – with 20,000 visitors on its best day. By the end of the fair, six months later, visitors had paid nearly 6 million Francs to ascend the world's tallest monument (the lifts were one of the tower's great attractions), and revenues proved more than adequate to repay investors. Continued public interest would make Eiffel a wealthy man.

Although the tower's main purpose was now accomplished, it was destined to remain the world's tallest structure for 42 years until 1930, when New York's Chrysler Building topped it by a mere 18 m (59 ft). Even after more than a century, Eiffel's tower still draws record crowds – over 5 million visitors per year, with a total of almost 200 million since its opening.

After the fair

The tower would prove to be the great engineer's last construction. In 1889, Eiffel found himself caught up in the financial scandal involving misappropriation of funds for the abortive Panama Canal project (p. 260). Originally engaged by Suez Canal builder de Lesseps in 1887 to advise on canal-lock construction, and confident in his abilities, Eiffel soon took on a larger role, only to find himself embroiled in a scandal which would see de Lesseps sent to prison and Eiffel condemned as well. In 1892 Eiffel was vindicated on appeal, but his spirit for construction was broken.

After the fair and the trial, Eiffel turned his

The inclined lifts were a novelty in themselves and were one of the attractions of a visit to the tower. Today, three lifts rise to the first and second levels, and another four ascend to the top. In total they travel 103,000 km each year. Otis inclined lifts (left) served the second level, while below is the Roux-Combaluzier-Lepape lift machinery.

attention – not surprisingly perhaps – to experiments to exploit the tower's height in testing the wind resistance of falling objects. A limited beginning quickly expanded and Eiffel went on to become a pioneer in the field of aerodynamics, first building a wind tunnel at the base of the tower and then another in nearby Auteil, which was still in service in the 1970s.

In 1903, with attendance dwindling after the 1900 World's Fair, and the end of his concession approaching, Eiffel turned to radio transmission experiments to forestall any temptation on the part of the City of Paris to dismantle the tower.

From 1926 to 1936 the French car manufacturer Citroën financed Italian designer Jacopozzi's lighting displays, containing upwards of 200,000 lamps.

(The cost of dismantling and rebuilding had already been estimated at 1 million Francs – a fraction of the original cost.) Radio transmission was a success, and by 1909 the tower had assumed a military role before, in 1912, confirming its utility by emitting the radio 'bip' signalling the hour, heard worldwide. The tower later became Paris's transmitting antenna for the first television experiments in 1935. By the outbreak of the Second World War, Paris would have nearly a thousand receivers and the tower had found a new function it still serves today.

A very Parisian tower

One of the tower's interesting attributes has been its close and continuous association with the artistic community of Paris: Robert and Sonia Delaunay, Jean Cocteau and many other artists, poets, photographers and musicians have celebrated its forms. Mountaineers have scaled the exterior, a cyclist has descended its stairs and hang gliders and parachutists have taken off from its heights. Over its century of existence, Parisians have regularly enjoyed the tower's pranksters and manifestations. The most spectacular have involved light: from 1926 to 1936 the tower wore a cascade of coloured lights, including publicity for sponsor Citroën, whose factory was nearby. In 1932 and 1934 first a large clock and then a tall thermometer joined its decorations. Paris's last World Fair of 1937 once again saw the Eiffel Tower and the Trocadéro as the centre of attraction for nightly fireworks and light shows.

Since the Second World War, limited ambitions have led to more modest schemes, though recently the tower featured a large millennium countdown calendar, culminating on 1 January 2000 with a gigantic fireworks display when the tower sparkled with 20,000 flashes. Eleven months later, Paris's mayor Jean Tiberi, recognizing that Parisians and visitors alike were enthralled by 10 minutes of sparkling lights every hour, from dusk to 1 a.m., signed a 10-year contract to maintain a display, once again confirming the Eiffel Tower's central place in the 'City of Lights'.

Exposition des Arts Décoratifs

ILLUMINATIONS DE LA TOUR EIFFEL exécutées et animées par LES ETABL ⁿᵗˢ JACOPOZZI

AN PARIS

The Empire State Building

Time: 1929–31   Location: New York City, United States

Building skyscrapers is the nearest peace-time equivalent of war …
Col. W. A. Starrett, 1928

When it was completed in 1931 the Empire State (the nickname of New York State) was the tallest building in the world, surpassing the recently finished Chrysler Building, also in New York City, by 61 m (200 ft). It retained this status for over 40 years, until it was outscaled by the World Trade Center Towers, New York City (p. 187) in 1973, followed by the Sears Tower in Chicago (p. 192) in 1974, and since 1996 by the Petronas Towers in Kuala Lumpur (p. 204).

Its designers, the well-respected New York architecture firm of Shreve, Lamb and Harmon, worked closely with the renowned general contractors, Starrett Brothers and Eken, and with the engineering firm of Homer G. Balcom. This team was one of the most successful in modern building history, achieving a still-unsurpassed record for construction speed for a building of this size – a mere 20 months from the start of design to finished building. The startling facts of its construction and engineering – it was completed ahead of schedule and, at $41 million (including the land), under budget – and the magic of its image have assured the Empire State's continuing iconic status as one of the world's most celebrated buildings.

The project was the brainchild of John Jacob Raskob, later head of General Motors, who, along

The Empire State Building almost half finished: the efficient and innovative system used in its construction meant that it was completed at an amazing speed.

with Pierre S. du Pont, was the major investor in the project. Lending cachet to the enterprise was Alfred E. Smith, former governor of New York and presidential candidate of the Democratic Party in 1928, who was named head of the Empire State Corporation. The aim of this august group was to build the world's tallest building, a goal they achieved in spite of the difficult mid-town location for an office building – Fifth Avenue between 33rd and 34th Streets – and the Great Depression, which cast its shadow over the economy.

The building is generally said to have 102 floors, although only 85 contain office space. The

An ironworker: one of Lewis Hine's celebrated photographs of the construction process of the Empire State Building.

61-m (200-ft) metal and glass mast, originally intended to moor airships, adds the equivalent of 17 storeys to the building. With the two sub-basements, the total height, excluding the mast, reaches 381.6 m (1252 ft), and the building boasts 189,000 sq. m (2.1 million sq. ft) of rentable area. The statistics relating to materials used in the Empire State are nothing less than astonishing. Workers laid 10 million bricks, installed 6400 windows, put in 1886 km (1172 miles) of elevator cable and 5663 cu. m (200,000 cu. ft) of stone. The construction technology used in the building – a riveted steel structure with masonry curtain walls and incorporating cinder concrete and draped mesh floor slabs – was common at the time, but the methods used to marshall these components at the site were highly innovative.

Simplified Art Deco flourishes, from the chevron-like patterns between the windows to the dazzling marble treatment of the lobby, which features a stainless steel portrait of the building, lend minimal decoration to an essentially simple design. The characteristic setbacks of the profile are a result of New York City zoning regulations that ensured that light and air reached the city's streets. It was in fact because of these same regulations that the Empire State could be built so tall – they stipulated that after setbacks were adopted at appropriate levels, a tower of unlimited height could rise over 25 per cent of the site. Many variables influenced the development of this skyscraper: economics, building codes, technology and, above all, the real estate market. In this regard, the Empire State Building represents the epitome of speculative development in the 1920s and 1930s. Its fame, however, was not matched by financial success. In fact, it was only fully occupied by tenants some 20 years after its completion.

A construction-driven design

Construction of the Empire State began after the demolition of the Waldorf-Astoria Hotel on the site at Fifth Avenue, with the first structural columns set in place on 7 April 1930. Just six months later, the steel frame was topped off at the 86th floor – a rate of more than one storey a day. This

The entrance façade, with some of the building's Art Deco flourishes clearly visible.

awe-inspiring speed of construction, still unequalled today, was achieved as a result of several interrelated factors. First, design choices, particularly those of the façade, were driven primarily by practical construction considerations. Second, there was a careful planning of the use of resources, both human and material. And third, the contractors adopted the then rather avant-garde technique of fast-tracking, which allows for the start of construction before the full design of the building is finished. This meant that when the erection of the structure was begun on the lower floors, working drawings of the structure of the top floors had yet to be completed.

The construction-driven design approach also addressed the substantial impact that the two major parts of the building – the steel structure and curtain wall – had on the speed of construction. In the Empire State, the curtain wall comprised a brick backing covered with limestone piers, window assemblies, decorative

aluminium spandrels and vertically placed stainless steel strips that mask the joints between the piers and the spandrels. This last innovation obviated the need for side-to-side connections between spandrels and piers. Consequently, less detailing of the limestone was required, saving a considerable amount of time. In addition, the decision to add a curtain wall spandrel beam fastened to the columns supported the brick wall directly, without the need for shelf angles and attendant time-consuming adjustments. In the Empire State, in addition, all the curtain wall components were installed from inside, greatly improving safety and contributing to the supremely efficient construction process.

The steel frame was designed by the office of Homer G. Balcom and consisted of 'I' steel sections for beams and upper-floor columns, and beams riveted together for lower-floor columns. With fast-tracking, instead of the usual sequence of completion of a full set of working drawings,

The plans of the floors change as the building rises, from the ground floor (bottom) to the 7th (centre), 30th (top left) and 61st (top right).

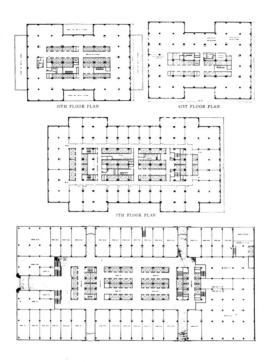

30TH FLOOR PLAN

61ST FLOOR PLAN

7TH FLOOR PLAN

Detail of the steel columns and their reinforced concrete piers at the base of the building.

development and approval of shop drawings, steel fabrication, steel delivery and erection, the entire steel structure was broken down into smaller packages. The timely completion of each package and its related process required considerable co-operation and co-ordination between the general contractor, architect, structural engineer, steel fabricators and erector, as well as the existence of precise planning by Starrett Brothers and Eken.

Finally, the designers and builders of the Empire State devised a careful planning process for the efficient transport of people and materials. For example, in order to reduce the number of elevator trips made to the ground level by workers, whose numbers at the height of construction totalled around 3500, makeshift cafeterias were set up on appropriate floors during the erection of the steel frame. The builders were also faced with the difficulties of working on an extremely restricted building site – under 1 ha (2.4 acres) – in a major urban area. Particular problems were the transportation, storage and handling of materials, which were brought to the site by about 500 trucks a day at the peak of construction. They came up with brilliant solutions, such as the delivery of materials directly into hoppers in the basement structure. From here there was quick vertical delivery within a few days, with fast unloading and handling of materials at the proper locations. In addition, concrete was produced by a plant at the site, avoiding any delays. Steel beams arrived at the site from Pittsburgh only hours after they had cooled, and were almost immediately riveted in place. At each level of the structure, materials were also speedily distributed horizontally, using an ingenious narrow gauge railway system with hand-powered cars.

In terms of the distribution of the many building tasks, Starrett Brothers and Eken in effect acted more as construction managers than as builders, subcontracting a good part of the work. This approach differed from the practice of the

Opposite *Completed in 1931, the Empire State Building held the title of the tallest building in the world for over 40 years and still retains its iconic status.*

times, when general contractors performed most of the work themselves.

With their innovative practices, Starrett Brothers and Eken helped to establish the foundations of modern construction management. Their organizational innovations meant that the building was completed in record time, on 11 April 1931; its much-heralded inauguration took place on 1 May of that year.

The Empire State Building as icon

The Empire State Building is extraordinary not only for the ingenious organization of its construction, but also for the unfailing charm and mystery of its image. It has entered the popular imagination through both fiction and fact; since its starring role in the film *King Kong* in 1933, it has appeared in almost 100 films up to the present. The building has also seen tragedy, from suicide leaps to the horror of the B-25 bomber that crashed into the 79th floor on a foggy Saturday morning in 1945, killing 14 people. Visiting dignitaries have ranged from Winston Churchill to Helen Keller. This mythic structure continues to elicit tributes – prosaic, poetic, cinematic, photographic and pictorial. Most famous, perhaps, are Lewis W. Hine's more than 1000 breathtaking photographs documenting construction of the building. More recent images by many artists attest to this spectacular building's continued and ineffable hold on its observers' imaginations.

FACTFILE

Height (to 102nd floor observatory)	381.6 m
Weight	331,000 tonnes
Materials	aluminium, brick, limestone, steel
Bricks used	10 million
Lifts	67
Steps	1860
Windows	6400
Workforce	3500
Cost (building alone)	$24,718,000

The Gateway Arch

Time: 1948–65 Location: St Louis, Missouri, United States

The arch is in a sense a vertical monument on one axis and a wide monument in another. I think now we have the approaches worked out just right so that in a thousand years this will still be the right relationship between the monument, the river, the park, and the city.

EERO SAARINEN, 1962

In 1948 a national architectural design competition was held for the proposed Jefferson Westward Expansion Memorial. Planned for a site on the western bank of the Mississippi River in the city of St Louis, the memorial was to be a monument to Thomas Jefferson, America's only architect-President, and a symbol to commemorate the importance of this particular city as the place from which Meriwether Lewis and William Clark embarked on their historic journey to map the American West.

The memorial was conceived as a marker in the vast and predominantly flat landscape of America's mid-west and, at a more local scale, as a city landmark. The competition-winning submission by the notable Finnish-American architect Eero Saarinen consisted of a 180-m (590-ft) high parabolic arch to be built on the levee. The form of the tall free-standing arch was a symbol of modernism which had been used by other architects. Most notably it was a dominant element of

Le Corbusier's influential though unbuilt competition design for the Palace of the Soviets in 1931.

There was a long delay between the selection of Saarinen's design and the construction of the arch, and this provided an opportunity for the designers to study and refine their scheme. The final design was completed in 1958.

The memorial, which was to be located on an axis with the Old Courthouse, formed the focus of a new 33-ha (82-acre) riverside park. With the approval of proposals to relocate the existing railway lines back from the levee and to place them within a tunnel, the design for the park was also revised. The new park had curving paths and walls and a planting scheme which created a small forest, recalling the American wilderness. The arch was resited at a higher level and planned within a clearing – a reference to the clearings of the first encampments of the explorers. The arch also became taller and wider. As if to reaffirm the sweeping magnificence of a single gesture, it was reformulated as a catenary curve that extended its height to 192 m (630 ft), making it the tallest monument in America.

Design and construction

The detailed design of the monument was developed in close collaboration between the architect and the engineer – Saarinen worked with his architect colleague John Dinkeloo and structural engineer Fred Severud. Together they developed a structural concept based on a single, hollow, curving tube to be constructed in one material and with deep foundations to stabilize the form.

A drawing of Saarinen's design for the Gateway Arch: it was intended as a civic monument at the centre of a newly constructed riverside park.

The cross-section of the arch is an equilateral triangle which tapers from 16.45 m (54 ft) on a side at the base to 5.2 m (17 ft) at the apex. Stainless steel was selected as the main cladding material because of its tensile strength, finish and resistance to corrosion. The outer leaf is thus of 0.6-cm (0.25-in) stainless steel, while the inner skin is of 1-cm (0.4-in) carbon steel. Steel tension bolts tie the two skins together and force the bond between the steel and the concrete which is placed in the space between them. Both steel skins have additional stiffeners and the concrete is prestressed.

The wall panels were prefabricated in segments, using 886 tonnes of material, and the sections were then welded together on site.

Some 90 m (300 ft) above the ground, at a point where the lateral loads decrease and the dead weight is more critical as the arch becomes more horizontal, the concrete is eliminated and the

The Gateway Arch frames the view of the city of St Louis from across the Mississippi River.

FACTFILE

Height	192 m
Width at base	192 m
Foundations	c. 13.7 m deep
Materials	reinforced concrete, steel
Weight	43,000 tons
Cost	$13,000,000
Capacity at top	160 people

inner and outer metal skins are connected by steel diaphragms.

The construction of the arch was a complex and difficult process and special systems had to be devised to fabricate and transport each of the segments. The first six steel sections were lifted into place using ground-based cranes, while the remainder were put into position using two special cranes on mobile derricks which moved up the arch as each triangular steel section was put into place. With the construction of the two sides of the structure finished, the keystone – which was 2.6 m (8.5 ft) wide and weighed 80 tonnes – was inserted to complete the arch.

To achieve this a special horizontal jack had to be designed to hold the two legs of the arch apart as the gap was only 0.6 m (2 ft). In addition, fire hoses were used to pour water on to the stainless steel covering to minimize thermal expansion. After numerous delays – several lawsuits, a labour strike brought about by fear of collapse and an attempt to climb the arch by civil rights protesters – the last segment of the arch was set in place on 20 October 1965.

Like many other architects and designers at this time, Saarinen was interested in transferring technological expertise from other industries to the construction of buildings. In developing the form and constructional details of the arch he came close to applying stressed skin fabrication techniques developed by the aircraft industry to the design of this exceptional monument.

The development of the winning competition design for the Jefferson Westward Expansion Memorial almost extended throughout Eero Saarinen's career. The processes of redesign and refinement are symptomatic of his approach to design. He died in 1961; the project was seen through to completion under the supervision of his colleagues and successors Kevin Roche and John Dinkeloo.

Above *The installation of the specially fabricated keystone saw the completion of the arch on 20 October 1965.*

Left *The cranes on the mobile derricks were designed to move progressively up the arch during the later stages of construction.*

The World Trade Center

Time: 1962–73   Location: New York City, United States

*As I learned to understand the purpose of the project, it became clear that the Trade Center,
with its location facing the entry to New York harbour, could symbolize the importance
of world trade to this country and its major metropolis and become a physical expression of
the universal effort of men to seek and achieve world peace.*
MINORU YAMASAKI, ARCHITECT, 1979

U pon their completion, the 110-storey twin towers of the World Trade Center in New York City became the tallest man-made structures in the world, surpassing the 381.6-m (1252-ft) Empire State Building (1931) by over 30 m (100 ft). The World Trade Center successfully revived the flagging downtown financial district at a time when many businesses were relocating to mid-town Manhattan. Until their destruction by terrorists on 11 September 2001, the towers served as the focus of a multi-block development surrounded by five lower buildings and a plaza, with a working population of 50,000 occupying 929,000 sq. m (10 million sq. ft) of office space. A shopping concourse level below the plaza provided links to three New York subway lines and commuter trains to New Jersey. The unprecedented scale of the project fostered important engineering innovations in the foundations, the structural support system and the lift arrangements.

The foundations
The site was originally salt marsh, only 1 m (3 ft) above sea-level, with the granite bedrock layer 21 m (70 ft) below grade. Such tall towers required

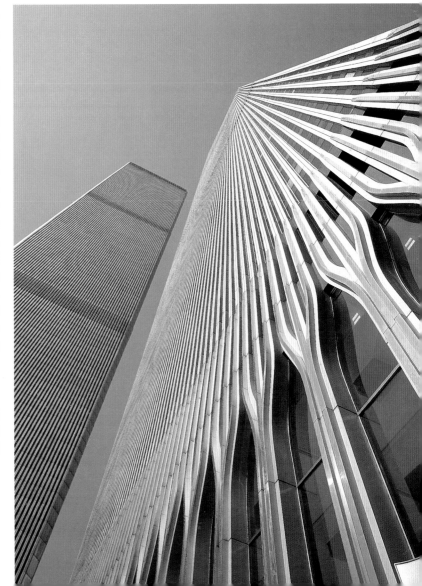

The twin towers of the World Trade Center were the focus of a commercial development in downtown Manhattan, intended to bring new life to the area.

The load-bearing box columns on the exterior shared support with the columns of the structural core where lifts and services were located. The floors on hollow trusses (bottom) acted as diaphragms.

very deep foundations resting on bedrock, but the swampy conditions prohibited excavation by conventional means. Instead, the engineers proposed a slurry trench system. In order to keep water from seeping into the excavations, an area 152 × 305 m (500 × 1000 ft) was surrounded with a slurry wall. Sections 1 m (3 ft) wide and 7 m (22 ft) were dug down to bedrock and filled with slurry (bentonite clay and water), which helped to maintain the shape of the excavation until a steel reinforcing cage could be inserted and concrete

poured; being heavier, this sank to the bottom, displacing the slurry.

The sections were then joined to form a wall, creating what was known as the 'bathtub'. This was stabilized against external water pressure with steel cables, creating a dry zone allowing further excavations for the foundation pilings. The excavated soil was transferred to Manhattan's west side where it was used as fill for the site of Battery Park City. Subway tunnels and subterranean utility lines crossed the site, causing further complications that required delicate manoeuvering during excavations.

Support and bracing

Such exceptionally tall buildings require additional support and wind bracing. Greater heights also mean more lifts, thereby reducing the amount of space available for office use. Conventional skyscrapers employ skeletal construction, in which the structure resembles a steel cage of vertical supports and horizontal girders. Their exterior 'curtain' walls have no supporting function, rather they are hung from the structural skeleton. Lifts, stairs and other services occupy the core of any tall building, but with skeletal construction, the percentage of space occupied by them increases significantly with building height. Necessary cross-bracing both stiffens the core to counteract greater wind shear forces and further diminishes office space.

To maximize usable space, the Center engineers recommended abandoning conventional design for a new form of load-bearing construction. Traditional load-bearing walls can be seen in any simple masonry building, where bricks or stone support their own weight. However, the load-bearing exterior walls of the Center towers employed a novel self-supporting system of hollow, square supports, called box columns. These steel columns, 30 × 35 cm (12 × 14 in), carried much of the weight of the building and all the wind loads; their squarish shape offered maximum resistance to twisting and bending. While columns on the first two floors were considerably thicker and spaced 3 m (10 ft) apart, at the third floor, the columns transformed into 'trees',

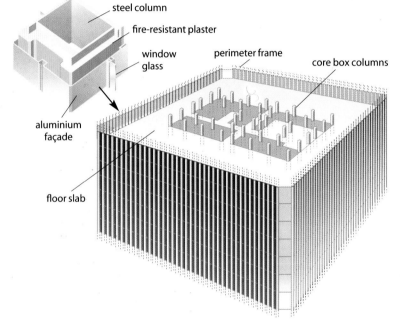

steel column

fire-resistant plaster

window glass

perimeter frame

core box columns

aluminium façade

floor slab

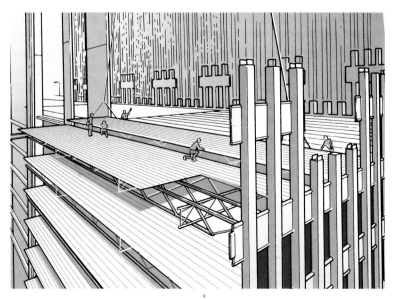

with three smaller box columns branching upwards. The upper columns were placed at intervals of 1 m (3 ft), on centre, and welded to horizontal spandrel beams to create a strong but flexible external matrix, much like a stiff tube. The architect, Minoru Yamasaki, who had a fear of heights, noted that the proximity of the columns, less than a shoulder width (56 cm/22 in) apart, also helped to alleviate acrophobia for the occupants.

The floors also contributed to the structure. Designed as a series of hollow trusses, they acted as stiffened diaphragms, helping to redistribute wind forces from each external wall to its two perpendicular walls, where forces were transferred down through the external columns to the ground. This system allowed for considerable flexibility. Utilities were easily threaded through the hollow trusses of the floors. Placing the dominant supports on the external walls opened the interiors, allowing for flexible layouts.

Lifts and services

As in conventional buildings, the core housed lifts and services, while also providing a second important source of structural support for the building. Yet, rather than waste valuable space on a vast vertical transportation network, Yamasaki economized with three zones of express and local lift service, serving sky lobbies at the 44th and 78th floors. Larger express lifts operated as shuttles, whisking passengers up to these lobbies, where local lifts serving groups of floors delivered them to their final destinations.

By treating the building like three smaller buildings stacked one on top of the other, Yamasaki reduced the amount of space normally consumed by lifts by 15 per cent, and at the same time improved transport speed and efficiency.

Efficiency in design and materials

At every opportunity, the structure was made stronger and lighter. Structural steel was deployed in grades varying according to the gravity (building weight) and wind loads expected at different levels. Heavier grades were used at the bottom, with lighter ones near the top, thus reducing both cost and weight overall.

The load-bearing external walls were erected in prefabricated sections two storeys high and three columns wide that were welded together and bolted into place during construction. These aluminium-clad steel columns reduced glass by 20 per cent compared with most curtain wall skyscrapers. Less glass meant a decreased need for air conditioning in the summer and for heating in the winter. To clean the 43,000 windows of the twin towers, a remarkable computerized cleaning system was developed. Thin tracks built into the external columns enabled an automated cleaning unit to pass down from the roof, spraying detergent solutions or rinses, and cleansing the glass with brushes and squeegees.

The construction process

Construction on such a mammoth scale necessitated careful orchestration of arrival and departure times for materials, delivery vehicles, machinery and workers at the cramped site. Building materials for the towers came from across the United States. For example, the prefabricated sections of structural steel came from 14 separate plants in such far-flung locales as St Louis, Los Angeles and Seattle. Because of the limited space on the site, the pieces, shipped via rail, were kept across the Hudson River at one of the Pennsylvania Railroad yards until needed. They were then trucked to the site through the Holland Tunnel. Eight hydraulic cantilevering cranes called 'jumping kangaroo cranes' were

The World Trade Center under construction. The innovative structural system is clearly visible: the load-bearing columns on the first two floors were thicker and spaced further apart; at the third floor, they branched out into three smaller columns which continued up the height of the towers.

The towers survived after the impact from the planes for at least an hour. As the supports for the floors failed in the intense heat, the floors collapsed, driving down on those below.

specially built in Australia for the construction of the towers. They derived their name from the fact that they were placed on top of the buildings, and could 'jump' or rise to upper floors as the buildings grew higher.

Demolition, foundation work and construction of the towers involved 4000 workers over a seven-year period. The general contractors were Tishman Realty & Construction Co., Inc. of New York. Foundation work began in August 1966. Though the first tenants took occupancy in the North Tower in December of 1970, construction continued, and the two towers were not officially dedicated until 4 April 1973. Work continued on the five adjacent buildings of the Center into the early 1980s.

While organizing such a complex project required considerable design and planning skills, the engineering innovations at the Center were even more noteworthy. Although they were soon eclipsed in height by Chicago's Sears Tower (p. 192) and then Kuala Lumpur's Petronas Towers (p. 201), the World Trade Center towers remained the tallest structures in Manhattan. The observation deck in Tower Two was one of New York's most popular tourist destinations, offering unparalleled views of Manhattan and New York Harbour.

FACTFILE

Height: Tower One	417 m (without transmission tower)
Tower Two	415 m
Depth of foundations	21 m
Dimensions of floors	63 m x 63 m
Total of steel box columns	35,000
Windows	43,000 (approx. 55,740 sq. m)
Weight of structural steel	90,720 kg
Total workforce	50,000
Cost	$400 million

Why the towers fell

On 11 September 2001, two fully fuelled Boeing 767 jets were hijacked en route to Los Angeles from Boston and flown into the towers. The North Tower was struck first, near the 95th floor. Some 20 minutes later, the South Tower was hit near the 60th floor. News videos reveal that, on impact, several external box columns were breached in each tower on a number of levels. Key floor support systems and elements of the structural core were also damaged on several levels. The ensuing explosion of some 20,000 gallons of jet fuel destroyed additional columns on the opposite sides of the towers and probably caused further internal structural damage.

Despite these initial impacts, each tower survived for at least an hour. While structural engineers still debate the precise cause of the collapse, some feel that the immense damage from the collisions alone may have led to the building failures. However, most agree that the jet fuel fires, reaching temperatures of 1649–1927°C (3000–3500°F), would have fatally compromised the remaining components. At 800°C (1472°F) steel softens, losing its ability to function as a support. Although the towers had sprinkler systems designed to withstand normal office fires for up to three hours, they were useless against the petroleum-based fires.

When the structural supports of each tower failed, the weights of the floors above the crash sites suddenly functioned like giant hammers, driving down on the floors below. As the supports of each subsequent floor failed, a chain reaction developed, fed by gravitational forces and leading to a catastrophic collapse. Each tower folded like a stack of cards, much as it would have done in a controlled demolition. Because the South Tower was struck near the 60th floor, closer to the corner of the building, its upper floors initially fell diagonally, like a felled tree. The tubular structure may have helped to guide the subsequent collapse vertically downwards.

Skyscrapers as symbols

Drawing on the co-ordinated efforts of thousands of individuals in engineering, building technol-

ogy, business, government and the design professions, the Trade Center towers represented one of the greatest human accomplishments of the 20th century. With a working population of 50,000 persons, the towers functioned as vertical cities within a larger metropolis. Their effectiveness as symbols of America's global achievements in technology and finance attested to the realization of Yamasaki's vision. While their destruction at the hands of terrorists underscored their effectiveness as symbols, it also inaugurated extensive debate on the security of such structures in the contemporary geopolitical climate. In an age of increasing globalization, the survival of the skyscraper depends more than ever on the achievement of international harmony.

Symbols of America's global achievements in technology and finance, the twin towers were victims of their iconic status.

The Sears Tower

Time: 1970–74   Location: Chicago, Illinois, United States

The tall building is the landmark of our age.
LOUISE HUXTABLE, 1984

The Sears Tower marked the climax of the development of the skyscraper in the United States and, for over 20 years, held the record as the world's tallest building. Soaring 110 storeys to a height of 443 m (1454 ft), it is a striking landmark in the skyline of downtown Chicago, the city where many innovations in high-rise buildings were pioneered. The tower was designed for Sears, Roebuck and Company, a mail-order catalogue business, to consolidate its 7000 employees in one location. Sears purchased a city block and commissioned Skidmore, Owings & Merrill (SOM), an international corporate practice of architects and engineers, to design the building.

SOM's team was led by architect Bruce Graham and structural engineer Fazlur Khan. Together with architect-engineer Myron Goldsmith, they had already established an outstanding reputation for the design of high-rise buildings. Using new computer-aided methods of quantitative structural analysis, the engineering concepts that they pioneered spawned a generation of skyscrapers of unprecedented size, beyond the realm of previous structural or economic feasibility.

Opposite *The Sears Tower belongs to a generation of very tall buildings that required the development of new structural concepts to deal with wind loads.*

FACTFILE

Height	443 m
	520 m with antennae
Total floor area	409,000 sq. m
Weight	222,500 tons
Workforce	16,500
Cost	$150 million

Braced and bundled tubes

The taller the building, the greater the effect of wind. To resist wind loads, smaller-scale structures are typically stiffened by diagonal bracing or shear walls around the cores of lifts and stairs. However, using this method to brace a steel frame to achieve adequate stiffness in a high-rise building is very costly. Consequently, new structural concepts had to be developed for such buildings that would use the same amount of structural material as conventional buildings and thereby incur no cost premium for height. The work of SOM is a chronicle of these new concepts. In 1971, their 100-storey John Hancock Building in Chicago utilized Fazlur Khan's new 'braced tube' concept with diagonal bracing at the perimeter of the frame instead of at the central core.

Sears did not want to see diagonal bracing on the face of their building, however, and in addition required a wide range of floor sizes, both to meet their own needs for very large floor plates and to provide smaller areas for tenants who were to occupy part of the building. To satisfy these requirements, Fazlur Khan developed the structural concept of 'bundled tubes'. Instead of lateral bracing at the small scale of the core or at the large scale of the building perimeter, the Sears Tower is a bundle of mid-scale tubes – in a sense individual towers – tied together. Nearly 30 per cent taller than the John Hancock Building, the structure of the Sears Tower is only 14 per cent heavier.

At its base, the tower consists of nine tubes, each 22.9 m (75 ft) square, which ascend to different heights: two stop at level 50, two at level 66 and three at level 90, leaving only two tubes to

ascend the final 20 storeys. In addition to becoming more slender and visually lighter as the building ascends, this solution provides floor plates ranging from 3800 to 1100 sq. m (41,000 to 10,000 sq. ft).

Each tube is free of internal columns to provide total flexibility for office layouts and is framed on all four sides by steel columns at 4.6-m (15-ft) centres connected by perimeter steel beams. In place of a bolted frame with diagonal bracing that would reduce the flexibility of the interior space, the frame has only vertical and horizontal members stiffened by fully welded connections. Columns and beams are built up members of steel plate welded in the form of W-sections. The thickness of the plate varies from 25 mm (1 in) at the top of the building to 100 mm (4 in) at the base, where the accumulated gravity loads are greatest. The steel superstructure sits on a 1.5-m (5-ft) thick concrete mat on underlying caisson foundations. These concrete caissons in steel shells range from 2.2 to 3 m (7 to 10 ft) in diameter and average 20 m (65 ft) in length to reach bedrock.

Materials and construction

The steel superstructure was prefabricated in 7.6 by 4.6 m (26 by 15 ft) modules – the largest that could be transported to site by truck. Each module consisted of a two-storey column with shop welded half-length beams on either side. After being craned into place on site, mid-span beam-to-beam connections were field bolted. By eliminating 95 per cent of field welding, the frame was erected rapidly at the rate of 8 storeys per month, with significant savings in labour costs.

To increase the stiffness of the building, the tubes are joined along column and beam lines shared by adjacent modules. In addition, the tubes are strapped together by two storey bands of trusses around the perimeter of the bundle at levels 29–31, 64–66 and 88–90. The truss diagonals are concealed behind louvred cladding that provides air intake for mechanical equipment on these floors. The stiffness of the tubes is further augmented by the floors of the building, which work as structural diaphragms. Concrete slabs on corrugated steel decking are supported by 1-m (40-in) deep trusses. Each truss is bolted directly to a column, making the structure more efficient by avoiding the indirect transfer of floor loads through girders. The direction of the spanning trusses is alternated every six floors to equalize the loading on the perimeter frame of the tube.

The Sears Tower has 102 lifts for its working population and is divided vertically into three zones of 30–40 floors, with a two-storey sky lobby at the base of each zone. The 16,500 occupants of the building are shuttled to the sky lobbies by 14 double-deck, mass-transit express lifts. From these points, passengers transfer to banks of local lifts to arrive at their own floor. A public observation deck on the 103rd floor is served by two dedicated express lifts from the ground that rise at 9.15 m (30 ft) per second .

In addition to marking a significant advance in the optimization of structural systems for high-rise buildings in order to achieve greater height with less material, the Sears Tower exemplifies the way in which International Style modernism was appropriated in the United States to become a symbol of corporate power. The taut curtain wall of black aluminium and bronze-tinted glass is understated, revealing nothing of the structural ingenuity which enabled the building to soar to a previously unattainable height.

Providing a very stiff structure with a minimal weight of structural steel, the bundled tubes generate a range of floor plate sizes and configurations as well as large areas of column-free space.

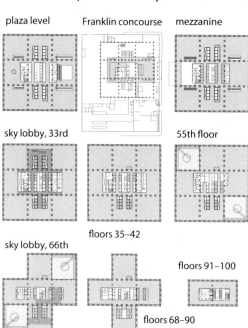

plaza level   Franklin concourse   mezzanine

sky lobby, 33rd   55th floor

floors 35–42

sky lobby, 66th

floors 91–100

floors 68–90

The CN Tower

Time: 1973–75   Location: Toronto, Ontario, Canada

Building high or, more correctly, building higher, continues to offer a compelling challenge to contemporary constructors, not only the structural engineers who devise the means of attaining increased height and those who organize the construction process, but also the promoters and financiers of the enterprise. Extreme height can bring substantial financial rewards by ensuring the tower's status as a potential tourist destination, with the further possibility of the building gaining an iconic role as symbol or emblem for the city itself.

The CN Tower in Toronto's downtown, rising 553.3 m (1815 ft) from the ground to the tip of its lightning rod, achieves not only supremacy as the world's tallest free-standing structure – a record it has retained since its completion in 1975 – but also memorably defines the skyline profile of that city, so much so that it is a copyrighted structure, images of which cannot be reproduced without permission. By comparison, Moscow's Ostakino Tower, a near contemporary and direct rival of the CN Tower, rises to a lower height of 535 m (1762 ft). London's Post Office Tower, one of the earliest built to support microwave transmission equipment, rises a mere 176 m (580 ft).

Nearly two million tourists a year ride the lifts to the observation deck near the summit, or stop off at the restaurant and disco 365 m (1200 ft) above ground level, ensuring that the CN Tower is financially as well as structurally self-supporting on the

The CN Tower still dominates the skyline of Toronto today, a quarter of a century after it was built. Depending on how it is reckoned, it is also the tallest structure in the world.

A helicopter was used to lift in the television antenna that tops the tower.

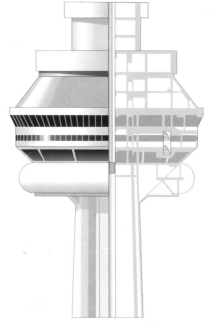

Right *A revolving restaurant, disco and observation deck have proved popular visitor attractions.*

basis of its construction cost of $63 million dollars. Visitors continue to provide the lion's share of the revenue for the building; smaller contributions are made by rentals from television, radio and telecommunications companies for space to deploy their microwave aerials in the zone below the observation deck.

It was the need to improve television reception during the high-rise boom in Toronto in the 1960s – which caused disruption of signals – that prompted the project initially. The Canadian Broadcasting Corporation decided to team up with the two railway companies, Canadian Pacific and Canadian National, who had already combined to promote a Metro Centre based on Union Station which could also include a tower for CBC's microwave antennae. When this joint project foundered in 1971, Canadian National decided to proceed on their own, with a free-standing tower to be sited amidst their railway tracks.

Construction

After reviewing a number of options, structural engineer Mulcahy Grant proposed a single shaft, hexagonal in plan and stiffened by tapering concrete fins. Sitework began in 1973, with the removal of over 56 tonnes of earth and shale for the foundations – a concrete foundation pad 6 m (20 ft) thick, sunk 17 m (55 ft) below the city centre. The shaft of the tower was cast on site using a 300-tonne slipform mould, which climbed in step with the concrete pours, the structure rising 6 m (20 ft) a day. Work was carried on 24 hours a day, five days a week, to complete the structure in 40 months. It is proof against impacts from birds, planes and tornados, with a predicated lifespan of three centuries. After the shaft was complete, work began on the tower sphere for the observation decks and revolving restaurant. The antenna was lifted into place in 44 pieces by helicopter.

Visitors ascending in the glass-fronted lifts to the tower's Space Deck can view the sunlit snow and ice of Lake Ontario to the south, while the northern panorama includes the downtown Sheppard and Yonge towers, with the plains of Southern Ontario in the far distance. Despite various more recent upstarts on the Toronto skyline, the CN Tower remains pre-eminent.

The fashion for free-standing Observation Towers carrying equipment and doubling as microwave platforms may have passed in favour of visitor facilities on the upper levels of standard commercial office towers, as in the Sears Tower in Chicago (p. 192), but there will always remain a lingering respect and affection for that brand of transparent and unadulterated one-upmanship exemplified by Toronto's lone 'skypricker'.

The Hongkong and Shanghai Bank

45

Time: 1979–86   Location: Hong Kong, People's Republic of China

… the firm met the bank's brief to build the 'best bank headquarters in the world'
MARTIN PAWLEY, 1999

The Hongkong and Shanghai Banking Corporation has been established in the former colony since 1864, and is one of two banks authorized to issue currency. On a favoured site overlooking Statue Square, its 1935 headquarters building was designed by the architects Palmer and Turner, who were instructed by the chairman to design 'the best bank in the world'. The result was a handsome building, with a steel frame clad in stone, and with some innovations for its time, such as air conditioning and high-speed electric lifts. The Bank duly placed a picture of the new building on its bank notes.

By the late 1970s, however, the Palmer and Turner building had become outdated, due primarily to the sheer growth of the Corporation, and the difficulty of adapting it to new technology. In June 1979 the Bank held a competition for the design of a replacement, which was won by Foster Associates, who were once again briefed to design the world's best bank. The competition scheme which they had submitted relied on strong 'masts' on each side of the site, supporting a series of bridges. This idea allowed the possibility of a phased regeneration of the site – building a bay at a time while progressively demolishing the original building – and opening-up the ground floor to the public at large. It also allowed

The building is suspended from pairs of steel masts and divided into three sections, or bays, 35, 47 and 28 floors high. The masts are connected at five points by two-storey trusses from which the floor clusters are suspended.

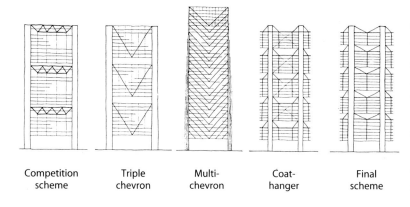

| Competition scheme | Triple chevron | Multi-chevron | Coat-hanger | Final scheme |

Above *Drawings of various schemes for the structure, with the final version of five two-storey trusses on paired masts.*

the engineers for the project, Ove Arup & Partners, to develop the idea of a 'minimum footprint', which would correspondingly maximize the plan area available for bank accommodation.

Almost as soon as they appointed Foster Associates, the Bank abandoned the idea of phased retention of the original building, both from the point of view of its own activities and because the scheme would in practice make it difficult to develop any significant basement area, needed as a way of fully realizing the almost astronomic value of this central site. Although the competition design underwent several modifications before the final contract scheme was arrived at, the mast and bridge principle continued to prove viable as a basic design concept.

Below *Cut-away diagram of the bank, showing the structure of the building. The floors are 'suspended' from the huge trusses.*

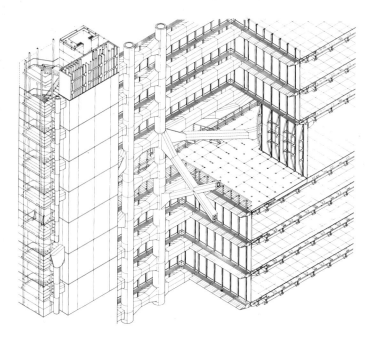

The structure

The final structural solution was a development of the 'coat-hanger' scheme. The whole of the superstructure is supported on four frames, each frame consisting of two masts which support suspension trusses at five discrete levels. The double-height spaces formed by the trusses become the focal point for each group of floors, and contain circulation and social spaces, as well as providing a refuge in case of fire.

Each mast is made up of four tubular steel columns, interconnected by haunched rectangular beams at each storey. This arrangement maximizes the load-carrying capacity of the mast, while minimizing its plan area. It is conventionally said that engineers design logical structures, and then architects alter them to make them more interesting. Here, however, is a structure which is both logical and interesting, and the only obvious architectural intervention has been to remove the top boom of the outermost truss (made possible by its lighter loading) in order to make the logic of the hanger system clearer.

The cladding

As the frames can be seen from outside the building, the design team would have liked simply to expose the basic structure. However, the need for both durability and fire resistance called for protective coatings, which in their turn would require some form of cladding. The cladding has to fit the structural members tightly, so that their form is still revealed, and it must also have an inherent durability in the wet climate of the South China Sea. The solution was to prefabricate panels of aluminium fixed by cleats attached to the frame, and sealed at the edges. Aluminium cladding has been used on many buildings, but it is often thought to give a slightly 'quilted' effect, due to a lack of complete flatness. For the Bank, however, perfection was demanded, and achieved by the subcontractor with the use of 5-mm thick material (five times thicker than conventional panels),

Opposite below *A popular public plaza runs beneath the building, covered by a glass ceiling – this soon became known as the 'underbelly'.*

FACTFILE

Height	179 m
Building form	3 stepped towers 29, 36, 44 storeys
Height of atrium	52 m
Total floor area	99,000 sq. m
Banking hall	0.4 ha, 81 tellers, 8000–1000 transactions per day

and by the development of computer-controlled welding machinery to attach the edge flanges, which left the panels virtually distortion free.

The external walls are generally of glass, used to further the idea of transparency, supported on a system of vertical mullions. Because of the greater flexibility associated with a hanging structure (and the effects of typhoon winds) both mullions and glass are designed to accommodate small floor-to-floor movements. Sun visors, intended to cut glare, double as walkways for window cleaning.

Opening up the ground floor as a public thoroughfare (a generous gesture by the Bank, which also brought it certain gains in terms of permitted development) necessitated some form of separating membrane at first-floor level, in order to contain the interior conditioned air of the building. The form finally chosen – a minimum weight structure of catenary framing members with glass infill – quickly earned it the name of the 'underbelly'.

Above *The bank while under construction: the steel structure was covered by close-fitting aluminium cladding.*

Left *The main floors of the building are mostly open plan, allowing great flexibility; the massive structural elements are left very visible.*

instinctively looks up, and suddenly the 10-storey atrium comes into view.

It is this atrium that finally confirms the Bank's particular qualities: the design aims of slender masts, thin floors, floor-to-ceiling glazing and an open-plan layout have achieved the effect of an almost weightless structure, with a transparency unequalled in any other building of this height.

By contrast, the structural elements of the main trusses are a formidable presence in the circulation levels, and the ruthless pursuit of perfection in all details (almost all the surfaces above floor level are either metal, in various shades of grey, or glass) leaves employees rather limited options for personalization of their space. But the building has worn well, and while it was never the tallest structure in Hong Kong, it remains a unique building of outstanding quality. And on Sundays, expatriates from the Philippines give it the popular vote by gathering in the shade of the ground floor for picnic lunches, watched over by Stitt and Steven, the two bronze lions retained from the former building.

Below *The central atrium rises up through 10 floors which are open to it. An escalator penetrates the glass ceiling from the plaza below.*

The interior

Employees gain access by means of lifts at each end of the building between the masts. There is, however, a more interesting option for the general public – the central escalator, which penetrates a small aperture in the underbelly. It is an old theatrical trick, but it works. The visitor

Petronas Towers

Time: 1991–96   Location: Kuala Lumpur, Malaysia

The space between is my greatest interest in this project.
CESAR PELLI, 1996

Completed in 1996, the twin Petronas Towers in Kuala Lumpur currently holds the title of the world's tallest building, reaching 451.9 m (1482 ft), and containing 88 floors of rentable space in each tower. Designed by Cesar Pelli & Associates, the building combines innovative technology with Islamic symbolism, and represents a departure from the Malaysian capital's International Style-inspired tall buildings. Significantly, for the first time in over 100 years, the prize for the world's loftiest building has been taken away from the United States. Title holders have included such New York architectural luminaries as the Empire State Building (p. 179) and the World Trade Center (p. 187), and, most recently, Chicago's Sears Tower (p. 192).

The significance of the Petronas Towers goes beyond its spectacular height, however. It is the major building in a $2-billion project for the development of the Malaysian capital, comprising a 20-ha (50-acre) park, and office, commercial and apartment buildings, a mosque and other structures, which the Malaysian government hopes will be the centrepiece in the country's move towards becoming a fully industrialized nation by 2020. The construction of the Petronas Towers, sponsored by the country's national oil company (after which it is named) and the government, has also brought about welcome technology transfer, with teams of international engineers and general contractors working closely with their Malaysian counterparts.

The concrete structure of two towers rising together. Two different general contractors built the towers, creating a spirit of competition – both were completed at the same time.

Imagery

In terms of its architectural imagery, the architect was given the task, after winning an international competition in 1991, to create a building that would have specifically Malaysian resonance. An initial scheme with a 12-pointed star as the basis of the plan was changed at the suggestion of Malaysia's prime minister, Datuk Seri Dr Mahathir Mohamad, to an eight-pointed star because of its Islamic symbolism. The star shape is visible on the scalloped curtain wall with its highly sculptural surface, shimmering with glass and stainless steel. The building is also appropriately sensitive to the local climate: the façades incorporate stainless steel sunshades in keeping with the tropical conditions of the city, located just two degrees from the equator.

Structure

If the imagery in the plan and general elevation of the building is specifically Malaysian, and hence a far cry from the abstraction of most tall buildings around the world today, the structure of the building is an example of technology transfer. Because of the enormous expense of importing steel to Malaysia, it was decided that the building should have a concrete structure and composite floors composed of metal decking and steel infill beams. This necessitated the devising of a high-strength concrete, the first of its kind in Malaysia, that would reduce the diameter of the columns, in order to fulfil the architect's wish to create slender towers. The structural engineers could thus reject the commonly used structural tube concept, as employed in the Sears Tower (p. 192), in order to free the building as much as possible from perimeter columns. Each tower has 16 perimeter columns with diameters of up to 2.4 m (7.8 ft), which are connected by a haunched ring beam at each floor. The feeling of open space is created by the generous interval, of 8 or 10 m (26.25 or 32.8 ft), between columns. Adding to the svelte appearance of the towers is the fact that only a small slice of each column is visible on the façade. The lateral load is carried by the columns and the structural core. The pinnacle of each tower contains a tuned mass damper to minimize the swaying of the buildings in the wind.

A two-level skybridge, 58.82 m (193 ft) long, connects the conference centre on the 41st and 42nd floors of the towers. This is an important element in the overall design, both in terms of its use as a fire exit from one tower to the other and as a breathtaking signpost. Made in almost 500 pieces in South Korea, it was assembled on site and

Above left *The evolution of the building geometry of the Petronas Towers, based on an eight-pointed star which is visible in the towers' exterior curtain walls.*

Left *View of the towers nearing completion. The use of high-strength concrete in the construction meant that the diameter of the supporting columns could be reduced and spaced at wide intervals.*

Opposite *The completed Petronas Towers glowing in the dusk light of Kuala Lumpur.*

The Skybridge
connects the two
towers at the 41st
and 42nd floors
and is supported
by two legs that
are attached at the
29th floor.

raised to its final position. It is supported on two slender legs attached to the 29th floor.

The international nature of the enterprise was further enhanced by the unusual fact that the two towers each had different general contractors – one Korean and one Japanese. These teams pursued their projects in a spirit of elevated competition.

The Petronas Towers thus stand as a manifestation of technology transfer, national pride and an unusually sensitive attention to local religious and cultural issues. Their extraordinary design, with its references to Islamic tradition, and the ingenious technological story behind their construction, will ensure their place as one of the outstanding examples of the tall building in the late 20th century. As the architect Cesar Pelli has remarked, 'These towers are not monuments but living buildings that play a symbolic role. We worked hard to make them alive.'

FACTFILE

Height	451.9 m
Floors	88 per tower
Area of each tower	218,000 sq. m
Materials	concrete, steel, glass, aluminium
Windows	32,000
Cost	$1.6 billion

New York-New York

Time: 1996–97   Location: Las Vegas, Nevada, United States

The biggest piece of pop art in the world.
NEAL GASKIN, ARCHITECT, 1998

Las Vegas reinvents itself every decade or so. The latest phase began in 1989 with the opening of the Mirage and Excalibur – two enormous hotel-casinos, each as complex and detailed as small cities, and as fantastic in appearance as fairy tales. Their purpose: to ensure people gamble and spend as much money as possible.

Though not the largest when it opened in 1997, the New York-New York hotel and casino (NYNY) is certainly one of the most audacious, transporting the fabled skyline of Manhattan to the Nevada desert. It stands at the corner of Trop-icana Boulevard and the Las Vegas Strip, on one of the busiest intersections in the city.

Taking advantage of the quicksilver boom in Las Vegas tourism in the 1990s, NYNY was built on a fast track in one and a half years for $460 million. The structure rose one floor per week for 48 weeks. Sitting on 7 ha (17 acres) – small for a Las Vegas hotel – NYNY squeezes in all the require-ments: a 7804-sq. m (84,000-sq. ft) ground-level casino with restaurants, bars and theatres; a high-rise tower for the rooms; a swimming pool; space for 3800 cars in a structure linked by bridges to

The famous Manhattan skyline is transplanted to the Nevada desert in a fanciful but functional casino-hotel. The low buildings behind the half-size Statue of Liberty contain casino, restaurants and theatres; the high-rise towers contain the guest rooms.

the main hotel and a *porte cochère* to handle 100 vehicles. And true to the one-upmanship required of a great Las Vegas hotel, it added a roller-coaster: thrill-seekers step into its cars inside the casino and ride outside, rising over 20 storeys as it circles the main tower before dipping low over the *porte cochère*, traversing several loops and returning to the casino and safety.

Form follows fantasy

The spires of the 'Empire State' and 'Chrysler' buildings (their pinnacles contain the luxury suites reserved for high-roller gamblers) rise out of a collage of other skyscrapers – most recognizable, although each has been altered with brighter resort colours or scaled down. But these are not individual buildings at all; the 47-storey room tower is a standard concrete frame structure with post-tensioned slabs. But where the geometry of a typical concrete frame office or hotel is usually simple, NYNY's surface and skyline are carved and articulated to mimic the appearance of the skyscrapers of Manhattan. The floor plate's edge is angled and jagged to give depth and definition to what on the exterior appear to be separate vertical structures, each with its own surface material.

FACTFILE

Area	7 ha
Cost	$460 million
Ground floor	704 sq. m
Rooms	2034

Around the base of the tower, the casino forms a separate low-rise steel-framed structure. As the foreground for the replicated skyscrapers, its exterior is designed to imitate older New York landmarks, including Grand Central Station, the Whitney Museum and Ellis Island; a free-standing Brooklyn Bridge becomes part of the sidewalk path. At the corner rises a half-scale copy of the Statue of Liberty, surrounded by spraying harbour fire boats, made of carved styrofoam covered in a mesh and fibre coating.

Two design firms collaborated on the design. The architect is Gaskin & Bezanski, who provided the architecture and oversaw the structure and exterior. The realization of the hotel's overall image, including the all-important casino, is the work of Yates-Silverman, an established Las Vegas firm specializing in interior design. They created the scenographic environment of intentionally aged Greenwich Village brownstone façades in the casino's food court, scale reproductions of the signs of Times Square, and details such as manhole covers with steam rising from them.

NYNY is a miniature city in more than its appearance: 1500 people work here daily on round the clock shifts; over 100,000 people come and go every day as hotel guests, convention-goers, gamblers, or for entertainment at the restaurants, showrooms and lounges. Circulation becomes critical with such huge numbers of people and vehicles. The main public vehicle entry is on Tropicana Boulevard, with arriving taxis, cars, shuttle vans, valet parking, baggage handling and limousines. A separate entry on the other side of the building services tour buses bringing large groups of people to the hotel and casino.

After a century of 'form following function' in architecture, NYNY represents a shift: now form follows fantasy. Its design is governed more by a romanticized New York as pictured in dozens of movies than the design criteria of traditional modern architecture. Yet the complex functions of greeting, pleasing, directing and serving tens of thousands of people are still provided for. The mirage of Manhattan in the desert becomes a very practical public building that responds with deep understanding to the culture it serves.

The London Eye

Time: 1999   Location: London, England

There is an innate desire in all men to view the earth and its cities from 'exceeding high places', to feel the pleasure of beholding some broad landscape spread out like a brightly coloured carpet at their feet.
HENRY MAYHEW, 1862

As an attraction, a skyline-breaking landmark and a public-pleasing feature of many a World's Fair or Pleasure Gardens, the Ferris Wheel, to give it its generic title, has enjoyed continuous popularity for the last century and a half. Observation wheels of various designs have also been celebrated in art, most famously in Carol Reed's film of Graham Greene's novel *The Third Man*, in which a critical scene takes place on the Riesenrad in Vienna's Prater.

The latest – and largest – addition to this select circle is the British Airways London Eye, also known as the Millennium Wheel. At 135 m (443 ft) tall, it is the world's highest observation wheel, rotating with a maximum of 800 passengers for a circuit of some 30 minutes, high above the heart of London. On a clear day the view extends for 40 km (25 miles), as far as Windsor Castle.

In its first year of operation (2000) the London Eye succeeded in attracting over three million passengers, and it is likely to remain on its site on the South Bank of the Thames, facing the Houses of Parliament to the northwest, long after its temporary five-year planning permission has expired.

Created by the husband-and-wife team of David Marks and Julia Barfield, the London Eye was first conceived by its architects in 1993, as their response to an open competition promoted by *The Sunday Times* and The Architecture Foundation in London for ideas for new structures to celebrate the Millennium. What amounts to a large new 'building' on this site of national importance and sensitivity required a public consultation process of unusual length and complexity, but Marks and Barfield won a strong consensus that the structure should go ahead. It

Sixteen wheel sections were floated upstream on the Thames and then assembled, before being raised to the vertical.

The central spindle was cast in the Czech Republic and its bearings machined in Germany.

was also seen to have value as a catalytic element in the regeneration of the South Bank, with the additional attribute of continuing the tradition of innovative structures in this quarter which began with Powell & Moya's 'Skylon', the landmark of the 1951 Festival of Britain just east of the London Eye site in Jubilee Gardens.

Innovative design

From the outset of the design process, Marks and Barfield were determined to introduce significant technical innovations in the hitherto standard configuration of a Ferris Wheel, which had changed little in a century. Most crucially, rather than being suspended as in a ski-lift, each of the 32 passenger capsules, 8 m (26 ft) in length and 4 m (13 ft) in diameter, is supported on the rim of the wheel by two ring bearings and fitted with a mechanical drive stability system to keep the capsule floor constantly level. This design avoids the problem of swaying and allows maximum visibility from within, unimpeded by structure. Protected by this patented stabilization system, the capsules are formed of three layers of laminated and curved, optical-quality glass with the minimum of framing members.

The London Eye was raised slowly in stages – the heaviest lift to date.

Outstanding views over and across the capital – the main selling point of the London Eye – were also enhanced by the early decision to support the wheel from the landward side only, with just three points of contact with the ground in Jubilee Gardens. To ensure a smooth and safe ride, various damping devices were built into the design and a new form of boarding platform was devised to allow easy entry to each capsule as it moves round and begins its upwards journey. Relative movements in the wheel's structure due to thermal expansion and wind forces are also taken into account.

Construction of the London Eye became a genuine example of European co-operation. The capsules were built by a ski-lift specialist in France, while their laminated glass panels were shaped in Italy. The 23-m (75-ft) long, 335-tonne central spindle and hub was cast in the Czech Republic and the steel rim and the 310-tonne 'A'-frame legs supporting the whole structure were fabricated in the Netherlands using steel from Britain. Finally, the bearings keeping the Wheel turning smoothly were made in Germany.

Quite apart from the necessity for all the parts to be manufactured to demanding tolerances and then fit smoothly together, individual components, such as the 16 sections which together

form the rim of the wheel, were problematic in terms of their sheer size – 8.5 m (28 ft) wide, over 6 m (20 ft) deep and 22 m (72 ft) long, as well as their weight – 36 tonnes each. Other challenges were posed by such logistical factors as the need to find a road route for the capsules from the factory in Grenoble to Zeebrugge, their port of embarkation, avoiding all bridges on the way because the loaded transporters turned out to be higher than French motorway bridges.

Because the Thames is a fast-flowing, working river, sailing the rim segments under the low headroom of Southwark Bridge, with clearances reduced to as little as 40 cm (15 in), required particular expertise. The whole rim and 'A'-frames were assembled flat on the water and then raised into place – the heaviest such structure ever lifted from the horizontal. The erection process was not without incident; the first attempt to raise the Eye saw failure of a cable mount, followed by postponement. But on the second attempt, it rose smoothly from the Thames into the sky.

Once the wheel had been raised and secured, the drive mechanism and the capsules were installed in turn. What had begun as an architect's visionary design had become a stunning landmark shining white in the London sunshine.

From the top of its rotation, the London Eye offers spectacular views over London – at night too.

FACTFILE

Height	135 m
Weight (wheel+capsules)	2100 tonnes
Circumference	424 m
Total capacity	800 people
Time to revolve	30 minutes
Cost	£75 million

Bridges, Railways & Tunnels

Rivers, seas, mountain ranges or canyon depths – such natural barriers represent obstacles to the free passage of people and trade, which economic imperatives insist must be overcome. Existing geography seldom presents easy solutions or an unimpeded right-of-way for modes of transport such as railways, where gradients need to respect mechanical limitations. Meeting the challenge of forging new transport links has always called for vision and dogged determination of the highest order.

These imperatives can range from ending the lucrative transit monopoly enjoyed by 400 Thames ferrymen by building the Thames Tunnel, breaking through the long legacy of Anglo-French rivalry by promoting the Channel Tunnel, or taking the bold decision to build the Brooklyn Bridge when the freezing over of New York's East River in the winter of 1866/67 halted all ferry traffic. Pressures for new links may also be starkly political. Witness the young Province of British Columbia's insistence that a transcontinental rail route – what was to become the Canadian Pacific Railway – be completed within ten years of their signing the treaty of Union. As a further incentive to signature, the CPR was seen by politicians and promoters as a powerful agent in the opening up of the Canadian West, bringing in new settlers and stimulating rising land values as the railway spikes were driven in.

The construction challenges posed by the Forth Rail Bridge were immense: it was the first cantilever bridge in the United Kingdom and the first to be built of steel rather than iron.

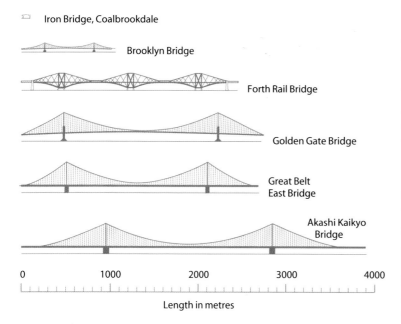

Iron Bridge, Coalbrookdale

Brooklyn Bridge

Forth Rail Bridge

Golden Gate Bridge

Great Belt
East Bridge

Akashi Kaikyo
Bridge

0   1000   2000   3000   4000

Length in metres

Diagram to show the comparative lengths of bridges.

Railway building brought its own particular challenges, both in the design of routes and in the logistics of construction. Work was often strictly seasonal, as in the case of Switzerland's Jungfrau Rail System, where the requisite materials and food for the workforce had to be in place before the onset of snowfalls. Huge workforces were needed: up to 12,000 men were required to forge a passage for the Canadian Pacific Railway through Kicking Horse Pass, and 70,000 to build the Moscow Metro during the 1930s. Gradients acceptable to high-speed trains have meant that tunnels needed to extend far beyond the obstacle above – a full 54 km (33.5 miles) for the Seikan Tunnel to link two islands a mere 23 km (14 miles) apart at their closest point. The Channel Tunnel also goes to earth some distance inland from the coasts of Britain and France.

Great bridges are the most visible and consistently memorable of engineering feats. Their sites are fully exposed to the elements, frequently inaccessible and yet they have to be built while maintaining a clear channel for vessels to pass beneath, as was the brief for the Akashi Kaikyo Bridge with up to 1400 ship movements below it each day on Japan's Inland Sea. The builders of San Francisco's Golden Gate Bridge were faced with a site directly fronting the Pacific Ocean, 19 km (12 miles) from a major earthquake fault and buffeted by gale-force winds, while the geology and tidal regime in the Firth between Edinburgh and Fife prompted the designers of the Forth Rail Bridge to devise a form of cantilever construction which did away with the need for temporary supports and allowed construction to proceed outwards from each pier before the central spans were lowered into place.

While bridge builders in France could draw upon the researches of their École des Ponts et Chausées, British designers proceeded initially by trial and error. Structures such as the Iron Bridge, spanning the Severn in Shropshire, despite being built of iron, owed much to the traditional assembly techniques of timber construction. A century later, Sir Herbert Baker, the designer of the Forth Rail Bridge, was able to credit its success to the 'resolute application of well-tested mechanical and experimental results'. Innovation has continued to this day, with bridge structures exploiting advances in metallurgy and the results of wind-tunnel testing to achieve once undreamt of clear central spans as part of structures which safely bend and flex in response to the enormous natural forces bearing upon them.

The construction of these huge bridges has spanned nations and continents. The steel towers of the Golden Gate Bridge were fabricated in Pennsylvania and shipped to site via the Panama Canal; the casting yard for the concrete components of the Great Belt East Bridge in Denmark lay over 70 km (43.5 miles) from the bridge site, and the steel girders for its deck travelled from rolling mills in Italy and Portugal.

What does not change in the history of these structures, railways or tunnels is the epic endurance of those who saw them through. The great engineer Marc Brunel worked for periods of up to 20 hours a day beneath the Thames in his tunnel, and Washington Roebling contracted 'caissons disease', or 'the bends', while overseeing the foundations of the Brooklyn Bridge. Those who promoted and engineered the structures described here have all been driven by the pressures of time, cost and the high public visibility of the projects to which they committed so much of their professional lives.

The Iron Bridge, Coalbrookdale

Time: 1779 Location: Telford, Shropshire, England

*There are few places where rural prospects and scenes of hurry and Business
are so happily united as at Coalbrookdale.*
LOCAL IRONMASTER, QUOTED BY ASA BRIGGS, 1979

By modern standards, the Iron Bridge across the River Severn at Telford in Shropshire is tiny – hardly 30 m (100 ft) in its span and rising a mere 15.35 m (50 ft) above the water. Yet this single structure, more than any other, exemplifies the revolution in constructional techniques made possible by developments in ironmaking which drew contemporary visitors from around the world to the Coalbrookdale Company, founded by the greatest ironmaker of his age, Abraham Darby I.

Today, visitors to this dramatic and densely wooded stretch of the Severn Gorge are rewarded by the prospect of a bridge supported on an elegant set of parallel arches – now reserved for pedestrians but until the 1950s still

The Iron Bridge provided an essential crossing between the settlements on both banks of the River Severn.

Iron developments

Iron had been used as a construction material in the form of minor components such as tie-rods, cramps and hinges, but brick, stone and timber continued to predominate well into the 19th century. The manufacturing innovations pioneered by Abraham Darby from the foundation of his company on its present site in 1708 helped transform the small castings and blacksmith's works into the engineering iron elements of the early 1800s which were, in the estimation of the structural engineer and historian James Sutherland, 'effectively new materials, mass produced on an industrial scale'.

The key to these developments was Darby's successful smelting of iron with coke instead of charcoal in 1709. Cast iron is coarsely granular in texture, as brittle as chalk yet strong in compression and readily cast. Modern applications of cast iron on the scale of the Iron Bridge include the external structural nodes which help to support the Pompidou Centre in Paris (p. 156).

The prime mover for the Iron Bridge was another owner of ironworks, John Wilkinson, also dubbed 'Iron-Mad Wilkinson' because of his energetic promotion of the material – he wore an iron

used by motor vehicles – high enough to allow the passage of vessels on the river below. Two centuries earlier, the Iron Bridge's setting was not so peaceful; furnaces roared, the hillsides seemed to be aflame and a veritable Vulcan's forge had been created in the shadow of the bridge.

Top *In his painting* Coalbrookdale by Night *(1801), Philip de Loutherbourg depicted forges at work – perhaps the arches for the Iron Bridge had been cast in them.*

Above *Elias Martin clearly depicted the method of construction of the bridge: the main arch frames were erected before the stone abutments were built.*

Right *The Iron Bridge had to be high enough to allow vessels to pass beneath.*

hat, designed boats made of iron and was buried in an iron coffin. It appears that the idea of a Severn bridge was put before the ironmaster by Thomas Farnolls Pritchard, the Shrewsbury architect and bridge designer, in 1773, and Wilkinson then drew support from other local industrialists.

Structure and innovation

The bridge consists of masonry piers set into each river bank, and across the central, clear navigation span the bridge deck is supported by a set of five parallel arches of cast iron. Almost semicircular in profile these are linked sideways to each other by a filigree of smaller structural members. Each arch was cast in two halves, a process which, in 1778, required Abraham Darby III to extend his Old Furnace. The manufacturing process was rationalized, relying on casting a very limited number of different components. Tried and tested assembly techniques were used, such as interlocking joints and wedges rather than direct bolt connections between the cast iron elements.

A recently rediscovered watercolour overturns the hitherto accepted sequence of construction. It now appears that the main arches were erected first, and the masonry abutments later. This new theory was successfully tested by building a half-scale model.

Unlike France's engineers of the same period, who were massing a corpus of knowledge of the performance of engineering structures through specialist educational establishments, manufacturers/constructors in the mould of the Darbys made progress – or failed to do so – by more empirical means. Their designs, however, did reflect architectural fashions both in their broad lines and in detailing. The circular rings in the spandrels of the central arch serve an undoubted functional purpose as well as pleasing the eye.

The sequence of erection was undertaken with great care. It required a mere 12 weeks to place and connect up the roughly 378 tonnes of cast iron components forming all the elements of the arches – a process simplified by the limited number of individual types. In this respect the Iron Bridge anticipates modern standardization, but the bridge's immediate legacy was limited.

FACTFILE

Length	30.6 m
Height above summer river level	16.75 m
Main ribs x 5	
length	21 m
weight	6 tonnes
Cost	
estimated	£3200
actual	£6013

Manufacturing techniques in cast iron continued to be refined by the Coalbrookdale Company throughout the 19th century and their products were notable exhibits at the 1851 Great Exhibition in Hyde Park. Yet it was the new breed of distinguished British engineers such as Thomas Telford, George and Robert Stephenson, and the Brunels, father and son, who seized upon the potential of the newly improved cast and wrought iron to build structures of hitherto unattainable dimensions.

The Iron Bridge remains as a landmark and the centrepiece of the extensive Ironbridge Museums complex, a UNESCO World Heritage Site and an important tourist destination.

Five parallel arches of cast iron, linked sideways by cross members, carry the bridge deck above. The circular ring was both functional and decorative.

The Thames Tunnel

Time: 1825–43   Location: London, England

Never was an honour [knighthood] more richly deserved, for without the tunnelling shield allied to the dauntless courage and tenacity of purpose of Marc Brunel, the work would never have been completed at all.
L. T. C. ROLT, 1970

A cross-section of the Thames Tunnel, heading towards Rotherhithe, with the shield visible at the right. On the left are the access shaft and engine house.

Few engineering projects have sprung from a more pressing need, a stronger commercial imperative and such straightforward, dogged determination to resolve the deficiencies of geography. By the start of the 1800s, over 4000 horse-drawn wagons and carts were crossing London Bridge over the River Thames every day, and nearly 400 watermen plied their lucrative ferry trade with passengers and goods. A secure and permanent crossing of the river in the form of a tunnel through its bed to avoid impeding the passage of vessels above had become an attractive if totally unknown prospect for investors. The consulting engineers would have to construct the world's first underwater tunnel.

FACTFILE

Length	356 m
Cost	£468,249
Workforce	2 shifts of 16 hours per day, 36 miners on each

A Thames crossing from Limehouse on the north bank to Rotherhithe on the south was actually begun – and substantial progress made – by the Cornish engineer Robert Vazie, succeeded by Robert Trevithick, also Cornish and one of the most notable engineers of his generation. But on the night of 26 January 1802, disaster struck – the tunnel roof collapsed, over 300 m (1000 ft) from the safety of the vertical shaft on the north bank, and with it the Thames Archway Company, the promoters of the venture. Trevithick proposed an alternative approach which involved coffer dams driven into the river bed. Within the relatively dry trench thus formed, cast iron tunnel sections could be laid, but this idea also foundered in the soft Thames mud.

Enter Marc Isambard Brunel, born in 1769 to a French family of tenant farmers in Gissors, Normandy, and subsequently, as a refugee from the French Revolution of 1789, City Engineer of New York. By the time he settled in Britain, Brunel had already proved himself a prolific inventor, with numerous patents to his name and contracts for his block-making machines from the Royal Navy at Chatham Dockyard.

His response to the challenge of a Thames tunnel seems to have been inspired almost incidentally by his experiences at Chatham. The best solution to a bored underwater tunnel through variable strata, he surmised, would be to imitate the action of the shipworm, *Terado navalis*, whose counter-rotating jaws could bore a precise circular passage through the hardest of ship's oak, forming a rigid tunnel lining as it went from its own hardened excrement. Brunel transformed this concept into his patent for a Great Shield, which he later described in an address to the Institution of Civil Engineers as 'an ambulating coffer dam travelling horizontally'.

The Great Shield

As initially patented by Brunel, and refined by Rennie and Company for the final assault on the Thames, the Great Shield was a mechanical device consisting of a cast iron, vertical frame with sections which allowed 36 miners standing on three tiers or platforms to excavate the working face by hand in a controlled sequence. Each miner stood in a compartment facing wooden planks which they removed one by one, digging away the soft mud behind and replacing

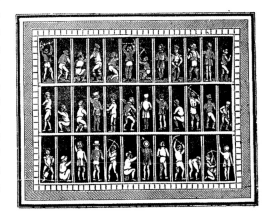

A contemporary diagram of the tunnelling shield, with a workman in each of the compartments.

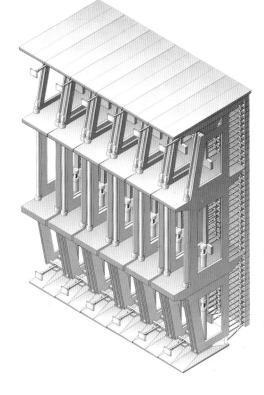

Brunel's invention of the Great Shield was the key to building the Thames Tunnel. It enabled faster progress to be made by a well-organized workforce of tunnellers.

A design proposed by Brunel for the south-side Tunnel entrance, with sweeping pedestrian staircases.

Below *Sir Marc Isambard Brunel, in a portrait by Samuel Drummond, c. 1835. In the background are various objects related to his inventions and projects, including a picture of the Thames Tunnel.*

the plank. As the Shield moved slowly forward, bricklayers followed close behind to form the tunnel lining, almost 1 m (3 ft) thick, bound together with Roman cement. In the course of development, Brunel's original circular tunnelling shield evolved into a rectangular assembly of frames, each 6 m (19 ft) high and 1 m (3 ft) wide, giving access to a large area of excavation face.

What proved to be the crucial difference between Marc Brunel's original patent for the Great Shield and the version actually put to work under the Thames was the omission, for cost reasons, of the diaphragm. This was to have served the vital function of supporting and sealing off that section of excavation between the face of the Shield and the completed brickwork following behind. Without this protection, in the uncertain strata through which the tunnel proceeded, periodic inundation of the works was inevitable, leading at one point to a seven-year hiatus, during which Marc's son Isambard, later to eclipse the fame of his father as an engineer of genius, was to despair of its successful completion.

The personal toll on both the Brunels was daunting. Marc himself would spend up to 20 hours a day for periods of nine days or more down in the tunnel workings; Isambard combined intensive site responsibilities at Limehouse with his own nascent engineering career and family life.

The Thames Tunnel, begun in 1825, was completed in 1843. In that year, on 26 July, it was graced by a visit from the young Queen Victoria and her consort Prince Albert. And in the first 15 weeks after its opening it attracted over one million paying customers. Marc Brunel was subsequently honoured with a knighthood and enjoyed a well-deserved retirement until his death at the end of 1849.

In 1865 his beloved tunnel was adopted by the East London Railway, and it continues to this day to serve passengers on the London Underground. Brunel's brickwork is as firm as ever, but commuters may find it hard, during their brief transit, to visualize the tunnel as the one-time venue for uproarious candlelit dinners of the Tunnel Club, with the Brunels acting as hosts.

Brooklyn Bridge

Time: 1869–83   Location: New York City, United States

The bridge could never have been built by mere knowledge and scientific skill alone….
The faith of the saint and the courage of the hero have been combined in the
conception, the design and the execution of this work.
HON. ABRAM. S. HEWITT, AT THE OPENING OF THE BRIDGE ON 24 MAY 1883

The Brooklyn Bridge, built by father and son, is the product of revolution: a repressed liberal uprising in France and Germany in 1830 that led to John Roebling's emigration to America in 1831; the American Civil War, in which John's son, Washington, was a colonel; and the Industrial Revolution, which in many ways is epitomized by the Roeblings and by the Brooklyn Bridge.

John Roebling was educated in engineering, architecture and philosophy in Berlin, but on arriving in America he established a farming community. Realizing the frugal limitations of this life, he returned to engineering, becoming a civil engineer on the construction of the Pennsylvania Canal. Here he noticed how unreliable were the hemp ropes used to haul barges up inclines. Recollecting a German article on wire ropes, he set up a rope walk on his farm and manufactured the first wrought iron wire rope in America.

Roebling's graduation thesis had featured a suspension bridge in Bavaria, and in 1844 he

Brooklyn Bridge originally carried pedestrians, horse-drawn vehicles and a short tramway over the East River. In the foreground of this view of around 1883 is the New York end-station, near City Hall Park.

made a proposal for a suspended canal across the Allegheny River. Four more followed before he was commissioned, in 1851, to build the Niagara Falls Rail Bridge, and, in 1856, the Ohio Bridge in Cincinnati. The Civil War interrupted the building of the Ohio Bridge, which was not finished until 1866. Roebling's son Washington played a significant role in this project, a working relationship recalling that of Isambard Kingdom Brunel and his father Marc on the Thames Tunnel (p. 216).

Schemes for a bridge

The idea of a bridge between New York and Brooklyn had been suggested on a number of occasions, but until the completion of the Cincinnati Bridge the scale of the undertaking had been considered impractical. The East River was a turbulent tidal strait, full of shipping traffic, so the roadway would have to be high enough to give the necessary clearance for the masts of sailing ships. The economic justification for the project was underlined in the winter of 1866–67 when the East River froze, blocking all ferry traffic. The following summer, a state bill incorporating the New York Bridge Company was passed, and on 23 May John A. Roebling was appointed chief engineer.

Roebling's proposal was for a suspension bridge with a central span of 486 m (1595 ft), 50 per cent greater than the Cincinnati Bridge – the longest yet built. Many doubted its feasibility and it was two years before the designs were approved and construction started. Weeks later, in the course of surveying the site, John Roebling injured his foot. This did not cause much concern at the time but, through his stubborn disregard of doctors' advice, it was to lead to Roebling's death from tetanus a few weeks later. He was 63.

His son Washington now inherited the project. He was well prepared. Not only had he worked on the Cincinnati Bridge and been educated at the Rensselaer Polytechnic Institute (America's first school of civil engineering), he had also been sent to Europe to study caisson construction. While the feasibility of the bridge had been established by his father, the detail and its construction were to become the work of Washington Roebling.

Sinking the foundations

As in so many engineering projects, much of the effort and innovation is hidden. The sinking of the caissons and the excavation of the foundations for the 82-m (268-ft) towers that support the bridge were in themselves tasks of such heroic and unprecedented scale that is still hard to appreciate them.

The caissons were huge airtight boxes built of timber and iron, open at the bottom so that labourers could dig out the riverbed. Like great ships, the caissons for both piers were constructed in dry docks, launched and then towed

Washington Roebling was one of the pioneers of caisson development. This simplified diagram shows many of the grabber arms, dirt chutes and other equipment, which were the first to be built into such an underwater structure.

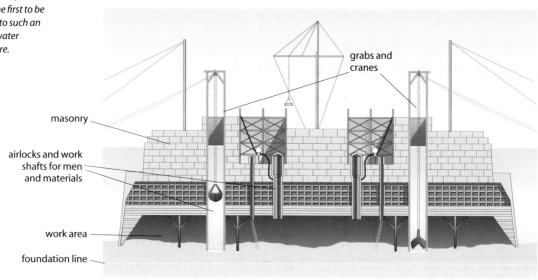

grabs and cranes

masonry

airlocks and work shafts for men and materials

work area

foundation line

Apart from a church spire in Manhattan, the towers of Brooklyn Bridge were the tallest structures in New York at the time. In 1877 a wooden-slat footbridge was suspended between them and opened to the general public – ladies were advised not to cross.

to their sites. They were weighted down with layers of stone and sunk at their appointed positions. Material at the base of the caissons was excavated, allowing them to settle inch by inch to their final position. By pumping air into the caissons, the working space within was pressurized and the water kept out; an air lock enabled workers to get in and out. Shafts were constructed through the masonry that built up progressively on top to remove excavated materials and deliver the components of the concrete that would eventually fill the caisson and form the foundation of the granite towers.

The whole operation was not without considerable risk and exceptional discomfort, though there was no shortage of labour. On one occasion, a blow-out of the air within the caisson threw a column of rock and water over the neighbourhood and caused the caisson to settle dramatically, but fortunately not out of line. On another occasion, a labourer using a candle to look for his lunch-box set fire to the caulk in a joint of the massive timber structure. Air leaking out drew the fire into the caisson timbers. Despite many days fighting the fire, the project could only be saved by flooding the caisson completely.

For the New York caisson this problem was avoided by lining the inside with tin.

The pressures inside were so high that it was impossible to whistle, and as the caisson sunk deeper the workmen were to experience a problem that had first been noted on James Eads' Bridge in St Louis. Caisson's disease, or 'the bends' as it was nicknamed, was a disabling, often fatal disease that struck some of the workmen soon after leaving the pressure chamber. We now know that it is caused by nitrogen bubbles in the blood or tissues. A company doctor observed that the problem was the result of over-rapid decompression and got close to understanding how it could be prevented when he noted that the

FACTFILE

Central span	486 m
Total length (including approaches)	1825 m
Height of roadway above river	41 m
Height of towers	82.6 m
Cables	40 cm diameter
Cost	$9,000,000

The famous elevated walkway takes pedestrians right into the lattice of the hanger ropes and inclined stay ropes – which John Roebling had designed to be strong enough to hold up the roadway in the absence of the main cables.

wife Emily became both interpreter and emissary, and only a few of his most able assistants had contact with him. Despite this, he orchestrated in absolute detail the construction of the bridge, watching progress from his bedroom window through a telescope. His bridge was the world's first steel-cable suspension bridge and pioneered a series of details and techniques that were to become standard solutions for future bridges.

Principal among these was the system of spinning and anchoring the four great suspension cables. These each contained 5282 galvanized steel wires bound into 19 strands arranged to form a cable 40 cm (15.75 in) thick. Each of the strands in a finished cable is in fact a continuous wire, 298 km (185 miles) long, that was repeatedly drawn out from one anchorage, between the masonry towers, down to the other anchorage and then back. At the anchorages the cables were fixed to huge iron chains tied to four cast iron anchor plates embedded in the granite. The same system can be seen on the Golden Gate Bridge (p. 234), built 60 years later, and the Great Belt East Bridge, Denmark (p. 244). In addition to these great suspension cables, a series of steel ropes radiates from the towers, anticipating the technology of contemporary cable-stayed bridges.

The bridge in fact comprises two bridges, with an elevated walkway down the centre between the two carriageways. From clamps around the main cables, steel ropes suspend trusses that support the deck. These ropes develop a variable grid pattern with the inclined stay ropes, giving the bridge much of its aesthetic character. Along the centre, the trusses were twice the depth of the perimeter trusses because of the additional load of the trams that the bridge was designed to carry on its inner carriageways.

symptoms abated when men re-entered the chamber. He even suggested that a pressure capsule be built above ground for the treatment of the afflicted workmen. Roebling himself was not immune, developing the illness through a punishing work schedule.

Despite being near to physical collapse, Roebling persisted, working on the New York caisson, where he agreed to found the pier on the hard sand layer rather than taking it further down to rock and risk exposing the workers to greater pressures and the bridge company to further expense and delay. Over 2500 people had worked to sink the two sets of foundations over two years.

Innovations in bridge-building

Both sets of foundations were complete by July 1872. At this point, exhausted and ill, Roebling withdrew to his house on Brooklyn Heights. His

The ribbon to open the bridge was cut on 24 May 1883, when over 150,000 people and 1500 vehicles made the crossing. It was a great event, with businesses and schools closing for the day.

Six lanes now carry modern traffic and the outer trusses have been extended and strengthened with the addition of an upper level. Hangers and stays have been replaced, but the bridge remains essentially as the Roeblings conceived it.

The Canadian Pacific Railway

Time: 1871–87   Location: Montreal to Vancouver, Canada

All I can say is that the work has been done well, in every way.
CORNELIUS VAN HORNE, CRAIGELLACHIE, 7 NOVEMBER 1885

For the new Confederation of Canada, formed in 1867, an urgent need was to expand its transport links. This was to be achieved by the building of a trans-continental railway, for which there was much support. In particular, British Columbia, isolated on the Pacific Coast, insisted that it should be connected to the rest of Canada by rail if it was to join the fledgling state. This bargain was struck in 1871; the aim was to start work within two years, and complete it within ten. An early government survey concluded that it was possible, but difficult, and the exact locations of the mountain crossings remained essentially unresolved.

Early progress was modest, but in 1881 the Canadian Pacific Railway was formally incorporated. As the immediate prospects of a return on capital were far lower than the anticipated social benefits, the project was heavily supported from government funds. The 1126 km (700 miles) already completed or under construction were handed to the CPR, along with $25 million in cash. In addition the CPR was granted over 10 million ha (25 million acres) of land, divided into parcels of 260 ha (640 acres). The aim was to give the CPR a source of profit, and to encourage the railway to attract immigrants to the west. This, it was argued, would increase the value of all the land and create railway traffic.

Above *A train passing the Kicking Horse Pass Monument, marking the Continental Divide; this was one of the greatest challenges to be overcome in the entire route of the railway across the continent, shown in the map (right).*

Yet engineering costs were going to be unavoidably high. Men and materials had to be paid for and transported great distances, and hazards included 320 km (200 miles) of granite rock

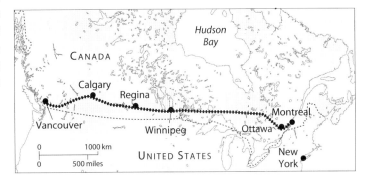

The task accomplished: the ceremony of 'driving the last spike' took place at Craigellachie, Eagle Pass, in the Rocky Mountains, on 7 November 1885. The very final stretch of the railway to Vancouver opened in 1887.

and treacherous bog north of Lake Superior. These could have been avoided by a route further south, but this would have taken the railway into the United States. Such difficulties had to be overcome while virtually no revenue accrued to the company.

The right manager was essential. An American of Dutch descent, William Cornelius Van Horne, was appointed General Manager of the CPR at the age of just 38. It was his amazing display of energy and tenacity which was to see the project through to completion. Construction began in 1882, with 13,050 km (900 miles) of track needing to be laid within ten years.

To general astonishment, Van Horne declared that the first 800 km (500 miles) would be laid by the end of 1882, and that the whole railway would be complete by 1887. Floods prevented

him from reaching his initial target, but 670 km (418 miles) of track were laid.

Crossing mountains

The question of the crossings over – or through – the Rocky and Selkirk mountains still had to be faced, and Major A. B. Rogers was dispatched to find a route. It took him one-and-a-half years to achieve this task, and he chose Kicking Horse Pass across the Rockies and what was to be named Rogers Pass in the Selkirks. Meanwhile, the prairie section to Calgary was finished by August 1883.

But finances were precarious, time was precious and economies were urgently needed. Very steep gradients restrict the haulage ability of locomotives and may require extra safety measures. To avoid the need for tunnelling at Kicking Horse Pass, however, a 13-km (8-mile) stretch of line was built at a gradient of 1 in 22. Named the Big Hill, this had to do; it was later replaced by two spiral tunnels.

Again in the Selkirks, a less than ideal surface route was adopted, and avalanche shelters were required. This was replaced in 1916 by the Connaught Tunnel which lowered the summit of the line by 164.6 m (540 ft) and shortened the route by 7.25 km (4.5 miles).

The spring of 1885 saw an uprising in Manitoba; Van Horne put the as-yet incomplete railway at the disposal of the military and the rebellion was crushed in four days. After that, how could the Government refuse the CPR another, and final, loan? The Great Lakes section was finished that same year.

Completion was within reach, and the rails met at Eagle Pass. The last spike was driven at a ceremony at Craigellachie on 7 November 1885. The Canadian Pacific opened to traffic with a train from Montreal on 28 June 1886. It reached the outskirts of Vancouver on 4 July. The final 20-km (12-mile) link to Vancouver itself opened on 23 May 1887.

The distances in Canada are huge and the scale of the work was immense. Building the CPR was one of the great epics of railway construction, for which Van Horne, its creator, was knighted by Queen Victoria in 1894.

FACTFILE

Distance, Montreal to Vancouver	4700 km
Height of Kicking Horse Pass	1628 m
Workforce on Kicking Horse Pass	12,000

The Forth Rail Bridge

Time: 1882–90   Location: Firth of Forth, Scotland

*The merit of the design, if any, will be found not in the novelty of the principle underlying it,
but in the resolute application of well-tested mechanical laws and experimental results.*
SIR BENJAMIN BAKER, 1941

The Firth of Forth bridge is one of the great monuments of 19th-century British engineering. Before the bridge was proposed, however, the problems of developing a reliable and secure method of crossing the Forth had exercised the minds of some of the greatest names in engineering. A re-design of the ferry system and proposals for tunnels were produced by John Smeaton (1772), Hugh Baird (1807), John Rennie (1809), Robert Stevenson (1817) and Thomas Telford (1828), among others.

By the early 1800s, bridge design was considered the solution by forward-thinking minds. Various schemes were considered and rejected

An icon of both Scotland and 19th-century engineering, the Forth Rail Bridge is still the second longest bridge of its type.

before Parliament intervened in 1865 and authorized the North British Railway and its engineer Thomas Bouch to construct a crossing over the Forth. Bouch, also the designer of the Tay Bridge, proposed a suspension bridge with twin spans of 488 m (1600 ft). Construction began on the scheme in 1878 but was halted following the Tay Bridge disaster of 28 December 1879, in which 75 railway passengers were swept to their death when the central spans collapsed in a gale. A year later, Bouch's Forth Bridge design was rejected.

The cantilever principle

New proposals emerged from Sir John Fowler, W. H. Barlow and T. E. Harrison. The design was based on the 'continuous girder principle' – essentially a continuous girder with definitive breaks at chosen points of contraflexure. The original proposal was modified by Fowler and his junior partner, Benjamin Baker, to the form we know today.

Speaking to the Royal Institution in 1887, Baker described the cantilever principle:

'Two men sitting on chairs extend their arms, and support the same by grasping sticks which are butted against the chairs. There are thus two complete piers, as represented in the drawing above their heads. The centre girder is represented by a stick suspended or slung from the two inner hands of the men, while the anchorage provided by the counterpoise in the cantilever end piers is represented here by a pile of bricks at each end.

'When a load is put on the central girder by a person sitting on it, the men's arms and the anchorage ropes come into compression.

'The chairs are representative of the circular granite piers. Imagine the chairs one-third of a mile apart and the men's heads as high as the cross of St Paul's, their arms represented by huge lattice steel girders and the sticks by tubes 12 feet in diameter at the base, and a very good notion of the structure is obtained.'

The first modern cantilever had been built in 1867 by Heinrich Gerber across the River Main at Hassfurt in Germany, with a central span of 130 m (425 ft). Named after him, cantilevers were initially called Gerber bridges. In the United States, the earliest bridge of the type was built in 1876 by Charles Shaler Smith over the Kentucky River, and in 1883 a notable cantilever bridge was built over the Niagara River by C. C. Schneider. This was the first to be called a cantilever.

Building the bridge

The construction challenges posed by the Forth Bridge were immense. The spans necessary were almost four times as large as any railway bridge previously built in the United Kingdom, which as yet had no cantilever bridges. Also, steel, the proposed material, was considered relatively untried for bridge applications. From the mid-1800s most railway bridges were of cast iron, although steel could offer a 50 per cent increase in maximum working stresses, clearly a great attraction with long spans. Safety was a primary concern after the Tay Bridge disaster, which had been caused by high winds. A new wind loading of 56 lb per sq. ft (previously 10 lb per sq. ft) had been imposed and the Board of Trade stated that the bridge: 'should gain the confidence of the public, and enjoy a reputation of not only being the biggest and strongest, but also the stiffest bridge in the world'.

The human model used by Benjamin Baker to demonstrate the cantilever principle to the Royal Institution in 1887, with a diagram to show the forces at work.

The construction of the colossal spans was a tremendous task that was undertaken by William Arrol of Glasgow, who had also worked on the massive new Tay Bridge. Initial site work involved building the support piers. No special difficulty arose with the work executed either in tidal conditions, or in half-tide or full-tide cofferdams. Each of the three main towers is supported on four separate granite foundations, constructed within iron caissons 21 m (70 ft) in diameter. The caissons were founded at depths varying from 4.25 m (14 ft) to 27 m (89 ft). A delay was caused when one of the caissons accidentally tilted and, through a combination of very high and low tides, sank unevenly into the mud. It took ten months before it was refloated and sunk again in the correct position.

FACTFILE

Overall length	2465 m
Maximum span	521 m
Height of towers	104 m
Height above river (high tide)	46 m
Steel in superstructure	50,000 tons
Rivets	6,500,000
Workforce (maximum)	4600
Cost	£2½ million

By 1887, the year of Queen Victoria's Golden Jubilee, the core of the towers had reached their full height and it remained to extend their arms towards each other and close the gap. It was the task of constructing the cantilever sections that

The design of the bridge minimized the need for temporary support structures during construction, as is graphically shown in this photograph.

The Forth Rail Bridge is still in use today; the enormity of the task of building it can be fully appreciated from this view from the top of one of its towers.

fully demonstrated the practicality and buildability of cantilever design. Because construction takes place by building out from one support to the next, no temporary support structure is needed. This dramatically reduces the amount of material required and the time taken. All the steel superstructure, which used large riveted tubes for the compression members, was fabricated on site.

In September 1889, a bridge worker clambered from the Queensferry to the central Inchgarvie cantilever across a ladder placed between crane jacks, working some 60 m (200 ft) above the water. On 15 October a more secure and formal crossing was made, and by 6 November the central girder was ready to be connected. This was delayed for over a week until the temperature changed sufficiently to cause the necessary expansion that would allow the key plates to be driven in and the girder fixed between its supporting cantilevers. The bridge was opened by the Prince of Wales on 5 March 1890 and is still in use today. It held the world record for a cantilever bridge until 1917.

Not only is the Firth of Forth Rail Bridge still in use today, it is also a structure that will continue to inspire generations of engineers. And how long might such a monument last? 'Forever if you look after it' according to the Firth of Forth Bridge Engineer in 1890.

The Jungfrau Rail System

Time: 1896–1912   Location: Bernese Oberland, Switzerland

The Swiss landscape is beautiful, but it is not the ideal terrain for the building of railways.
SWISS TRANSPORT MUSEUM GUIDEBOOK, 1987

The mountains of Switzerland have long been a major tourist attraction: who could stand in the small town of Interlaken (567 m (1860 ft) above sea level) in the Bernese Oberland, and fail to be impressed with the mountains which surround it? Access is another matter. To reach the pass of Kleine Scheidegg (2061 m/6760 ft) it is necessary to take first one and then a second rack railway. The Wegneralp Railway had been opened to this point in 1893; to this day, there are no roads at all at this altitude, and access is exclusively by train or on foot. It is thus the railway which transports all construction materials, as well as supplies for the hotels and cafés.

Kleine Scheidegg was seen by Adolf Guyer-Zeller, a Zurich engineer, as the ideal point from which a railway could ascend further towards the mountain peaks. Together with the Eiger and the Monch, the Jungfrau is the third of the peaks dominating the area, all around 4000 m (13,000 ft) high. This was in 1893.

Guyer-Zeller's spectacular creation, the metre-gauge Jungfrau railway, starts out from Kleine Scheidegg in the open and turns quickly towards the mountains. For the first 2.2 km (1.4 miles) it climbs steadily along the ridge to Eigergletscher (at 2320 m/7600 ft), where it enters the main

tunnel. The remaining stretch of 7.1 km (4.4 miles) to Jungfraujoch is completely underground.

Construction work started in 1896, and Eigergletscher was reached by 1898. This was to serve as the base during construction, and is still the site of the line's only workshop. An immediate problem was its inaccessibility during the winter months; all the required materials had to be in place before the snows of winter, including food

In order to climb the 1393 m to the Jungfraujoch (altitude 3454 m) from Kleine Scheidegg, the line had to wind across the mountain; the maximum gradient is 25 cm per metre. Much of the route is in a tunnel, though two stations on the route allow passengers to disembark and enjoy the spectacular views.

The railway was planned to be powered by electricity from the beginning – steam trains could not run through the tunnels. Capacity has steadily increased: more than 4000 passengers are carried up to the Jungfraujoch on the busiest days.

for the workforce. Even water is a problem, since it takes 14 litres of snow to produce 1 litre of water, for which electricity is also required.

The railway was designed to be electric from the beginning, and the pair of vehicles are powered from the overhead line. Throughout, the railway is fitted with the Strub rack system, in which steel teeth on the track engage pinion wheels, or cogs, in the vehicles. This enables steeper gradients to be climbed in safety – a maximum of 1 in 4 in the case of the Jungfraubahn. Even at this gradient, the railway cannot take a direct line inside the mountain.

Electric drills were used to cut the tunnel through malm, a hard mountain limestone; no tunnel lining was needed. At Eigerwand (4.4 km/ 2.75 miles; 2865 m/9400 ft) a platform and passing loop were constructed. But, equally importantly, a lateral tunnel was built to the edge. From this, a magnificent panorama of the mountains of

central Switzerland is visible, from behind solid plate glass. Trains on the upward journey stop here to allow passengers to disembark and admire the view. Blasting created most of this complex and the station was opened in June 1903.

Next stop is Eismeer (5.7 km/3.5 miles; 3160m/ 10,368 ft), where passengers again disembark to view, this time close to the ice and a different set of mountains. There is a passing loop here, too. The railway was opened to this point in July 1905, the builders having taken seven years to reach it from Eigergletscher.

In the long final section to Jungfraujoch (9.3 km/5.7 miles; 3454 m/11,300 ft) the malm gives way to gneiss, a much harder rock. A change was made to the more powerful pneumatic drills, but progress was considerably slowed. The air was also becoming more rarified. An additional problem was the disposal of the excavated waste; for this a horizontal passage was blasted about 3 km (2 miles) beyond Eismeer station.

The opening of the last section of line from Eismeer, up to and including the terminus, took place on 1 August 1912. This lies on the snow- and ice-covered saddle between the Jungfrau (4158 m/ 13,600 ft) and the Monch (4099 m/ 13,450 ft). Although the station platforms are below ground level, a hotel and other facilities are immediately above, in the open, and there are many walks possible for those suitably equipped. Welcome to the highest railway station in Europe, whose terminus is permanently above the snow line!

FACTFILE

Height of Jungfraujoch station	3454 m
Height of Kleine Scheidegg	2061 m
Distance Kleine Scheidegg to Jungfraujoch	9.3 km
Journey time	c. 50 mins
Maximum gradient	25%
Tunnels	2

The Moscow Metro

Time: 1931 onwards   Location: Moscow, Russia

The thousands of people crowding the platforms day and night went crazy with delight.…
It was difficult to believe that one was beneath the soil of Moscow.
ALEXEI DUSHKIN, ON THE OPENING OF THE MAYAKOVSKAYA STATION, 1938

Cities all over the world discover that movement within them becomes increasingly difficult as they expand. Put simply, there is just not enough space on the surface to cope with large commercial buildings, high levels of economic activity, dense populations and the huge volumes of traffic which result. Road traffic is always a problem, whether it be horse-drawn or internal combustion. While Moscow makes use of trams and trolleybuses as well as buses, moving

Mayakovskaya Station, designed by Alexei Dushkin, is unusual in being completely Art Deco in style.

arrangements for connections between the lines were made, so that interchange was relatively painless. The first section to be opened was that from Sokolniki in the northeast to Krinskaia Place in the southwest, with a branch to Smolensia Rinok. The work was carried out under the personal direction of Nikita Kruschev, who later achieved greater fame as the Soviet leader. At its peak, Metro construction was estimated to have employed as many as 70,000 men.

Methods of construction

Tunnel building was carried out using two methods. One was cut-and-cover, which consists of digging a huge open trench, building the station platforms and laying the track, and then covering the work over. The other is deep construction, using access shafts and a tunnelling shield to join up the shafts at low level, thus creating the railway. In both cases, the construction teams had to contend with a mixture of loams and limestone, but also quicksands which brought the very real risk of flooding. There was also the winter cold. Spoil was brought to the surface and dumped, usually by wheelbarrow, but had to be removed before it froze solid.

Decoration

Perhaps the main claims to fame of the Moscow Metro are its monumental scale and the elaborate decoration of its stations, at least on the earlier parts of the system. On descent by escalator to platform level, the traveller enters a wide concourse between the platforms, which sometimes incorporate statues. The walls are clad in marble, usually pink but sometimes black. Lighting is provided by chandelier, and heroic sculptures, mosaics, paintings, carvings and decorative plasterwork adorn the walls.

The platforms themselves are wide and straight, stretching to a generous 150 m (490 ft) in length. This is a quarter as long again as usually found in London. Moscow's trains were equipped with four pairs of double doors, on each side of each vehicle. In short, the whole was designed to impress visitors to Moscow, whether they were from overseas or from the provinces.

Mosaic panel in the ceiling of the Novokuznetskaya Station, begun during the Second World War but not finished until 1978. It is by Alexander Deinaka, and depicts the Soviet construction industry.

as many people as possible by underground railway is very effective.

Moscow was fairly late in constructing its first underground railway, which was begun under the communist regime. The city council had discussed the idea as early as 1900, but the combined opposition of the Russian Imperial Archaeological Society and the Archbishop of Moscow, who both feared the effects of tunnelling on the foundations of churches and other buildings, ensured that no progress was made.

Yet the traffic problems did not diminish, and a planned Metro scheme was sanctioned in 1931. Broadly, this consisted of a series of a dozen radial routes, linked in pairs to provide for journeys from one side of the city to the other. Extensive

FACTFILE

Overall length of system	262 route km
Workforce	70,000
Metro stations	160
Metro cars	4218
Employees	34,000

Later construction included a belt, or Circle, line. This intersects all the radial lines at about 5 km (3 miles) from the centre of Moscow, meaning that many journeys can be made without entering the central area. It also joins seven of the city's nine railway termini. Completed in 1954, 'the architectural and artistic motifs were devoted to the military glory of the Soviet people in the Great Patriotic War and their peaceful creative toil', according to a 1985 publication celebrating the half century of the undertaking. The system continues to expand. Today, around 3.2 billion passenger journeys are made each year on Moscow's Metro, a city of 9 million people. This makes the Moscow system the busiest in the world, easily exceeding Tokyo, Mexico City and Seoul. Next comes New York with just 1.2 billion, then Paris and Osaka. London appears as number eight on this list, with 930 million passengers, although numbers are rising fast.

Komsomolskaya Station of 1952, one of the most lavish of all the stations. The architects were V. Kokovin, A. Zaboltnaya and A. Shchusev, the designer of Lenin's Mausoleum.

The Golden Gate Bridge

Time: 1933–37   Location: San Francisco, United States

… the largest bridge of its kind ever attempted, with the tallest steel towers ever erected, the longest, largest cables ever spun, and the most enormous concrete anchorages ever poured.
JOHN VAN DER ZEE, 1986

Extraordinary natural obstacles stood in the way of the construction of the Golden Gate Bridge at the entrance to San Francisco Bay. The site is within 20 km (12 miles) of a major earthquake fault and directly fronts the Pacific Ocean. Seismic loads, tidal waves, ocean currents and gale-force winds placed unprecedented demands on both substructure and superstructure. Yet, completed, its span of 1280 m (4200 ft) between towers, was larger than any suspension bridge in the world at the time.

Joseph Strauss, the chief engineer, had only a modest amount of formal engineering training but acquired extensive practical knowledge of bridge design and construction by working for the New Jersey Steel and Iron Company before setting up his own bridge design practice. He was joined in the design team by Charles Ellis, a professor of engineering at the University of Illinois, and by Leon Moissieff, designer of the Manhattan Bridge over the East River in New York.

The final design illustrates how bridge engineering had progressed over the previous 20 years. Discoveries regarding the measurement and distribution of wind loads were integrated in the design, which was also influenced by advances in metallurgy and the drawing and spinning of cables. The old generation of rigid and solidly functional bridges was giving way to a new generation characterized by flexibility and elegance.

A view of the Golden Gate Bridge looking south towards San Francisco. The engineers had to take into account the possibility of earthquakes and gale-force winds in building this elegant structure.

FACTFILE

Total length	2740 m
Longest single span	1280 m
Height of towers	225 m
Cost	$27 million

The piers and anchorages

The construction of the bridge was not for the faint-hearted. The steel towers – each weighing around 22,200 tonnes and sustaining 61,500 tonnes force from the cables – soar 150 m (500 ft) above the roadway, which is itself 75 m (245 ft) above the water. Foundations for the towers reach 34 m (110 ft) below mean water level.

The founding of the San Francisco tower pier was one of the most complex construction problems encountered. The site was in virtually open sea and a concrete fender had to be built to act as a cofferdam within which the pier could be built. The construction below water level of a space the size of a football field was a tremendous feat. First, explosives were used to excavate the rock on which the pier was founded; these were dropped down a tube and timed to detonate automatically. This was hazardous work, as was the erection of the construction trestle that stretched from shore to pier site 335 m (1100 ft) away. Storms, tides and shipping accidents all delayed progress.

When the fender ring was completely sealed, 20 m (65 ft) of concrete was placed under water to form the base. The water was pumped out, leaving an oval cavity in which labourers set to work. To ensure that the ocean floor was strong enough to support the load, engineers inspected the rock base using shafts in the concrete to visit eight dome-shaped steel chambers 4.5 m (15 ft) wide on the ocean floor. After they pronounced it satisfactory, the inspection shafts and chambers were pumped dry and concreted.

The rock formation on the Marin side was quite different. Here, cofferdams were installed to provide a dry base from which the sandstone and shale could be quarried to expose firm rock for founding the tower's pier. In some parts, drilling and blasting went on over 10 m (33 ft) below the water level outside the cofferdam before a sufficiently solid foundation was encountered.

Excavation was also underway at the hillsides for the anchorages for the cables that hold the bridge up. These exert a pull of more than 280,000 kN, and to withstand the enormity of this force each anchorage was built in three interlocking blocks, ascending like steps.

The towers

The steel towers were the largest and highest in the world, making fabrication a challenge. The tower legs were made up of plates and angles, shop-riveted to form a cellular design. To check for straightness and accuracy of manufacture, 60 per cent of one tower leg was riveted together at the fabrication shops in Pennsylvania. Because of its size, this was done outdoors. It was then dismantled and sent by rail and ship through the Panama Canal and up the Pacific coast.

The towers were set on 19 base plates, each 125 mm (5 in) thick. Each section was hoisted into place by a giant movable crane that climbed

Constructing the piers and towers for the bridge: the cranes lifting the sections of the towers rose with the structure.

along with the tower. Every piece was assembled, inspected and, if not perfect, ground to fit. Rivets were heated by coal forges set on scaffolds outside the tower, and sent via a pneumatic tube to be fitted into a hole and forged into place.

The work was stressful and dangerous. Riveters worked both inside and outside the tower, often in poorly ventilated semi-darkness. The noise was terrific and many suffered from the fumes of the red lead paint given off when the hot rivets hit the painted sections.

The cables

With the towers complete, the cables to suspend the bridge decks could be strung; these were supplied and installed by the Roebling Company. From the anchorage on each shore, steel wire was reeled into place and gathered into strands that were then splayed out and anchored through eyebars to the shore. Each cable comprised over 25,000 wires in 61 strands, which were bunched together and compacted using hydraulic jacks.

At the top of each tower a saddle was installed on giant bearings to allow flexibility as the tower and cables responded to changes in stress and temperature. This was bolted in place after the cables had been strung. The effect of temperature on the long cables was visually evident in their relative tautness in the early morning and greater sag by midday. Grooved bands were clamped around each cable along its length so that the wire suspender ropes could be fitted. From these paired suspenders was hung the steel structure to support the roadway, which grew outwards from the towers.

Both cablers and steelworkers were grateful for the safety net, which was used here for the first time on a major construction project. It saved 19 lives, but on 17 February 1937, just months before the completion of the project, the net broke when a platform being used to strip wooden forms from beneath the road bed fell, killing 10.

The project was still completed early. The final coat of International Orange paint was applied and the bridge opened on 27 May 1937: 200,000 pedestrians crossed it before it was taken over by vehicles. It has remained an icon of bridge design.

Left *One of the two giant open portal towers that hold up the bridge. At the time the Golden Gate Bridge was built, these were the largest and highest in the world.*

Opposite above *Spinning the cables from which the bridge is suspended: the cable passed from the anchorage on the shore, over the towers and back again in a continuous loop.*

Opposite below *The steel decks for the bridge were assembled in sections and were attached outwards from the towers.*

The Seikan Rail Tunnel

Time: 1964–88 Location: Honshu to Hokkaido, Japan

We have now realized the people's dream to connect Honshu and Hokkaido by land.
TRANSPORT MINISTER SHINTARO ISHIHARA, ON OPENING THE SEIKAN RAIL TUNNEL, 13 MARCH 1988

Because of the great length of the tunnel, safety precautions were of paramount importance. This is one of two emergency tunnel stations which would allow passengers to be evacuated from a train in case of fire.

Water barriers between separate islands of the same nation represent a particular inconvenience. Japan consists of four principal islands: Kyushu, Shikoko, Honshu (with the capital Tokyo) and Hokkaido. In the 1930s, there had been plans to link them by rail using the high-speed 'bullet' trains – the Shinkansen concept.

To join Hokkaido and Honshu across the Tsugaru Strait it was decided to build a tunnel, though this was never going to be an easy task. The narrowest distance between these two islands is 23 km (14 miles), but the hilly nature of the terrain of each, combined with the requirement for trains to run on reasonable gradients,

meant that any tunnel had to be a great deal longer – over twice as long in fact.

The approach gradients of the Seikan are built at 1 in 85, with a gentle 1 in 330 in the underwater section. To minimize problems of seepage, the running tunnels for the trains are 100 m (330 ft) below the sea bed, which itself is 140 m (460 ft) below sea level at its deepest point. This is twice as deep as the Anglo-French Channel Tunnel. The result is that the Seikan is the world's longest and deepest railway tunnel.

Geology and tunnelling

Surveys showed that geological conditions were not at all favourable. Investigative works from 1964 on involved the excavation of inclined shafts from each side and a start on the horizontal pilot tunnel between them. This was not holed through until early 1983, a full 19 years after this part of the project began. Reports showed that the tunnel would have to be bored through badly faulted granite. The rock contained water-filled fissures which had to be sealed, or 'grouted', by spraying concrete at great pressure, and the tunnel reinforced with steel where necessary. Tunnel-boring machines could not be used in this situation, and tunnelling was moved forward by explosives and drilling.

Construction of the tunnel works proper began in 1972. It was always expected that it would take seven years to complete; in the event, it took nearly twice as long. Undetected faults in the rock and extensive flooding were early

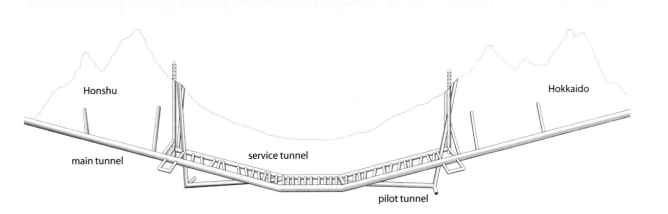

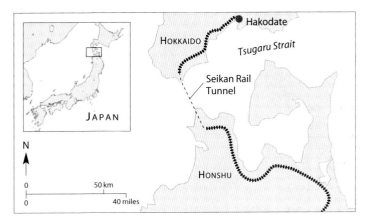

problems. Four major flooding incidents took place, each delaying work. Flooding still deposits earth and sand in the tunnel, which has to be cleared. Extensive and continuous pumping, right from the earliest construction, has been needed to keep the tunnel dry.

The main running tunnel for the trains was built for double track – both the Shinkansen and and narrow gauge – within a single bore of 11.3 m (37 ft) diameter. In addition to this, in the underwater section there are also the original pilot tunnel, which houses two pumping stations, and a service tunnel. A series of passages between the running and service tunnels were built for escape and rescue.

Safety measures

Two tunnel 'stations' have also been constructed for the evacuation of passengers from a train in case of fire or in other major difficulties. The running tunnel at these points is equipped with sprinklers. In such an event, passengers would be led to the service tunnel and then proceed through a fire shelter to a sealed air lock. This is at the base of the inclined shaft used in construction. These shafts now form the forced air ventilation intake, as well as a passageway for maintenance, escape and rescue. They are supplemented by vertical shafts, used to remove exhaust air (and any smoke) from the tunnel. Heat detection systems guard against train fires, and the whole of the tunnel operation is overseen from a control centre at Hakodate.

Tunnelling was completed in 1985. It took three years to fit out and complete the connecting lines before the tunnel opened to rail traffic on 13 March 1988. Although it was designed and built to Shinkansen standards, the necessary connecting lines have not been constructed and only narrow gauge track was laid. Air travel between the two islands has also taken passengers away from the rail system, but nothing can detract from the achievement of building the Seikan tunnel.

The Seikan tunnel between Hokkaido and Honshu consists of the main running tunnel, the original pilot tunnel and a service tunnel. There are also numerous links between the tunnels for access and escape.

FACTFILE

Total length	53.85 km
Length underwater	23.3 km
Max. depth below sea level	240 m
Diameter of main tunnel	11.3 m
Cost	$7 billion

58 The Channel Tunnel

Time: 1987–94   Location: The Channel, Britain–France

What a cursed thing to live in an island! This step is more awkward than the whole journey.
LETTER FROM EDWARD GIBBON TO LORD SHEFFIELD, 1783

On 30 October 1990, an exploratory probe broke through the short length of ground between two tunnelling machines in the chalk beds below the English Channel. Britain was, in strict terms, no longer an island, and, at 51.5 km (32 miles), the world's longest underwater tunnel was almost complete.

The history of the project

Proposals for some sort of fixed link between Britain and France go back to Napoleon's time; indeed Napoleon himself looked favourably on the idea (although he changed his opinion in later years). In 1802, Albert Mathieu proposed a tunnel which was ventilated by chimneys and lit by gas

One of the massive and complex tunnel-boring machines seen passing through one of the crossovers. These were specially built for the project and each one cost £10 million.

lamps, although such a design is not technically feasible. In the 1880s short sections of a tunnel were built under Shakespeare Cliff, in England, and on the French side of the Channel. The promoter, Sir Edward Watkins, wined and dined VIPs underground to demonstrate how well the work was going, but the Government withdrew their support due to the British military's fear of invasion. Another initiative in 1974 was again scuppered by the British, who this time lacked financial commitment. Eventually, after Britain's entry into the Common Market (as the European Union then was), it was finally realized that a fixed link made commercial sense, and so in 1986 a contract was awarded to Eurotunnel, a joint Anglo-French consortium, to design, build and operate a tunnel with provisions for both a rail shuttle service for vehicles and for through trains for passengers.

It had always been clear that the tunnel would be designed for rail, rather than road transport. The longest Alpine road tunnel, the St Gothard, is only 16 km (10 miles) long, but approaches the limit for effective ventilation without intermediate vent shafts. Its length is also around the maximum which the average motorist can drive in a tunnel without becoming disorientated. A rail tunnel also has a much smaller diameter – compare the land-take of a railway with a motorway – plus the potential for accidents is greatly reduced.

Geology
A tunnel on the necessary scale would simply not have been possible had the ground conditions not been favourable. Ideally, tunnellers like a material which is consistent, requires little

FACTFILE

Tunnels	3, one in each direction for trains, plus service tunnel
Length	51.5 km, 37.5 km undersea
Depth	average 50 m below seabed
Diameter	running tunnels 8.2 m outer 7.6 m inner; service 5 m inner
Distance apart	30 m
Workforce	13,000
Cost	$15 billion
Passenger train time in tunnel	20 minutes

support in the short term, and has a low permeability to minimize water ingress. In all these respects, the chalk beds of the region, and in particular the Chalk Marl, presented an ideal tunnelling medium. As long ago as the 17th century, a writer had commented on the similarity of the chalk outcrops at Dover and Calais, but this was not confirmed until the geologists of the 19th century made palaeographic comparisons. The continuity of the chalk beds under the Channel was finally confirmed in 1959 by initial geotechnical investigations for the tunnel. Later, more detailed surveys established the level and thickness of the beds along the route. The aim would be to drive the tunnel through the Chalk Marl, maximizing the thickness of rock cover which could be obtained below the Channel.

After investigation of the geology of the Channel it was decided to excavate the Tunnel through the Chalk Marl bed as this was the most suitable medium. (The vertical scale of the diagram is exaggerated.)

The design

The 'tunnel' is actually made up of two running tunnels of 7.6 m (25 ft) diameter, which are 30 m (98 ft) apart, and a central service tunnel connected to them by cross-passages at 375-m (1230-ft) centres. The running tunnel diameter is the minimum which can accommodate a shuttle car carrying heavy goods vehicles, below overhead electricity supply cables. The service tunnel provides access to the main tunnels under both normal and emergency conditions, and allows a train to be evacuated, as the cross-passage spacing is linked to the train door spacing. It also acts as the fresh-air supply duct, being kept at a positive pressure in relation to the running tunnels to prevent smoke ingress. There are also two crossover points which mean that, should it be necessary, the trains can change tunnels.

The service tunnel was also designed to act during construction as a pilot tunnel, allowing ground conditions to be investigated more thoroughly in advance of the running tunnel drives. Pressure-relief ducts, at 250-m (820-ft) intervals, reduce the air pressure build-up due to the 'piston effect' of the trains travelling at speed through the long tunnels. There is also a cooling system to counteract the temperature rises caused by the fast-moving trains.

Constructing the tunnels

The tunnel-boring machines (TBMs) are complex and expensive (each one cost around £10

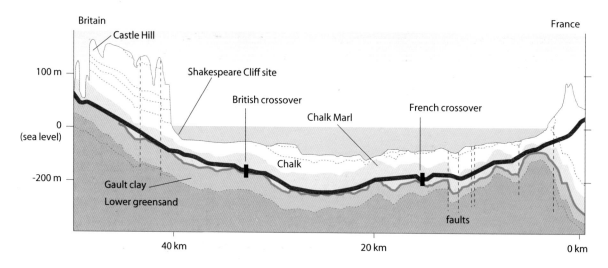

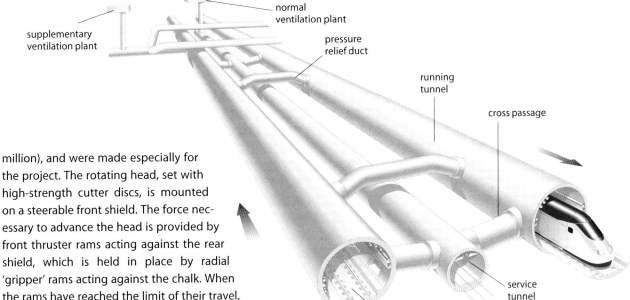

supplementary
ventilation plant

normal
ventilation plant

pressure
relief duct

running
tunnel

cross passage

running tunnel

service
tunnel

million), and were made especially for the project. The rotating head, set with high-strength cutter discs, is mounted on a steerable front shield. The force necessary to advance the head is provided by front thruster rams acting against the rear shield, which is held in place by radial 'gripper' rams acting against the chalk. When the rams have reached the limit of their travel, the grippers are withdrawn, and the rear shield moved forward by rear thruster rams acting against the pre-cast concrete lining segments. This cycle is then repeated. Initial progress was slow due to local ground inconsistency, but record progress was eventually achieved, with one TBM travelling 428 m (1400 ft) in a week.

Despite this, the overall programme could only be achieved if boring proceeded simultaneously from both sides of the Channel. The need for accurate control of the tunnelling operations was therefore paramount, both to keep the tunnel in the Chalk Marl bed, and, more stringently, to ensure that the two tunnels met accurately, despite the total tunnelling distance between the access shafts of 38 km (23.6 miles). This required the establishment of accurate base lines in each country, with their relative position established by observation of signals from overhead satellites. The base lines were then projected down the access shafts and along the tunnels by very accurate optical instruments. Observation of a target on the rear of the TBM allowed continuous monitoring and correction of its alignment. The final closing errors, after 38 km (23.6 miles) of 'blind' tunnelling, were 350 mm (under 14 in) horizontally, and an incredible 58 mm (2.3 in) vertically – an accuracy of 1 in 650,000.

From a start in December 1987, the combined length of the three tunnels, around 153 km (95 miles), had been driven in just $3^1/_2$ years. While this was a significant step, the tunnels were of little use without the installation of the track and overhead line equipment, drainage and the auxiliary services. The tunnel was finally handed over at the end of 1993, only three months behind the initial programme, with services starting running in the following year.

On 18 November 1996, a train carrying cars and lorries from France to England caught fire. It came to a halt 19 km (12 miles) from the shore and over 30 people were trapped. Fortunately, despite problems, the safety precautions built into the design worked and all the passengers escaped into the service tunnel. The fire was put out after six hours; the heat had been so intense that the train became partly welded to the tracks.

As well as being an astonishing technical achievement, the Channel Tunnel is a triumph of organization, since most of the work took place in confined spaces remote from the points of access. Equally, however, it represents an example of international co-operation, which overcame problems of language and custom.

Schematic diagram of the elements of the Channel Tunnel: the two running tunnels are on either side of the central service tunnel. Pressure-relief ducts and cross-passages are repeated along the length of the tunnel at intervals.

The Great Belt East Bridge

Time: 1988–98   Location: Zealand–Funen, Denmark

Beautiful to behold and excellently executed.
HM QUEEN MARGRETHE II OF DENMARK, ON THE INAUGURATION, 14 JUNE 1998

From the flat Danish landscape surrounding the Great Belt (Storebælt) – one of three straits linking the North and Baltic seas – the majesty of the East Bridge is clear for all to see. One of the largest suspension bridges in the world, the East Bridge is second only to Japan's Akashi Kaikyo Bridge (p. 248), which opened in the same year as the Great Belt Bridge, 1998.

The construction of the bridge, beginning in 1988, was an element of one of Europe's greatest engineering projects of modern times: a fixed link carrying a motorway and railway across the approximately 18-km (11-mile) wide Great Belt between Halsskov on Zealand and Knudshoved on Funen. The link would close the gap that had for so long existed in the Danish motorway and railway network.

The island of Sprogø connects the East Bridge, on the right, and the railway tunnels to the West Bridge (not visible). The portal for the railway tunnel is seen on the left.

Despite ferry services, which operated until 1998, the Great Belt had always been seen as a barrier to trade and communication – a view the new bridge seems to have borne out. Three years after its opening, traffic across the Great Belt has more than doubled. Currently an average of 21,500 vehicles cross the East Bridge each day.

Plans and designs

Although several projects for a bridge or tunnel link had been suggested over the years, none had got beyond the planning stage. In the 1980s, however, after years of deliberations, the Danish parliament finally approved the construction of a link. Due to a political wish to favour public transport, it was decided to complete the railway two to three years ahead of the motorway. This meant that two parallel, yet separate, links had to be constructed, one for the railway and the other for the motorway. In the event, flooding of the tunnel tubes halfway through the project caused serious delays and meant that the railway section could not be commissioned until one year before the inauguration of the road link.

In the middle of the Great Belt is the island of Sprogø. East and west of the island the water flow is virtually identical, but the main navigation route passes through the eastern channel. It was therefore decided that the motorway should cross the eastern channel on a high, suspension bridge with a wide span to allow shipping to pass below, while it would cross the western channel on a low bridge. The railway would cross the

eastern channel through a tunnel and run parallel with the motorway on a low bridge across the western. Sprogø had to be enlarged in order to form the link between the two bridges as well as between the West Bridge and the tunnel.

The construction of the East Bridge began in late 1991 following a three-year investigation and project design phase, during which a number of general requirements were defined. It was particularly important to determine the optimum length of the main span (the distance between the pylons or towers) across the eastern navigation channel.

Navigation simulations were carried out for a number of different designs with main spans ranging from 900 m (2950 ft) to 1800 m (5900 ft). The results showed that the span width had to be no less than 1600 m (5250 ft). Accordingly, a 1624-

m (5328-ft) span was selected, approximately 15 per cent longer than the world's largest existing suspension bridge span at the time, the 1410-m (4625-ft) Humber Bridge in Britain. To meet this requirement two tall pylons would have to be constructed. With a height of 254 m (830 ft) above

The principle of the suspension bridge allows for a light and elegant design, clearly illustrated by the East Bridge.

FACTFILE

Total length	6790 m
Suspension bridge	2700 m
Main span	1624 m
Side spans (2)	535 m
Height of towers	254 m above sea level
Cost	$645 million

Above *A steel bridge girder is lifted into position on two concrete pillars. One of the anchor blocks is visible on the left.*

Opposite *The two main cables rest on steel saddles on top of the pylons and carry the weight of the bridge deck through the vertical cables. Positioned some 275 m (900 ft) above sea level, the crane operator had a stunning view of the construction area.*

Right *During the spinning of the cables, two wire-mesh catwalks connected the anchor blocks, via the pylons.*

sea level, the East Bridge pylons exceed those of San Francisco's Golden Gate, the record holder for the previous 50 years, by around 29 m (95 ft).

Building the bridge
In almost all respects, the task confronting the contractors was an immense one. In addition to the large middle span and two side spans of 535 m (1755 ft) each, the design comprised 23 approach spans, 14 to the east and 9 to the west of the high bridge – in all adding up a total length of 6790 m (22,275 ft).

The East Bridge has a concrete substructure (caissons, pillars and pylons) and a steel superstructure (bridge girders and the cables carrying the motorway deck). About 40 per cent of the concrete casting took place at a site in Kalundborg; the concrete elements were then towed 70 km (44 miles) to the bridge site. The steel bridge girders travelled even further, from welding yards in Livorno and Taranto in Italy and Sines in Portugal, to final assembly in Aalborg, Denmark.

The classic suspension bridge design requires the main cables to be anchored deep inside large blocks at the end of side spans. For this bridge, a considerable effort was made to improve the anchor block design, which is often massive and dominating. The architects broke down the block into separate elements – triangular trestles for cable anchorage and a vertical pier shaft supporting the approach spans. The result is a surprisingly light construction, considering the forces it has to withstand from the pull of the weight carried by the two main cables.

The well-established air-spinning method, in use since the construction of the Brooklyn Bridge in New York (p. 219), was used to create the East Bridge's two main cables in situ. A cable strand with a thickness of only 5 mm (0.2 in) was pulled by a spinning-wheel riding on a temporary tramway erected along the alignment of the main cables. The spinning-wheel ran from one anchor block across the cable saddles of both pylons to the opposite anchor block and back again in one continuous loop. When completed, 18,648 parallel strands made up the 85-cm (34-in) thick, heavy, main cable, which is carried by the pylons and held in place by the anchor blocks. Vertical cables were then installed from the main ones, and the bridge girders were fastened to the vertical cables. Cable spinning of the two 3-km (2-mile) main cables for the East Bridge was completed in record time, just four months, in 1996.

In building the Great Belt, the combined endeavours of architects and engineers have created one of the most elegant bridges anywhere – a clean and deceptively light design which exemplifies the true principles behind the construction of suspension bridges.

The Akashi Kaikyo Bridge

Time: 1988–98   Location: Kobe to Awaji Island, Japan

… every new structure which projects into new fields of magnitude involves new problems for the solution of which neither theory nor practical experience furnish an adequate guide.
OTHMAR H. AMMANN, 1953

One of the most recent in a long line of structural engineering masterpieces, the Akashi Kaikyo suspension bridge is the continuation of the engineering leap that began during the Industrial Revolution. Suspension bridges take advantage of the superior tensile strength of steel and represent a radical change from the arch concept of bridges, based on the compressive strength of traditional structural materials such as masonry.

The spectacular Akashi Kaikyo Bridge is a fascinating case study in the overcoming of terrific natural forces and awe-inspiring structural exigencies. Spanning Japan's Akashi Strait between the city of Kobe and Awaji Island, the Akashi Kaikyo is now the longest suspension bridge in the world at 3910 m (12,828 ft), and lays claim to other titles as well.

It is ranked as the most expensive suspension bridge ever built ($4.3 billion), and the bridge with the longest centre span (1991 m/6532 ft) and highest towers (283 m/928 ft), almost as tall as the Eiffel Tower (p. 174). It is considerably longer than its two closest rivals, the Great Belt East Bridge in Denmark (p. 244) and the Humber Bridge in Britain, finished in 1981. Designed and built by the Honshu-Shikoku Bridge Authority over a period of ten years, in collaboration with many teams of Japanese consultants and building consortia, the Akashi Kaikyo holds pride of place in the vast building programme of the Authority, which has constructed 18 major bridges over the Inland Sea. This achievement also includes the Tatara Bridge, the longest cable-stayed span in the world.

Challenges

The designers and builders of the Akashi Kaikyo faced many challenges, both natural and structural, including poor supporting conditions. In addition, the severe weather in this part of the country presented problems of unprecedented magnitude for the design and construction of a bridge of this size. Typhoons and earthquakes are frequent, and rainfall averages 23 cm (57 in) per year. Testing carried out in a specially built wind-

Opposite and below *Currently the longest suspension bridge in the world, the Akashi Kaikyo Bridge is one of a series of major bridges built over the Japanese Inland Sea to connect the islands of Japan.*

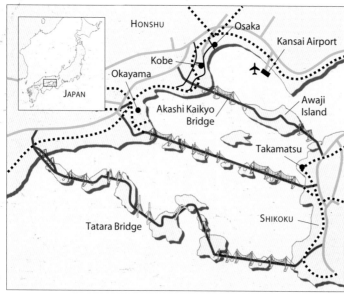

tunnel, the largest in the world, indicated the need for a vertical stabilizer in the form of a steel 'fin' located just below the bridge deck along the central line of the entire centre span in order to counter typhoon-level winds. There are also strong tidal currents in the strait.

Local history, in fact, includes a tragic impetus for the project: in 1955, two ferries sank in an attempted crossing of the strait during a storm, with considerable loss of life. Four decades later, this engineering wonder masterfully addresses the transport and safety concerns of the local inhabitants.

FACTFILE

Total length	3910 m
Length of main span	1991 m
Length of approach spans	960 m
Height of towers	283 m
Total length of wire in cables	300,000 km
Total cost	$4.3 billion
Steel used	200,000 tonnes
Concrete used	1,250,000 tonnes

Construction

A number of five-company consortia were organized for construction of the main elements of the bridge and approach tunnels. Construction entailed a decade of arduous site work, which began in May 1988 when an enormous reclamation project of the shallows was carried out near the anchorages for each end of the bridge. In 1989, huge caissons for the two central towers were floated and sunk, then filled with concrete. In 1992, tower erection began – the cells were fabricated on land, then carried by barge to the site and raised into position, where they were welded. The contractor teams had to accommodate an important economic factor: construction

Above *The foundations for the main towers consisted of prefabricated circular caissons. They were filled with a special new concrete that was manufactured and cast on site.*

Right *One of the huge anchorages at each end of the bridge. Built on reclaimed land, they represented a massive engineering challenge in themselves.*

Opposite, left *Newly developed high-tensile strength wire was used for the strands of the cables; this made it possible to have only two cables instead of the four originally intended.*

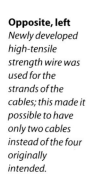

had to avoid disrupting the daily passage of more than 1400 ships through the strait.

For this reason also, a helicopter was used in 1993 to begin to pull aramid-fibre pilot suspension ropes. Once these were strung, a catwalk could be put in place; in order to maintain the 60-tonne tension needed for these ropes, special high-capacity winches were created. With the catwalk installed, the main cable could begin to be pulled across.

The long story of construction of the Akashi Kaikyo contains dramatic moments. In 1995, during construction, the 7.2-magnitude Great Hanshin Earthquake struck Kobe. The epicentre of the earthquake was a mere 10 km (6.2 miles) away, while the bridge had been designed to hold up against an 8.5-magnitude earthquake 150 km (93 miles) away. Miraculously, there was relatively little damage. While the foundations were intact, the anchorage and pier on the Awaji side of the structure had moved 1.3 m (4.25 ft) perpendicular to the centreline of the bridge. Steps were subsequently taken to adjust the truss members that support the deck, while all work on the bridge was halted for one month. The sections of the bridge were then put in place, starting from the towers and working in both directions. Despite having once again to avoid interrupting ship traffic, this work went so smoothly that the delay was made up.

Not surprisingly, a project of this magnitude featured a number of new concrete and steel technologies in its construction. The massive tower foundations used a newly developed silica

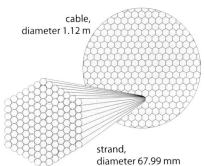

cable,
diameter 1.12 m

strand,
diameter 67.99 mm

maintenance
road

NTT
equipment

vertical stabilizer ('fin') open grating

maintenance
roads

water pipe

maintenance
road

Kansai Electric
equipment

fume concrete designed to avoid segregation under water. Another advance was a new admixture that obviated the need to vibrate the concrete used for the anchorages.

In addition, the cables benefited from a high-strength steel wire, used here for the first time, boasting a tensile strength of 1765 newtons per sq. mm, as opposed to 1570 newtons in the Authority's other bridges. This improvement meant that only two cables were eventually used instead of the four originally projected by the designers. Another innovation was the adoption of a prefabrication method to construct the cables, in which 127 wires were brought together into strands in the factory and then transported to the site, instead of adopting the usual spinning method.

Such striking technological advances were only one aspect of the design and construction of this magnificent structure. In pushing engineering to new limits by successfully confronting challenging site conditions, a devastating earthquake, typhoon-force winds and fierce currents in the strait, the designers, engineers and builders of the Akashi Kaikyo Bridge succeeded not only in creating the world's longest and most breathtaking span, but also an object of incontestable beauty.

Top *A section of the bridge deck being lifted into position.*

Above *Cross-section of the bridge deck, stabilized by the combination of the steel fin and open grating to cope with potentially typhoon force winds.*

Canals & Dams

Succeeding civilizations have put water to good use for transport, as a support for agriculture and even as a source of primary power. Our ascendancy over this element now includes engineering projects on a massive scale which harness and tame mighty rivers, open up new passages between seas or protect whole countries from the cataclysmic effects of inundation. These never fail to impress by their sheer size and audacity.

The statistics relating to such projects are on an equally impressive scale. Take, for instance, power generation. Giant artifacts such as the Hoover Dam can generate sufficient electricity to meet the needs of over 1.3 million domestic and commercial customers, while the Itaipú Dam can deliver 24 per cent of Brazil's and 95 per cent of Paraguay's power requirements, at the same time avoiding the output of 81 million tonnes of carbon dioxide emissions which would be produced by the equivalent coal-fired generating plants. Future prospects are yet more breathtaking, with China's Three Gorges Dam, now under construction on the Yangtze River, expected to supply over 10 per cent of that most populous nation's electricity.

What these water management projects can offer at their best is a truly all-embracing strategy for regional, even national regeneration. Cheaper electricity, secure supplies of fresh water, improved navigation for vessels further inland, millions of acres now under irrigation and security from flooding – these are the benefits most

Hoover Dam on the Colorado River: the benefits from this massive piece of engineering are many, including power generation, flood control and irrigation for farmland.

The spillway of the Itaipú Dam releases water from the reservoir behind the dam in a controlled though spectacular way, providing a vivid picture of the forces held in check.

Storm Surge Barrier in the Netherlands which, in addition to bringing security to a large part of the southwestern Netherlands, managed to add a new positive element to the land- and sea-scape. The Dutch government even changed the plan for this project in the course of its construction so that it was both less destructive of natural habitats and brought new opportunities for wildlife conservation and leisure facilities.

Great canals often slide through the landscape rather than transform it. More often the products of the last 200 years, especially the 19th century, these new water highways consumed in their making considerable quantities of men and money. Ferdinand de Lesseps' Suez Canal cost the lives of 125,000 of the 1.5 million labourers conscripted by the Egyptian government for the transit of 190 km (120 miles) from the Mediterranean to the Red Sea.

De Lesseps then turned his attention to the Isthmus of Panama and the challenge of forging over 80 km (50 miles) of canal through inhospitable jungle terrain and 26 m (85 ft) of level change between the Atlantic and the Pacific. Dogged by tropical disease and mounting debts, the de Lesseps venture foundered incomplete. It took the determination of Theodore Roosevelt and the US Corps of Engineers – and doctors – to drive the project through.

Both the Suez and the Panama canals continue to prosper as essential commercial links, but earlier projects such at the Erie Canal, which links the River Hudson at Albany with Lake Erie, proved vulnerable to mounting competition from the railways, which could offer faster and cheaper transit for goods. But the Erie route had served its initial purpose – New York eclipsed Boston, Baltimore and Philadelphia as the leading east coast port, and subsequent upgrading of the canal allowed larger vessels to use it.

The upgrading of canal networks such as those of Britain and France, parts of which date from the 18th century, has promoted a return to the waterways, albeit largely for recreational uses. In our age, it is rivers, rather than canals, which call for large-scale engineering projects to harness their huge forces for the good of mankind.

often cited by governments and politicians as the justification for new heights and widths of dam building.

If the economic and social gains flowing from such projects are laudable, their price, not merely in steel and concrete but in terms of existing communities, has sometimes proved high enough to give pause to their promoters. While the flooding of valleys to create dam-retained water reservoirs has been common engineering practice for over a century, the scale of resettlement required in the wake of the rising waters can be enormous. China's Three Gorges Dam, as an example, has caused the displacement of the population of some 19 towns and 326 villages, as well as raising the unanswered question of the potential build up of pollutants in the Yangtze upriver of the dam which are normally flushed out to sea.

At this scale, engineering becomes synonymous with regional ecology. Yet there are notable projects such as the Eastern Scheldt

The Erie Canal

Time: 1817–25   Location: Lake Erie to Hudson River, New York, United States

See! through thy streets, how Erie's waters come, Wafting the golden wealth of the great west,
And dashing down thy mountain, bear away a tide of plenty on to Hudson's tide.
NIAGARA DEMOCRAT, 1 NOVEMBER, 1843

A paradox of progress, the Erie Canal is not as much an engineering wonder as it is a socio-political event facilitated by engineering. Before roads or railroads, and triggered by the unforeseen demands of the war of 1812 against Britain, it became abundantly clear that Great Lakes' commerce from the interior of the young America needed a good connection to Atlantic trade.

On 4 July 1817, work commenced to build a canal to link Lake Erie at Buffalo with Albany, 480 km (300 miles) to the east on the Hudson River which was then navigable south to the city of New York. The date of 4 July was specially chosen because on that day in 1776 the American Congress approved the Declaration of Independence. On the very same day, in London, John Smeaton hung out the first ever sign proclaiming to the public his practice as being a 'Civil Engineer'.

Development of the canal

As early as 1792, the Western Inland Lock Navigation Company was incorporated to develop a canal from the Hudson River to Lake Ontario. In its first 10 years, a grand total of 3.2 km (2 miles) was built. Then, in 1808, Jesse Hawley published an essay advocating the feasibility of a canal west to Lake Erie. By 1811 a Canal Commission sought

financial aid from the US government and neighbouring states. The war of 1812 ironically quashed that plan, although it emphasized the need for the canal.

President James Madison vetoed federal funding for the project in 1817, but DeWitt Clinton (just elected New York's governor on the sole issue of the canal) authorized New York State financing, and added a spur to Lake Champlain, to bring in St Lawrence River shipping.

As planned and originally built, the Erie Canal was 12 m (40 ft) wide at the surface and 8.5 m (28 ft) wide at the bottom, with a depth of 1.2 m (4 ft). To accommodate the difference in elevation of 134 m (440 ft) between Lake Erie's surface and the Hudson at Albany, the system incorporated 83 locks to raise and lower cargo barges and passenger packets. Canal-lock technology was already well developed in 18th-century Europe

A map of the route of the Erie Canal, which stretched from Buffalo on Lake Erie to Albany on the Hudson River, which was then navigable to New York. The difference in elevation between the two towns was accommodated by 83 locks; the gradient was particularly steep at the Albany end, as shown in the diagram below.

and excavation was simply a matter of the number of men employed to move the earth. There is no real record of the total number of construction workers – thousands were hired locally as the digging passed through. Lines and grades were determined from an 1812 survey by James Geddes and Benjamin Wright, made easier by Simeon DeWitt's 1802 mapping of western New York.

Work began in 1817 on the middle section, which was relatively flat, and progressed in both directions simultaneously. In places aqueducts were needed, including one near Cohoes Falls 362 m (1188 ft) long. At Lockport in the west, a flight of five locks was constructed. Workers built bridges to carry foot and horse traffic; barges were hauled by mules trudging the marginal towpaths. In many places the clearance did not allow much headroom. Carl Carmer observed '… riders on the slow canal boats got many a bruised head from failing to heed the warning cry of the "hoggie" or mule driver, "Low bridge, everybody down".'

Quickly gaining in popularity and regarded as a triumph of art over nature, the Erie Canal made New York the predominant east coast port, superseding Boston, Baltimore and Philadelphia. When interior people became exuberant about being able to savour fresh oysters from the Atlantic in

FACTFILE

Length	495 km
Original width	12 m (surface) 8.5 m (bottom)
Original depth	1.2 m
Locks	83
Difference in elevation Buffalo–Albany	134 m
Cost	$7,143,000

under three days, a newsman from Batavia reminded them '… that Providence is the author of the ocean, and DeWitt Clinton the Projector of the Erie Canal'.

Enlargement and decline

In less than a decade the canal became too small for its traffic. Work began in 1836 to enlarge it to 21 m (70 ft) at the top and 16 m (52 ft) at bottom, and to a depth of 2 m (7 ft). The initial building cost, estimated at $6 million, was over $7 million. The enlargement was estimated at $23.5 million, but cost $36.5 million. A major economic slump, taxes and still more politics halted the enlargement project from 1842 to 1847. Then the Irish potato famine brought hordes of immigrants who became a copious source of cheap labour.

At about the time that President Abraham Lincoln issued his initial Emancipation Proclamation in 1862, the New York State Legislature declared the Erie Canal Enlargement Project complete. But by now the New York Central Rail Road, consolidated in 1853, was hauling more freight and passengers both quicker and cheaper. That brought about the bigger but already obsolescent N.Y. State Barge Canal.

Inevitably the same demands that created the need for the Erie Canal grew to outrun it. But from 29 October 1825, when the vessel *Seneca Chief* delivered a barrel of Lake Erie water to Governor DeWitt Clinton to pour into New York Harbour for the 'Grand Celebration of the Wedding of the Waters', the Erie Canal opened up the great American west for both the east coast and the rest of the world.

Syracuse, 1917, looking west on the enlarged Erie Canal system. Engine-driven barges had long replaced the mules, but the towpaths remain.

The Suez Canal

Time: 1859–69   Location: Mediterranean to Red Sea, Egypt

A pickaxe has just been swung in Africa, and the sound of it hitting the ground will resound the world over.
MONDE ILLUSTRÉ, MAY 1859

The need for a direct route from the Mediterranean to the Red Sea was first recognized in antiquity. In the 6th century BC the Egyptian pharaoh Necho began a canal link, and in the same century, during his invasion of Egypt, the Persian king Darius I ordered a canal to be cut from the Red Sea to the Great Bitter Lakes and a second canal from there to the eastern branch of the Nile Delta. Later, the Greeks and then the Romans are credited with re-excavating the channel on a number of occasions, but each time it became unnavigable and was abandoned. After the Arab conquest of Egypt it was again excavated and once more abandoned after some years. No further attempts were made for some time after navigation around Africa proved possible.

The idea of a short route to the east persisted, however. It resurfaced in 1798, during Napoleon's campaign in Egypt, though his engineers considered the idea to be impracticable, believing as they did that the Red Sea was some 9 m (30 ft) higher than the Mediterranean and that extensive flooding of Egypt would occur if the two seas were joined without numerous locks. Surveys proved this wrong, of course, and in 1854 the French diplomat and engineer Vicomte Ferdinand Marie de Lesseps convinced the Egyptian Viceroy that a canal was indeed practicable.

In 1858 La Compagnie Universelle du Canal Maritime de Suez was formed to cut a canal joining the two seas and to operate it for 99 years,

at the end of which ownership was to pass back to the Egyptian government. The Company was originally Franco-Egyptian, but Britain later bought the Egyptian shares.

Cutting the canal

The entire canal route across the desert is some 190 km (118 miles) long, of which several stretches run through or alongside natural lakes, including the Great Bitter Lakes which extend for about 35 km (22 miles). Around 60 m (196 ft) wide at the water surface and 25 m (82 ft) wide at the base, the canal was 8 m (26 ft) deep. In all, more than 35 million cu. m (1236 cu. ft) of excavation was required to complete the work.

A total of about 1.5 million Egyptians, provided by the government as forced labour, were engaged in cutting the canal, and more than 125,000 of them lost their lives. In those days, a team of seven labourers would excavate and move about 26 cu. m (918 cu. ft) of soil in a day; thus the labour force would have been fully engaged for the duration of construction. The soil was excavated by pick and shovel and then moved by hand or small barrow.

In 1859 work started on the main navigation canal and on a

Map showing the route of the canal from the Mediterranean to the Red Sea. With a total length of 190 km, the Suez is the longest canal without locks.

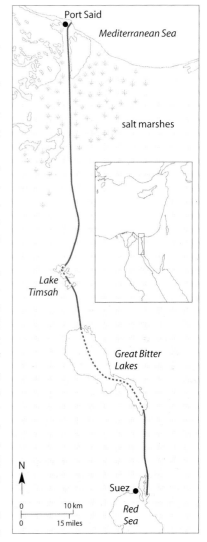

FACTFILE

Total length	190 km
Length through lakes	90 km
Original width	60 m (surface)
	25 m (bottom)
Depth	8 m
Workforce	1.5 million
Cost	£19 million

The Empress Eugénie in the imperial yacht Aigle *leads the flotilla of boats down the canal at its opening in 1869, while crowds of Egyptians line the banks.*

smaller canal parallel to it, designed to carry fresh water for the workmen and for the half-way port of Ismailia. By 1865, seven years after the start, a shallow canal capable of carrying a small boat had been completed. Two years later, in 1867, the canal had been widened and deepened to allow boats of up to 40 tonnes to transit across the desert. Later, machine dredging was used and this allowed the material removed from the canal bottom to be placed directly on the canal banks greatly speeding up the work. The canal was completed in 1867 and formally opened in 1869, 10 years after work started.

The cost of the canal amounted to almost £19 million, including interest charges during construction. This was more than double the original estimate. Later repairs and maintenance have cost three times that amount.

Inauguration

On 17 November 1869, the Suez Canal was officially inaugurated by Khedive Ismail in an extravagant ceremony. French, British, Russian and other royalty were invited and a highway was built linking Cairo to the new city of Ismailia, midway along the canal. In Port Said, an arsenal of fireworks assembled for the occasion accidentally blew up a few days before the opening, very nearly demolishing the town.

Four days of festivities were planned and 500 cooks and 1000 servants were imported from

Ships in convoy passing through the canal shortly after it opened. It was an immediate success and a great source of revenue for Egypt.

France and Italy to cater for the 6000 invited guests. The canal was blessed by Muslim, Greek Orthodox, Coptic and Roman Catholic priests and every available cannon and gun was fired, 20 military bands struck up, and through the drifting smoke of gunpowder the Empress Eugénie of France in the imperial yacht *Aigle* led the way into the canal. A smaller flotilla sailed from Suez and the two fleets met at Ismailia at sunset. Africa could now be considered an island. A banquet, a fireworks' display and a ball in the viceroy's new palace, illuminated by 10,000 lanterns, followed. The guests enjoyed the lavish festivities, unaware of the fact that the Egyptian national debt, which had stood at £3 million at Ismail's accession, had now, after construction of the canal, reached £100 million.

Later developments

Today the Suez Canal is 180 m to 200 m (590 to 656 ft) wide at water surface and 60 m (196 ft) wide at the bottom, and ships of 16-m (52-ft) draft and as large as 150,000 deadweight tonnes fully loaded, can make the transit at speeds of up to 13.5 km (8 miles) per hour. Most of the canal is limited to a single lane of traffic, but several passing bays exist, along with two-lane bypasses in the Bitter Lakes and elsewhere.

The Suez Canal is the longest canal without locks in the world, and third in length only to the St Lawrence Seaway in North America and the White Sea–Baltic Canal in Russia. It brings in nearly $2 billion a year in tolls, making it Egypt's third-largest source of foreign currency, behind tourism and money sent home by Egyptians working abroad. Nearly 15,000 vessels pass through the canal each year.

In the past, the Suez Canal's greatest strategic importance was its role in world trade. It transported 14 per cent of total world trade, 26 per cent of oil exports and 41 per cent of the total volume of goods and cargo that reach Arab Gulf ports. In recent times, as a result of tensions in the Gulf area, its importance has declined.

The canal shortens considerably the route between east and west – for instance, 86 per cent of the distance between the Saudi port of Jeddah and the Black Sea port of Constanza is saved if compared to the route round the Cape of Good Hope – this is equivalent to the distance between Tokyo and Rotterdam.

A ship traversing the Suez Canal today. Nearly 15,000 vessels still pass through the canal each year.

The Panama Canal

Time: 1907–14   Location: Colon–Panama City, Panama

*No single great material work which remains to be undertaken on this continent
is of such consequence to the American people.*
PRESIDENT THEODORE ROOSEVELT, 1901

*A diagram
showing the route
of the canal,
northwest to
southeast across
Panama, with sets
of locks near each
end to overcome
the difference in
elevation along
the route.*

In Panama the morning sun rises in the east over the Pacific Ocean; and sets in the west over the Atlantic. Westbound ships enter the Panama Canal from the Atlantic at Colon in the northwest and exit to the Pacific at Panama City in the southeast, after the 8-hour, 80-km (50-mile) transit, due to the fact that the isthmus connecting North and South America makes a reverse 'S' curve.

Hewn out of hostile earth a century ago, the Panama Canal has served the world longer than any other public work built on such a massive scale. It was a nearly impossible construction effort, but the largest engineering project ever undertaken was completed successfully, three years ahead of schedule. Its positive results have been enormous: transportation (military and commercial), and thus economics, politics and world order, were all enhanced. American civil and construction engineers, aided by medical pioneers, overcame every conceivable natural obstacle to complete the Panama Canal, without dispute the world's greatest construction accomplishment. Now, 100 years after it was built, the canal's capacity has essentially been doubled without interrupting service, constituting a second construction victory.

The French attempt

In 1552 Padre Francisco Lopez de Gomera published a book in which he identified Panama as the preferred site for a short cut from the Atlantic to the Pacific, avoiding having to sail around the whole of South America. It took nearly 350 years for construction technology to catch up, but in the first century of the canal's operation, about half a million vessels benefited from that saving.

The first actual attempt to build the canal was made by the great French promoter Ferdinand de Lesseps, who had earlier built the Suez Canal (p. 257). Despite their technical expertise, the French canal builders were unable to finish the Panama task because of two major problems. First, tropical diseases, mainly yellow fever (to which the French had no immunity) decimated them, and second, there were ceaseless landslides in Culebra Cut, the 13-km (8-mile) segment where the canal crosses the Continental Divide. Both complications proved insurmountable to the

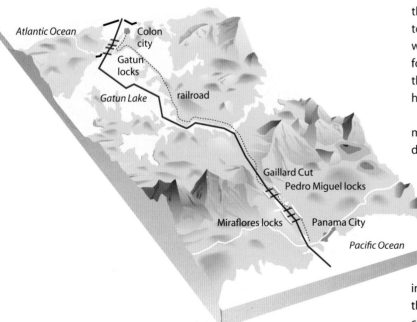

Atlantic Ocean

Colon city

Gatun locks

Gatun Lake   railroad

Gaillard Cut
Pedro Miguel locks

Miraflores locks   Panama City

Pacific Ocean

resources of the French-funded private enterprise. Bankruptcy and scandal ended the effort.

In eight years the French had accomplished an impressive amount of work, although only 13 per cent of the French excavation was useful for the present canal; the rest followed an inadequate route. And much of the topographical, geological and other information gathered by the French was of little use when, guided by the vision of President Theodore Roosevelt, the US government took over and supported the project.

Enter the Americans

De Lesseps failed in Panama because he was unable to surmount the particular difficulties posed by the undertaking. At Suez he had faced no jungles, mountains, diseases, access difficul-

ties, labour shortages, weather extremes or subsurface surprises. Panama presented all these, plus the immutable fact that ships had to be raised 26 m (85 ft) to cross the Continental Divide, then lowered again to exit.

Before any earth was moved, the American approach, initially under John Stevens, was to procure and deploy the necessary equipment, provide proper food and shelter for the army of labourers and ensure that the railroad – the lifeline of the project – was in working order. The American team was led by Colonel George W. Goethals, while Dr (Colonel) William Crawford Gorgas quelled yellow fever and malaria – essential if the work was to succeed.

To overcome the important elevation differential of the Continental Divide, three sets of locks –

The cutting of the Panama Canal to join the Atlantic and Pacific oceans was one of the world's greatest engineering achievements, overcoming huge problems in the process. It was such a commercial success that its capacity has virtually been doubled since its completion in 1914.

Bucyrus-Erie steam-engine conveyors were used to build the side slopes for the Gaillard Cut in 1912.

the Miraflores, Pedro Miguel and Gatun – were constructed, through which every vessel is raised or lowered. The locks, still the most massive concrete structures ever built, are especially noteworthy in the light of early 20th-century concrete technology and the speed with which they were constructed.

Each lock measures 305 by 33.5 m (1000 by 110 ft) and is 26 m (85 ft) deep, with walls up to 15.25 m (50 ft) thick at the bottom and 2.5 m (8 ft) at the top. The paired lock gates made of steel plate on a steel framework are another marvel – each is 20 m (65 ft) wide and 2 m (7 ft) thick. The tallest gates, at Miraflores, weigh 745 tonnes and tower 25 m (82 ft) high. All ships are hauled through the locks by small towing locomotives to avoid accidents.

A dam was built to control the flow of the Chagres River, thereby creating the Gatun Lake, which became the world's largest man-made lake. The dam itself, 2.4 km (1.5 miles) across at the crest and 50 m (165 ft) high, was at that time the largest earth-fill dam.

The problem of the landslides in Calebra Cut still had to be overcome. Colonel David Dubois Gaillard finally conquered this by opening out the channel's profile to reduce the slope of the sides. Sadly, Gaillard died in 1913, and the Culebra Cut was renamed in his honour.

The official opening of the Panama Canal took place on 15 August 1914, with the inaugural transit of the US steamship, *Ancon*. Problems remained, but the challenge had been met: the canal was opened to world traffic three years early and under its original estimated budget.

Recent changes

The canal was an immediate success and has since seen an increase in both ship size and traffic volume. In 1996 the Panama Canal Commission embarked on a $1-billion dollar modernization programme, to increase capacity by installing new equipment and technology. An enhanced tracking system now monitors the position of

FACTFILE

Total length	80 km
Height of Gatun Locks	26 m
Gaillard Cut	13 km long
Workforce, August 1913	39,962
Cost	$366,650,000

vessels, tugboats, locomotives and other mobile units. The system uses a Global Positioning System (GPS) to track all movements. The information is then used by Marine Traffic Operation to optimize scheduling vessels through the canal. Meteorological technology maximizes water resources, and protects canal installations against heavy floods or extended droughts. An earlier Gaillard Cut widening programme increased capacity by 20 per cent more ships per day – this project involved four times more excavation than the Anglo-French Channel Tunnel (p. 240).

Ship size is limited by that of the locks. The ships, known as 'Panamax' type, can navigate through the Gaillard Cut only one vessel at a time. Two-way Panamax traffic in a 152-m (500-ft) channel would generate hydrodynamic forces that would render navigation unsafe. The PCC approved a $200-million second widening in June 1991, with a completion date set for 2012. Drainage and monitoring of previous excavations in the Gaillard Cut have proved to be the most cost-effective solution to the landslide problem.

The PCC performed studies on how best to construct a new third lane of locks. There are several exciting possibilities: build new locks, with bigger chambers for ships larger than Panamax, or with Panamax chambers, or with smaller chambers; or build synchrolift locks (to conserve water) for smaller vessels.

The Republic of Panama has now assumed the responsibility of administering and managing one of the world's two great interoceanic canals, the other being Suez. With the 1989 signing of the Torrijos-Carter Treaty, the United States committed itself to transfer the administration and control of the Canal to Panama. That occurred at noon on 31 December, 1999.

The three sets of locks on the canal remain the world's most massive concrete structures, and are still in use.

64 Hoover Dam

Time: 1931–35 Location: Black Canyon, Nevada, USA

The building of Hoover Dam belongs to the sagas of the daring.
SCULPTOR OSKAR J.W. HANSEN, 1950

Now a part of the landscape, Hoover Dam was built across the Black Canyon of the Colorado River. Nevada is on the left, Arizona on the right.

In 1994 the American Society of Civil Engineers named Hoover Dam a national Historic Civil Engineering Landmark – 'one of America's Seven Modern Civil Engineering Wonders'. Hoover Dam (called Boulder Dam until 1947) was the greatest dam of its day.

For thousands of years, the Colorado River has followed its course from its Rocky Mountain rise to the Gulf of California, a distance of 2250 km (1400 miles). All life along its route has depended upon its waters for existence; but it would exact its toll in return. Each spring and early summer,

melting snow, the Colorado's principal source, regularly caused devastating floods in the low-lying lands, destroying the lives, crops and property it also nurtured. Then, after the summer and early autumn, the river would dry to a trickle. To improve and stabilize life along the Colorado, the river had to be tamed.

As early as 1920, the authorities realized that besides flood control, harnessing the Colorado would add the further benefits of a stable fresh-water supply, irrigation to create and water farm-land, hydroelectric power and public recreation.

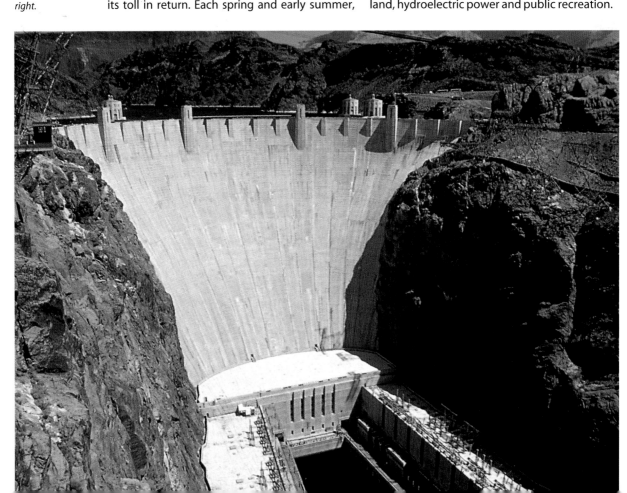

Long a distant dream, the process actually began in 1922 with the signing of the Colorado River Compact. This provided for an equitable allocation of the river's water to the seven states along its banks, and led to the 1928 Congressional Boulder Canyon Project Act authorizing construction of a dam in Black Canyon, between Arizona and Nevada.

Building the dam

Work began in 1931 with the building of a full, working railroad, needed to move men, machines and materials to the inaccessible site. (Three of the most significant modern construction miracles: this dam, the Panama Canal (p. 260) and the Channel Tunnel (p. 240), could not have been built without a dedicated work area railroad.)

A consortium of constructors, 'The Six Companies', combined in a joint effort to build the dam. They began by blasting tunnels through both rock canyon walls; coffer dams were then built upstream and downstream of the dam site and the waters diverted through the tunnels. Work could then begin on the dam in the dry. Despite temporary stoppages and a relatively high casualty count the project continued apace.

Hoover Dam is a concrete gravity-arch dam – the weight of water is held by both the weight of the wall and its curve, which transmits the load to the canyon sides, keeping the wall in compression. Concrete was poured into the wall in blocks or columns, which were then keyed together. By the time the last concrete increment was placed, two years ahead of schedule in mid-1935, 2.6 million cu. m (3.25 million cu. yd), weighing 6.6 million tonnes had been used – enough concrete to pave a two-lane road from New York to San Francisco, a distance of 4622 km (2872 miles).

On 30 September 1935, President Franklin D. Roosevelt dedicated the project to the American people. Within a year the first generators were operational in both power plant wings. Electrical generators continued to be added, with the last one going on line in 1961. The dam impounded Lake Mead, named for Dr Elwood Mead, then US Reclamation Commissioner. It is the largest man-made reservoir in the United States, storing about

35.2 million cu. m, or 28.5 million acres feet of fresh water (1 acre foot of water would cover a football field to a height of 1 foot).

Benefits of the dam

The new visitor centre provides a first-hand view of this project's powerful presence, as it fulfils its multi-purpose role. Irrigation of more than

The dam under construction: the retaining wall consists of reinforced concrete block columns which were poured in place and built up incrementally. A steel pipe section is being moved by crane in the foreground.

FACTFILE

Height	221 m
Crest length	379 m
Width at top	13.7 m
Width at bottom	201 m
Weight	6,600,000 tonnes
Average workforce	3500
Cost	$165 million
Capacity of lake	35.2 million cu. m

Lake Mead, with the four upstream intake towers visible, was created behind the dam. Below the dam are the power plants, with the controlled flow of the Colorado River released between them. On the left, Nevada, side is the visitor centre.

Below *Diagram to show the original workings of the Hoover Dam, including the water intake through great towers, the power plants and spillways to drain off excess water from the dam.*

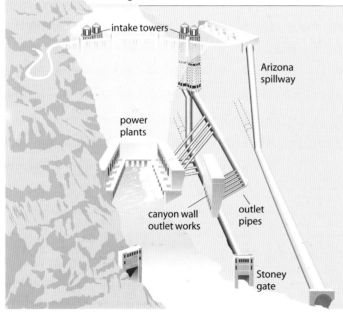

405,000 ha (1 million acres) of once arid wasteland in southwestern America (and in Mexico) created some of America's richest croplands, producing millions of dollars for local economies.

A dependable, clean, fresh-water supply meets the ever-increasing domestic and commercial needs of over 20 million people living and working in the area served. Reliable low-cost hydroelectricity powers the Arizona, California and Nevada region. The station annually generates over 4 billion kilowatt hours, enough to serve 1.3 million people's domestic and commercial needs. Between 1939 and 1949 it was the world's largest hydro-power plant. Finally, boating, swimming, water-skiing, camping and fishing in Lake Mead and the lesser lakes in the watershed provide a year-round recreation area for more than 9 million annual visitors, all administered by the US National Park Service.

From its outset, the total project cost $165 million. Most, with interest, has been repaid to the US Treasury through the sale of power generated by the dam. Hoover (Boulder) Dam, a thing of majestic beauty, has reclaimed and given life to a vast sector of the United States, and promises a long and useful future.

Itaipú Dam

Time: 1975–91   Location: Parana River, Brazil–Paraguay

A pool is … a symbol not of affluence but of order, of control over the uncontrollable.
JOAN DIDION, 1977

Itaipú Dam and its associated hydroelectric power plant on the Parana River – which forms the border between Brazil and Paraguay – is currently the largest renewable power development in operation in the world, and is one of the wonders of the 20th century. It also represents a successful project achieved through the close co-operation of two neighbouring countries.

Everything connected with the project is on a vast scale. Itaipú Dam is some 7.7 km (4.8 miles)

FACTFILE

Total length	8 km
Maximum height	196 m
Cost	$18 billion
Workforce	30,000
Generators	18 (20 planned)
Power generated	1 million kw/hour
Capacity of reservoir	29 billion cu. m

Blowing up one of the cofferdams protecting the construction site by diverting the waters of the Parana River.

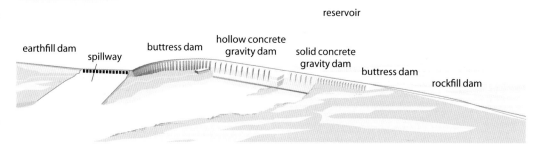

earthfill dam spillway buttress dam hollow concrete gravity dam reservoir solid concrete gravity dam buttress dam rockfill dam

View over the site while the dam was still under construction. The spillway is on the left and the main dam is right of centre. Other concrete dams are between these two structures, with embankments to left and right, as shown in the diagram.

long in total and comprises five linked dams of different types, both concrete and embankment. The main dam is a hollow concrete gravity dam: the centre is hollow to minimize the amount of concrete required, though this was still enormous, yet the structure is sufficiently strong to withstand the pressure of the water held behind it. The various individual dams range in height from 25 to 162 m (82 to 530 ft).

The powerhouse at the toe of the main dam holds the turbine generators, each of which produces 715 megawatts (MW). In 2000, the power produced by the plant represented about 24 per cent of Brazil's total electricity requirements and about 95 per cent of Paraguay's, and capacity is scheduled to increase when the last remaining generators are commissioned.

Building and materials

Construction began in 1975 with work to divert the Parana River from the dam site. The Parana is the seventh largest river in the world, with an average flow of about 8300 cu. m (2930 cu. ft) per second – this was the first time that such a large river had been diverted. It took almost three years to excavate the diversion channel, 2 km (1.25 miles) long, 150 m (490 ft) wide and 91 m (298 ft) deep and involving the removal of around 50 million tonnes of material. Cofferdams were then built upstream and downstream of the works to divert the flow through the new channel. At 100 m (330 ft) high and 550 m (1805 ft) long, these are among the largest ever built.

Once the river had been diverted from the construction site, its original bed was drained and excavated prior to the building of the dams and spillway. To construct these required a total of 8.8 million cu. m (310 million cu. ft) of concrete and 13.2 million cu. m (466 million cu. ft) of soil and rock. A total of seven overhead cableways, fed from three concrete production plants on each bank, kept up the flow of concrete to the site.

At the height of construction, work continued uninterrupted around the clock and some 30,000 people were employed. The amount of concrete consumed was 15 times that used to build Channel Tunnel (p. 240) and the quantity of iron and steel involved would be enough for 380 Eiffel Towers (p. 174).

With the dam completed on 13 October 1982, the sluice gates of the diversion channel were closed and the waters of the reservoir began to rise. The lake formed covers some 1350 sq. km (14,530 sq. miles), with a maximum depth of 170 m (558 ft) at the dam; it took 14 days to fill. Projects on such a scale are bound to have an impact on the environment. As the waters rose, teams in boats went out and collected hundreds of animals that were in danger of drowning and areas of wildlife habitat were created elsewhere.

Excess water from the dammed lake is allowed to escape in a controlled, though spectacular way

Construction continued by night at Itaipú – here cranes lift materials into place in the main dam.

View over the dam from Paraguay. Excess water from the dammed lake is allowed to escape through the spillway in the foreground.

over the spillway on the right bank. Its maximum discharge capacity is twice the flow of the highest flood on this river on record. Fourteen steel radial gates, each around 21.3 m (70 ft) wide and high, regulate the amount of water discharged.

Power and pleasure

The first generator began operation in May 1984; the last came into operation some seven years later in July 1991. Each of the 18 Francis turbine-generator assemblies weighs about 3300 tonnes and generates 715 MW at full load. To produce this amount of power, 645 cu. m (22,770 cu. ft) of water per second flow through each machine. Power output from the plant has increased each year – the maximum has been over 90 billion kilowatt hours of electricity in 2000. This repre-

sents a saving in carbon dioxide emissions of 81 million tonnes per year compared with electricity generated by coal-powered plants. Two more generators are planned to come into operation in 2004. Brazil and Paraguay operate different power systems, and the turbines are equally divided between the two systems. Brazil at present consumes the larger share of power produced, mostly in São Paulo.

The project is not only a commercial success in providing a source of power for Brazil and Paraguay, it also ensures a dependable water supply for homes and factories and for irrigation. The dam has become a major tourist attraction too – more than 10 million visitors have travelled to see it, bringing much needed income to the local community.

The Dutch Sea Barrier

Time: 1977–87   Location: southwest Netherlands

*Although our enemy Oceanus seems to be at rest,
he will come like a roaring lion to destroy everything …*
ANDRIES VIERLINGH, 16TH CENTURY

FACTFILE

Total length of barrier	6.8 km
Piers	
number	65
height	53 m
weight	18,000 tons
Cost	$325 million

On 1 February 1953, a storm-driven high tide brought disaster to the southern coastal region of the Netherlands known as the Delta area. Over 200,000 ha (494,200 acres) of farmland were flooded and 1835 people drowned, tragically revealing the inadequacy of the Dutch defences against the 'eternal friend and enemy' – the sea.

As a result, a special committee was set up and in 1958 the Dutch parliament passed the Delta Act. The Delta Project proposed the construction of major dams across the tidal channels to the Rhine, Maas and Scheldt Delta on the coastal perimeter, in effect shortening the total defence line against the sea by almost 700 km (435 miles). In addition, the existing defences – the dikes – would be heightened, and a series of smaller dams, surge barriers, sluices and locks would connect most of the islands. The drawback was that in the process an important natural estuarine environment would be completely cut off from the sea; the plan put safety for the human inhabitants above environmental conservation.

The Eastern Scheldt Storm Surge Barrier

Beginning in 1958, various elements of the Delta Plan were built, leaving the longest and most difficult dam – closing the mouth of the Eastern Scheldt – until last. The dam would have to

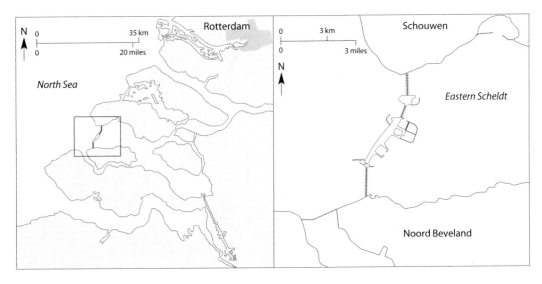

The Dutch Sea Barrier is part of a coastal defence system protecting the southwest Netherlands. It spans the Eastern Scheldt delta between man-made islands.

The 65 concrete piers of the barrier were constructed in batches in dry docks. The vehicles give a good indication of the scale.

stretch for 8 km (5 miles) across the inlet, which was 40 m (130 ft) deep at its maximum and had strong tidal currents. Construction began in 1969 and by the end of 1973 three construction islands had been built, two of which were later joined, as well as around 5 km (3 miles) of dam. But growing concerns about the loss of a unique natural environment as well as economic considerations – shellfish culture and fishing are important sources of local income – finally forced the government to abandon the initial plan in 1977.

Filter mattresses were laid on the sea bed to provide a firm foundation for the structures of the dam before they were put in place.

Instead of a solid dam, the engineers came up with a new design for an innovatory open storm-surge barrier. Movable shutters would be open under normal conditions, allowing the water to flow through, but could be lowered to protect the area during periods of strong winds and high tide.

The project team, comprising the Rijkswaterstaat (Public Works Department) Delta Division and a consortium of Dutch contractors, was faced with an unprecedented challenge. Such a design had never been built before and so new technical solutions and construction methods had to be devised. All major elements were tested in a scale model under laboratory conditions, but nature is not as predictable as civil engineers would like.

The construction process

After numerous tests, the proposed solution consists of a line of 65 huge concrete piers, in three sections across the channels between the two artificial islands, with 62 movable steel gates or shutters hung between the piers. The total length of the barrier system is 6.8 km (4.2 miles).

The first step was to prepare solid foundations on the sea bed for the piers. The underwater subsoil had to be compacted to a depth of 15 m (50 ft). Steel needles driven into the sea bed from a specially designed vessel were vibrated, forcing out water and settling the sand. This alone took three years. To protect the sand bed from scouring by the strong currents, filter mattresses filled with graded layers of sand and gravel were laid on the estuary bottom. The mattresses were rolled out from huge drums on board another vessel designed specifically for this task.

At the same time, the massive concrete piers, each weighing 18,000 tonnes, were constructed in three dry docks on one of the islands in the delta. Each pier took about 18 months to complete and they were produced continually in batches. Once completed, the dry dock was flooded and two other special vessels lifted the piers, towed them out and placed them precisely in position. The piers were then grouted to the mattresses and internal spaces were filled with sand to increase their stability. Sills consisting of graded layers of stone – smallest at the bottom – were placed around the base of each pier. A total of 5 million tonnes of stone was used in this operation.

Next, the piers were connected by concrete sills and the box girder bridges for the roadway that runs along the top were installed. And, of course, the movable steel gates had to be fitted. These are 5 m (17 ft) thick and 40 m (130 ft) wide and vary in height between 6 m (20 ft) and 12 m (40 ft), depending on their position in the barrier. The largest, in the deepest part of the delta, weighs 480 tonnes. They take about an hour to open or close and are regularly tested. The barrier is closed on average twice a year to counter high

water levels and has proved to be extremely effective.

The Eastern Scheldt storm-surge barrier was officially opened in 1987. It is the only protective system against the sea in the world of this type, and provides security for a large region of the Netherlands. It has helped in the environmental management of the Delta area, as well as providing traffic links between the islands, and has been central to the development of the recreational use of the area. Finally, although the system is a modern, technologically advanced structure, it blends extremely well into the landscape.

Above *After the dry docks were flooded, the piers were lifted by a specially made vessel, Ostrea, and transported and positioned in the barrier.*

Below *An aerial view of the barrier in open position, allowing free flow of water into and out of the Eastern Scheldt.*

The Three Gorges Dam

Time: 1994– Location: Yangtze River, China

In the world there is nothing more submissive and weak than water.
Yet for attacking that which is hard and strong, nothing can surpass it.
LAO-TZU, 6TH CENTURY BC

Opposite
Construction of the shiplock at the dam. Barges of up to 10,000 tonnes will be able to navigate upstream when it is complete. The lift will raise the vessels a total of 87 m.

Below *Location map showing the Yangtze and the site of the Three Gorges Dam.*

The Three Gorges hydroelectric project currently being built on the Yangtze River in China can be described as a modern Great Wall of China, so large is the project and the effort required to build it. On completion – scheduled for 2009 – this will be the biggest hydroelectric project in the world and will supply about 10 per cent of China's energy needs.

The Yangtze River, properly called the Chang Jiang or Long River, is the longest river in Asia and the fourth longest in the world. Floods on the Yangtze have always caused great damage – in the 20th century alone, they killed more than a million people and resulted in huge losses to farming and industry. In addition to producing electricity, the Three Gorges Project aims to control such floods and provide irrigation. A channel and ship lock to allow navigation in the river above the site are also part of the scheme, opening the way into central China for large ships, helping industry and improving living standards.

The dam – a hollow gravity dam – will be 175 m (574 ft) high and over 2 km (1.25 miles) long. A total of 102.8 million cu. m. (3630 million cu. ft) of soil and rock have had to be excavated and 27.9 million cu. m (985 million cu. ft) of concrete – three times that required at Itaipú – and 354,000 tonnes of steel reinforcement, along with a further 265,000 tonnes of metal, will be consumed. The amount of materials could build the Great Pyramid 44 times over, and a workforce of 28,000 is being employed.

Building the dam

Before construction of the dam itself could begin, it was first necessary to divert the river around the site. The average flow in the Yangtze at this point is between 14,000 and 19,000 cu. m (494,400 and 670,975 cu. ft) per second, making this the largest river diversion project yet built, at a cost $3.7 billion alone. The cofferdams to achieve this were major civil engineering works in themselves. The upstream cofferdam was constructed in 60 m (197 ft) of water and required some 10.3 million cu. m (363,740 cu. ft) of material.

The main dam will be fitted with low-level gates to allow sediment to be flushed downstream during the flood season. To achieve this,

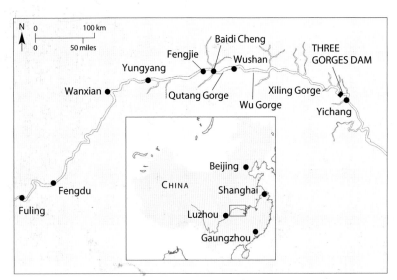

Right *The water intakes of the left bank power house are clearly visible as construction continues.*

23 gates, each 7×9 m (23×30 ft), will be installed along the bottom of the dam. Each year the reservoir water level will be lowered at the start of the flood season and the gates opened, flushing out the silt. At the end of the season the gates will be closed to catch and store mainly clean water in the reservoir, which will be filled by the last floods of the season. Even so, some 50 million tonnes of silt a year will be deposited into the reservoir.

To prevent floods spilling over the dam, an overflow designed to handle four times the average flow at the river mouth and comprising 22 gates, each 7×17 m (23×56 ft), will be built in the centre of the dam.

Power capacity and flood control

There are two powerhouses at the downstream toe of the dam with 26 turbine generators each of 700 megawatt (MW) capacity, producing a total of 18,200 MW – 50 per cent greater than that at Itaipú. A second phase is planned to add capacity, taking the total to 22,400 MW. The first stage alone is equivalent to half the production capability of the largest power company in America, and each generator will produce nearly the same amount as a modern nuclear power station. The power generated will save burning about 50 million tonnes of coal each year.

Operation of the reservoir will also assist flood control. The total volume of the reservoir will be 39.3 billion cu. m (1388 billion cu. ft) and the flood control capability of the reservoir will be 22.15 billion cu. m (782 billion cu. ft). The frequency of flooding downstream will be reduced from once in every 10 years to less than once in every 100 years, which should greatly

increase the safety of some 15 million people living downstream.

Another benefit will be the improvement of navigation in the upper reaches of the Yangtze. At present large barges can only travel as far inland as Wuhan, some 250 km (155 miles) below the dam, and only barges under 6000 tons can pass upstream of the site. After building the ship locks, barges of up to 10,000 tons will be able to navigate as far inland as Chongquing, some 2500 km (1555 miles) inland from the sea for six months of the year.

A ship lift – the largest in the world to date – will also be built. This will be capable of transporting passenger ships or cargo vessels up to 3000 tonnes over the dam, opening up a large area of China to economic development. The ships will be transported in a container 120 m (394 ft) long, 18 m (59 ft) wide and 3.5 m (11 ft) deep.

The construction of a project of this size is not without its costs, both economic and environmental. Construction cost is presently estimated

FACTFILE

Length	2 km
Height	175 m
Cost	$75 billion
Workforce	28,000
Generators	26 currently
Capacity of reservoir	39.3 billion cu. m

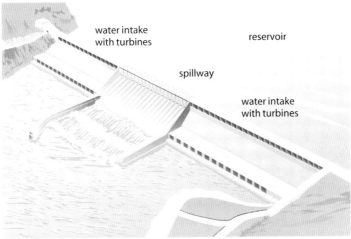

water intake
with turbines

reservoir

spillway

water intake
with turbines

Left *A diagram of the finished project, with the two power houses at the downstream toe of the dam on either side of the central spillway.*

at $75 billion. In addition, the reservoir will force the displacement and resettlement of some 1.1 to 1.9 million people, inundate an area of around 632 sq. km (244 sq. miles), including 27,000 ha (66,716 acres) of farms and orchards as well as 19 cities, 326 villages and numerous ancient sites. Water pollution in the river could increase, as the dam will trap pollutants that were formerly flushed out to sea.

In spite of all this, China considers that the project is a worthwhile investment. The construction by Chinese resources of a project this size is surely an impressive achievement, well worthy of the people who built the Great Wall.

Colossal Statues

Gigantic human forms – figures many times larger than life-size – have continued to exercise a compelling fascination for those intending to commemorate a great national event or celebrate a ruling dynasty, a favourite hero or a newly minted republic and, in the process, stamp the commanding presence of mankind on the natural landscape. Such monuments are not only the products of the period which now ranks as the heyday of huge statues, the half century spanning the late 1880s, when New York's Statue of Liberty was completed, through to the 1930s with the consecration of Rio's Statue of Christ the Redeemer and the Mount Rushmore National Memorial, dedicated in 1941. Their pedigree stretches back to such wonders of the ancient world as the Colossus of Rhodes and the giant statues erected by Egyptian pharaohs.

In all three cases in this book, their primary purpose was to embody or encapsulate at monumental scale a long-held sentiment which seemed to call for a more permanent form of expression. For the Statue of Liberty, that purpose was the expression of amicable feelings from the people of France to the citizens of the young sister republic, the United States of America. The Rio Christ came about largely through the efforts of the Catholic Circle of that city, intended to serve as a highly visible source of inspiration to local believers as well as signalling a welcome to visitors with its wide open arms. Mount Rushmore's genesis stemmed from an idea hatched by the state historian of South Dakota to promote

The colossal heads of four of the early presidents of the United States were carved from the living rockface of Mount Rushmore in South Dakota using dynamite and drills.

The gigantic arm and hand of the statue of Christ the Redeemer in Rio de Janeiro, Brazil. The statue is made from cast concrete supported on a steel armature.

interest in his region through commemorative sculptures of the men who opened up the West. The likenesses of Kit Carson and Buffalo Bill were subsequently replaced by Presidents Washington, Jefferson, Lincoln and Theodore Roosevelt.

Today, these original motivations may be forgotten, but the potency of the statues as proxies for the cities or nations they have come to represent remains undiminished with the passage of time. Restorations have been needed to repair the ravages of age and exposure, yet they continue to be honoured and promoted – and enjoyed – as national emblems.

The process of designing and building – or carving out – these colossal statues on what were very exposed, open sites called for an unusual degree of collaboration between the sculptor and his chosen engineer, such are the enormous wind forces bearing upon the structure, the limited area available to sink foundations and construct a plinth or, in the case of sculptor John Gutzon Borglum on Mount Rushmore, the demanding logistics of transferring the desired three-dimensional form from his studio to the rock face. Often the statue was required to reach as high or higher than the latest buildings of the host city, a feat which Gustave Eiffel, engineer of the eponymous tower, was able to achieve with his braced steel frame which supports the

puddled iron members holding up the 'skin' of the Statue of Liberty, an innovatory technique which was to be taken up by the next generation of New York's skyscraper builders.

Each artist began with a small-scale maquette, allowing the form of the statue to be refined and options for its assembly reviewed. The external profile of the structure was then broken down into a set of components for manufacture, transport and subsequent assembly on site. At Mount Rushmore, where material was to be blasted and chiselled away rather than built up to form the four presidential profiles, the sculptor devised an ingenious method of scaling up the heads from his maquette on to site, so that the existing rock was removed only where necessary. But the eye of the artist still prevailed. Paul Landowski, the French/Polish sculptor of the Rio Christ, insisted that he refine the design of the head and hands of the figure at full size to avoid the inevitable distortions which arise in the process of scaling up from a model.

Statues on this scale are perhaps unlikely projects today. Instead, there has been a recent series of iconic buildings such as the Sydney Opera House and Bilbao's Guggenheim, which serve much the same purpose, in terms of the international celebrity of a city, as did these three giants of statuary.

The Statue of Liberty

Time: 1875–86   Location: New York City, United States

One hundred years ago, thousands upon thousands of the sons and daughters of France presented the United States of America with this Statue of Liberty, today the symbol of our common values.

PRESIDENT MITTERAND OF FRANCE, STATUE OF LIBERTY RE-DEDICATION CEREMONY, 1986

The Statue of Liberty, the gigantic figure constructed on Liberty Island in Upper New York Bay, symbolizes the gateway to the New World. The monumental sculpture, the inspiration of a prominent French legal scholar and politician, Edouard-René Lefebvre de Laboulaye, was given to the people of the United States by the French in 1884 to commemorate a hundred years of American independence. Sited to face the city's harbour, the copper-sheathed figure represents a woman draped in Classical robes and wearing a crown with seven spikes. The broken shackles of slavery lie at her feet and in her uplifted right hand she holds a torch. In her left hand she holds a book which is inscribed with the date of the Declaration of Independence – 4 July 1776. The statue itself is 46 m (151 ft 5 in) high, comparable in size to the highest skyscraper at that time, and with its base it towers 93 m (305 ft).

Design and construction

The figure, originally called 'Liberty Enlightening the World', was the work of the French sculptor Frédéric Auguste Bartholdi. Money for the statue was raised by subscription from the people of France, and Bartholdi began working on the sculpture in his studio in Paris in 1875. He first built a small terracotta maquette and went on to increase the statue's size through three meticulously scaled and successively larger versions.

The Statue of Liberty, towering over Liberty Island and facing New York's harbour, has become widely recognized as a symbol marking the gateway to the New World.

Right *A view of the full-scale assembly of the Statue of Liberty that was first constructed near Bartholdi's studio in Paris.*

Opposite *The Statue of Liberty is sheathed in around 300 copper plates that were hammered into moulds to create the shape and fine details.*

Below *The figure stands on a stone-faced pedestal constructed within the star-shaped fort at one of the major entrances to New York city.*

Finally, full-scale wooden models of sections of the statue were built. Each section was then covered with plaster, and carpenters made wooden forms that followed the shape of the plaster. Copper sheets were placed in the forms and hammered into the desired shape, before being attached to the support-frame constructed in a yard near the sculptor's studio as part of a full-scale assembly. After the statue had been successfully erected at full size in Paris it was dismantled, packed in 214 wooden crates and shipped aboard the *Isère* for America. It arrived in New York on 17 June 1885.

The construction of this giant, free-standing figure presented particular structural design problems. In order to solve them, Bartholdi commissioned the French engineer Gustave Eiffel (builder of the Eiffel Tower, p. 174) to design the internal supporting system. Since the sculpture was relatively light, the problem was not so much one of supporting vertical loads; rather, it was that the extensive surface area enclosing the hollow interior made the sculpture vulnerable to the force of the wind.

Eiffel's design for the interior of the Statue of Liberty proposed a structural frame with a central tower made up of four vertical columns connected by horizontal and diagonal crossbeams. This central pylon provided the primary support and was tied to the ground through a stone pedestal. The pedestal, made of reinforced concrete faced with granite, was reputed to have a foundation that was the largest single concrete structure in the world at the time. It was designed by the American architect Richard Morris Hunt and sat within the walls of a star-shaped fort that had been built on the island almost 80 years earlier to defend New York City against naval attack.

The central tower supported the sculpted external skin of the monument on a strong but flexible framework of 1350 ribs and verticals made of puddled iron, a contemporary material similar to cast iron. These were fixed to the external skin of copper using copper saddles and copper rivets. This detail allowed for movement resulting both from wind loading and temperature differentials. Eiffel also recognized the

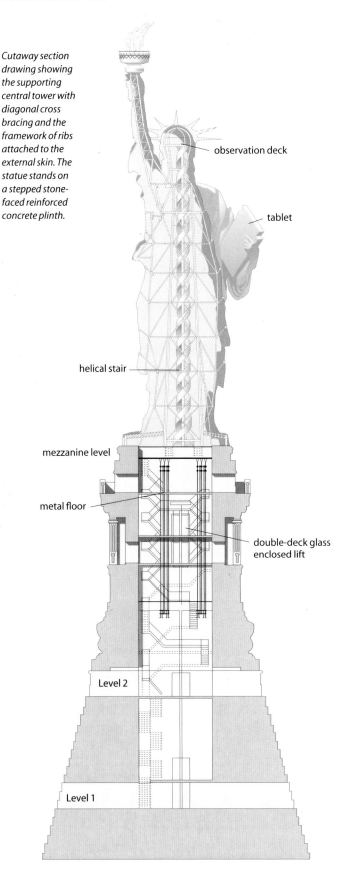

Cutaway section drawing showing the supporting central tower with diagonal cross bracing and the framework of ribs attached to the external skin. The statue stands on a stepped stone-faced reinforced concrete plinth.

observation deck

tablet

helical stair

mezzanine level

metal floor

double-deck glass enclosed lift

Level 2

Level 1

electrolytic incompatibility of iron and copper and placed a barrier between the two.

The sculpted external skin consisted of some 300 plates of copper. Each was only 0.2 cm (0.09 in) thick and had been produced, as noted above, by hand hammering each plate into a mould – a technique called repoussé. This helped to create the delicate shaping of the figure while also making the envelope more rigid. The many folds in the drapery also helped to distribute stresses and minimize sagging.

Eiffel's design for the Statue of Liberty introduced at least two innovations which were to prove extremely valuable for construction in America. First, the diagonally braced frame which he designed inside the figure represented the most extensive system of wind bracing that had been incorporated in any structure in America at that time, with the exclusion of bridges. Secondly, his use of steel for the posts that are the major bearing members of the frame was the first time that this metal had been specified for a structure in New York other than a bridge.

The Statue of Liberty thus represented not only an exceptional structural solution and a technical innovation in its own right, but liberated the designers of skyscrapers by introducing the braced frame and demonstrating the potential of steel. The building usually regarded as the first work of skeletal construction in New York was the Tower Building at 50 Broadway, designed by Bradford Gilbert and built in 1888–89.

After delays created by the need to raise funds, the statue was finally completed in 1886 at a cost of $800,000. About half the total was donated by the French. On 28 October 1886, the Statue of Liberty was dedicated. There was a grand parade in New York City and the harbour was filled with boats. President Grover Cleveland and members of his cabinet, together with representatives of the French government and the French-American Union, were present for the dedication ceremonies. Subsequently the monument became a powerful national symbol. Its image has been used extensively and many millions of immigrants have passed by the statue as they entered the United States at nearby Ellis Island.

Repair and restoration

Over the years the statue has undergone a series of minor changes. The flame in the torch, which Bartholdi had originally created in solid copper with gold leaf, was pierced with portholes and Gutzon Borglum (the sculptor of Mount Rushmore; p. 288) introduced larger areas of glass to create a lighted beacon. There was also extensive water penetration in both the flame and the torch, as well as movement in the structure and internal failures in the construction of the overall skin. After almost a century of intense use and weathering in the wind, rain and salt air, it was agreed that the Statue of Liberty required major repairs.

After a two-year study, a repair programme was initiated in 1983. Sponsored by the French-American Committee for Restoration of the Statue of Liberty Inc., the programme was designed to repair extensive damage caused by corrosive electrolytic reactions that had led to failure in almost half of the 'saddles' that connected the external skin to the internal structural skeleton. New ribs of stainless steel were installed and new copper 'saddles' and rivets fitted. The internal face of the skin, which had been painted several times over the years, was also cleaned. Using a spray of liquid nitrogen seven layers of paint were removed.

Other problems created by errors in the alignment of the head and the connection of the framework supporting the right arm when the statue was first constructed were repaired, with the addition of new structural framing, while the torch and flame were entirely rebuilt. Facilities for visitors were also improved. The provision of new lighting and an integrated ventilation system improved environmental conditions in the monument, while new glass lifts and a central stair fitted within the pedestal and the statue made them more easily accessible for visitors.

Official ceremonies marking the opening of the newly restored Statue of Liberty were held on 4 July 1986 and a grand ceremony was held on 28 October of that year to celebrate the 100th anniversary of its original dedication.

FACTFILE

Height	
foundation to torch	93 m
statue	46 m
Length of hand	5 m
Steps to crown	354
Weight	
overall	204 tonnes
copper skin	91 tonnes
Rivets	300,000
Cost	$800,000

As a part of the major repair programme that was completed in 1986, new lifts and a central stair were constructed within the plinth and the framework of the statue to provide improved access for visitors.

The Statue of Christ the Redeemer

Time: 1926–31 Location: Rio de Janeiro, Brazil

I adore this tourist Christ with open arms searching for equilibrium on the Brazilian mount.
JORGE DE LIMA

Standing on the top of Mount Corcovado, the Statue of Christ the Redeemer towers over the city of Rio de Janeiro and has become a symbol of the city.

The monumental figure of Christ the Redeemer has graced the highest promontory overlooking Rio de Janeiro since its completion in 1931. With arms outstretched, the statue promises redemption for Christians while also symbolizing Rio's openness to visitors. As a monument, it shares the welcoming aspects of the Statue of Liberty in New York (p. 281) and the spiritual reassurance of Christ of the Andes, and its size recalls the Colossus of Rhodes, one of the Seven Wonders of the ancient world. Its dramatic site, Mount Corcovado ('hunchbacked'), is an irregular outcropping of rock with views stretching over the city to the Atlantic Ocean. A popular sightseeing spot since the 19th century, Corcovado stands in Tijuca Forest, a 5-sq. km (13-sq. mile) national rainforest. Most visitors reach the statue via the Corcovado Railway, built in 1884. The statue's wonder is matched only by the difficulties it posed to modern engineers.

Discussions about a monument to inspire local Catholics and to commemorate the 100th anniversary of Brazilian independence (1922) began in 1921. The Catholic Circle, led by important clergymen and prominent politicians, determined the location and general form of the statue. Partly inspired by the existing cross-shaped radio transmitter on Corcovado's summit, engineer Heitor da Silva Costa suggested combining early designs for a standing figure of Christ holding an orb and cross with another in the form of a cross. Although the transmitter was soon removed because of public protests, the statue of Christ with open arms that replaced it serves as a reminder of the impact of technology on the local landscape. Money to support the construction of the figure was donated by individuals from all walks of life, rich and poor.

Parisian sculptor Paul Landowski was chosen to design the statue, and his Art Deco style, with its simplification of forms, facilitated its construction. Landowski collaborated with Brazilian architects and engineers to develop the structure and the final statue from reduced-scale plaster models. Most sections were enlarged from the scale models, but Landowski designed the head and the hands at full scale to avoid distortions. The hands of Christ are modelled after those of a Brazilian sculptress.

In designing the base, supervising architect Heitor Levy was restricted by the size of the site – it could be no more than 15 m (50 ft) in diameter. Engineer da Silva Costa designed an internal armature to support the pieces of cast concrete from which Landowski fashioned the statue. This armature stabilized the giant figure, supporting the weight of its concrete sections and resisting wind pressures. Knowing that a metal armature would be vulnerable to being melted down in times of war, da Silva Costa instead designed a reinforced concrete armature. This was also less expensive to erect and to maintain.

Four pillars inside Christ's robe support the sculpture, with cross-braces tying the pillars together and stiffening the whole against wind pressure. The pillars are sunk into the pedestal base and intermediate platforms connect them at regular intervals as they rise toward the figure's shoulders. Where necessary, the pillars curve to conform to the external shape of the statue. Cantilevered supports connected by transverse joists inside the neck help support the weight of the head while withstanding four times the expected pressure of the winds that often swirl violently at that height. The arms rest on a reinforced concrete trellised girder terminating in steel trellised girders that support the hands.

The concrete shell of the statue was formed in sections and covered with small triangular tiles of greenish soapstone (steatite). Soapstone does not conduct electricity, fade or crack, and so is an ideal substance. A system of lightning rods was integrated into the head and arms to deflect storm charges. Until recently cleaning was done manually, but mechanical spray apparatuses have now eased the monumental task. Restoration in 1990 repaired many of the damaged sections and thoroughly cleaned the statue, making it more popular than ever.

The statue was designed by the sculptor Paul Landowski. He worked on the head at full size to avoid potential problems of distortion caused by the statue's great height and scaling up from a model.

FACTFILE

Height	
statue	30 m
monument, base to top of head	38 m
Height of head	3.75 m
Length of hand	3.2 m
Span fingertip to fingertip	28 m
Height of Mount Corcovado	710 m

Mount Rushmore

Time: 1927–41 Location: South Dakota, United States

The Memorial at Mount Rushmore is the first monument erected in the Western hemisphere dedicated to a conception and the organization of this great Western Republic.
GUTZON BORGLUM

Opposite above
A three-figure plaster model of Jefferson, Washington and Lincoln in the artist's studio, with Gutzon Borglum standing in front. Unforeseen problems with the rock mean that the arrangement of the heads in the finished sculpture is different.

Opposite below
Aerial view of Mount Rushmore National Memorial near its completion in 1941. Buildings on top of the carving housed equipment and served as workshops.

The Mount Rushmore National Memorial is a monumental sculpture which honours four American presidents. The gigantic faces of George Washington, Thomas Jefferson, Abraham Lincoln and Theodore Roosevelt were carved out of a mountainside in the Black Hills of South Dakota between 1927 and 1941 by a team led by the sculptor John Gutzon Borglum. These particular figures were chosen as they represented the birth and the ideals of the nation.

Although Borglum was to be a key figure in the realization of the project, the idea for the memorial grew out of a suggestion made by Doane Robinson. Robinson was the State Historian of South Dakota and in 1923, anxious to promote the region, record its history and encourage visitors, he proposed the creation of a monumental sculpture at the Needles. His idea was that this group of tall granite spires in the Black Hills be carved to create statues of western heroes. The idea of having large figures of Kit Carson, Buffalo Bill Cody and others was an appealing one to some, but others felt that neither the site nor the subject were appropriate. Borglum, who had been engaged as the sculptor for the scheme, suggested that if such an ambitious project was to be undertaken it should be made into one of national significance.

Gutzon Borglum, the son of a Danish immigrant, was born in Idaho. He studied art in San Francisco and at the Académie Julian in Paris before receiving a commission to carve a huge memorial to the Confederate Army at Stone Mountain in Georgia. However, after disputes with his sponsors, Borglum left before that project was completed and went to work in South Dakota. The idea initially suggested by Robinson, and subsequently developed with Borglum, became formalized in a proposal to create a memorial at Mount Rushmore which would show the faces of the four presidents. The proposal was approved by both the federal and state governments in 1925, and when, two years later, President Calvin Coolidge officiated at the formal dedication ceremonies he was the first person to refer to Mount Rushmore as a 'National Shrine'.

Mount Rushmore had been selected as the site for the memorial because of its fine-grained granite, and at the dedication Borglum climbed the 1745-m (5725-ft) high mountain and began carving the bust of George Washington. It was a task which was to last for more than 14 years, require a workforce of more than 350 people and which Borglum was never to see completed. The project cost just under $1 million, of which the federal government contributed about 84 per cent, the remainder coming from private donations. The actual carving of the monument took about $6\frac{1}{2}$ years, but the intermittent lack of funding extended the work over a considerably longer period of time.

FACTFILE	
Height of heads	18 m
Height of Mount Rushmore	1745 m
Workforce	350
Cost	$990,000

Carving the monument

Borglum decided to carve one head at a time and for the first he made a plaster model in the studio which was $1/12$ of the actual size of the head on the mountain. On top of the 1.5-m (5-ft) high model of Washington's head the sculptor fixed a flat plate which was marked in degrees. A 76-cm (30-in) long horizontal steel bar was pivoted from the centre of the plate. The bar was marked off in inches and a sliding plumbline, also marked in inches, was suspended from the bar. By moving the bar and sliding out the plumbline to any point on the face it was possible to record the relevant measurements. A similar device, but 12 times larger, was constructed on the cliff top at the place which was selected to be the top of Washington's head and this enabled measurements to be transferred through the plotting of a series of points. Borglum called this device a 'pointing machine' and the men whose job it was to measure and mark out the shaping points on the rock became known as the pointers.

After the points had been selected on the surface of the mountain, the granite was drilled to

the depth indicated and dynamite charges used to blast away the outer rock. The rock was blasted to within 15 cm (6 in) of the final face, which meant that the drilling had to be very precise. Fortunately, many of the men working on the project with Borglum had experience in local mines or quarries, though the conditions on the cliff face were very different and presented particular difficulties. Each driller was strapped into a leather-lined seat hung by cables from a winch. The drill, weighing about 39 kg (85 lb) was also hung from the same cable. As the winchman was too far back from the edge of the cliff top to be able see the driller, whom he had to move from one point to another, a call boy in a safety harness was positioned on the cliff edge and relayed messages between the driller and the winchman.

Operating a pneumatic drill while dangling in space hundreds of feet below the cliff top was not an easy task. In order to exert enough pressure to drill deep horizontal holes, the drillers first set up a length of chain that they could brace the back of their seat against. The chain was slung from steel pins fitted into holes drilled into the rock face.

As the drillers moved across the face of the mountain they were followed by powdermen who inserted dynamite into the prepared holes. They placed 60 or 70 small charges at a time and blasting took place twice a day – once at lunchtime when the workmen had left the face, and again at the end of the working day. In a second operation which followed the blasting the drillers honeycombed the granite with rows of closely spaced holes, striking off the final layer using steel wedges and hammers and leaving the face smooth by using special finer drills.

The granite was so hard that the drill bits blunted relatively quickly. A blacksmith was employed to work on site permanently, while a group of other workers moved up and down among the drillers helping to replace drill bits.

Above *James 'Jim' Larue, left, and Lincoln Borglum, right, standing on one of the heads next to a pointing machine.*

Left *Carving the face of Abraham Lincoln: scaffolds and suspended cradles were used at this stage of the process.*

A monument for the nation

The work was difficult and the weather often caused problems. In 1929 President Coolidge signed the Rushmore Bill to establish the Mount Rushmore National Memorial Commission and allocate $250,000 towards its completion; this was matched by funds from private sources. With the stock-market failure adversely affecting peoples' personal finances, however, Borglum had to seek increased government funding, and with amended legislation in 1934 the memorial became a federal project.

The completed head of Washington was finally dedicated on 4 July 1930. Borglum and his team then started on Jefferson. This second face was originally planned to be on Washington's left. But because of the poor quality of the rock – and after four years of work – it had to be blasted away and carving started again to relocate it on the opposite side.

The rock here was badly fissured, however, and had to be cut back substantially before detailed carving could start; later, the discovery of a long crack where the nose was to have been forced Borglum to adjust the angle of Jefferson's head. It was completed in 1936 and President Franklin Roosevelt attended the ceremony. In the following year Lincoln's head was dedicated, and Theodore Roosevelt's was finally completed on 2 July 1939.

Borglum had also designed a Hall of Records which was to be cut into the mountain and connected to the outside by a 33-m (100-ft) long tunnel. Although 23 m (68 ft) of the tunnel was cut, it was never completed as Gutzon Borglum died on 6 March 1941. Work continued on the rest of the project until October of that year under the direction of Borglum's son Lincoln, who had worked on the project from the outset, aged 15, as a pointer.

With the outbreak of the Second World War, the dedication ceremony of the world's largest sculpture was postponed indefinitely, only to be eventually celebrated on 4 July 1991 – the occasion of the 50th anniversary of the completion of the Mount Rushmore National Memorial.

Mount Rushmore floodlit at night. Washington, Jefferson, Lincoln and Theodore Roosevelt were chosen as representing the birth and ideals of the United States.

Further Reading

Churches, Mosques, Temples & Shrines

1 Hagia Sophia

Krautheimer, R., *Early Christian and Byzantine Architecture* (Harmondsworth, 1965)

Lethaby, W. R. & Swainson, H. , *The Church of Sancta Sophia Constantinople. A Study of Byzantine Building* (London, 1894)

Mainstone, R. J., *Hagia Sophia. Architecture, Structure and Liturgy of Justinian's Great Church* (London & New York, 1988)

Mango, C., *Byzantine Architecture* (New York, 1976/London, 1979)

Mathews, T. F., *The Early Churches of Constantinople: Architecture and Liturgy* (University Park, 1971)

Van Nice, R. L., *St Sophia at Istanbul; An Architectural Survey* (Washington, DC, 1965 & 1986)

2 The Temple at Tanjavur

Balasubrahmanyam, S. R., *Middle Chola Temples, Rajaraja I to Kulottunga I (AD 985–1070)* (Faridpur, 1975)

Dehejia, V., *Indian Art* (chapter 9) (London, 1997)

Michell, G., *The Hindu Temple, An Introduction to Its Meaning and Forms* (Chicago, 1988)

Pichard, P., *Tanjavur Brhadisvara, An Architectural Study* (New Delhi & Pondicherry, 1995)

Volwahsen, A., *Living Architecture: India* (reprint Lausanne, 1999)

3 The Temple of Byodo-in

Fukuyama, Toshio, *Heian Temples. Byodo-in and Chuson-ji* (New York & Tokyo, 1976)

Paine, Robert Treat, Soper, Alexander & Waterhouse, David, *The Art and Architecture of Japan* (Harmondsworth, 1974)

Soper, Alexander, *The Evolution of Buddhist Architecture in Japan* (Princeton, 1942)

4 St Mark's Cathedral

Lorenzetti, *Venice and its Lagoons* (Trieste, 1975)

Masalino, G., *The Basilica of St Mark's in Venice* (Venice, 1955)

Norwich, John Julius, *A History of Venice* (London, 1977 & 1981)

Ruskin, J., *The Stones of Venice* (London, 1851–53)

Ruskin, J., *St Mark's Rest* (London, 1877)

Vio, Ettore (ed.), *St Mark's Basilica in Venice* (London, 2000)

5 The Leaning Tower of Pisa

Burland, J. B., 'Propping up Pisa – Part I', *Journal of Architectural Conservation*, 2;7–21 (1997)

Burland, J. B., 'Propping up Pisa – Part II', *Journal of Architectural Conservation*, 3;7–21 (1997)

Ministero dei Lavori Pubblici, *Ricerche e studi sulla Torre di Pisa ed i fenomeni connesi alle condizione di ambiente*. 3 Vol., I. G. M. (Florence, 1971)

Sanpaolesi, P., *Il campanile di Pisa* (Pisa, 1956)

torre.duomo.pisa.it/index_eng.html (official website)

6 Chartres Cathedral

Adams, Henry, *Mont Saint-Michel and Chartres* (original ed. 1913, reprinted London, 1980)

Branner, Robert, *Chartres Cathedral* (London & New York, 1969)

Favier, Jean, *The World of Chartres* (London & New York, 1990)

Henderson, George, *Chartres* (Harmondsworth, 1968)

James, John, *Chartres, the Masons who Built a Legend* (London, 1982)

Wilson, Christopher, *The Gothic Cathedral* (London & New York, 1990)

7 King's College Chapel

Heyman, Jacques, *The Stone Skeleton, Structural Engineering of Masonry Architecture* (Cambridge & New York, 1995)

Wayment, Hilary, *King's College Chapel Cambridge, The Great Windows, Introduction and Guide* (Cambridge, 1992)

Willis, Robert & Willis Clark, John, *The Architectural History of the University of Cambridge and of the Colleges of Cambridge and Eton* (Cambridge, 1988)

Woodman, Francis, *The Architectural History of King's College Chapel and its Place in the Development of Late Gothic Architecture in England and France* (London, 1986)

8 St Peter's Basilica

Ackerman, James S., *The Architecture of Michelangelo* (Chicago & London, 1981)

Argan, Giulio & Contardi, Bruno, *Michelangelo Architect* (London & New York, 1993)

Bruschi, Arnaldo, *Bramante* (London, 1977)

Hibbard, Howard, *Carlo Maderno and Roman Architecture* (London & University Park, 1971)

Hibbard, Howard, *Bernini* (Harmondsworth, 1963)

Lees-Milne, James, *St Peter's* (London & Boston, 1967)

9 The Mosque of Selim II

Goodwin, G., *A History of Ottoman Architecture* (London & New York, 1972)

Goodwin, G., *Sinan, Ottoman Architecture and its Values Today* (London, 1993)

Kuran, A., *Sinan, the Grand Old Master of Ottoman Architecture* (Washington, DC, 1987)

Yetkin, S. K., *Turkish Architecture*, trans. Ünsal (Ankara, 1965)

10 The Taj Mahal

Begley, W. E. & Desai, Z. A., *Taj Mahal: The Illumined Tomb. An Anthology of Seventeenth-Century Mughal and European Documentary Sources*, The Aga Khan Program for Islamic Architecture (Cambridge, MA, 1989)

Koch, Ebba, *Mughal Architecture: An Outline of its History and Development: 1526–1858* (Munich, 1991 & 1998)

Okada, Amina & Joshi, M. C., *Taj Mahal* (New York, London, Paris, 1993)

Qaisar, Ahsan Jan, *Building Construction in Mughal India: The Evidence from Painting* (New Delhi,1988)

'Tadj Mahall' in *Encyclopaedia of Islam*, 2nd ed., vol. 10 (2000)

11 St Paul's Cathedral

Beard, Geoffrey, *The Work of Sir Christopher Wren* (London, 1956)

Downes, Kerry, *Christopher Wren* (London, 1971)

Fürst, Viktor, *The Architecture of Sir Christopher Wren* (London, 1956)

Seckler, E., *Wren and his Place in European Architecture* (London, 1956)

Summerson, John, *Sir Christopher Wren* (London, 1971)

Whinney, Margaret, *Wren* (London & New York, 1971)

12 The Panthéon, Paris

Le Pantheon: symbole des revolutions: de l'Eglise de la Nation au Temple des grands hommes. Published on the occasion of an exhibition held at the Hotel de Sully, Paris, and at the Centre Canadien d'Architecture, Montreal (Paris, 1989)

Sharp, Dennis, *The Illustrated Encyclopedia of Architects and Architecture* (New York, 1991)

13 The Sagrada Familia

Bonet, J., *The Essential Gaudí: The Geometric Modulation of the Church of the Sagrada Familia* (Barcelona, 2000)

Burry, M. C., *The Expiatory Church of the Sagrada Familia* (London, 1993)

Gomez, J., Coll, J., Melero, J. C., Burry, M. C., *La Sagrada Familia: De Gaudí al CAD* (Barcelona, 1996)

McCully, M., et al, *Homage to Barcelona: The City and its Art 1888–1936* (London, 1986)

Thiébaut, Philippe, *Gaudí. Builder of Visions* (London & New York, 2002)

Van Hensbergen, Gijs, *Gaudi: A Biography* (London & New York, 2001)

Zerbst, R., *Gaudí 1852–1926: Antoni Gaudí y Cornet, a Life Devoted to Architecture* (Cologne, 1990)

14 The Chapel of Notre Dame du Haut

Cohen, Jean-Louis (ed.), *Le Corbusier. Catalogue de l'exposition*, Centre Georges Pompidou (Paris, 1991)

Curtis, William J. R., *Le Corbusier Ideas and Forms* (Oxford, 1986)

Girsberger, Hans (ed.), *Le Corbusier 1910–60* (New York, 1959)

Kidder Smith, G. E., *Looking at Architecture* (New York, 1990)

Régnier, Bruno & McClure, Bert, *Le Corbusier. Promenades dans son oeuvre en France* (Paris, 1991)

Serenyi, Pete (ed.), *Le Corbusier in Perspective* (Englewood Cliffs, NJ, 1975)

Palaces & Castles

15 The Alhambra

Barrucand, M. & Bednorz, A., *Moorish Architecture in Andalusia* (Cologne, 1992)

García Gomez, E., *Poemas árabesen los muros y fuentes de la Alhambra* (Madrid, 1985)

Grabar, O., *The Alhambra* (London, 1978)

Jacobs, M., *Alhambra* (Milan, 2000)

Raquejo, T., *El palacio encantado. La Alhambra en el arte británico* (Madrid, 1989)

Zuylen, G. van, *Alhambra, a Moorish Paradise* (London & New York, 1999)

16 The Forbidden City

Ledderose, Lothar, *Ten Thousand Things: Module and Mass Production in Chinese Art*, The A.W. Mellon Lectures in the Fine Arts, 1998, The National Gallery of Washington, DC. Bollingen Series XXXV: 46 (Princeton, 2000)

Wan Yi, Wang Shuqing, Lu Yanzhen (chief compilers), translated by Rosemary Scott & Erica Shipley, *Daily Life in the Forbidden City: The Qing Dynasty 1644–1912* (Hong Kong, 1988)

17 The Topkapi Palace

Goodwin, G., *Topkapi Palace* (London, 1999)

Miller, B., *The Palace School* (Cambridge, MA, 1941)

Negipoglu, G., *Architecture, Ceremonial and Power* (New York, 1991)

18 The Kremlin

Brumfield, W. C., *Gold in Azure: One Thousand Years of Russian Architecture* (Boston, 1983)

Brumfield, W. C., *A History of Russian Architecture* (Cambridge & New York, 1993)

Hamilton, G., *The Art and Architecture of Russia* (Harmondsworth, 1983)

Riasanovsky, N., *A History of Russia* (New York & London, 1999)

Wortman, R., *Scenarios of Power* (Princeton, 1995)

19 The Escorial

Bury, J. B., 'Juan de Herrera and the Escorial', *Art History*, IX 4 (December 1986)

Kubler, George, *Building the Escorial* (Princeton, 1982)

Mulcahy, Rosemarie, *The Decoration of the Royal Basilica of El Escorial* (Cambridge, 1994)

Taylor, René, 'Architecture and magic: considerations on the idea of the Escorial' in *Essays in the History of Architecture Presented to Rudolf Wittkower* (New York, 1967)

Wilkinson-Zerner, Catherine, *Juan de Herrera, Architect to Philip II of Spain* (New Haven, 1993)

20 Versailles

Gourcuff, Alain de, *The Gardens of Le Nôtre at Versailles* (Paris, 2001)

Lablaude, Pierre-André, *The Gardens of Versailles* (London, 1995)

Leveque, Jean-Jacques, *Versailles* (Paris, 2000)

Montclos, Jean-Marie Perouse de, *Versailles* (New York, 1991)

Saule, Béatrix & Corbiau, Gérard, *Versailles, La Visite multi-lingual* DVD vidéo (Paris, 1999)

The Palace of Versailles (Paris, 1998)

www.versailles.fr

21 The Potala Palace

Baker, Ian A., *The Dalai Lama's Secret Temple* (London & New York, 2000)

David-Neel, Alexandra, *My Journey to Lhasa* (London, reprint, 1983)

Fisher, Robert E., *Art of Tibet* (London & New York, 1997)

Kemp, Richard, *The Potala of Tibet* (London, revised ed., 1988)

Montgomery MacGovern, William, *To Lhasa in Disguise* (London, 1924)

22 Schloss Schönbrunn

Aurenhammer, Hans, *J. B. Fischer von Erlach* (London, 1973)

Lanchester, H.V., *Fischer von Erlach* (London, 1924)

23 The Winter Palace

Brumfield, W. C., *Gold in Azure: One Thousand Years of Russian Architecture* (Boston, 1983)

Brumfield, W. C., *A History of Russian Architecture* (Cambridge & New York, 1993)

Hamilton, G., *The Art and Architecture of Russia* (Harmondsworth, 1983)

Massie, S., *Land of the Firebird* (New York, 1980)

Orloff, A. & Shvidkovsky, D., *St Petersburg: Architecture of the Tsars* (New York, 1996)

Wortman, R., *Scenarios of Power* (Princeton, 1995)

24 Neuschwanstein Castle

Blunt, Wilfrid, *The Dream King. Ludwig II of Bavaria* (London & New York, 1970)

Burg, Katerina von, *Ludwig II of Bavaria: The Man and the Mystery* (Windsor, 1989)

Hojer, Gerhard & Jervis, Simon, *Designs for the Dream King: the Castles and Palaces of Ludwig II of Bavaria* (London & New York, 1978)

King, Greg, *The Mad King: The Life and Times of Ludwig II of Bavaria* (New Jersey & London, 1996)

Knapp, Gottfried, *Neuschwanstein* (Stuttgart & London, 1999)

25 The Viceroy's House, New Delhi
Hussey, Christopher, *Life of Sir Edwin Lutyens* (London, 1950, repr. 1984)
Irving, Robert Grant, *Indian Summer. Lutyens, Baker and Imperial Delhi*
(New Haven & London, 1982)
Lutyens, exhibition catalogue (London, 1981)
Morris, Jan, *Architecture of the British Empire* (London & New York, 1986)

26 La Cuesta Encantada: Hearst's Castle
Aidala, Thomas, *Hearst Castle, San Simeon* (New York, 1981)
Boutelle, Sara Holmes, *Julia Morgan, Architect* (New York, 1988)
Kastner, Victoria, *Hearst Castle: The Biography of a Country House* (New York, 2000)
Loe, Nancy E., *Hearst Castle: An Interpretive History of W. R. Hearst's San Simeon Estate* (Santa Barbara, 1994)
Nasaw, David, *The Chief, The Life of William Randolph Hearst* (New York, 2000)
Swanberg, W. A., *Citizen Hearst: A Biography of William Randolph Hearst* (New York, 1961)
www.hearstcastle.org/history/the_castle.asp

Public & State Buildings

27 The Houses of Parliament
Colvin, H. M. (ed.), *The History of the King's Works*, 6 vols (London, 1963–1982)
Fell, B. H. & Mackenzie, K. R., *The Houses of Parliament: A Guide to the Palace of Westminster* (London, 1930, rev.14, 1988)
Gerhold, D., *Westminster Hall* (London, 1999)
Port, M. (ed.), *The Houses of Parliament* (New Haven & London, 1976)
Riding, Christine & Riding, Jacqueline, *The Houses of Parliament. History, Art, Architecture* (London, 2000)
www.parliament.uk/hophome.htm

28 The Crystal Palace
Beaver, P., *The Crystal Palace, A Portrait of a Victorian Enterprise* (Chichester, 1970)
Downes, C. & Cowper, C., *The Building Erected in Hyde Park for the Great Exhibition of the Works of Industry of All Nations*, 1851 (London, 1852)
McKean, J., *Crystal Palace* (London, 1994)
Sennett, R., 'The Crystal Palace' in *Palais-Royal* (London, 1986, Pt 2)

29 The Opéra, Paris
Blaser, Werner & Stucky, Monica, *Drawings of Great Buildings* (Boston, 1983)
Fontaine, Gérard, *Palais Garnier. Le Fantasme de l'Opéra* (Paris, 1999)
Mignot, Claude, *Architecture of the Nineteenth Century in Europe* (New York, 1984)
Sharp, Dennis, *The Illustrated Encyclopedia of Architects and Architecture* (New York, 1991)

30 The Pentagon
Congressional Quarterly's Washington Guidebook, Congressional Quarterly (Washington, DC, 1990), 119–21
Headquarters of the United States Department of Defense: The Pentagon, www.defenselink.mil/pubs/pentagon
Pentagon Renovation Program, http://renovation.pentagon.mil./history.htm
The Pentagon, Office of the Assistant Secretary of Defense for Public Affairs, Washington, DC (n.d)
Winston, S., 'Pentagon Contractors Divide and Conquer', *Engineering News-Record*, vol. 245, no. 9, 4 (September 2000), 58–63

31 The Guggenheim Museum, New York
Kidder-Smith, G. E., *Source Book of American Architecture* (Princeton, 1996)
McCarter, Robert, *Frank Lloyd Wright* (New York & London, 1997)
Pfeiffer, Bruce Brooks & Larkin, David, *Frank Lloyd Wright. Master Builder* (New York & London, 1997)
Storrer, William Allin, *The Architecture of Frank Lloyd Wright* (Chicago, 3rd ed., 2002)
www.guggenheim.org

32 Walt Disney World Resort
Dunlop, Beth, *Building a Dream: The Art of Disney Architecture* (New York, 1996)
Fjellman, Stephen M., *Vinyl Leaves: Walt Disney World and America* (Boulder, 1992)
Francaviglia, Richard V., 'Main Street U.S.A.: A Comparison/Contrast of Streetscapes in Walt Disney World', *Journal of Popular Culture* (Summer 1981), 141–45
Marling, Karal Ann (ed.), *Designing Disney's Theme Parks: The Architecture of Reassurance* (Montreal, 1997)
Mosley, Leonard, *Disney's World: A Biography* (Latham, MD, 1985)
Thomas, Bob, *Building a Company: Roy O. Disney and the Creation of an Entertainment Empire* (New York, 1998)

33 The Sydney Opera House
Drew, Philip, *The Masterpiece: Jorn Utzon A Secret Life* (Melbourne, Australia, 1999)
Duek-Cohen, Elias, *Utzon and the Sydney Opera House: Statement in the Public Interest* (Sydney, 1967)
Fromonot, Francois, *Jorn Utzon The Sydney Opera House* (Corte Madera, CA, 1998)
Ove Arup Partnership, 'Sydney Opera House Special Issue', *The Arup Journal*, 8, 3 (October, 1973)
'Sydney Opera House Commemorative Issue', 106, Royal Society of New South Wales (Sydney, 1973)
Utzon, Jorn, *Descriptive Narrative with Status Quo: Sydney Opera House, January 1965* (Sydney, 1965)
www.soh.nsw.gov.au/

34 The Louisiana Superdome
Mule, M., *Superdome*, (New Orleans, 1996)
www.superdome.com

35 The Pompidou Centre
Campbell Cole, Barbie & Rogers, Ruth Elias (eds), *Richard Rogers + Partners* (London, 1985)
Clark, Roger H. & Pause, Michael, *Precedents in Architecture* (New York, 1985)
Russell, Frank (ed.), *Architectural Monographs: Richard Rogers + Architects*, (New York, 1985)
Sharp, Dennis, *Twentieth-Century Architecture: A Visual History* (London, 1991)
Silver, Nathan, *The Making of Beaubourg*, (Cambridge, MA, 1994)
www.cnac-gp.fr/

36 Kansai International Airport
Buchanan, Peter, *Renzo Piano Building Workshop* (London, 1993–97)
Eco, Umberto, *The Making of Kansai International Airport Terminal, Osaka, Japan. Renzo Piano Building Workshop* (Tokyo, 1994)
Piano, Renzo, *The Renzo Piano Logbook* (London & New York, 1997)
www.kansai-airport.or.jp/english/

37 The Guggenheim Museum, Bilbao

Dal Co, F. & Forster, K. W., *Frank O. Gehry* (New York, 1998)

Forster, K. W., *Frank O. Gehry, Guggenheim Bilbao Museoa*, (Stuttgart & London, 1998)

Iyengar, H., Novak, L., Sinn, R. & Zis, J., 'The Guggenheim Museum, Bilbao, Spain', *Structural Engineering International* (1996), 227–29

Jencks, C. (ed.), *Frank O. Gehry, Individual Imagination and Cultural Conservatism* (London, 1995)

Van Bruggen, Coosje, *Frank O. Gehry. Guggenheim Museum Bilbao* (New York & London, 1997)

www.guggenheim.org

Towers & Skyscrapers

38 The Washington Monument

Allen, T. B., *The Washington Monument: It Stands for All* (New York, 2000)

Gallagher, H. M. P., *Robert Mills: Architect of the Washington Monument 1781–1855* (New York, 1935)

Tamaro, M. J. & O'Connor, J. G., 'Scaling the Monument', *Civil Engineering*, vol. 69, no. 4 (April 1999), 36–41

Torres, L., *"To the immortal name and memory of George Washington": The United States Army Corps of Engineers and the Construction of the Washington Monument* (Washington, DC, 1984)

39 The Eiffel Tower

Architectural Guide to the Eiffel Tower (Monticello, 1981)

Cate, Phillip Dennis (ed.), *The Eiffel Tower: A Tour de Force. Centennial Exhibition* (New York & Paris, 1989)

Denker, Winnie & Sagan, Françoise, *The Eiffel Tower* (London, 1989)

Harriss, Joseph, *The Eiffel Tower. Symbol of an Age* (London, 1976)

Loyrette, Henri, *Gustave Eiffel* (New York, 1985)

www.tour-eiffel.fr/teiffel/uk/

40 The Empire State Building

Friedman, D., '"A Story a Day": Engineering the Work', in Willis, C. (ed.), *Building the Empire State* (New York & London, 1998), 33–46

James, T. J. Jr., *The Empire State Building* (New York, 1975)

Langer, F., *Lewis W. Hine: The Empire State Building* (Munich, 1998)

Tauranac, J., *The Empire State Building: The Making of a Landmark* (New York, 1995)

Willis, C., 'Building the Empire State', in Willis, C. (ed.), *Building the Empire State* (New York & London, 1998), 11–32

www.esbnyc.com/

41 The Gateway Arch

Ford, Edward R., *The Details of Modern Architecture, Volume 2: 1928 to 1988* (Cambridge, MA, 1996)

Peter, J., *The Oral History of Modern Architecture* (New York, 1994)

Saarinen, Eero, *Eero Saarinen on His Work* (New Haven, 1962)

www.stlouisarch.com

42 The World Trade Center

Clifton, G. Charles, 'Collapse of the World Trade Center Towers' http://www.hera.org.nz

Department of Civil Engineering, University of Sydney, Australia, 'World Trade Center-New York-Some Engineering Aspects' http://www.civil.usyd.edu.au/wtc.htm

Darton, Eric, *Divided We Stand* (New York, 1990)

Gillespie, Angus, *Twin Towers* (New Brunswick, NJ, 1999)

Leary, Warren E., 'Years to Build and Moments to Destroy: How the Twin Towers Fell', *The New York Times*, 25 September, 2001

The Port of New York Authority, *The World Trade Center in the Port of New York, New York* (New York, 1967)

Robins, Anthony, *The World Trade Center: Classics of American Architecture* (Englewood, NJ & Fort Lauderdale, FL,1987)

Ruchelman, Leonard I., *The World Trade Center: Politics and Policies of Skyscraper Development* (Syracuse, NY, 1977)

Seabrook, John, 'The Tower Builder', *New Yorker*, November 19, 2001, 64–73.

Tarricone, Paul, 'After the Blast', *Civil Engineering* May 1993, 44–47

'The Tallest Steel Bearing Walls', *Architectural Record*, vol. 135 (May 1964), 194–96

Yamasaki, Minoru, *A Life in Architecture* (New York & Toronto, 1979)

43 Sears Tower

Eggen, A. P. & Sandaker, B. N., *Steel, Structure and Architecture* (New York, 1995)

Huxtable, A., *The Tall Building Artistically Reconsidered: The Search for a Skyscraper Style* (New York, 1984)

Marlin, W., 'Sears Tower: The mail-order approach to urban form', *Architectural Forum* (January–February 1974) 25–31

Tigerman, Stanley, *Bruce Graham of SOM* (New York, 1989)

www.sears-tower.com/

44 The CN Tower

Dendy, William & Kilbourn, William, *Toronto Observed* (Toronto, 1986)

McHugh, Patricia, *Toronto Architecture – A City Guide* (Toronto, 1986)

Whiteson, Leon, *Toronto: The Liveable City* (Toronto, 1982)

www.cntower.ca

45 The Hongkong and Shanghai Bank

Foster, Norman, *Norman Foster: Catalogue of Work* (Munich & London, 2000)

Jodidio, Philip, *Sir Norman Foster* (Cologne & London, 1997)

Lambot, Ian (ed.), *Norman Foster, Foster Associates. Buildings and Projects, Vol. 3, 1978–1985* (Hong Kong, 1989)

Pawley, Martin, *Norman Foster. A Global Architecture* (London, 1999)

www.fosterandpartners.com

46 Petronas Towers

Crosbie, M. J., *Cesar Pelli: Recent Themes* (Basel, 2000)

Pearson, C. A., 'Other than their status as the world's tallest buildings, what else do Cesar Pelli's Petronas Towers have going for them?' *Architectural Record*, 187, no. 1 (1999), 92–101

Petroski, H., 'The Petronas Towers', in *Remaking the World: Adventures in Engineering* (New York, 1997), 203–12

47 New York-New York

Anderton, Frances & Chase, John, *Las Vegas: The Success of Excess* (London, 1997)

Earley, Pete, *Super Casino: Inside the 'New' Las Vegas* (New York, 2000)

Hess, Alan, *Viva Las Vegas: After-Hours Architecture* (San Francisco, 1993)

Hess, Alan, 'New York, New York', *Architectural Record* vol. 185, no. 3 (March 1997)

Izenour, Steven & Dashiel, David A. III, 'Relearning from Las Vegas', *Architecture* (October 1990)

48 The London Eye

Architecture Today 108 (May, 2000)

Civil Engineering, 144, 2 (May, 2001)

Journal of the Institution of Structural Engineers, 'The British Airways London Eye', vol. 79, no. 2 (January 2001)

Lambot, Ian & Wood, Nick, *Reinventing the Wheel. The Construction of British Airways London Eye* (Haslemere, 2000)
Powell, Kenneth, *New London Architecture* (London, 2001)
Rattenbury, Kester, *The Essential Eye* (London, 2002)

Bridges, Railways & Tunnels

49 The Iron Bridge, Coalbrookdale
Briggs, Asa, *Iron Bridge to Crystal Palace* (London, 1979)
Clark, Catherine M., *Ironbridge Gorge* (London, 1993)
Giedion, Sigfried, *Space, Time, Architecture* (Oxford & Harvard, 1962)
Great Engineers: The Art of British Engineers (London, 1987)
Joedicke, Jurgen, *A History of Modern Architecture* (London, 1959)
www.ironbridge.org.uk

50 The Thames Tunnel
Clements. Paul, *Marc Isambard Brunel* (London & Harlow, 1970)
Lampe, David, *The Tunnel. The Story of the World's First Tunnel under a Navigable River, Dug beneath the Thames, 1824–42* (London, 1963)
Overman, Michael, *Sir Marc Brunel and the Tunnel* (London, 1971)

51 Brooklyn Bridge
McCullogh, David, *The Great Bridge: The Epic Story of the Building of the Brooklyn Bridge* (New York, 1983)
Shapiro, Mary, J., *A Picture History of the Brooklyn Bridge* (New York & London, 1983)
Trachtenberg, Alan, *Brooklyn Bridge, Fact and Symbol* (Chicago, 1979)

52 The Canadian Pacific Railway
Graham, Melissa, *Trans-Canada Rail Guide* (Hindhead, 1996)
Marshall, John, *The Guinness Railway Book* (London, 1989)
Mitchell, Robert D. & Groves, Paul A. (eds), *North America. The Historical Geography of a Changing Continent* (London, 1987)

53 The Forth Rail Bridge
Koerte, Arnold, *Two Railway Bridges of an Era. Firth of Forth and Firth of Tay. Technical Progress, Disaster and New Beginnings in Victorian Engineering* (London & Basle, 1992)
Mackay, Sheila, *Bridge Across the Century. The Story of the Forth Bridge* (Edinburgh, 1985)
Mackay, Sheila, *The Forth Bridge. A Picture History* (Edinburgh, 1993)
Murray, Anthony, *The Forth Railway Bridge. A Celebration* (Edinburgh, 1988)
Paxton, Roland *100 Years of the Forth Bridge* (Telford, 1990)

54 The Jungfrau Rail System
Allen, Cecil J., *Switzerland's Amazing Railways* (London, 1960)
Cooling, Maureen G., *Ticket to the Top* (London, 1986)
Jungfraubahn, Jungfrau Railway, Switzerland (undated, *c.* 1920)
www.jungfraubahn.ch

55 The Moscow Metro
Garbutt, Paul, *World Metro Systems* (Harrow, 2nd ed., 1997)
Nock, O. S., *Underground Railways of the World* (London, 1973)
Tarkhanov, Alexei & Kavtaradze, Sergei, *Stalinist Architecture* (London, 1992)
Urban Public Transport Statistics, UITP (Brussels, 1997)

56 The Golden Gate Bridge
Chester, M., *Joseph Strauss, Builder of the Golden Gate Bridge* (New York, 1965)

Dillon, Richard H., *High Steel. Building the Bridges across San Francisco Bay* (Berkeley, 1979)
Horton, Tom & Wolman, Baron, *Superspan. The Golden Gate Bridge* (New York, 1998)
Van der Zee, John, *The Gate: The True Story of the Design and Construction of the Golden Gate Bridge* (New York, 1986)
www.goldengate.org

57 The Seikan Rail Tunnel
Chadwick, Roy & Knights, Martin C., *The Story of Tunnels* (London, 1988)
Modern Railways, *Railway Gazette International*, various issues
www.pref.aomori.jp/newline/newline-e/sin-e08.html

58 The Channel Tunnel
Anderson, G. & Roskrow, B., *The Channel Tunnel Story* (London, 1994)
Bonavia, Michael R. *The Channel Tunnel Story* (Newton Abbot, 1987)
Eurotunnel, *The Official Channel Tunnel Factfile* (London, 1994)
Grayson, Lesley, *The Channel Tunnel. Le Tunnel sous la Manche* (London, 1990)
Hunt, Donald, *The Story of the Channel Tunnel, 1802–1994* (Upton-upon-Severn, 1994)
Kirkland, C. J., *Engineering the Channel Tunnel* (London, 1995)
Wilson, Keith, *Channel Tunnel Visions, 1850–1950* (London, 1995)

59 The Great Belt East Bridge
Gimsing, Niels J., *Design of a Long-Span Cable-Supported Bridge Across the Great Belt in Denmark – 25 Years of Experience and Evolution* (Yokohama, 1991)
Gimsing, Niels J., *The Akashi Kaikyo Bridge and the Storebælt East Bridge – the Two Greatest Suspension Bridges of the 20th Century* (Kobe, 1998)
Gimsing, Niels J. (ed.), *East Bridge* (Copenhagen, 1998)
Holmegaard, Karsten (ed.), *Storebælt 1988–1998* (Copenhagen, 1998)
Selsing, Jo, *Brobyggerne/Bridgebuilders* (Copenhagen, 1998)

60 The Akashi Kaikyo Bridge
Dupre, J., *Bridges: A History of the World's Most Famous and Important Spans* (New York, 1997), 114–15
Fujikawa, H., Kishimoto, Y. & Nasu, S., 'Aesthetic Design for Akashi Kaikyo Bridge', *Transportation Research Record*, no. 1549 (1996), 12–17
Normile, D., 'Spanning Japan's Inland Sea: Akashi Kaikyo's Record-Length Suspended Span Caps Program', *Engineering News-Record*, vol. 237, no. 19 (4 November 1996), 30–34
Ochsendorf, J. A. & Billington, D. P., 'Record Spans in Japan', *Civil Engineering*, vol. 68, no. 2 (February, 1998), 60–63
www.hsba.go.jp/bridge/e-akasi.htm

Canals & Dams

61 The Erie Canal
Chalmers, Harvey, *The Birth of the Erie Canal* (New York, 1960)
Shaw, Ronald E., *Erie Waterwest; a History of the Erie Canal, 1792–1854* (Lexington, KY, 1966)
Sheriff, Carol, *The Artificial River: The Erie Canal and the Paradox of Progress* (New York, 1996)
www.canals.state.ny.us/

62 The Suez Canal
Burchell, S. C., *Building the Suez Canal* (London, 1967)
Farnie, D. A., *East and West of Suez: The Suez Canal in History, 1854–1956,* (Oxford, 1969)
Lord Kinross (Patrick Balfour, Baron Kinross), *Between Two Seas: The*

Creation of the Suez Canal (London, 1968)

Wilson, Arnold T., *The Suez Canal: Its Past, Present, and Future* (London, 1933, reprinted 1977)

63 The Panama Canal

Haskin, Frederic J., *The Panama Canal* (New York, 1914)

Howarth, David, *Panama, Four Hundred Years of Dreams and Cruelty* (New York, 1966)

McCollough, David, *The Path Between the Seas* (New York, 1977)

www.pancanal.com

64 Hoover Dam

Dunar, A. J. & McBride, D., *Building Hoover Dam, An Oral History* (New York, 1993)

Woodbury, David Oakes, *Colorado Conquest* (New York, 1941)

Woollett, William, *Hoover Dam: Drawings, Etchings, Lithographs* (Los Angeles, 1986)

65 Itaipú Dam

'$18-billion Itaipú Dam sets new hydroelectric records', *Engineering News-Record* (January, 1999)

www.itaipu.gov.br/homeing.htm

66 The Dutch Sea Barrier

De Haan, H. & Haagsma, I., *De Deltawerken; techniek, politiek, achtergronden* (Delft, 1984)

'Eastern Scheldt Storm Surge Barrier', Proceedings of the Delta Barrier Symposium (Rotterdam, 1982)

Huis in 't Veld, J.C. et al, *The Closure of Tidal Basins* (Delft, 1987)

Nienhuis, P. H. & Smaal, A. C., *The Oosterschelde Estuary (the Netherlands): A Case-Study of a Changing Ecosystem* (Dordrecht, 1994)

Rijkswaterstaat, 'Ontwerpnota Stormvloedkering Oosterschelde' ('Design Report of the Eastern Scheldt Storm Surge Barrier') in 5 volumes, *Projectorganisatie Stormvloedkering*, Ministerie van Verkeer en Waterstaat (1987)

67 The Three Gorges Dam

Heersink, Paul, *Three Gorges Dam* (Lindsay, Ontario, 1996)

Qing, Dai, *The River Dragon has Come! The Three Gorges Dam and the Fate of China's Yangtze River and its People* (Armonk, 1998)

www.chinaonline.com/refer/ministry_profiles/threegorgesdam.asp

Colossal Statues

68 The Statue of Liberty

Boime, Albert, *The Unveiling of the National Icons* (Cambridge, 1998)

Condit, Carl W., *American Building* (Chicago, 2nd ed., 1982)

Trachtenberg, Marvin, *The Statue of Liberty* (New York, 1976, rev. ed.1986)

69 The Statue of Christ the Redeemer

Motta, Edso, (ed.), *O Cristo do Corcovado* (Rio de Janeiro, 1981)

Pedreira, Mauricio, 'Rio recovers the mantle of Christ', *Americas* (English edition), vol. 42, no. 5 (Sept.–Oct., 1990) 26–29

Wilson, M. Robert & Landowski, Paul, *Le Temple de l'Homme* (Paris, 2000)

www.corcovado.com.br

70 Mount Rushmore

Boime, Albert, *The Unveiling of the National Icons* (Cambridge, 1998)

Chidester, David & Linenthal, Edward T., *American Sacred Space* (Bloomington, 1995)

Shaff, Howard, *Six Wars at a Time: the Life and Times of Gutzon Borglum, Sculptor of Mount Rushmore* (Darien, Conn., 1985)

Sources of Illustrations

Joseph/Robert Harding; 89 © Michael Jenner; 90 P. Winton; 91t © Adam Woolfitt/Robert Harding; 91b © Jayawardene Photo Library; 92 © Michael Jenner/Robert Harding; 93 © W. C. Brumfield; 94 © Robert Francis/Robert Harding; 95 P. Winton; 96 © W. C. Brumfield; 97 © Dave Jacobs/Robert Harding; 98 © AISA-Archivo Iconográfico; 99t © Adam Woolfitt/Robert Harding; 99c from *Architettura Libro IV (Regole generali)*, 1537. Folio LIII recto; 99b engraved by Pierre Perret, 1587; 100 Reproduced courtesy of The Marquess of Salisbury; 101 © AISA-Archivo Iconográfico; 102 © Photo RMN-Arnaudet; 103 Photo RMN-J. Derenne; 104, 105 Photos RMN; 106 Photo Harry Bréjat - RMN; 107 Photo Hugh Richardson; 108 © N. Blythe/Robert Harding; 109 P. Winton, after F. Meyer; 110t Photo Erich Lessing/AKG London; 110b © Jane Sweeney/Robert Harding; 111 © AISA-Archivo Iconográfico; 112 Photo Erich Lessing/AKG London; 113 © AISA-Archivo Iconográfico; 114 © W. C. Brumfield; 115 © AISA-Archivo Iconográfico; 116, 117, 118 © Achim Bunz; 119, 120, 121 © Country Life Picture Library; 122 Photo A. F. Kersting; 123 © Leslie Woodhead/Hutchison Picture Library; 124 © Emily Lane; 125 © Doug Traverso/Robert Harding; 126–27 Photo A. F. Kersting; 128 © Jean-Pierre Delagarde & © Jacques Moatti; 129 © Jason Hawkes; 130 Photo A. F. Kersting; 131t Public Record Office. Work 28/895; 131b © Michael Jenner; 132t lithograph published by Vacher & Son, 1854; 132b Courtesy Palace of Westminster; 133 © Simon Harris/Robert Harding; 134 Guildhall Library, Corporation of London; 135, 136t, 136b *Illustrated London News*, 1849–52; 137 Guildhall Library, Corporation of London; 138 Photo Jean Schormans - RMN; 139, 140t © Jean-Pierre Delagarde & © Jacques Moatti; 140b Pascal Lemaître © Centre des Monuments Nationaux, Paris; 141t P. Winton; 141b, 142 Courtesy Department of Defense, Washington, DC; 143 Photo Hulton Archive, London; 144t Photograph by William Short © The Solomon R. Guggenheim Foundation, New York; 144b, 145 Photograph by David Heald. © The Solomon R. Guggenheim Foundation, New York; 146, 147 © Disney Enterprises, Inc.; 148 News Ltd.; 149t © Jeremy Horner/Hutchison Picture Library; 149b News Ltd; 150 NAA: A1500, 1966/15925; 151 Courtesy Ove Arup & Partners; 152 News Ltd; 153 © Troy Gomez; 154 Courtesy Curtis and Davis Office Records, Southeastern Architectural Archive, Tulane University Library; 154, 155 © Troy Gomez; 156, 157 Photo Georges Meguerditchian © Centre Georges Pompidou, Paris; 158t © John Donat. Photo courtesy Rogers Partnership; 158b Photo G. Meguerditchian © Centre Georges Pompidou, Paris; 159 © Philip Craven/Robert Harding; 160 Renzo Piano Building Workshop architects (Noriaki Okabe Associate Architect) in association with Nikken Sekkei Ltd., Aéroports de Paris and Japan Airport Consultants Inc. Drawing courtesy RPW; 161t © Dennis Gilbert/VIEW; 161b Renzo Piano Building Workshop architects (Noriaki Okabe Associate Architect) in association with Nikken Sekkei Ltd., Aéroports de Paris and Japan Airport Consultants Inc. Drawing courtesy RPW; 162t Photo Susumu Shingo Photo © RPW; 162b Renzo Piano Building Workshop architects (Noriaki Okabe Associate Architect) in association with Nikken Sekkei Ltd., Aéroports de Paris and Japan Airport Consultants Inc. Photo courtesy RPW; 163 © Dennis Gilbert/VIEW; 164–65 © C. Bowman/Robert Harding; 165, 166t Courtesy Gehry Partners; 166b, 167 © Timothy Hursley; 168–69 © AISA-Archivo Iconográfico; 170 P. Winton; 171 © Timothy Hursley; 172t Library of Congress, Washington, DC; 172b Photo by Mathew Brady, 1879. © The National Archives, Washington, DC; 173tc, 173tr P. Winton; 173b Library of Congress, Washington, DC; 174 © Roger Viollet; 175 © Jean Bernard 176 © ND-Viollet; 177t Anne Ronan Picture Library; 177b © ND-Viollet; 178 © Roger Viollet; 179, 180 Photos Lewis Hine; 181 © Nigel Francis/Robert Harding; 182t *Architectural Forum*, June 1930; 182b From *Notes on Construction of Empire State Building*, Starrett Brothers and Eken 1956–57; 183 © Jeff Greenberg/Robert Harding; 184 Jefferson National Expansion Memorial/National Park Service; 185 © Schuster/Robert Harding; 186t, 186b Jefferson National Expansion Memorial/National Park Service; 187 © Walter Rawlings/Robert Harding; 188t, 188b P. Winton, after *Architectural Record*, 135; 189 © Emily Lane; 190 AP Photo Archive; 191 Photo © H. Block/AKG London; 193 © Timothy Hursley; 194l, 194r P. Winton; 195 © Roy Rainford/Robert Harding; 196t Copyright of TrizecHahn Tower Limited Partnership; 196b P. Winton, after Nigel Hawkes, *Structures* (Macmillan 1990), 111; 197 Photo Ian Lambot; 198t, 198b © Foster and Partners; 199t Photo John Nye; 199b, 200t, 200b Photo Ian Lambot; 201 Photo Uwe Hausen. Courtesy of J. A. Jones; 202t P. Winton; 202b Photo Uwe Hausen. Courtesy of J. A. Jones; 203 © Jayawardene Photo Library; 204 Courtesy of J. A. Jones; 205 © Gavin Hellier/Robert Harding; 206 © Gavin Hellier/Robert Harding; 207, 208t, 208bl, 208bc, 208br, 209 © Nick Wood; 210–11 © John Tickner; 212 P. Winton; 213 Photo A. F. Kersting; 214t Science Museum, London UK/Bridgeman Art Library; 214c Private Collection, Sweden; 214b Collection Allied Ironfounders Ltd; 215 © Jean Williamson/Mick Sharp; 216 Lithograph by Trautmann after Bönisch. Guildhall Library, Corporation of London; 217t British Museum, London; 217b P. Winton; 218t Elton Collection,

Ironbridge Gorge Museum Trust; 218b By courtesy of the National Portrait Gallery, London; 219 Private Collection/Bridgeman Art Library; 220 P. Winton; 221 Photo Hulton Archive, London; 222 © Ethel Davies/Robert Harding; 223t © Paolo Koch/Robert Harding; 223b P. Winton; 224 Canadian Pacific; 225 © John Tickner; 226t P. Winton; 226b, 227 History Collection of the Civil Engineering Library, Imperial College London; 228 © John Tickner; 229 P. Winton; 230 © MPH/Robert Harding; 231 © Christopher Rennie/Robert Harding; 232 © Emily Lane; 234 © Nick Wood/Robert Harding; 235, 236t, 236b San Francisco History Center, San Francisco Public Library; 237 © Robert Aberman/Hutchison Picture Library; 238 © Paul van Riel; 239t P. Winton, after Nigel Hawkes, *Structures* (Macmillan 1990), 208–09; 239b P. Winton; 240–41 QA Photos; 242, 243 P. Winton; 244 Photo Jan Kofoed Winther; 245, 246t Photo Søren Madsen; 246b, 247 Photo Jan Kofoed Winther; 248 P. Winton; 249, 250t, 250b, 251tl, 251tr Courtesy Honshu-Shikoku Bridge Authority, Kobe; 251bl, 251br P. Winton; 252–53 © Nicholas Hall/Robert Harding; 254 Courtesy Itaipú Binacional; 255l, 255r P. Winton; 256 Photo Erie Canal Museum, Syracuse, N.Y; 257 P. Winton; 258 From *The Inauguration of the Suez Canal* by Marius Fontaine. Illustration by M. Riou; 259t Photo Fleming; 259b © David Clilverd/Hutchison Picture Library; 260 P. Winton, after Nigel Hawkes, *Structures*, (Macmillan 1990), 136–37; 261 © Mike Garding/South American Pictures; 262 Photo AKG London; 264 © Robert Francis/Robert Harding; 265 Library of Congress, Washington, DC; 266t United States Department of the Interior Bureau of Reclamation. Photo Andrew Pernick, March 31 1996; 266b P. Winton; 267, 268t Courtesy Itaipú Binacional; 268b P. Winton; 269, 270 Courtesy Itaipú Binacional; 271 P. Winton; 272t, 272b, 273t © Ovak Arslanian; 273b © Michael St. Maur Sheil; 274 P. Winton; 275, 276–77 © Andy Ryan; 277 P. Winton; 278–79 © Tom Till; 280 © Sue Cunningham/SCP; 281 © Simon Harris/Robert Harding; 282t Elton Collection, Ironbridge Gorge Museum Trust; 282b © Schuster/Robert Harding; 283 © Simon Harris/Robert Harding; 284 P. Winton, after Nigel Hawkes, *Structures* (Macmillan, 1990), 27; 285 Photo © Dan Cornish/Esto All Rights Reserved; 286 © Jason P Howe/South American Pictures; 287 © Sue Cunningham/SCP; 289t Courtesy National Park Service, Mount Rushmore National Memorial; 289b Photo Rise Studio. Courtesy National Park Service, Mount Rushmore National Memorial; 290t, 290b Bell Photo. Courtesy National Park Service, Mount Rushmore National Memorial; 291 Courtesy National Park Service, Mount Rushmore National Memorial.

Sources of quotations
31 John Ruskin, *The Stones of Venice* (London, 1851–53); 34 Jean Kerisel, *Down to Earth* (Rotterdam, 1987); 39 Henry Adams, *Mont-Saint-Michel and Chartres* (Boston & New York, 1913); 48 Madame de Staël, *Corinne*, 1807; 57 W. E. Begley, & Z. A. Desai, *Taj Mahal: The Illumined Tomb: An Anthology of Seventeenth-Century Mughal and European Documentary Sources* (Cambridge, MA, 1989); 84 Pierre Loti, *The Last Days of Pekin* (Boston, 1902); 99 William Lithgow, *Discourse of a Peregrination*, 1623; 107 W. Montgomery McGovern *To Lhasa in Disguise* (London, 1924); 116 Richard Wagner, *Das Rheingold*, 1852; 119 Robert Byron, *Country Life* (June 1931); 123 quoted in Sara Holmes Boutelle, *Julia Morgan Architect* (New York, 1988); 143 Bernard Levin, *A Walk Up Fifth Avenue* (London, 1989); 157 Nathan Silver, *The Making of Beaubourg*, (Cambridge MA,1994); 164 Kurt W. Forster, 'The Museum as Civic Catalyst', *Frank O. Gehry, Guggenheim Bilbao Museoa*, 1998; 171 L. Torres, 'To the immortal name and memory of George Washington':The United States Army Corps of Engineers and the Construction of the Washington Monument (Washington, 1984); 179 Col. W. A. Starrett, *Skyscrapers and the Men Who Build Them* (New York, 1928); 187 Minoru Yamasaki, *A Life in Architecture* (New York & Toronto, 1979); 192 Ada Louise Huxtable, *The Tall Building Artistically Reconsidered: The Search for a Skyscraper Style* (New York, 1984); 195 Leon Whiteson, *The Liveable City* (Oakville, 1982); 197 Martin Pawley, *Norman Foster. A Global Architecture* (London, 1999); 201 Cesar Pelli *Engineering News-Record*, vol. 326, No. 2, 15 January 1996, 39); 213 Asa Briggs, *Iron Bridge to Crystal Palace* (London, 1979); 216 L. T. C. Rolt, *Victorian Engineering* (London, 1970); 225 Sir Benjamin Baker, in David Steinman & Sarah Watson *Bridges and their Builders* (New York, 1941); 234 John Van Der Zee, *The Bridge* (New York, 1986); 248 Othmar H. Ammann, 'Present Status of Designs of Suspension Bridges with Respect to Dynamic Wind Action', *Boston Society of Civil Engineers* 40 (1953). Reprinted in D. P. Billington, *The Tower and the Bridge: The New Art of Structural Engineering* (Princeton, New Jersey, 1985); 264 Oskar J. W. Hansen, *Sculptures at Hoover Dam* (Washington, 1950); 267 Joan Didion *The White Album*,'Holy Water' (New York & London, 1979; first published 1977); 274 Lao-Tzu (6th century BC), *Tao-te-ching* (tr. by D. C. Lau, Baltimore, 1963); 286 from Edson Motta (ed.), *O Cristo do Corcovado* (Rio de Janeiro, 1981).

Index

Page numbers in *italics* refer to illustrations

Aalto, Alvar 143
Abbot Suger 43
aerodynamics 178
Agha, Ala'ettin 91
Agha, Davut 90, 91
Agha, Mehmet 56
Agra 60; *see also* Taj Mahal
Ahmet I 92
air conditioning 159, 162, 189, 197, 199
Akashi Kaikyo Bridge, Japan 16, *212*, 212, 244,
    248–51, *249, 250, 251*; steel 'fin' 249, 251
Al-Andalus 79
Albert, Prince 134, 218
Alexandria, Egypt 30
Alhambra Palace, Granada *12*, 14, 78, 79–83, *79–83*;
    construction 80–81; palace of Charles V 79
Allegheny River 220
Allen, George 133
aluminium 173, 181, 189, 198
American Civil War 172, 220
American Society of Civil Engineers 264
Amiens cathedral 13, 39
anchorage 222, 236, 246, 249, 250
anchoring cables 222, 236
Annunciation Greek Orthodox Church, Milwaukee
    143
Anston, Yorkshire 133
antennae, radio 170, 287; television 170, 178; *see
    also* radio transmission
Anthemius of Tralles 22
Apollo 106
apse 22, 39, 48, 56, 68, 70
arch 24, 40, 48, 55, 64, 67, 96, 184, 186; brick jack-
    arches 132; cast iron 215; Gateway Arch, St Louis
    1, 169, *170*, 184–86, *184–86*; moulded 42; parallel
    213, *215*; pointed 39; Romanesque round 39
Archigram Group 157
architectural competition 156, 157–58, 160, 172,
    184, 197–98, 207; drawings 20, 172, *184, 198*;
    models 20, 143, 158, *158*
Armoury, Moscow 97
Art Deco 180, 231, 287
Art Nouveau 69
Atlantic Ocean 15, 286
atrium 23, 31, 33
Austro-Hungarian monarchy 111
Avalokiteshvara 107, 108
Awaji island, Japan 248

Baird, Hugh 225
Baker, Benjamin 226
Baker, Sir Herbert 120, 122, 212
Balcom, Homer G. 181
Barfield, Julia 207
Barlow, W. H. 226
Baroque 50, 51, 62, 63, 91, 97, 103–04, 104, 106;
    Austrian 111; Italian 65, 102, 103
Barozzi da Vignola, Giacomo 101
Barry, Charles 128, 131, 133
Bartholdi, Frédéric Auguste 175, 281, 282, 285

basalt 26
Basilica of Loreto, Italy 68
Bath Abbey 46
Bauhaus 157
Bautista, Juan 78, 100
Beaubourg, Paris 156, 157
Beauvais cathedral 13, 39, 67
'bends' *see* 'caissons disease'
Bennelong Point, Sydney 148
Bergstrom, George Edwin 141
Bernini, Gianlorenzo 20, 52, 111; *see also* St Peter's
    Basilica, Rome
Bilbliothèque Nationale, Paris 156
Bird, Francis 63
Black Canyon, Arizona/Nevada 265
Black Hills, South Dakota 288
Black Sea 259
Bocabella, Josep Maria 68
BOCAD 166; *see also* computers, application of
Boleyn, Anne 47
Bordaz, Robert 159
Borglum, John Gutzon 280, 285, 288, 289, 290, 291
Borglum, Lincoln 290, 291
Borromini, Francesco 65, 111
Bosporus 89
Boston 254
Bouch, Thomas 226
Boulder Dam *see* Hoover Dam
Bourges cathedral 39
Bramante, Donato 20, 48, 50, 62, 66
Brasilia 122
brick 24, 32, 60, 80, 84, 86, 88, 94, 95, 131, 132, 133,
    180, 181, 188, 214
bridges 12, 16, 17, 53; Akashi Kaikyo 16, 212, *212*,
    244, 248–51, *249, 250, 251*; arch concept 248;
    Brooklyn Bridge 176, 211, 212, *212*, 219–22, *219,
    221, 222*, 246; Büyükçekmiçe, Turkey 53;
    construction 158; Gerber 226; Golden Gate *2–3*,
    16, *212*, 212, 222, 234–37, *234–37*, 246; Forth Rail
    6, 176, *210–11*, 212, *212*, 225–28, *225–28*; Great
    Belt (Storebælt), East Bridge, Denmark 212, *212*,
    222, 244–47, *244–47*; Humber Bridge,
    England 245, 248; Iron Bridge 213–15, *213–15*;
    London Bridge 90, 216; Manhattan Bridge, New
    York 234; Niagara Falls Rail Bridge 220; Ohio
    Bridge, Cincinnati 220; Tatara Bridge 248; Tay
    Bridge, Scotland 226, 227; *see also* cantilever
    bridges
Brihadishvara *see* Tanjavur, temple at
British Columbia 211, 223
British Museum, London 131
Brooklyn Bridge, New York 176, 211, 212, *212*,
    219–22, *219, 221, 222*, 246
Brunel, Isambard Kingdon 215, 218, 220
Brunel, Marc Isambard 16, 212, 215, *218*, 218, 220;
    Brunel's tunnelling 'shield' 16, 217, *217*, 218
Brunelleschi 62
Buddhism 28, 29; Tibetan 107
'bundled tubes' concept 170
Burghley, Lord 100
Bustamante, Agustin 100
buttresses 24, 44, 67, 69; flying 39, 40, *40*, 42, 65, 66,
    130

Byodo-in temple, Kyoto 19 , 28–29, *28, 29*
Byzantine 22, 24, 33; style 89, 117, 125; Russo- 95
cables 234, 246, 250, 251; steel 188, 222, 235
caissons 194, 221, 227, 246, 249, 250; construction
    of 220–21, 249; 'caissons disease' 212, 221
Cambiaso, Luca 101
Canadian Pacific Railway 15, 196, 211, 212, 223–24,
    223, 224
canal lock construction 177, 255–56, 261–62
canals 12, 15; Erie 254, 255–56; Panama 15, 177,
    212, 235, 254, 260–63, *261–63*, 265; Suez 15, 16,
    177, 254, 257–59, *258, 259*, 260, 263; suspended
    220
Canterbury cathedral 46
cantilever bridges 211, 212, 228; principle 226, 227
capitals 24, 81, 91
Capitol, Washington, DC 169
Carpeaux, Jean-Baptiste 140, *140*
carvings 26, 42, 44, 46, 52, 55, 81, 232, 290, 291; by
    machine 128, 133
Casey, Lieutenant Colonel Thomas Lincoln 172
Castello of Bergamo, G. B. 100
castles: Chantilly 104; Hohenschwangau 116;
    Neuschwanstein 78, *78*, 116–18, *116–18*; Saint-
    Cloud 104; Windsor Castle 207
catenary arch 69
catenary curve 184
cathedrals 12, 13, 54, Amiens 13, 39; Beauvais 13,
    39, 67; Bourges 39; Canterbury 46; Chartres 13,
    17, 19, 20, 39–43, *39, 40, 41, 42, 43*; Florence 62, 64;
    Laon 39; La Ronda 124; Le Mans 39; Peterborough
    46; Pisa 20, 34, *35*; Reims 39; Sagrada Familia 16,
    20, 68–71, *68–71*; St Denis 13, 39, 43; St Mark's 20,
    30–33, *30–33*; St Paul's 13, 20, 62–65, *63–65*, 66,
    67; St Peter's *4*, 13, 20, 48–52, *49, 50–52*, 62, 64, 67,
    98; Sens 13, 39
Catherine the Great 96, 115
CATIA 166, 167 *see also* computers, application of
cement 81; lime and hydraulic 172; Roman 218
Central Park, New York 144
Cerdà, Ildefons 68
Chagres River 262
chaharbagh 58, 59
chalk 240, 242; Chalk Marl 242, 243
Chance, Robert Lucas 135
chancel 31
Chandigarh 122
Chang Jiang *see* Yangtze River, China
Channel Tunnel 211, 212, 238, 240–43, *240–41*, 263,
    265, 269; construction of 242–43; cooling system
    242; fire 243; geology 241–42; safety 243
Chantilly, chateau of 104
Chaplin, Charlie 123
Charlemagne 43
Charles V, Emperor 82, 98
Chartres cathedral 13, 17, 19, 20, 39–43, *39, 40, 41,
    42, 43*; construction 40–43; 'the Chartres master'
    40; 'Portail Royal' 40, 42, 43; stained glass 43, *43*
Chateaubriand 82
Chatham Dockyard 217
Chatsworth House, Derbyshire 128, 135
chattri 122
Chirac, Jacques 67

choir 42, 44
Chola dynasty 25; building techniques of 27
Christ the Redeemer, statue of, Rio de Janeiro 279, *280*, 280, 286–87, *286–87*; restoration 287
Chrysler building, New York 13, 177, 179
chujja 120
churches 13, 19–20, 22, 68; Hagia Sophia 20, 21–24, *21–24*, 32; St Mark's 20; St Peter's Basilica 20, 48–52, *49, 50–52*; King's College Chapel, Cambridge 13, *13*, 19–20, 44–47, *45, 46, 47*; Kremlin, Moscow *76–77*, 78, 89, 93–97, *93–97*; Muscovite churches 95; Notre Dame du Haut, Ronchamp 13, *18–19*, 19, 72–75, *72–75*; Panthéon, Paris (church of St Geneviève) 13, 20, *20*, 66–67, *66, 67*; Russian Orthodox church 95
Citroën 178
cladding 167, 198–99
Classical architecture 66, 79, 78, 82, 102, 104, 122
classicism 33, 47; French 102, 103
clay 35, 160; marine 35
clearstorey 40, 42, 43, 65
Cleveland, Grover 284
Clinton, DeWitt 255, 256
CN Tower, Toronto 169, 170, *170*, *195*, 195–96; construction 196, *196*
CNC (computer numerically controlled) milling data 166, 167 *see also* computers, application of
Coalbrookdale Company 213, 215
'coat hanger' scheme 198
Coburn, John 151
Cocteau, Jean 178
cofferdams 131, 217, 227, 235, 265, 267, 268, 274
college of St. Nicholas 44; *see also* King's College Chapel, Cambridge
colonnades 24, 26, 34, 112, 123; Bernini's, Rome 49, 51, *51*, 52; Doric, Kremlin, Moscow 97; Washington Monument 172
colossal statues: Christ the Redeemer 279, 280, *280*, 286–87, *286–87*; Mount Rushmore *278–79*, 279–80, 285, 288–91, *289–91*; Statue of Liberty *7*, 174, 175, 279, 280, 281–85, *281–85*, 286
Colossus of Rhodes 279, 286
columns 24, 31, 50, 54, 63, 67, 81, 82, 91, 114, 202; box 188–89, 190; Corinthian 97; steel frame 155, 158, 170, 181, *182*, 192, 194
Common Market *see* European Union
computers, application of 16–17, 37, 69, 128, 160, 164, 166–67, 192; CAD (computer-aided design) 69, *165*
concrete 71, 74, 75, 80, 131, 132, 141, 172, 185, 194, 196, 201, 202, 206, 234, 238, 243, 246, 249, 250, 262, 265, 268, 272, 274, 287; cinder 180, 182; reinforced 16, 17, 67, 144, 182, 274, 282, 287; silica fume 150–51
Connaught Tunnel 224
Constantine the Great 21–22, 48
Constantinople 20, 22, 24, 30, 31, 33, 89; Church of the Holy Apostles 31; Great Palace 22; Hippodrome 22; Patriarch of 24; S.S. Sergius and Bacchus, church of 22; *see also* Hagia Sophia
construction costs 14, 20, 22, 48, 61, 114, 118, 134–35, 154, 159, 160, 175, 179, 205, 223, 254, 255, 256, 258, 262, 266, 276, 281, 284, 288
construction methods and technology 13, 15, 16, 17, 25, *27*, 27, 34–35, 42–43, 51, 60, 127–28, 167, 208, 272; Chinese 84; ironmaking 213, 214–15; Italian fortification engineering 94; stressed skin fabrication techniques 186; traditional 78, 131
Coolidge, Calvin 288, 291
copper 281, 282, 284, 285

Cordoba 79
cornices 24, 96
Cortona, Pietro da 65
Costa, Heitor da Silva 287
Costa, Lucio 122
Cotte, Robert de 103
Council of Trent 99
Council on Tall Buildings and Urban Habitat 170
courtyard 26, 44, 55, 58, 86, 112, 114, 141
Couturier, Father Alain 72, 75
craftsmen 20, 22, 59–60, 80, 100, 110, 125; carpenters 55, 65, 282; gilders 51; glaziers 51; iron workers 177; masons 20, 51, 65, 133; painters 51; plumbers 65; sculptors 65, 282, 287, 288; stone-carvers 65, 133; stuccoists 51; *see also* workforce
Craigellachie 224
crossing 31, 39, 42, 46, 52, 62, 63
Crusades, the 33, 43
crypt 32, 67
Crystal Palace, London 13, 134–37, *134–37*
cupola 65, 66, 70, 95
Curie, Pierre and Marie 67
curtain wall 188, 189; masonry 180, 181

d'Orbay, François 103
Dalai Lamas 107, 108
dams 12, 16, 262; embankment 26; gravity-arch 265; hollow concrete gravity 26, 274; Hoover Dam, Colorado River, Nevada 16, *252–53*, 253, 264–66, *266*; Itaipú Dam, Brazil-Paraguay *7*, 253, 267–70, *267–70*, 274, 276; Three Gorges Dam, China 16, 253, 254, 274–77, *275*, *276–77*
Darby I, Abraham 213, 214
Darby III, Abraham 215
Darius I 257
Davis, Arthur Q. 154
Declaration of Independence 255, 281
Deinaka, Alexander 232
Delaunay, Robert 178
Delaunay, Sonia 178
Delta Project 271
DeWitt, Simeon 256
diagonally braced frame 284
Dinkeloo, John 186
disease 260, 261
Disney Concert Hall, Los Angeles 164
Disney, Roy O. 146
Disney, Walt 118, 146
Disneyland, Anaheim 146; Adventureland 146; Magic Kingdom 146; Tomorrowland 146; Frontierland 146
Disneyworld *see* Walt Disney World Resort, Florida
Dixon, Dave 154
Doge's Palace, Venice 30
domes 13, 20, 21, 22, 23, 24, 31, 46, 50, 53, 54, 55, 56, 60, 62, 63, 64, 65, 66, 67; semi-domes 23, 24, 54; collapse 24; hemispherical 48
Donne, John 98
Dover 242
draughtsmen 128, 131
dredging machine 258
dry docks 220, 272, 273
Dushkin, Alexei 231
Dutch Sea Barrier 254, 271–73, *272, 273*; construction 272–73

Eagle Pass 224
earthquakes 16, 24, 28, 162, 212, 234, 248; Great Hanshin Earthquake, Kobe 162, 250, 251
East River, New York 211, 219, 220, 234

Eastern Scheldt Storm Surge Barrier, Netherlands *see* Dutch Sea Barrier
École des Beaux-Arts, Paris 125, 138, 140
École des Ponts et Chaussées 212
Edirne 54; Mosque of Selim II 19, 53–56, *53–56*
Edward the Confessor 130
Egyptian temples 153
Eiffel Tower, Paris 16, 169, *170*, 171, *174, 175, 177*, *178*, 174–78, 248, 269; lifts 177, *177*; light shows *178*, 178
Eiffel, Gustave 174, *176*, 280, 282, 284
Eiger 229
Eigergletscher 229, 230
Eigerwand 230
Eisenstein, Sergei 77, 114
Eismeer 230
El Greco *Martyrdom of St Maurice* 101
electricity 230, 242, 253, 256, 287 *see also* power generation
elevators *see* lifts
Elizabeth I 92, 100
Elizabeth II 151
Elizabeth, Empress of Russia 14, 77, 113
Ellis, Charles 234
Ellis Island, New York 284
Ely, Reginald 44, 46
Empire State Building, New York 13, *170*, 168–69, 169, 170, 179–83, *179–83*, 187; construction 179, *180, 182*, 180–83; materials 180–82
enamel 33, 75
English Channel 16, 240
English Perpendicular 44
environmental conservation 269, 270, 271, 273
Erie Canal 254, 255–56, *256*; decline 256; Erie Canal Enlargement Project 256
Erlach, Johann Bernard Fischer von 14, 78, 111
Ermolin, Vasily 94
Escorial 78, 98–101, *98–101*; church *101*; construction 99–101, *100*; gardens 101; mausoleum 98–99, *99*; monastery 98, 99, 100; Philip II 78, 98, 101
Estaing, Giscard d' 159
Eugénie, Empress 140, 259
European Union 241
Eurotunnel 241
Expressionism 69

fantasy architecture 206
Faraday, Michael 133
fast-tracking 81
Ferdinand of Aragon 79
Festival of Britain (1951) 208
Fioravanti, Aristotle 95
fire 243; control systems 155; risk 28, 84, 88, 162; resistance 131, 132, 158, 198
fireworks 178, 259
flooding 224, 232, 238–39, 244, 254, 264, 271, 274; protection from 16, 252, 263, 264, 276
Florence Cathedral 62, 64
Flower, Barnard 46–47
Fontainebleau 47, 104
Forbidden City, Beijing *5*, 14, 77, 84–88, *84–88*; construction 85, 88; Hall of Central Harmony 86; Hall of Supreme Harmony 86–88; Nine Dragon screen 85, *88*; Palace of Heavenly Purity 88; reconstruction of *87*
Forth Rail Bridge, Scotland *6*, 176, *210–11*, 212, *212*, 225–28, *225–28*; construction of *226*, 226–28
Fossati, Gaspare and Giuseppe 24, 91
Foster Associates 187, 188

Foster, Norman 170
Foucault's Pendulum 67
foundations 34, 42, 60, 90, 172, 175, 187–88, 196, 220, 235, 250, 272
fountains 55, 91, 106, 112; Lion fountain, Alhambra Palace 82, *83*; Viceroy's Palace, New Delhi 120
Fowler, Sir John 226
Fox Henderson and Co. 135, 136
Francis I of France 90
French Academy, Rome 138
French Revolution 67, 217
fresco 96, 101, 104; *see also* wall paintings
Friazin, Bon 96
Friazin, Marco 94, 95
Friday Mosque (Jumma Masjid), Shahjahanabad 120

Gabriel, Jacques-Ange 104
galleries *see* museums and galleries
Garabit Viaduct, Auvergne 175
gardens 82, 85, 86, 99, 101; design 105; Islamic 82; Mughal 120
Garnier, Charles 128, 129, 176
gas lighting 133, 240–41
Gaskin & Bazanski 206
Gateway Arch, St Louis *1*, 169, *170*, 184–86, *184–86*
Gatun Lake 262
Gaudí, Antoni 20, *68*, 68–69
Gautier, Théophile 82
Geddes, James 256
Gehry, Frank O. 17, 69, 164, 166
Generalife, Granada 82; *see also* Alhambra
geodesic globe 147
Gerber, Heinrich 226
gerberettes 158
Gherardesca, Alessandro della 37
Gibbons, Grinling 65
Gilbert, Bradford 284
glass 135–37, 150, 167, 189, 199, 202, 208, 285; stained 19, 40, 42, 43, 44, *46*, 46–47, 75
Global Positioning System (GPS) 263
gneiss 230
Godunov, Boris 96
Goethals, Colonel George W. 261
gold 22, 26, 91, 285
Golden Gate Bridge, San Francisco *2–3*, 16, *212*, 212, 222, *234–37*, 234–37, 246; construction of *235*, *236*, 235–36
Golden Section 73
Goldsmith, Myron 192
Gomera, Padre Francisco Lopez de 260
Gothic 97, 131, 151; architecture 66, 67, 68, 69, 116, 117; early phase 40; late 44;
Graham, Bruce 192
Granada 80; *see also* Alhambra
Grand Théâtre, Bordeaux 138
granite 24, 26, 27, 131, 173, 187, 221, 222, 227, 238, 282, 289, 290; Guadarrama 101
Great Belt (Storebælt), East Bridge, Denmark *212*, 212, 222, 244–47, *244–47*, 248; construction 245, *246*, *247*; West Bridge 244
Great Bitter Lakes 257, 259
Great Depression 180
Great Exhibition (1851) 13, 128, 134, 135, 137, 215
Great Fire of London 62
Great Hanshin Earthquake, Kobe 162, 250, 251
Greek cross plan 20, *31*, 31, 48, 62
Greek temples 153
Guggenheim Museum, Bilbao 16, 17, *17*, 128, 152, 164–67, *164–67*, 280

Guggenheim Museum, New York 128, 143–45, *144*, *145*
Guggenheim, Solomon R. 143
Guinness World Record 155
Gurney, Goldsworthy 133
Guyer-Zeller, Adolf 229
Gwathmey Siegel & Associates 145
Gyatsho, Sangye 108

Hagia Sophia, Istanbul 20, 21–24, *21–24*, 32; Baptistery 23; Patriarch's Palace 23, 24
Hall, Peter 150
Hall, Sir Benjamin 133
Hall, Todd and Littlemore 150
Halloway, Christopher 94
Happold, Edmund 158
Hardouin-Mansart, Jules 103, 104
Harrison, T. E. 226
Haussmann, Baron 138
Hawksmoor, Nicholas 65
Hawley, Jesse 255
Hearst, William Randolph 14, 78, 123
Hearst's Castle *see* La Cuesta Encantada
Henri IV 140
Henry VI 19, 44
Henry VII chapel at Westminster 46
Henry VIII 19, 44, 47
Hermitage State Museum, St Petersburg 56, 113
Herrera, Juan de 100
Heyman, Jacques 46
Hindu 13, 26, 60
Hine, Lewis W. 180, 183
Hohenschwangau castle 116
Hokenberg, Ferdinand von 112
Hokkaido, Japan 238, 239
Holanda, Rodrigo de 100
Homer G. Balcom 179
Hongkong and Shanghai Bank, Hong Kong 152, *170*, 170, 197–200, *197–200*
Honshu, Japan 238, 239
Honshu-Shikoku Bridge Authority 248
Hoover Dam, Colorado River, Nevada 16, *252–53*, 253, 264–66, *266*; construction of *265*, 265
Horne, William Cornelius Van 224
Houses of Parliament, London *126–27*, 129–33, *129–33*, 207; Big Ben 129–30, *133*, 133; Central Tower 129, 132–33; Clock Tower 129, 132, 133, *133*; House of Commons 130, 131; House of Lords 130, 131, *131*; Victoria Tower 129, 132, 133; *see also* Old Palace of Westminster *and* Westminster Hall
Houte, Adrian van den 47
Hudson River 189, 254, 255
Hugo, Victor 67
Humber Bridge, England 245, 248
Hunt, Richard Morris 282
Hyde Park, London 13, 128, 134, 137, 215

Ibn al-Yayyab 79, 80
Imperial Hotel, Tokyo 143
Indian architecture 120
Indiana Hoosierdome 155
Industrial Revolution 147, 219, 248
Interlaken 229
International Style modernism 194, 201
iron 16, 17, 24, 60, 67, 173, 175, 211, 212, 220, 254; cast 131, 132, 133, 136, 214, 215, 217, 222, 226, 282; framework 173, 176, 282; puddled 282; smelting 214; wrought 131
Iron Bridge, Coalbrookdale, Shropshire 213–15, *213–15*; construction 214–15

irrigation 16, 253, 264, 265–66, 270, 274
Irving, Washington 82
Isabella of Castile 79
Isidore of Miletus 22
Isidore the Younger 24
Islam 53, 79; influence on design 201, 202, 204
Ismail, Khedive 259
Ismailia 258, 259
Istanbul 53, 54, 56; mosque of Suleyman the Magnificent 54; *see also* Hagia Sophia, Topkapi Palace
Itaipú Dam, Brazil-Paraguay *7*, 253, 267–70, *267–70*, 274, 276; construction of *268*, *269*, 268–70; environmental impact 269; reservoir 269
Ivan II, Grand Prince 95
Ivan III 93, 96
Ivan IV 96

Jahangir 59
Jamiolkowski, Professor Michele 38
Janissary Corps 90
Jank, Christian 117
Japanese architecture 124, 161
Jeanneret, Charles-Édouard *see* Le Corbusier
Jefferson Westward Expansion Memorial *see* Gateway Arch, St Louis
Jefferson, Thomas 184, 280, 288, 291
Jiaqing emperor 85, 88
Joche (sculptor) 29
John Hancock Building, Chicago 192
Jones, Owen 82
Joseph I 111, 112
Jungfrau Rail System 212, 229–30, *230*; construction 229–30
Jungfraujoch 230
Justinian, Emperor 22, 23, 31

Kahn, Louis 144
Kalim, Abu Talib 60
Kansai International Airport, Osaka 127, 160–63, *160–63*; plans *160*, *161*
Karim, Mir Abdul 59
Kaveri River 26
Kazakov, Matvei 96
Khan al-Shirazi, Amanat 61
Khan, Fazlur 170, 192
Khan, Gushri 108
Kicking Horse Pass 212, 224
King's College Chapel, Cambridge 13, *13*, 19–20, 44–47, *45*, *46*, *47*; choir 44; construction of 44
Kingdome, Seattle 155
Knudshoved, Funen, Denmark 244
Koechlin, Maurice 175
Kokovin, V. 233
Kremlin, Moscow *76–77*, 78, 89, 93–97, *93–97*; Annunciation Cathedral 95; Arsenal tower 94; Beklemishev tower 94; Bell Tower of Ivan the Great 96, 96; Cathedral of the Archangel Michael 96; Church of the Deposition of the Robe 95; Church of the Twelve Apostles 96; construction 93–95; Dormition of the Mother of God 85; Frolov tower 94; Lenin mausoleum 94, 233; Palace of Congresses 97; reconstruction of *95*; rebuilding by Nicholas I 97; Senate building 96–97; Spassky (Saviour) tower 94
Kuwait Parliament House 149
Kyushu, Japan 238

La Cuesta Encantada, San Simeon 123–25, *123–125*; Casa Grande 123; construction 125

La Ronda cathedral 124
La Tourette monastery, Lyons 72, 74
Laboulaye, Edouard-René Lafebvre de 281
Lahauri, Ustad Ahmad 59
Lake Champlain 255
Lake Mead 265, 266
Lake Ontario 196, 255
Lake Superior 223
Landowski, Paul 280, 287
landslides 260, 262, 263
Laon cathedral 39
Las Navas de Tolosa, battle of 79
Las Vegas Strip 205
Latin cross plan 39, 50, 62
Le Corbusier 13, 19, 72, 75, 122, 143, 149, 184
Le Mans cathedral 39
Le Nôtre, André 103, 104, 105
Le Nôtre, Jean 104
Le Vau, Louis 103
lead 24
Leaning Tower of Pisa 20, 34–38, *34, 35, 36, 37*; bell
   chamber 35, 37; construction of 34–35;
   stabilization of 20, 37–38
Lebrun, Charles 103, 104
Lee, John 46
Lemercier, Jacques 62
Leoni, Pompeo 101
Leopold I, Emperor 14, 78, 111
Les Halles, Paris 156
Lesseps, Ferdinand Marie de 177, 254, 257, 260, 261
Levin, Bernard 145
Levy, Heitor 287
Lewis, John Frederick 82
Liberty Island, New York 281
lifts 189, 194, 196, 197, 200
lightning rod 195
limestone 24, 54, 94, 95, 96, 181, 230, 232; Indian
   142; malm 230
limewash 110
Lincoln, Abraham 256, 280, 288, *290*, 291
linga 25, 26, 27
locks 271, 276; *see also* canal locks
Lohengrin, legend of 117, 118
London Bridge 90, 216
London Eye *16, 170,* 170, 207–09, *207–09*
London Underground 218
Louis VIII 102, 103, 104
Louis XIV 77, 102, 103, 104, 105, 112, 140
Louis XV 66, 103, 140
Louis XVI 103
Louis, Victor 138
Louisiana Superdome, New Orleans 127, 153–55,
   153–55
Louis-Philippe 103, 104
Loutherbourg, Philip de *214*
Louvre, Paris 102, 156
Ludwig II 78, 116, 117, 118
Luther, Martin 20, 48
Lutyens, Edwin 14, 77, 119, 120, 122

Machuca, Pedro 82
Maderno, Carlo 20, 48, 51, 52
Madison, James 255
Maisonnier, André 72
Makrana, Rajasthan 60
Malraux, André 67
Manhattan Bridge, New York 234
Mansart, François 62, 103, 104
maquette 280, 281
marble 20, 22, 23–24, 31, 32, 33, 34, 55, 56, 60, 61,

81, 82, 86, 88, 138, 139, 140, 172, 173, 180
Maria Theresa, Empress 112
Marks and Barfield 207
Marks, David 207
Marsh, George Perkins 172
Martin, Elias *214*
materials 139; advances in 16; glass 135; reinforced
   concrete 71, 124, 142; steel 250; titanium 164,
   167; traditional 17, 24, 78; wood 135, 164
Mathieu, Albert 240
Matisse, Henri 72
Mattarnovi, Georg 113
mausoleums 20, 57, 58, 59, 78, 94, 98–99, 108, 171
Maximilian II 116
Mecca 24, 56, 91
Mehmet II, Sultan 78, 89
Michelangelo 20, 48, 50, 51, 52, 62, 66, 98
mihrab 24, 56
Milan, fortress at 94
Millennium Wheel *see* London Eye
Mills, Robert 171, 172
mimbar 24, 56
minarets 24, 53, 54
Ming Dynasty 77, 85, 88
Mississippi River 168, 184, 185
moat 85, 86
Modernism 148, 184
Mohamad, Datuk Seri Du Magthir 202
Mohammad II, Sultan 82
Moisssieff, Leon 234
monastery 28, 78, 99
Monch 229
Mongols 85
Montserrat 70
Morgan, Julia 14, 78, 124, 125
mortar 24, 26, 35; lime 60
mosaic 20, 22, 30, 31, *31*, 32, *32*, 33, 51, 52, 139, 140,
   140, 232
Moscow Metro 212, 231–33, *231–33*; decoration of
   232–33
Moscow river 97
mosques 19–20, 201; Suleyman the Magnificent,
   Istanbul 54; *see also* Hagia Sophia; Mosque of
   Selim II, Edirne
Mosque of Selim II, Edirne 19, 53–56, *53–56*;
   construction of 54–55; courtyard 56; plan *55*
Mount Corcovado, Rio de Janeiro 286, 287
Mount Rushmore National Memorial, South Dakota
   278–79, 279–80, 285, 288–91, *289–91*; carving
   289–90; dedication ceremony 291
Mughal 57, 58; architecture 120
Muhammad 91
Muhammad I 78, 79, 80
Muhammad IV 80
Muhammad V 80, 81, 82
Mumtaz Mahal 20, 57, 58, 60, 61
muqarnas 81; *see also* stucco
Murat III 90, 91, 92
Murat IV 92
museums and galleries 24, 33, 85, 156; British
   Museum 131; Guggenheim, Bilbao 16, 17, *17*, 128,
   152, 164–67, *164–67*, 280; Guggenheim, New
   York 128, 143–45, *144, 145*; Hermitage State
   Museum 56, 113; Louvre, Paris 102, 156; Orsay
   Museum, Paris *138, 140*, 156; Pompidou Centre *5*,
   128, 152, 156–59, *156–59*, 214
Mussolini 51

Nandi 25, 27
Nanjing, China 85

Napoleon I 203, 240, 257
Napoleon III 138
narthex 23, 31, 33, 151
naves 13, 23, 24, 31, 39, 42, 48, 51, 62, 70; aisled 64;
   linear 20; longitudinal 66
Necho, pharaoh 257
Neo-baroque 139
Neoclassicism 66, 96, 97, 103, 112, 115, 123, 130,
   138, 141
Nervion River 165
Neuschwanstein Castle *78*, 78, 116–18, *116–18*;
   Singers' Hall 117, 118; Throne Room 117
Neva river, St Petersburg 113
New Palace of Westminster *see* Houses of
   Parliament, London
New York-New York hotel-casino, Las Vegas 170,
   205–06, *205, 206*; roller–coaster 206
Niagara Falls Rail Bridge 220
Niagara River 226
Nicholas I 97
Niemeyer, Oscar 122
Nikon, Pariarch 96
North Sea 244
Notre Dame du Haut, Ronchamp 13, *18–19*, 19,
   72–75, *72–75*; construction 72
Nougier, Émile 175
Novy, Aleviz 96

Obayashi 163
obelisk 172, 173; Egyptian 172
Ogurtsov, Bazhen 94
Ohio Bridge, Cincinnati 220
Old Courthouse, St Louis 184
Old Palace of Westminster 130
Opéra, Paris *128*, 128, 138–40, *138–40*, 176
Orissa 26
Orsay Museum, Paris *138, 140*, 156
Osaka Bay 160, 163
Ostakino Tower, Moscow 195
Ottoman architecture 92; Empire 55
Ove Arup & Partners 127, 148, 157, 158, 159, 160,
   198

Pacassi, Nikolaus 111, 112
Pacific Ocean 15, 212, 260
Paciotto of Urbino, Francesco 100
Palace Museum *see* Forbidden City, Beijing
Palace of the Soviets 184
palaces *12*, 14, *14*; Alhambra, Granada *12*, 14, 78,
   79–83, *79–83*; Escorial 78, 98–101, *98–101*;
   Forbidden City *5*, 14, 77, 84–88, *84–88*; Kremlin
   76–77, 78, 89, 93–97, *93–97*; Doge's Palace 30;
   Potala *14*, 78, 107–10, *107, 108, 110, 111*; Schloss
   Schönbrunn 14, 78, 111–12, *111–12*; Topkapi
   Palace 78, 89–92, *89–92*; Versailles 77, 102–06,
   102–06, 112, 122; Winter Palace 14, 77, 113–15,
   113–15
Palais Garnier, Paris *see* Opéra, Paris
Palazzo Farnese, Piacenza 101
Panama Canal 15, 177, 212, 235, 254, 260–63,
   261–63, 265; construction *262, 263*; Gaillard Cut
   263; Lesseps attempt 260–61; locks 261–62;
   modernization 262–63; opening 262
Panama City 260
Panthéon, Paris (church of St Geneviève) 13, 20, *20*,
   66–67, *66, 67*
Parana River 267; diversion of 268
Pavia, bell tower 38
Paxton, Joseph 13, 128, 134, 135, 136, 137
Pearce, Edward 65

Pellegrini, Pellegrino (Tibaldi) 101
Pelli, Cesar 170, 204; & Associates 201
pendentives 32, 67
Pennsylvania Canal 219
Pentagon, Arlington 128, 141–42, *141–42*
Percy, Dr John 133
Perpendicular 129
Peter the Great 93, 113
Peterborough cathedral 46
Petronas Towers, Kuala Lumpur *15*, 16, 170, *170*, 179, 190, 201–04, *201–04*; skybridge 202–04, *204*
Pevsner, Nikolaus 44
Philip II 78, 98, 101
Piano, Renzo 157, 158, 159
piers 226; masonry 215
pietra dura 61, *61*
Pisa 20; baptistery 34; cathedral of 20, 34, *35*; cemetery (Camposanto) 34; Leaning Tower (belltower) 20, 34–38, *34, 35, 36, 37; see also* Leaning Tower of Pisa; Piazza del Duomo 34
Pisano, Bonanno 36
pollution 254, 277
Pompidou Centre, Paris *5*, 128, 152, 156–59, *156–59*, 214
Pompidou, Georges 156, 157, 159
Pont, Pierre S. du 179–80
Pope John Paul II 153
Pope Julius II 48
Pope Leo X 20, 48
Pope Paul III 50
Port Said 257
Porta, Giacomo della 50, 51
portcullis 44
Posokhin, Mikhail 97
Post Office Tower, London 195
Potala Palace, Lhasa *14*, 78, 107–10, *107, 108, 110, 111*; Red Palace 108; White Palace 108, *110*
Potomac river, Washington, DC 141, 142
Poussin, Nicolas 104
Powell & Moya 208
power generation 253; coal-fired 253, 270; electricity 253, 265, 266; hydroelectric 16, 264, 266, 267, 270, 274
prefabrication 176, 185, 189, 198, 250
Pritchard, Thomas Farnolls 215
Pritzker Prize 164
Protestantism 50
Pu Yi, Emperor Aisin Gioro 85
Pugin, A. W. N. 64, 65, 128, 131
pyramidion 173
pyramids, Egyptian 12

Qianlong emperor 84, 88
Qing dynasty 85, 86
Quarenghi, Giacomo 115
quicksand 232

railways *15*, 136, 165, 174, 244, 254, 265; Canadian Pacific *15*, 196, 211, 212, 223–24, *223, 224*; Jungfrau Rail System 212, 229–30, *230*; Niagara Falls Rail Bridge 220; Wegneralp Railway 229
Rajarajeshvara *see* Tanjavur, temple at
ramps 27, 42, 51, 88
Raphael 20, 48
Raskob, John Jacob 179
Rastrelli, Bartolomeo Francesco 113, 114, 115
Ravenna, Italy 33
Rebay, Baroness Hilla 143
Red Fort, Delhi 120
Red Sea 257

Red Square, Moscow 95
Redman, Henry 46
Reformation, The 20
Reid, Dr David Boswell 133
Reims cathedral 39
Renaissance 32, 33, 47, 48, 50, 103
Rennie, John 225
Rensselaer Polytechnic Institute 220
Renzo Piano Building Workshop 127, 160
reservoirs 254, 265, 276
Ricci, Sebastiano, *Apotheosis Joseph I* 112
Rice, Peter 158
Richard III 44
Richter, Friedrich 97
Riedel, Edouard 117
Rijkswaterstaat 272
Roberts, David 82
Robinson, Doane 288
Roche, Kevin 186
Rocky Mountains 224, 264
Rococo 92, 103, 112; Viennese 112
Roebling, John 219–20, 222
Roebling, Washington 219, 220
Rogers, Major A. B. 224
Rogers, Richard 157, 158, 159
Rohe, Mies van der 143
Romanesque 40
Romans 127, 257
Romanticism 82
Rome 49; the Colosseum 12; Sack of 50; St Peter's Basilica 20, 48–52, *49, 50–52*; S. Agnese 65; S. Maria della Place 65; Tomb of St Peter 48
roof structure 19, *28*, 28, 42, 44, 66, 74, 75, 84–85, 110, 132, 155, 161; barrel-vaulted 26; hammerbeam 130; shell 148, 149; wooden 109
Roosevelt, Franklin D. 265, 291
Roosevelt, Theodore 254, 261, 280, 288, 291
rose window 39
Rotherhithe 216, 217
Rousseau, Jean-Jacques 67
Rubens 101; *Adoration of the Magi* 47, 101
Ruskin, John 32, 64
Russian Orthodox church 95

Saarinen, Eero 169, 184, 186
safety 226, 239, 243, 290; net 236
Sagrada Familia, Barcelona 16, 20, 68–71, *68–71*; Nativity façade 69, 70, 71; Passion façade 71
St Denis cathedral 13, 39, 43
St Geneviève, church of *see* Panthéon, Paris
St Gothard road tunnel 241
St James's Park, London 104–05
St Lawrence River 255
St Lawrence Seaway, USA 259
St Louis 184
St Mark the Evangelist 30
St Mark's Cathedral, Venice 20, 30–33, *30–33*; plan of *31; see also* Pala d'Oro
Saint Paul de Vence, Dominican chapel 72
St Paul's Cathedral, London 13, 20, 62–65, *63–65*, 66, 67; the 'Great Model' 62, 64; plan *62*; screen wall 64–65; the Warrant Design 63–64
St Peter's Basilica, Rome *4*, 13, 20, 48–52, *49, 50–52*, 62, 64, 67, 98; Bernini's colonnade 49, 51, *51*, 52; phases of construction of 49–52; Piazza San Pietro *51*, 52; plans of 48, *50*; Tomb of St Peter, Rome 48
St Petersburg 91, 93
St Quentin 99
St Stephen's Chapel, Westminster 44

Saint-Cloud, chateau of 104
Saint-Germain-en-Laye 102; park 104
San Francisco 123; Bay 234
San Luis Obispo, California 123
San Simeon 78
sand 35, 54, 142, 272, 273
sandstone 60, 61, 235
Sangallo, Antonio da 48–50
Sarapallam 27
Sauvestre, Stephane 175
scaffolding 42, 136, 235; bamboo 27
Schloss Schönbrunn, Vienna *14*, 78, 111–12, *111–12*; Chinese Room 112; construction 112
Schneider, C. C. 226
sculpture 26, 27, 40, 43, 51, 52, 63, 115
sea defences 271, 273
Sea of Marmara 24, 89, 91
Sears Tower, Chicago *6*, 170, 170, 179, 190, 192–94, *193*, 201; floor plans *194*
Sears, Roebuck and Company 192
Second World War 142, 143, 178, 179, 291
Seikan Rail Tunnel, Japan 212, *238*, 238–39
Selim I 91
Selim II 53
Sens cathedral 13, 39
Seven Years War 77, 113
Severn River 212, 213
Seville 79
Shah Jahan 20, 57, 59, 60, 61
Shakespeare Cliff, England 241
shale 235
Shaw, George Bernard 123
Shchusev, A. 233
Sherborne Abbey 46
Shikoko, Japan 238
Shiva 25, 26, 27
Shreve, Lamb and Harmon 179
shrines 19–20, 26, 48
Shuvalov, Petr 114
Sierra de Guadarrama 78, 99
Sigüenza, José de 98, 100, 101
silver 22, 26
Simone, Giovanni di 36
Sinan 19, 24, 53, 54, 56, 90
Skidmore, Owings & Merrill (SOM) 192
'Skylon' 208
skyscrapers 169–70, 188, 192, 280, 281, 284; Chrysler building 13, 177, 179; Empire State Building 13, *168–169*, 169, 170, *170*, 179–83, *179–83*, 187; Petronas Towers *15*, 16, *170*, 170, 179, 190, 201–04, *201–04*; Sears Tower *6*, 170, *170*, 179, 190, 192–94, *193*, 201; World Trade Center 170, *170*, 179, 187–91, *187, 189, 191*, 201
Smeaton, John 225, 255
Smith, Adam 136
Smith, Alfred E. 180
Smith, Charles Shaler 226
Smith, Henry 46
soapstone 287
Solari, Pietro Antonio 94
Sommervell, Brigadier General Brehon B. 128, 141–42
Songtsen Gampo, King 107–08
Soufflot, Jacques-Germain 13, 20, 66
spandrels 24, 181
Spanish Civil War 71
Speiss, A. 117
spillways 266, 268, 270
spinning cables 222, 234, 246, 251
Sprogø, Denmark 244–45

Sri Lanka 26
Stalin, Joseph 97
Starrett Brothers and Eken 169, 179, 182–83
Starrett, Col. W. A. 169
Stasov, Vasilii 115
Statue of Liberty, New York 7, 174, 175, 279, 280, 281–85, *281–85*, 286; internal framework 282, 285; models of 282; opening 284; restoration 285
steel 142, 153, 155, 162, 166, 188, 189, 211, 212, 226, 228, 235, 238, 248, 249, 254, 270, 273, 284; cables 188, 222; carbon 185; frame 180–81, 182, 197, 262, 280, 287; riveted steel structure 180, 181; stainless 180, 185, 202, 285
Stevens, John 261
Stevenson, Robert 215, 225
Stockton, Thomas 44, 46
stone 17, 27, 28, 35, 42, 47, 52, 55, 91, 109, 127, 131, 132, 133, 168, 171, 180, 188, 197, 214, 220; Portland 64; red Dohlpur 122
Strauss, Joseph 234
stucco 52, 80, *80*, 81, 112, 115
Subirachs, Josep M. 71
Suez canal, Egypt 15, 16, 177, 254, 257–59, *258, 259*, 260, 263; cost of construction 258; inauguration 258–59; and world trade 259
Suffragettes 173
Suleyman the Magnificent 90, 91
Suleyman the Magnificent, mosque of 24, 54
Sumatra 26
suspension bridge 219, 220, 222, 245, 246, 248
Sutherland, James 214
Sydney Opera House 16, 128, 148–52, *149–52*, 157, 280; Concert Hall 151; Opera Theatre 151
Syracuse *256*

Taj Ganj, Agra 58
Taj Mahal, Agra 20, 57–61, *57–61*; *pietra dura* 61, *61*; plan *58*
Takinaka 163
Tanjavur, city of 25–26; Marathas of 27; Nayakas 27; Subrahmanya temple at 27; temple of 13, 20, 25–27, *25–27*
tapestries 112, 117
Tatara Bridge 248
Tavernier, Jean-Baptiste 60
Tay Bridge, Scotland 226, 227
Taylor, Williams & Jordan, Messrs. 133
Telford, Thomas 215, 225
temples 13, 19–20, 86; Subrahmanya temple at Tanjavur 27; Tanjavur 13, 20, 25–27, *25–27*; Byodo-in, Kyoto 19, 28–29, *28, 29*
terrorism 16, 142, 187, 190–91
Thames Tunnel 16, 211, 212, *216*, 216–18, 220
Thames, River 129, 131, 170, 207, 209, 212
Three Gorges Dam, China 16, 253, 254, 274–77, *275, 276–77*; environmental impact 276–77; power generation 274, 276; reservoir 276; ship lock 274, *275*
Tian'anmen Square, Beijing 85
Tianjin 85
Tiberi, Jean 178
Tijou, Jean 64
tiles 88, 90, 92, 125; Iznik 56, 91, *91*; ceramic 81, 85, 149; clay 88; roof 85, 88
timber 28, 32, 64, 84, 89, 109, 127, 136, 212, 214, 220; *see also* wood
tin 221
Tintoretto 33, 101
Tishman Realty & Construction Co. Inc. 190
Titian, *Martyrdom of St Lawrence* 101

Tivoli 52
Tokyo, Japan 238
Toledo, Juan Bautista Alfonsis de 99
Topkapi Palace, Istanbul 78, 89–92, *89–92*; Baghdad Kiosk 92; Barrack of the Halberdiers 90; Court of the Eunuchs 91; Divan Hall 90, 91; First Court 89–90; Fourth Court 92; Gate of Felicity 91; Gate of Welcome 90; Hagia Irene 89; Hall of the Throne 92, *92*; Harem 91–92; mosque 91; Pavilion of the Holy Mantle 91, *91*; Pearl Kiosk 90; reconstruction of *90*; Revan kiosk 89, *89*; Second Court 90–91; Third Court 91
Topkapisaray *see* Topkapi Palace, Istanbul
Tor, Konstantin 97
towers 15, 16, 17, 54, 70, 74; CN Tower 169, *170*, 170, 195–96, *195*; Eiffel Tower 16, 169, *170*, 171, 174–78, *174, 175, 177, 178*, 248, 269; Kremlin 93, 94; Leaning Tower of Pisa 20, 34–38, *34, 35, 36, 37*; Ostakino Tower, Moscow 195; Petronas Towers 15, 16, *170*, 170, 179, 190, 201–04, *201–04*; Post Office Tower, London 195; pyramidal 25, 26–27; Sears Tower *6*, *170*, 170, 179, 190, 192–94, *193*, 201
transept 31, 39, 42, 43; aisled 64
travertine 52
Trdat 24
Treaty of Versailles 106
Trevithick, Robert 217
triforium 40
Trocadéro, Paris 179
Tsugaru Strait 238, 239
tubular structure 190, 202; braced tubes 192–94; bundled tubes 192–94, *194*
tufa (stone) 52
tunnel-boring machines (TBMs) *240*, 242–43
tunnel building 238; cut-and-cover 232; deep construction 232
tunnels 16, 17, 184, 212, 224, 229; Channel Tunnel 211, 212, 238, 240–43, *240–41*, 263, 265, 269; Holland tunnel 189; St Gothard road tunnel 241; Seikan Tunnel 238–39, *238, 239*; Thames Tunnel 16, 211, 212, 216–18, *216*, 220
turbine generators 268, 270, 276
Twin Towers *see* World Trade Center, New York
tympana 24, 43
typhoons 16, 251

Uji River, China 28
UNESCO World Heritage sites 29, 82, 85, 215
United States Department of Defense 141
University of Illinois 234
urban icons, buildings as 16, 22, 183, 184
Utzon, Jorn *148*, 148, 149, 150, 152, 157

Vaccà, Giuseppe 34
Val-de-Grace 62
Vasari, Giorgio 101
vaults 33, 39, 40, 42, 44–46, 60, 67, 95; aisle 136; barrel 26; brick 24; ceiling 22; crossing 46; fan 13, 44–46; groined 131; lierne 46; quadripartite 46
Vaux le Vicomte 103
Vazie, Robert 217
Velàzquez 101
Vellert, Dierick 47
ventilation 133; upcast shaft system 133
Versailles 77, 102–06, *102–06*, 112; fountains 106; Grand Canal 105–06, *106*; Hall of Mirrors 103, 104, *105*; opera 104; orangery 103; Petit Trianon 104; Royal Chapel 103, *104*; Trianon Gardens 104; Trianon Palace 104

Vertue, William 46
Viceroy's House, New Delhi 14, 77, 119–22, *119–22*; Durbur Hall 122; grand staircase 120
Victoria, Queen 134, 137, 218, 224; Golden Jubilee 227
Villar y Lozano, Francisco 68
Viollet-Le-Duc 67
Vitruvian principles 12, 78, 99, 101
Vladimir, Cathedral of the Dormition 95
Voltaire 67
Vouet, François 104

Wagner, Richard 116
Waldorf-Astoria Hotel, New York 180
Walt Disney World Resort, Florida 128; 146–47, *146, 147*; Animal Kingdom 147; Epcot *146*, 146, 147; hotels 146–47; Magic Kingdom 128; Disney-MGM Studios 147; monorail 147
Washington Monument, Washington ,DC 169, *170*, 171–73, *171–73*; construction of 172–73; renovation 173
Washington, George 171, 173, 280, 288, 289, 291
Wastell, John 46
water 253; supply 86; table 35, 37, 155
Watkins, Sir Edward 241
weather, effects of 16, 196, 232, 248; lightning 287; snow 212, 229, 264; storms 235, 271; typhoons 248, 251; wind 212, 234, 272, 280, 282, 284, 287 *see also* wind tunnel testing
Wegneralp Railway 229
Westminster Abbey 131
Westminster Hall, London 130, *130*, 131
Wexler, Donald 147
Wilkins, William 44
Wilkinson, John 214–15
wind tunnel testing 76, 212, 248–49
Windsor Castle 207
Winter Palace, St Petersburg 14, 77, 113–15, *113–15*; construction 113; Jordan (Ambassador) staircase 115, *115*
Wittenberg 20, 48
wood 60, 81, 85, 92, 103, 109
Woodman, Francis 44
workforce 14, 15–16, 17, 22, 26, 42, 43, 51–52, 54, 60, 77, 88, 100, 114, 124, 133, 136–37, 142, 176–77, 180, 182, 186, 190, 194, 201, 206, 212, 217, 220, 222, 235, 249–50, 254, 255, 257, 261, 265, 269, 274, 288; deaths 254 *see also* craftsmen
World's Fair, Paris 1867 175; Paris, 1889 175, 176; Paris 1900 178; Paris 1937 179
World Trade Center, New York 170, *170*, 179, 187–91, *187, 189, 191*, 201; design of 188–89; construction of *189*, 189–90; destruction of 16, 187, *190*, 190–91; lifts 189; materials 188–89
Wren, Christopher 20, 62, 64, 66, 111
Wright, Benjamin 256
Wright, Frank Lloyd 128, 143, *143*, 165
Wyatt, Matthew Digby 136

Yamasaki, Minoru 170, 189, 191
Yamuna River 57, 60
Yangtze River 253, 274, 276
Yates-Silverman 206
Yorimichi, Fujiwara-no- 28, 29
Yusuf I 80

Zaboltnaya, A. 233
Zamaraev, Gavrill 97
Zhu Di, Emperor 85
ziggurat 144